PROFESSIONAL NEWS REPORTING

COMMUNICATION TEXTBOOK SERIES

Jennings Bryant — Editor

Journalism

Maxwell McCombs — Advisor

PROFESSIONAL NEWS REPORTING

Bruce Garrison
University of Miami

LEA LAWRENCE ERLBAUM ASSOCIATES, PUBLISHERS
1992   Hillsdale, New Jersey   Hove and London

Lawrence Erlbaum Associates, Inc., Publishers
365 Broadway
Hillsdale, New Jersey 07642

Library of Congress Cataloging-in-Publication Data

Garrison, Bruce, 1950–
    Professional news reporting / Bruce Garrison.
        p.   cm. — (Communication textbook series. Journalism)
    Includes bibliographical references and index.
    ISBN 0-8058-1020-X (c). — ISBN 0-8058-1021-8 (p)
    1. Reporters and reporting—Handbooks, manuals, etc.
    2. Journalism—Handbooks, manuals, etc. I. Title. II. Series.
    PN4871.G37 1992
    070.4'3—dc20   92

10   9   8   7   6   5   4   3   2   1

Contents

v

Foreword

Mike Foley, executive editor
St. Petersburg Times

If you've got this book in your hands, you must be thinking about ways to refine your skills as a journalist.

Yes, I meant to use the word "refine." You see, I agree with a colleague who once suggested we are all born journalists, although our early attempts are usually a bit crude. For example, one of your first news items probably was: "Mommy, I wet my pants!"

Most people go only slightly beyond this stage of the reporting and retelling process, choosing other careers, but still carrying on the practice. Their styles are often seen in the "Guess what?" or "Did you know that . . ." schools of storytelling.

But, you, it seems, are looking to move deeper into this art than most. Maybe you are thinking of journalism as a career? Or, at least, a discipline that will help in another path, the law, perhaps? Politics? Government work? Public relations?

Or, something worthwhile.

In any event, I assure you that you have come to the right place.

This book will not make you a good newsperson. I could not find any secret formulas, no magic incantations or even any sets of hard rules for how news should be handled.

If I had, I probably wouldn't recommend you spend your time with it.

Oh, you will find tips from successful editors and reporters. There is advice galore and lots of how-I-got-the-story stuff. Some of it might work for you. Some won't.

As I mentioned earlier, journalism is an art, not a science. The methods of obtaining information, the facts that make news stories worth reading or hearing, are as varied as the people who practice them.

Some reporters intimidate. They overwhelm situations and sources with their fearlessness, demanding to know everything immediately. They use their note pad, camera, or microphone as a weapon, and woe be unto the poor source who says "no comment."

Other reporters whine. They wheedle and stammer, seemingly on the verge of tears, begging for help in understanding what's going on. They are almost apologizing—and sometimes they do apologize—for bothering a source with so many dumb questions.

The best reporters probably do both, and just about everything else in between. Why, you ask. (A good question. Maybe you have talent, after all.)

The object of all this is not the big story, the Pulitzer Prize, or an anchor job at the networks. It is not about money or power or celebrity.

The point of it all is simply, truth. Or as close to truth as you can get in the time you have.

What this book will do is suggest ways to get closer to the truth. How to ask questions. What questions to ask. How not to worry about looking silly or stupid. How you can actually be compassionate and fair and (horrors!) *human* and still succeed.

The art and science of information gathering and dissemination has changed dramatically in the past decade or two. I see no reason that changes in the future will not be even more dramatic. The pace will be even quicker.

But, there is and was and always will be one constant. Good journalism is possible only if good journalists are committing it.

You can write with grace and wit. You can be drop-dead gorgeous with a voice that out-uncles Cronkite. You can charm the pants off Mister and Mrs. America. But if your top priority is anything but the truth, go into something else. Please.

On the other hand, if you like the idea of getting to the bottom of things, of knowing stuff first and enjoy telling other people about it; if you can stand a little heat when the truth you find and pass along isn't pretty (remember Mom's reaction to your early news reports?), then read on.

The profession might be able to find a spot for you. This book will help you get there.

Good luck.

Preface

Reporting is changing. The fundamentals will always be the fundamentals, but there are so many new reporting tools for reporters in the mid-1990s that to say that the process of reporting is different from what it was a decade ago is an understatement.

Like many aspects of journalism in the mid-1990s, some of the changes have been brought about by the ongoing social evolution in U.S. society. Other changes are technology related. Reporters carry out their jobs differently. It may be hard to imagine, but reporters once worked without telephones. That was just 115-plus years ago. Now it seems hard to remember when reporters worked without fax machines, answering machines, personal computers, tiny portable cameras, and hand-held tape recorders. It will soon be difficult to remember when reporters did not have their own cellular telephones and palmtop computers to go with them everywhere they go on assignment.

Yet reporters face other problems that seem as old as reporting itself. Reporters still often face difficulties with sources, with editors and producers, and with the public at large. There is an ethical and legal dimension of reporting that is rapidly maturing and changing the environment in which reporters must work in the United States.

This book is written for individuals interested in the process of news reporting. It is focused on both print and broadcast news reporting approaches. Ideas, techniques, and examples cover both forms of journalism not only because there are individuals interested in both subjects, but primarily because the news reporting techniques used in each are similar.

This book intends to provide a current presentation about news reporting processes. This book discusses reporting tools such as interviewing, observation, and research, including use of databases. Furthermore, there are discussions of reporting about the most common news story forms such as those based on press conferences, speeches, and meetings. Beginning students in reporting are also provided discussions of law and ethics as they impact on the daily work of news reporters.

This book is designed to serve the basic text of a two-volume set of reporting books. The second book of the set, *Advanced Reporting: Skills for the Professional,* is also published by Lawrence Erlbaum Associates (1992). It is designed to be a companion to this book and an extension of the introduction to news reporting offered here. Both books are part the Lawrence Erlbaum Associates Communication Textbook Series (Journalism Subseries). Two other LEA texts that I have authored, *Professional News Writing* (1990) and *Professional Feature Writing* (1989), provide additional background on the news gathering enterprise. Finally, it should be noted that portions of this book originally appeared in those two books.

ACKNOWLEDGMENTS

There are many professional journalists and mass communication educators who provided assistance that is deeply appreciated by the author. Their interest and generous gifts of time are valued. Without their willing support leading to completion of this work, the work would not be as useful. My sincerest thanks go to them.

Specifically, special thanks are extended to:

Dean Edward Pfister for his assistance in providing the research support of the School of Communication at the University of Miami, Coral Gables.

Alan Prince, journalism professor at the University of Miami and a former *Miami Herald* section editor and beat reporter, for his comments on the entire manuscript. His tireless efforts at copyreading the manuscript and his excellent ideas for improvements are deeply appreciated.

Mike Foley, executive editor of the *St. Petersburg Times,* for his foreword and overall encouragement for this project.

Jim Leusner, award-winning investigative reporter and federal courts beat reporter at the *Orlando Sentinel,* for his advice and assistance on research and on investigative reporting techniques. He also provided numerous items useful to reporters reproduced in this book. Furthermore, he generously gave his time to review several chapters of the manuscript prior to publication.

Nora Paul, chief librarian at the Poynter Institute in St. Petersburg, Florida, and former editor for information services at the *Miami Herald,* for her expert advice and unceasing assistance in writing the chapters about newsroom libraries and on database searching techniques. She also reviewed several chapters of the manuscript prior to publication.

Michael Carlebach, photography faculty member at the University of Miami, for his assistance in preparing some of the photographs used in this book.

Christine Davidson, broadcast journalism faculty member at the University of Miami and former producer at Cable News Network, for her suggestions for the chapter on interviewing for radio and television.

Kyu Ho Youm, journalism professor at Arizona State University and my former colleague at the University of Miami, for his review of the chapter on media law.

The *Miami Herald* and Knight–Ridder, Inc., for permitting access to their computerized reference database, Vu-Text. This courtesy made research easier and it certainly was a major timesaver.

Steve Rice, assistant managing editor/graphics at the *Miami Herald,* and Lissette Nabu, Rice's assistant, for providing many of the photographs used in this book and on the cover of the book.

To these professionals:

Bonnie Anderson, reporter, WTVJ-TV, Channel 4, Miami, for providing scripts from her reporting in the Persian Gulf during the war there in 1990–1991.

David Green, special projects editor, and Timothy Kelly, vice president and editor, the Lexington *Herald-Leader,* for their thoughts about the newspaper's award-winning series on education funding in Kentucky.

Dan Wadlington, news director, KWTO-AM, Springfield, Missouri, for background information about his award-winning series of stories about a cover-up in the Greene County sheriff's office.

Janine Wilhelm, Radio-Television News Directors Association staff, Washington, DC, for providing hard-to-find research materials.

For providing scripts, photographs, original materials reproduced in the book as figures, and other graphic or computer materials, I would like to thank:

Raymonde Bilger, Division of Student Affairs, University of Miami, Coral Gables.

Melba Calkins, assistant to the news director, KTUL-TV, Channel 8, Tulsa, Oklahoma.

Susan Carpenter, public relations office, the Los Angeles Kings hockey team.

John Culliton, former news director, WCCO-TV, Channel 4, Minneapolis.

And to my hard-working student assistants, without whose help I could not have finished this book in any reasonable amount of time:

Christina Henriques, journalism student and my research assistant at the University of Miami, for her editorial assistance and library research.

Joanne C. Acosta, broadcast journalism student and my research assistant at the University of Miami, for her editorial assistance and library research.

And finally, Mishi The Cat, for her constant companionship during the writing and research of this manuscript. This was her fourth book project. Thanks Mishi.

Bruce Garrison

INTRODUCTION TO REPORTING

1 | Life In The Newsroom

Life as a reporter these days is not easy. But oh, it can be exciting. Take veteran Miami television and newspaper reporter Bonnie Anderson, for example. Her work as a television reporter includes routine crime stories, local politics, and consumer scams. When Iraq invaded Kuwait, she was on a jet headed for Israel and Jordan to get the story for south Florida viewers. She returned after a month. But when war broke out in the Middle East, her station, WTMJ-TV, Channel 4, the National Broadcasting Company (NBC) owned-and-operated station in south Florida, sent Anderson to Saudi Arabia to get the war front story about south Florida soldiers for local viewers. Her stories offered local perspectives of the war in the Persian Gulf not provided by network coverage. She was there another month. Then, as the war ended, she returned to the Middle East, this time to Syria for the peace talks. Her previous experience as a foreign correspondent based in Beirut, Lebanon, for NBC helped her to provide strong, meaningful reporting. She knew local customs and had local contacts. But she also knew how to work safely in a dangerous region. "The random violence is the most dangerous aspect of working there," she explained. "You have to sleep with one eye open all the time" (B. Anderson, 1991).

Her weeks in a tension-filled region, hand-writing scripts, filing stories by telephone and by satellite, offered opportunities that many young reporters dream about. She had many problems, however, even with her extensive experience in the region. "Restrictions in the various countries are the worst thing," she said. "Censorship is a big problem in Iraq and in Israel. In Syria, it's hard to get the pictures, but not hard to feed them," she explained. "In Israel and Baghdad, a censor will look at the tape you want to feed and if he doesn't like what he sees, he'll blackburst (erase) it." Anderson also said the work is interesting because much of the reporting

---

A television director and producer mix sounds and pictures to create their final product (photo by Al Diaz, *Miami Herald* staff).

3

involves use of anonymous sources. "People are scared. It's tough trying to talk to people."

American Broadcasting Company (ABC) correspondent Chris Bury is based in Chicago. Bury spends most of his time in the Midwest covering stories such as the Clinton campaign in 1992, other benchmark regional elections, major breaking stories, and even occasional feature stories. But when the war broke out in the Middle East, Bury was dispatched as part of a rotating team of ABC correspondents in Saudi Arabia. Suddenly, he was preparing stories about U.S. troops in the desert. He was unable to spend the Christmas holidays with his family, because of his long-term assignment, but it was a sacrifice he was willing to make to do the job. Bury spent two stints in the Middle East before returning to his routine. But his daily routine would make many people dizzy. Bury often must run for an airplane at O'Hare Airport to cover a breaking story hundreds of miles from Chicago. On the Clinton campaign trail, he would visit a half dozen cities in one day. He's never quite sure when he will be able to catch up on things.

Associated Press (AP) reporter Sandra Jaramillo Walewski spends part of her time at work in the office as an editor, but she goes out on general assignment as needed. Based in AP's Miami bureau for 5 years, Walewski takes advantage of her Latin American heritage and bilingual abilities to move in and out of the different cultures of a diverse urban area such as Miami and Fort Lauderdale. She must spend most of her reporting time covering breaking stories, which means she is assigned major announcements at press conferences, visits by national and international figures, crimes and trials, and major traffic or industrial accidents, as well as generating "enterprise" stories and writing an occasional feature story. She also takes to the road when needed, driving to assignments where the news service needs a reporter. In 1991, for example, a 30-year-old woman told police she was sexually assaulted by a member of the Kennedy family at the Kennedy winter home in exclusive Palm Beach, about 80 miles north of Miami. Walewski was dispatched to get the national story for AP. Working with police and tough-to-reach sources within the Kennedy home, she filed her story by dictating over the telephone what she learned on the scene. Her "A" wire story was filed just a few hours after she finished her interviews. Walewski worked primarily with public relations people from the police department and spokespersons representing the Kennedy family, but also had to contend with dozens of competing reporters. "It was unbelievable," she said, recalling her arrival in Palm Beach the day after the story broke. "Trying to get something unique was difficult. There were too many people all going to the same places. And it was tough because I was not familiar with the town." Walewski also got help from the major Palm Beach-area newspaper, which frequently exchanges information as part of its arrangement with AP. To complete her story, Walewski talked to Palm Beach residents and tourists to get their reaction, and she added background information about previous incidents involving the Kennedys at Palm Beach, such as the 1984 drug-related death of Robert Kennedy's son, David.

Walewski wrote two versions of the same story, one for morning-cycle news organizations and one for evening-cycle news organizations (Walewski, 1991). Her story is reprinted at the end of this chapter.

When President George Bush visited Tulsa, Oklahoma, in 1990, ABC affiliate KTUL-TV, Channel 8, had on its hands a big story that one reporter alone could not handle. Instead, the station used a team approach, making the most of its 28 news staff members and 15 photographers. The president arrived in the morning, headed to Stillwater to give a speech, and returned to Tulsa late that afternoon just before the early evening newscast went on the air. Anchors introduced stories chronicling the day's excitement of a presidential visit. First, the president's commencement address at Oklahoma State University was highlighted. Then viewers saw reports on the president in Tulsa, preparing for an address at the city's convention center. Switched to reporter Steve Knight at the speech site, viewers were updated on activities and heard a live interview with Oklahoma Democratic Sen. David Boren. This is high-pressure instantaneous television news. "It is hectic, wild and a wonderful place to work," said Melba Calkins (1990), assistant to KTUL-TV News Director Michael Sullivan. The script of the KTUL-TV 5 P.M. report is reproduced at the end of this chapter.

At CBS affiliate WCCO-TV, Channel 4, in Minneapolis-St. Paul, reporter Darryl Savage was sent one morning to cover what seemed to be a routine fire for the evening newscasts. The fire had destroyed a houseboat moored in the Mississippi River in the middle of the night; firefighters had not been able to get to the scene on time. But the fire raised an even bigger safety issue for residents of the island where the fire occurred. Savage saw the bigger dimension in the story and highlighted this point in his "package." His story script, reprinted at the end of this chapter, shows a variety of sources needed for this basic television news story: effective video of the fire and the neighborhood, video of the blocked route and bridge, interviews that lead to strong natural sound—the broadcasting term for ambient sound—from witnesses and neighborhood property owners and residents, and information from authoritative sources such as the Minneapolis fire chief.

These five examples typify what reporting is about today. It is about working with and talking to people. It is doing research; understanding and explaining; stress; travel; facing danger; unusual working hours; long days; taking risks; writing and rewriting; acting and reacting quickly on deadline; and ad libbing.

This book introduces you to reporting in the mid-1990s. It gives you the foundation in reporting needed for careers in television or radio news as well as for magazine and newspaper careers. But first, let us discuss the environment of the news media in the mid-1990s.

NEWS MEDIA IN THE MID-1990s

Technology has reorganized and, in some cases, redefined what reporters do. Continuing fast-paced technological developments will make your work as a reporter in the mid-1990s both more difficult and much easier. In reporting, like other work in journalism, some things will change and others will remain the same. Newspapers, magazines, and newsletters are turning to fax distribution and to lasers for precision printing. Television and radio are placing greater emphasis on live satellite transmission of news. There will be newer ways to get information to consumers. Old ways will be improved. For example, television viewers will have high definition video, comparable to the 35 mm film used by theatrical motion pictures, available in the mid-1990s, and stereophonic sound will continue to grow in use (Rinehart, 1990). Wiring the United States for cable means better, more diverse news communication. News organizations will target specific audiences and personalize products to compete for the time of the information consumer. This trend toward audience fragmentation and personalizing the "news product" crosses all news media and will make a reporter's job even more challenging (Anderson, 1990; Criner, 1990). What was once a strategy for print media is now embraced by television news producers.

The health of the communications industry will be strong in the coming decade. Cable television news may offer the most growth and employment opportunities. As more local cable operations offer in-house produced news and information, additional career options will be available for entry-level journalists. Traditional broadcasters enjoy the largest audiences of all news providers today and this will gradually translate into greater financial success. Magazines will enjoy success through their targeted, specialized audiences. And newspapers, the original mass news providers, will appeal most to over 40-year-old audiences that will continue to swell in numbers as the "baby boomers" grow older in the next decade. Newspapers will also continue to take the lead in developing electronic, computer-based information sources for more sophisticated news consumers (Burke, 1990; Dennis, 1990).

You will continue to hold an important position in our society as an information provider in the news media. The efficient and accurate presentation of information to citizens depends on quick decisions and quick reaction to events by newsgatherers.

There will be a changing U.S. population to serve as we enter the 21st century. Three-quarters of the population growth in the United States in the mid-1990s will be minorities. Estimates suggest that the nonminority population in the United States will continue to drop in proportion to minorities. In 1980, 80% of the U.S. population was nonminority. In 1990, it was 76%. In 2000, it is projected to be 72%. And by 2010, it will drop to 68% (Swanston, 1990). What does this mean to journalism and reporting? It means new understanding on the part of reporters will be necessary, especially from "majority" group White males who have traditionally dominated U.S. newsrooms. It also means new opportunities for minority group members seeking careers in journalism as news organizations seek to increase proportions of minority employees to equal those of the populations of their communities.

There will be additional tests of the relationships between the press and

Knight-Ridder Inc. executive Tony Ridder poses with one group of his company's many newsroom computer terminals (photo by David Walters, *Miami Herald* staff).

society and between the press and government. Many times, public concern about the work of reporters will arise — such as criticisms of reporters for "giving away war secrets" during the Persian Gulf War. Ethics and general professional behavior of reporters continue to be a focal point for reporters of the mid-1990s. First Amendment issues will center on technological developments involving the distribution of information (Maguire, 1990).

SOCIAL RESPONSIBILITIES OF JOURNALISTS

You may already be aware of some of the duties of news and information providers — reporters by any other name — today. Their duties are important social responsibilities, as mass communication scholars Theodore Peterson, Jay Jensen, and William Rivers (1965) described them. The role of the news media is singularly important in today's complex U.S. democracy. People need the information to serve as good citizens and, because of the busy lives most people lead, they cannot always attend meetings and participate directly. People depend, instead, on their local news media to tell them what they need to know on a day-to-day basis.

Traditionally, 20th-century news media have been expected to provide at least five basic requirements to consumers. According to the historic

Commission on Freedom of the Press, headed by Robert M. Hutchins in 1947, these five obligations of the press are to:

- Provide truth and meaning in the news
- Serve as a forum for the exchange of ideas and commentary
- Provide a representative picture of the various groups and activities of society today
- Clarify the goals and values of our society
- Provide full access to the information, or news, of the day (Peterson et al., 1965)

This is a composite of ideas about the role of the news media in society. Peterson, Jensen, and Rivers maintained that social responsibility of the press "accepts the traditional functions of enlightening the public, servicing the political system, and safeguarding civil liberties. However, it reflects the belief that the media have not performed those tasks as capably as they should in a modern industrial democracy" (p. 109).

The social responsibility theory, these scholars maintained, also accepts the functions of serving the economic system, providing entertainment, and still making a profit to stay in business. "But it would subordinate those tasks to the more important ones of promoting democratic processes and public enlightenment" (p. 8).

CHARACTERISTICS OF JOURNALISTS

An Indiana University study of U.S. journalists tells us there are more journalists compared to the findings of a similar study conducted 15 years earlier. In their book, Weaver and Wilhoit (1986) estimated there were 112,000 full-time editorial employees in the news media. Two thirds of these work in the print media, with 46% at daily newspapers. Of the remaining one third, 17.5% work in radio and 13.6% in television or combined television-radio operations (p. 13).

The study also found that journalists are young (a median age of 32 years), mostly male (66%), caucasian (90%), Protestant (61%), "middle of the road" politically (58%), Independents (39%) or Democrats (39%), and readers of the *New York Times* (33%), the *Wall Street Journal* (25%), and *Time* (52%) (Weaver & Wilhoit, 1986, pp. 19–37).

More of today's journalists are better educated than the generation preceding them, Weaver and Wilhoit reported. A study in 1971 reported 58% of journalists held bachelor's degrees or higher, but the figure increased to 70% by 1982–1983 (p. 47).

College majors in journalism or communication seem to be important as well. Journalism and communication majors in the news media are increasing in proportion. Weaver and Wilhoit found more than half of journalists participating in their study held degrees in journalism/

communication. With the exception of news magazine journalists (only 26% held journalism/communication degrees), other news media are dominated by journalism majors, ranging from just more than half (weekly newspaper journalists) to nearly two thirds (television journalists).

QUALITIES EDITORS AND PRODUCERS SEEK IN REPORTERS

Your work as a reporter in the mid-1990s will be both easier and harder than your predecessors found the job to be. Technology such as laptop personal computers, lasers, satellite disks, and cellular telephones make work faster and easier. But the job is made more difficult because public expectations are higher and there is more information to gather in this computerized technosociety. You will probably not work 9 to 5 at first. You will work

---

SUE ELLEN CHRISTIAN, ASNE
SKILLS: WHAT DOES IT TAKE FOR A JOB?

What does it take to become a journalist today? The American Society of Newspaper Editors (ASNE) recently polled its members and the key criteria were rated. What's important in a candidate's background?

The scenario that was put to editors:

"Assume that you are interviewing someone for his or her first newspaper job (even if your newspaper doesn't usually hire entry-level people). How important to your decision to hire the applicant is each of the following?"

Here's what they are looking for, in order of characteristics they rated as "very important" or "important":

	Very Important (%)	Important (%)
Writing skills	86	14
Spelling and grammar	73	25
Newspaper internships	51	31
Knowledge of journalism ethics	35	46
Broad background in arts and sciences	33	48
Typing or word-processing skills	20	44
Journalism skills courses	19	47
Work on a school paper	21	40
Grade point average	6	47
Knowledge of media law	11	35
Business and economics courses	6	39
Hands-on experience with computers	6	31
Familiarity with communication theory	4	16

(continued)

SUE ELLEN CHRISTIAN, ASNE *(continued)*

Percent citing each as very or somewhat important:

	Total	Large newspapers	Medium newspapers	Small newspapers
Internships	82%	86%	83%	76%
Grade point average	53	63	47	46
Journalism skill courses	66	56	74	81
Business and economic courses	45	55	44	31
Broad background (arts and sciences)	81	89	81	69
Typing/word processing skills	64	51	68	71
Familiarity with communication theory	20	8	21	32
Knowledge of media law	46	36	50	54
Journalism ethics knowledge	81	80	85	79
Writing skills	100	100	100	100
Spelling and grammar	98	99	99	99
Work on school paper	61	60	68	52
Hands-on experience with computer	37	23	41	49
Number of newspapers	378	123	158	97

Source: Christian (1990).

nights and weekends. As a beginner at least, you will get the toughest shifts and the least challenging assignments. But if you can prove yourself under those conditions, opportunities will come your way.

It is important to emphasize the difficulty of being a successful professional news reporter these days. Yet, for those who do have the drive and talent to succeed, the rewards can be great—both personally and professionally. Your first newspaper "byline" or first television news "package" credit can be highly satisfying. The euphoria and high spirit you feel from this accomplishment at any level, from weekly student newspaper to major market television station, are equalled by little else in professional writing. And beginners do have a chance at success. With the right idea at the right time, you can become a successful reporter early in your career.

What motivates you to be a reporter? If you can answer that question by the time you finish this book, you might have the foundation for becoming a professional reporter.

You write to pass along information to your readers or listeners. You write to tell them what you have learned. They learn. They are entertained. They are thrilled. They are saddened. People react to what you have to say in print. At the same time, you have a tremendous responsibility to be accurate, concise, and timely.

You also have to know how to express yourself. This basic communication skill is your starting point in reporting. You must have the interest and you must have writing ability. At some point in your life, you began to think of yourself as a writing-oriented person.

NEWSROOM ORGANIZATION

Technology is tearing down walls in the communication industry. Previously sharp organizational divisions, with clearly defined areas of responsibility, are today not so distinct. Newspapers of all circulation sizes and publication cycles, for example, are affected by this era of reorganization. Television and radio newsrooms are now often experiencing a technological makeover called newsroom automation (Paulson, 1991).

The 1990s is a decade of high technological impact on organization of the news media. Technology is already redefining how news media are structured because it has changed how employees get work done and even the work they do. The most significant technological advancement that is bringing the most change is the computer.

News media were rather simply organized until the computer and other new technology of the past two decades came along. Sohn, Ogan, and Polich (1986) described a modern newspaper's approach that calls for five divisions: publisher's office and general management, advertising, circulation, news-editorial, and production. Sohn, Ogan, and Polich observed that "although demographics and philosophies may differ, most newspapers have a fairly similar departmental structure" (p. 4). They felt the computer has had significant impact on creation of new departments and new responsibilities for employees.

Undoubtedly the organizational plan for the newspaper of the 1990s has changed. Existing departments have changed structure. And new departments have appeared to fill new demands. Even the names of the departments have changed in startling fashion. For instance, fewer newspapers have "composing rooms" today. Instead, these "pre-press" functions are often controlled through the newsroom and a computer center. And the personnel department has grown to become an increasingly important human resources division responsible for, among other things, hiring and training, communication, testing and evaluation, child day care, workplace quality, health care, and continuing education.

In this decade, most newspapers will gradually eliminate the remaining portions of their operations that were formerly composing rooms. With pagination systems and desktop-publishing systems to "paste-up" or compose pages, the production process will become even more efficient and require even fewer people.

Desktop publishing has had its biggest impact on small operations such as weekly newspapers and newsletters (Genovese, 1987; Rykken, 1989). These new personal computer-based systems have strengthened weekly newspapers by lowering production and labor expenses. Combined jobs and responsibilities have contributed to fast growth in this publishing process for many weeklies. Desktop publishing has also led to consolidated production facilities in companies that produce more than one newspaper, such as community weeklies. By using telephone computer modem links as well as facsimile machines, publishers have reorganized and cut operation costs. Now production, circulation, and business/accounting departments at different locations can work more efficiently through a centralized facility linked in a network by computer and telephone lines.

Information systems comprise one of the newest divisions, serving many other divisions internal to the newspaper. This division maintains and operates computer and other systems for data processing and production of the newspaper. It often includes a systems engineering department as well.

The news–editorial division focuses on two areas of news gathering. The news department includes the traditional reporting and editing sections of the newspaper such as foreign, national, metro/city, sports, newsfeatures (life-style, arts, entertainment), business, Sunday magazine, food, such functions as the newspaper's reference, photographs, and clippings library, and the graphics (photography and art) departments. The editorial department, although smaller, reflects the opinion functions of the newspaper such as editorials, columns, letters to the editor, and special news analyses and interpretations.

Much of this discussion has focused on how technology has already affected the organization of newspapers. Considering the advice of communication consultant Wilson P. Dizard, Jr. (1985), we can expect even more realignment in the years ahead: "In little more than a generation, the technology to match this challenge [of the promise of our democratic society] has moved from the laboratories into everyday use. Our applications have been primitive compared to the potential of the new machines" (p. 17).

The broadcast newsroom is undergoing similar transformation caused by technology. Newsroom automation (NRA) is one significant transition. Radio and television stations have learned by the automation experience of newspapers, in fact. One station in Boston is an example: "WHDH-TV engineering, news, and production (note that!) staffers began their quest [for NRA] by painstakingly studying the ways in which newspaper publishers use computers in operations automation," wrote computer consultant Bob Paulson (1991). "They found many similarities between the two operations" (p. 16). Figure 1.1 shows a typical application of computers in the newsroom of WFAA-TV, Dallas (L'Amie, 1991).

New jobs have been created in engineering and production departments simply to cope with changing technology such as satellite and microwave links, portable video equipment, and computers. Computers and other automated systems are now critical in story identification and preparation, writing assignments, illustration production, story editing and headlining (called "billboarding" by broadcasters), newscast rundowns preparation, on-air live/tape playback integration, and story archiving (Paulson, 1991). In the newsroom, computers are replacing typewriters just as they have done at newspapers and magazines for many of those routine tasks. These

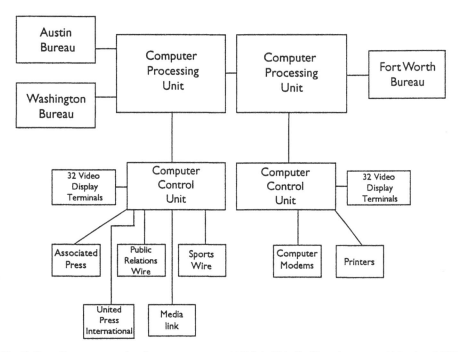

FIG. 1.1. Computers in the newsroom, WFAA-TV, Dallas (*source:* L'Amie, 1991).

tools for writing and research have changed news delivery and script preparation.

Desk-top personal computers have made it possible for broadcast newsrooms to produce "dramatic, telling packages," affirmed Bob Paulson (1991, p. 16), which include (a) written copy; (b) an edited list of live takes, tape clips, and soundbites; (c) graphics from established style sheets; (d) defined and timed video transitions; and (e) a shot list for robotic camera in the studio.

Technology, such as computers, is also forcing reorganization of the broadcast station, with new departments and positions created; old useless ones have been eliminated or scaled back. Technology, perhaps most of all, is causing changes in the competitive dimension to television. With cable systems, some experts believe there may be as many as 500 channels in a single system by the year 2000. With today's systems typically offering from 35 to 100 or more channels, viewers will have even more choices, making the job of attracting substantial audiences that more difficult for news programmers (Stumpf & Jessell, 1991).

THE ROUTINE OF A NEWSPAPER REPORTER

Newspaper reporters come in two varieties. The more common is the staff reporter, an individual who works full-time or steady part-time for a single

Women are finding more opportunities in the television industry, both in on-camera and in production positions such as camera operators and engineers (photo by Al Diaz, *Miami Herald* staff).

publication. Free-lance newspaper reporters often work for local newspapers, but most newspapers do not use their work as often as they use staff-written material.

Most newspaper staff members work regular schedules. Most work 40 hours a week, but some who work on a salary find their schedule and demands of the job require more than the conventional work week. The work of newspaper reporters is not limited to a 9-to-5, Monday-through-Friday schedule. Nor is the work limited to "scheduled" times. Most top print and broadcast journalists on a regular work schedule find they never really stop working, even when off duty. If you want to succeed, you must take advantage of the opportunity whenever a good story prospect presents itself.

Whether you work general assignment or on a beat, the intense nature of newspaper reporting requires that you be prepared at all times. With daily, two or three times a week, or even weekly deadlines, much story production is expected. You must have an endless stream of strong ideas to develop into stories. You cannot "switch off" your alertness as a reporter.

There are both challenges and rewards in this environment. One challenge is to know a great deal about a wide range of subjects in a given community. For specialists on beats at newspapers, the challenge is to know a great deal about a restricted range of subjects, but the news reporter carries the burden of responsibility for the entire publication.

As a reporter, you will take advantage of public familiarity with your newspaper. Few communities have more than one major newspaper today. If you work for that newspaper or your community weekly, readers and sources will recognize it immediately. This means you will have stories come to you, and you might find a higher level of cooperation from sources.

Eventually you will also enjoy the advantage of being known by your readers. Your name will become familiar to the community you serve as a journalist. If you are good, this can become a major asset in your work. But if you are not professional in your work, it becomes a liability.

THE DAILY ROUTINE OF A TELEVISION REPORTER

If you ask those persons who work in a broadcast newsroom about their work, they will respond with plenty of adjectives for what they experience. "Crazy," some say. "Chaotic," others tell you. "Stressful," still others contend. If you remember the *intensity* of some of the newsroom scenes in the Hollywood film, *Broadcast News,* you probably get the picture.

The immediacy of broadcast journalism, turned up several notches higher than print journalism, makes this an environment for persons who thrive on challenges, not for those who want to avoid stress. You have to enjoy the tension of broadcast news. The excitement of a breaking story, the demands of a long work day, and the satisfaction of a job well done combine to draw many people to the electronic news world.

Many broadcast news operations have combined commercial television and radio services. Although this varies, many commercial television newsrooms are affiliated with an AM, FM, or both types of radio stations. There are many more radio stations than television stations, so it follows that there are numerous radio stations that are not affiliated with television stations.

Most television newsrooms spring to life long before sunrise, especially if there is a live morning news program to air. Throughout the day journalists work to meet program deadlines. After the early morning newscast, a noon newscast may follow. Afternoon cut-in newsbreaks are prepared, and then early evening programs are produced. Work may slow a bit after the late evening news ends.

But at some major market television stations today, a 24-hour operation is required because of the volume of news that is produced for broadcast. At others, which may produce dinner-hour and late-night news programs only, the rigors begin a little later in the day, but these intensify as the afternoon speeds on.

Most broadcast news positions are full-time, but some entry-level opportunities are part-time. There is some free-lance work in broadcasting, but it is not as widespread as in the print news media. Most occurs in news centers such as New York or Washington, DC.

As with newspapers and magazines, broadcast newsrooms are organized into general assignment and specialized beats. Some reporters will handle both types of reporting and writing. But eventually, most broadcast journalists develop specializations.

The broadcast newsroom's center of activity, like the city desk in a newspaper newsroom or a department editor's desk in a magazine office, is the assignment desk. Here reporters and photographers are given stories and sent out with hours or minutes to get the work done. Assignment editors, working with producers, organize the next program as stories are being completed.

Reporters and tape editors work to match pictures and sound to create their 90-second stories, called *packages*. They write and rewrite scripts, timed to the second. They seek drama with accuracy. Producers write shorter stories, review network satellite feeds, and then combine all the elements for the total newscast. Anchors review their scripts for smooth presentation.

Upgraded equipment and facilities have been a priority for most radio news operations in the 1990s, according to Vernon Stone (1989b, p. 9). In a survey of radio and television news directors in 1988, he found the leading recent positive development in radio news was improved equipment, facilities, and news coverage. Decisions to add newsroom staff and additional news time were also credited as recent changes in the radio news industry.

The constant activity in a television–radio newsroom is dizzying for a casual visitor. During a live newscast production, pressure and intensity reach their peak. Precise timing, accurate reporting, and words merged with pictures – all dealing with the latest information wind up with 22 minutes or so of news for viewers each half hour.

Stone (1989a) also said the most common entry-level job in broadcast news is field reporting. Less often, he indicated, jobs are available in news production. Some beginning broadcast journalists find opportunities in photography (p. 8).

Radio journalists often combine news writing and reporting with newscasting, Stone noted.

THE SCOPE OF THE NEWS BUSINESS

There were 1,611 morning and evening daily newspapers with an average circulation of 38,530 copies in the United States in 1990, according to figures compiled by the American Newspaper Publishers Association (ANPA; Anon., 1991, April). More than 113 million U.S. adults read a daily newspaper on an average day. There were 865 Sunday editions averaging 72,150 copies. There were 7,476 weekly newspapers with an average circulation of 7,323 copies in 1990, including paid and free circulation newspapers, ANPA reported.

There are many more magazines; the total in the late 1980s was about 22,000. However, just 9,000 of these are sold to the general public, with

Although the pace of television news is often hurried, there are often long periods of time spent waiting for events to occur (photo by Al Diaz, *Miami Herald* staff).

others designated for restricted trade or company markets for employees or customers. About 20% of all magazines are weekly, 6% are published twice a month, 42% appear once a month, 11% are issued every 2 months, and 12% are quarterlies.

Reporters depend more and more on technology. Computers, fax machines, cellular telephones, microcassette recorders, and other hardware provide ways to gather information unavailable to reporters only a generation ago. You are able to work on machines that make story preparation easier than ever before.

News organizations are more sophisticated in production techniques. This means news reporters can produce and revise stories faster and closer to deadlines and supplement the usual news coverage of an event.

Trends in group ownership of news media have changed the nature of the business over the past two decades. The largest newspaper groups, such as Gannett and Knight–Ridder, have purchased major dailies, but many of these companies also own broadcast or other information services. Gannett, for instance, owns several broadcast stations. Knight–Ridder, for instance, owns several electronic information service companies and at one time also owned television stations. Other companies have gathered up available small dailies and weeklies. Magazines have experienced the same phenomenon. Companies have bought up independently owned magazines to form new or larger groups.

The effect has been less independent management of publications. At times, staff positions have been eliminated to create more profitable operations. It has meant a harder time to make a living for reporters in some markets and some specializations. It has also meant greater resources and new ideas. It has meant some publications near failure got a second chance. And this has helped reporters.

Newspapers are changing in the 1990s. They are using feature material in larger quantities, so they seek better quality from reporters to keep the demand for their editions high. Reacting to television and other electronic media vying for the growing entertainment and leisure time of Americans, newspapers are offering material once found only in magazines, such as longer, in-depth profiles or analyses. William Rivers and Alison Work called this phenomenon the "magazining of newspapers" (1986, p. 4). Recently, some newspaper feature sections have shown interest in shorter, tightly written pieces with the same "television story" flair of *USA Today*.

Magazines, as well, have changed in the past three decades. Television, film, and other influences changed them in the 1960s and 1970s. General interest consumer magazines closed when operations became more costly than circulation and advertising revenues could cover. More specialized magazines evolved in the 1960s and 1970s to replace the general interest publications. Suddenly, readers interested in health and medicine did not have to depend on news magazines or the coffee-table magazines of another era. They instead subscribed to *Prevention* or similar magazines.

City and regional magazines that became the rage of the late 1960s and 1970s remain significant today in many metropolitan areas. Entertainment and personality-celebrity publications were created and have grown.

John Mack Carter, editor-in-chief of *Good Housekeeping* and director of New Magazine Development for Hearst Corp., declared the magazine industry is strong today. "And, if my thesis proves correct, we will be doing even better in the future" (1986, p. 7). Carter pointed to a decline in television viewing because of dissatisfaction with network television and cable television programming, and use of VCRs and personal computers.

Sandra Kresch, director of Strategic Planning for Time Inc., agreed that print media are strong and vital. "All of the technological and social change of the last few decades has had very little effect on the magazine industry in recent years. Print is healthy and vital—and shows every sign of continuing to be so in the future" (1986, p. 7). Kresch noted that magazines have experienced circulation growth and healthy advertising since 1979.

"Both magazines and newspapers are responding to external forces that are beyond their control. Yet they are surviving through a long process of adaptation that is changing both their appearance and content," Rivers and Work (1986, p. 9) observed.

Broadcasting magazine reported in 1992 that there were 11,107 operating commercial and educational radio stations, 1,495 commercial and educational television stations, 1,210 low power television stations, and 11,254 cable television systems serving 55.8 million subscribers (Anon., 1992, March 23, p. 84).

There are slightly more commercial AM radio stations (4,984) in operation than there are commercial FM stations (4,605), or educational FM stations (1,518).

There are fewer commercial television stations. At present there are only 557 VHF (very high frequency, channels 2–13) stations and 581 UHF (ultra high frequency, channels 14–83). Of just 357 educational television stations, the majority (234) are UHF. The biggest area of television growth is commercial UHF television, which saw 168 construction permits issued in 1992.

Expansion in the area of low power television is apparent from these figures. Only 1,210 stations were on the air in 1992, but another 1,013 hold construction permits.

And cable television continues to grow rapidly in most parts of the United States. Penetration of households has passed halfway, with 60.6% of 93.1 million U.S. households receiving cable, according to *Broadcasting*. Of the 93.1 million households, almost all (92.0 million) now have the *capability* to receive cable telecasts.

Local television news is improving significantly—catching up with the level of news produced by the resource-laden networks and network owned-and-operated affiliates. After years of being considered "stepchildren" of the more serious-minded parents at the networks, local stations have made great strides in news programming in the 1970s and 1980s. "Today, local television news has more resources, has more viewers, and broadcasts significantly more news than ever dreamed of by its network counterparts," La Salle University Professor Richard Goedkoop (1988, p. vii) wrote. "This is not to say that local television news is *better* than that which we can view from ABC, CBS, NBC, or CNN. Both network and local television news are constrained by the nature of our broadcasting system to walk a fine line between journalism and entertainment" (p. vii).

With the new techniques in programming and technology, the debate continues over which reporting and writing methods work best in television news. "Broadcast journalists, by contrast [with print journalists], have had

TIMES MIRROR CENTER, WASHINGTON
AMERICA'S SOURCES OF DAILY NEWS

Persons who said they regularly consulted the media	National Findings (%)
Read a daily newspaper	54
Watch news on TV	74
Listen to news on the radio	46
Persons who used *each* source yesterday	
Newspaper	43
Television News	52
Radio News	53

Source: Anon., July 15, 1990.

TIMES MIRROR CENTER, WASHINGTON
USING MULTIPLE SOURCES OF DAILY NEWS

	National Findings (%)
Used one source yesterday	84
Used only three sources yesterday	15
Used only two sources yesterday	34
Television and Newspapers	12
Television and Radio News	13
Radio News and Newspapers	9

	% reporting regular viewership or readership
Used one or more "National" news source	51
Number of sources used:	
One	28
Two	14
Three	10
Uses print only	32
Uses electronic only	36

Source: Anon., July 15, 1990.

barely four decades to experiment with the potential of television news and to reach at best a limited understanding of how broadcast news content can most effectively be communicated," said Colorado State University Professor Frederick Shook (1989, p. xix).

New technology seems to be the catch-phrase in radio news in this decade. Reporters and editors are using computers and other equipment to

**NATIONAL CABLE TELEVISION ASSOCIATION
LEADING INFORMATION SOURCES ON CABLE**

According to the National Cable Television Association in 1990, these six news organizations are in the top 20 largest cable networks ranked according to the total number of subscribers:

1. ESPN (Bristol, CT)	55.9 million
2. Cable News Network (Atlanta)	54.4
8. C-Span (Washington, DC)	49.7
14. The Weather Channel (Atlanta)	43.0
15. Headline News Network (Atlanta)	41.8
18. Financial News Network (New York)	33.8

Source: Anon., October 1990.

improve their news production. Not only are stations remodeling facilities, they are adding computers with high speed information services, news vans for remote production, high quality recording equipment for improved actualities (sound clips), editing stations in the studio, and even cellular telephones for reporters to file from field locations (Courson, 1989).

Vernon Stone (1989b, March), in his study for Radio-Television News Directors Association (RTNDA), found radio news directors also saw improvement in news coverage in terms of production quality and air time given to news. He also saw some slight growth in staff size and some stations adding radio news departments.

CONTEMPORARY READERS AND AUDIENCES

Americans are busy people. But as their leisure time increases, there are more and more choices to consider (Garrison, 1991). Newspapers, magazines, radio, and television all compete for the rare few minutes each day that Americans find for leisure activities. Media audiences are constantly changing entities but the news media depend on them for their livelihood. Without them, there is no one for whom to gather information. Without them, in the U.S. system especially, there is no financial base for advertising revenue.

Research shows the majority of Americans get their daily information about what is going on in their world from television newscasts. One recent study by the Times Mirror Center for the People & the Press in Washington showed 74% of respondents said they regularly watch TV news, whereas just 54% said they regularly read a daily newspaper. Radio news was the third most-used source of information, listed by 46% in the national survey (Anon., 1990, July 15). Bogart (1989) cited a similar study, which found 68% of respondents in a national survey watched television news on a typical day, spending about 58 minutes viewing.

Perhaps even more important in this national study was the finding that

84% of the respondents used only *one source* for news and information. Of those few respondents who used multiple sources, television and radio were the most popular one-two punch, whereas television and newspapers were also a common combination (Anon., 1990, July 15). Most national media-use surveys since the mid-1960s have shown a clear preference by Americans for information from television over newspapers.

Young people are less inclined to consume news regardless of the medium. As adults get older, they spend more time both reading and watching news. And most (85%) literate U.S. adults read a newspaper at least on occasion, Bogart (1989) reported. He also noted that people of higher income and education "are most likely to be heavy users and seekers of information and regular newspaper readers. In fact, the differentiation begins in childhood" (p. 94).

CAREER PROSPECTS FOR REPORTERS

Journalists can begin their careers in a number of ways. Most journalists enjoy writing and communicating with others. If this sounds like you, then you might make a good journalist. There may be fewer opportunities in some news media today, but the diversity of opportunities has never been so great.

News is a business that demands both action and active people. It is a business of highs and lows. There are moments of great intensity and moments of sheer boredom. But it takes aggressive, people-oriented, curious individuals to be journalists. Good journalists never seem to outgrow the 3-year-old's favorite question: "Why?"

Students interested in newspaper reporting will probably not begin their careers as metropolitan daily reporters. A few extraordinary students will be able to start this high up the ladder. Most recent college graduates who seek newspaper jobs at major daily newspapers will begin as newsroom clerks or in part-time positions. Otherwise, the opportunities are best at small daily newspapers and weekly newspapers throughout the country. Furthermore, specialty newspapers such as those serving industry or ethnic groups (or those written in foreign languages) are also more open for entry-level employment.

When considering entry-level applicants, magazines today tend to hire clerical and research assistants instead of writers and reporters. Older, more experienced journalists get the most sought-after writing and reporting positions. The "behind-the-scenes" jobs are an opportunity to prove your abilities and to "be there" when a chance to write arises. As with newspapers, smaller magazines—those published for a specialized audience and with a regional circulation—offer a better chance to get started right out of college. Although there may be better chances to find jobs at specialized magazines, to be seriously considered these magazines usually require some expertise in that specialization.

Stone (1989a) writes a regular careers report in broadcast news for the RTNDA. In his opening paragraph, he pointed out, "There's no shortage of applicants for jobs in television and radio news" (p. 1). This should give you a clue to the competition you will be up against if you are thinking about a career in broadcast or cable journalism.

On-air broadcast news jobs are truly hard to find. You should not be fooled into thinking you will graduate and start to work as an on-camera reporter or anchor for a large market television station. Anchor jobs are not available to entry-level broadcast journalists. In most cases, these are earned by experienced reporters with 5 to 10 years or more of experience. It is almost as difficult to find a major market on-air reporting job.

Instead, most entry-level newsroom jobs at major market television stations are found in the off-camera production, research, reporting, and writing areas. These include work as an assignment desk assistant, an assistant producer, a staff researcher, a tape editor, or even a news cameraperson.

Most of these opportunities require good writing and organizing skills and can lead to chances to work on stories on a daily basis. They do not always offer the glamour of on-air work. With experience, those chances may come.

Just as in the print media described earlier, television news and radio news jobs are more easily found in smaller broadcast markets and in the growing area of cable television news. Even a medium-size market commercial television station may use only about two dozen full-time staff members ranging from news director to a roving general assistant/clerk (Stone, 1989a, 1991), and the national average commercial television news staff size is 21 full-time and 3 part-time news staff members. An average radio news operation has just 1 full-time and 1 part-time staff member. For a major market radio news operation, the average is slightly over 5 positions, including part-timers. For the smallest market stations, the average is slightly more than 2 persons, including part-time positions (Stone, 1989a, 1991).

Local origination cable news reporting is the best chance for entry-level work today if you have an interest in television news writing, reporting, and editing. Some universities and colleges have their own stations, either broadcast or cable channel, and most communities have cable systems today. This is the best place to start while in school or just after finishing school. You will need *experience* for the best entry-level jobs.

Commercial radio news opportunities are greater than those in commercial television. For one reason, there are simply more radio stations. In a major market, for example, there may be 30 to 40 radio stations, whereas there may be only 5 to 10 local television stations. However, many radio stations de-emphasize news and do not maintain large news staffs—some commercial stations may not have any news specialists at all. But, as stated earlier, the best chances in radio await you in smaller markets.

Stone (1989a) said jobs are found in at least nine types of electronic media:

- commercial television stations
- commercial radio stations

- public television
- public radio
- broadcast networks
- cable television
- corporate television
- wire services
- public relations (pp. 5–6).

There are 10 major jobs or positions found in typical broadcast newsrooms today:

- reporter
- cameraperson
- assignment editor
- news producer
- executive news producer
- writer
- tape editor
- anchorperson/newscaster
- news director
- assistant news director (pp. 6–7).

An advantage, of course, of starting with a small station is the diversity of experience. Newsroom job specialization, on the other hand, can become a potential liability for those starting with large stations. In other words, there's risk in doing too much of very little.

Starting in radio is good advice. "What of starting in radio and moving to television after a year or two? Radio can give solid experience in writing, on-air delivery, interviewing, first-hand reporting, and the live, on-your-feet reporting of spot news which is becoming more and more important in both radio and television," argued Stone (1989a, p. 9).

For certain groups in the population, there are special opportunities made available through industry programs. For minorities and women, for example, many news organizations have programs to identify and train talented individuals. These programs begin as early as high school, continue through college with internships and part-time jobs, and become full-time after graduation. If you qualify, you should begin looking into local opportunities today.

WHAT'S AHEAD IN THIS BOOK

This book describes and illustrates the most important reporting skills of print and broadcast journalists. If you master the material here, you will know the basics of reporting for newspapers, magazines, radio stations, and television stations.

This book is divided into three major sections:

Part I provides your introduction to reporting. This chapter has served as the starting point, but chapters 2 and 3 provide more depth. Chapter 2 discusses general assignment and beat reporting. Chapter 3 tells you how to develop sources for stories.

Part II is devoted to the techniques of reporting. For generations, reporters have refined skills for gathering information. These chapters offer you the best of reporting techniques today. Chapter 4 focuses on research for news stories. Chapter 5 goes further into that subject by looking closely at use of documents and computer databases in reporting news stories. Chapter 6 provides the basics of news story interviewing, and chapter 7 looks closely at special techniques needed for successful broadcast interviewing. Chapter 8 describes observational skills. Chapter 9 outlines the techniques used in group reporting settings such as press conferences and meetings.

Part III looks at the important areas of regulation and control of reporting. Chapter 10 gives you background needed to report within the law, and chapter 11 provides key points in the professional ethics of reporting.

Each chapter also offers a wide variety and a large number of examples in a section called "How Professionals Write It," to enhance your understanding of the material discussed. To get the most from these, study how the stories have been written and the sources that were used. Analyze the differing styles and approaches. Determine what worked well for each example. And try to take something from each example and apply it to your own writing.

In the appendices, you will find the internal media relations policy of a major university, the *Orange County Register*'s newsroom policy memorandum about confidential sources, the Society of Professional Journalists code of ethics, the Radio-Television News Directors Association code of ethics, and a reporter's bookshelf list of reference sources.

HOW PROFESSIONALS WRITE IT

SOURCE: KTUL-TV, Channel 8 (ABC), Tulsa, OK
AUTHOR: KTUL-TV news staff
DATE: Friday, May 4, 1990
TIME: 5 P.M. newscast

* * *

---

2 SHOT 2 BOX	JOINS US FROM THE NEWSROOM WITH SPECIFICS.

TO DON LIVE NEWSROOM	--------------DON LIVE-------------
	2 SHOT TOSS BACK
	------------------2------------------
	(LAT) THANKS DON . . . AS WE SAID . . . PRESIDENT BUSH IS IN TULSA TONIGHT . . .
	(ELY) HE ARRIVED THIS MORNING . . . AND WAS RUSHED TO STILLWATER . . . FOR COMMENCEMENT AT OKLAHOMA STATE.
TURN ELY--------------------------------1---------------------------------	
BUSH COMMENCEMENT ELY 5	
	3
ELY CLOSEUP	(ELY)
	AT O.S.U. . . . PRESIDENT BUSH INVITED NEW CUTS IN NUCLEAR WEAPONS . . . AND LAID-OUT AMERICA'S FUTURE STRATEGY . . . IN EUROPE.
VTR VO---	
CG____OKLAHOMA STATE UNIVERSITY	HE TOLD THE GRADUATES . . . THAT WE ARE COMMITTED TO EUROPE . . . AND NATO . . . FOR THE LONG RUN . . .
	FROM ECONOMICS . . . TO A MILITARY PRESENCE.
	HOWEVER . . . AS SOON AS A FINAL AGREEMENT IS REACHED ON CONVENTIONAL FORCES THERE.
	HE WANTS TALKS WITH THE 3 + 1
ELY VTR VO NATS	SOVIETS . . . ON TACTICAL NUCLEAR WEAPONS.
VTR SOT--------------------------------SOT---------------------------------	
NO CG	IN: AS DEMOCRACY BLOOMS IN EASTERN EUROPE . . .

RUNS :26   RUNS :26

OUT: CREDIBLE . . . AND EFFEC-TIVE."

VTR VO NATS TIED ON ---

MR. BUSH . . . SAYS U.S. INVOLVE-MENT IN EUROPE . . . HAS LED TO THE LONGEST PERIOD OF PEACE . . . IN THE HISTORY OF THAT CONTINENT. HE BELIEVES, CON-TINUED STABILITY . . . AND PEACE . . . ARE WITHIN REACH.

END VTR VO----------------------2 SHOT-STEVE------------------------

TWO BOX TOSS TO STEVE 5/4

5:00   KNIGHT

TWO SHOT: ------------------------SHOT------------------------ PAGE 04

(CHUCK) THE PRESIDENT NOW IS BACK IN TULSA.

(LEANNE) HE'S GETTING READY TO SPEAK AT THE ACADEMIC ALL-STATE BANQUET.

(CHUCK) THAT'S IN THE CONVEN-TION CENTER.

STEVE KNIGHT JOINS US NOW, FROM THERE, WITH "OKLAHOMA LIVE":

REMOTE FULL: ---

CG:_____DOWNTOWN
_____8-STEVE KNIGHT/LIVE

(AD LIBS TO ROLL CUE FOR LIVE VO/VTR "244 GUARDS": "THE PRESIDENT ARRIVED BACK IN TULSA ABOUT AN HOUR AGO.")

OKLAHOMA LIVE/BUSH
5:00   KNIGHT

5/4

PAGE 04 + 1

LIVE VO/VTR (REMOTE)---

REMOTE FULL: ---

CG:_____SEN. DAVID BOREN/ (D), OKLA.	(AD LIBS INTERVIEW WITH BO-REN) (TOSSES TO VTR PKG "TEACHER PROFILE" ROLL CUE:)
VTR PKG ---	
	(OUT: "NEWS EIGHT.")
REMOTE FULL ---	
	(AD LIBS WRAP UP AND TOSSES TO STUDIO)

Reprinted with permission of KTUL-TV.

• • •

SOURCE: WCCO-TV, Channel 4 (CBS), Minneapolis
AUTHOR: Darryl Savage, reporter
DATE: Friday, August 10, 1990
TIME: 6 P.M. newscast

* * *

NICOLLET ISLAND FIRE	(((DAVE //_____)))
INTRO 6PM (KH) × DAVE CU A	EARLY THIS MORNING, FIRE GUTTED A HOUSEBOAT THAT WAS DOCKED BY NICOLLET IS-LAND. FIREFIGHTERS WEREN'T ABLE TO REACH THE BOAT IN PART BECAUSE A TRAIN BLOCKED THE ROAD. ACCESS TO THE ISLAND, WHICH
TAKE ADDA FULL (nicollet)	IS JUST NORTH OF DOWNTOWN MINNEAPOLIS, IS A CONCERN OF THE FIRE CHIEF, AS WELL AS SOME OF THE 30 PROP-ERTY OWNERS ON THE ISLAND ... AS DARRYL SAVAGE RE-PORTS.
TAKE VT SOT ON 11	
	OUT: (((VT SOT)))
NICOLLET ISLAND FIRE (KH) 6PM	((NAT:fire))))
	((TRACK))))
TITLE: MPLS. tp 1 fire	WHEN MINNEAPOLIS FIRE-FIGHTERS ARRIVED ON THE

SCENE AT THREE A-M, ALL THEY COULD DO WAS BATTLE THE BLAZE FROM THE SHORE. BY THE TIME THEIR BOAT ARRIVED, THE HOUSEBOAT WAS CHARRED.

((SOT))))

NO TITLE

IN: we're lucky it's just	tp1
(a boat if it's a	7:52
home, we're in the	7:58

OUT: same situation.

(((TRACK)))))

tp 2 43:35 rr tracks

tp2
45:11 bridge

tp 2 19:38 bridge weight sign

A BURLINGTON NORTHERN TRAIN WAS BLOCKING EAST IS-LAND ROAD. A COMPANY SPOKESMAN SAID THE CREW AP-PARENTLY LEFT THE TRAIN WHEN THEY WENT OFF DUTY. THE ONLY OTHER ACCESS – THE NICOLLET STREET BRIDGE – ISN'T STRONG ENOUGH TO SUPPORT A 15-TON FIRETRUCK.

TITLE: TOM DICKINSON :08 IN_____   ((SOT))))
        MPLS FIRE CHIEF OUT_____

IN: well what we need	tp2
to have is this bridge	14:24
taken out and a suitable	14:32

OUT: bridge put in.

(((TRACK)))

tp 2 2 shot

tp 2 neighborhood shots

UNTIL A NEW BRIDGE IS BUILT, ALL FIRE CHIEF TOM DICKINSON CAN DO IS ASK BURLINGTON NORTHERN TO MOVE THEIR TRAINS. THIS MORNING, THAT TOOK 45 MINUTES – TOO LONG TO SAVE THE HOUSEBOAT. STILL, SOME RESIDENTS AREN'T CON-CERNED ABOUT THE TRAINS.

NICOLLET ISLAND 6PM

((((TRACK))))

STILL, NOT ALL RESIDENTS WANT THE OLD BRIDGE UP-GRADED.

((((SOT)))

TITLE: JUDY RICHARDSON :06
   NICOLLET ISLAND
   RESIDENT
IN_____
OUT_____

IN: "I want to see   tp2
emergency vehicles but   30:39
I don't want lots of   30:45
traffic.
OUT: keep it that way.

(((TRACK)))

FOR NOW, ISLANDERS ARE STILL
WORKING ON BALANCING
MODERN ACCESS AND
OLD-FASHIONED CHARM.

tp 2 32:59 sawing

DARRYL SAVAGE, WCCO TV
NEWS, NICOLLET ISLAND.

((NAT; SAWING)

Reprinted with permission of WCCO-TV.

• • •

SOURCE: The Associated Press
DATE: Wednesday, April 3, 1991, 12:03 A.M.
AUTHOR: Sandra Walewski, writer
STORY SLUG: Kennedy Compound Assault

* * *

PALM BEACH, Fla. (AP)—Police fended off a deluge of publicity Tuesday as they investigated an alleged rape on the Kennedy estate, saying they didn't want to compromise the case.

"This is definitely the clamor of the town the last two days," said Palm Beach police spokesman Craig Gunkel.

Investigators have not filed charges in the case and have declined to say whether anyone associated with the Kennedy family is a suspect, Gunkel said.

A spokesman for U.S. Sen. Edward Kennedy issued a statement Monday saying he was with his family in Palm Beach over the Easter weekend, but had nothing to do with the incident.

The victim of the alleged 4 A.M. Saturday assault at the compound was identified only as a 30-year-old woman who lives in Palm Beach County.

"We haven't made public any particular name as ruled out or in," Gunkel said. "It's a delicate case when you talk about sexual battery—you don't want to release something that could hinder your investigation."

Gunkel characterized the reported attack as a rape, saying it was not a less serious form of sexual assault. He also said alcohol was involved, including drinks consumed prior to the incident, but he would not elaborate.

Local newspapers reported Kennedy was with his son, Patrick, and nephew, William Kennedy Smith, Friday night at the Palm Beach lounge Au Bar. The newspapers quoted the manager, Stuart Lichtenstein.

Patrick Kennedy, 24, said Tuesday he knew nothing about the incident and was asleep at the time of the alleged rape.

"The girl is not someone I know. She was not a guest of mine. I assume she was a guest of one of my cousins," he said.

Smith, 30, a student at Georgetown University School of Medicine, stayed with friends Tuesday night and couldn't be reached for comment, the landlord at his Georgetown carriage house told the Palm Beach Post.

Patrick Kennedy is a member of the Rhode Island House and the youngest of Ted Kennedy's three children. Smith is the son of Ted Kennedy's older sister, Jean Kennedy Smith, and the late Stephen Smith.

Police Chief Joe Terlizzese, asked whether he was satisfied investigators have been able to question all members of the Kennedy family who might have information on the case, said: "We are not satisfied."

Shortly after the woman got in touch with police Saturday, investigators were sent to the Kennedy compound, but by then, the man the woman said assaulted her had left Palm Beach, Terlizzese said.

Terlizzese said the woman told investigators she met the senator and his party for drinks and later went to have "a couple of cocktails" at the Kennedy estate.

The rape report left local residents and tourists buzzing.

"It's deja vu for the family. I'm enthralled with them and everything that happens to them," said Ruth Kane, visiting from nearby Boca Raton. "I find them fascinating – not always admirable."

Lona Rosen, a tourist from Philadelphia, had mixed feelings about the case.

"They've had a lot of tragedies," she said. "This is another chapter in the family history."

The rape report came seven years after Palm Beach was shaken by another Kennedy family tragedy, the drug-overdose death of the late Robert Kennedy's son, David Kennedy.

David Kennedy had been kicked out of the compound by the family and moved to the nearby Brazilian Court Hotel, where his body was found April 25, 1984.

The $3 million Kennedy estate served as a winter White House for John F. Kennedy three decades ago and had been used by Rose Kennedy, the family matriarch, until her health declined recently.

The Kennedys "keep to themselves" for the most part, said Gunkel, and do not get special protection when they are in town. The only incidents they have had at the compound in recent years were trespassing reports, he said.

Reprinted with permission of the Associated Press.

• • •

2 General Assignment And Beat Reporting

The reporter is the most important man in the newspaper organization.
—Bush (1929, p. 1)

Chilton R. Bush, a University of Wisconsin journalism professor, wrote those words over 60 years ago. Reporters are the most important *men and women* in the *news organization*. The emphasis remains the same, although a few key things have changed. Women work side by side with men as reporters and news originates from more than just newspapers today, but the essence of Bush's words still rings true.

Reporters, Bush also wrote, must have a critical sense, be widely connected, know their territories, be resourceful and curious, have poise and enthusiasm, and, on top of all that, be able to write.

Put very simply, reporters are the arms, legs, eyes, and ears of their news organizations. Reporters are the individuals entrusted with the responsibility of gathering information for a given story or subject. They are the grass roots of the news organization. Without reporters, most news organizations lose their uniqueness and become no more than relay stations for other news sources.

Veteran newsmen John Chancellor and Walter Mears (1983) felt the essence of journalism is reporting. Journalism, they wrote, "is the craft of telling what happened. Telling what happened requires the journalist to tell how the information was gathered" (p. 139). Chancellor, anchor and commentator for the NBC Nightly News for many years, and Mears, a Pulitzer Prize-winning Associated Press Washington political reporter, summarized what the job of any reporter must be: "Who told you? How do you know? How reliable is the source? Is the source trying to peddle a point

For some news reporting specializations, such as the police beat, much of the newsmaking action occurs at night (photo by Jon Kral, *Miami Herald* staff).

of view, to build up, or knock down, someone or something? Those are basic questions to answer" (p. 139).

Denver's *Rocky Mountain News* shows how important reporters are to a newspaper. Reporters Ann Carnahan and Tony Pugh, with the guidance of assistant city editor Chris Broaderick, developed in a five-story series of articles that 85% of children from the city's nine low-income housing projects who should have graduated with their class dropped out or fell too far behind to graduate. The city reacted with disbelief and shock because no one really knew the educational plight of inner-city teenagers. Denver residents were made aware of this problem not because they saw the events behind the stories firsthand, but because of the enterprise of the city desk reporters for this newspaper. Minority groups picketed the school administration's offices. New programs were proposed to remedy the problem (Ambrose, 1991).

This is reporting. Reporters monitor their communities, gather and organize information about the activities they observe, and write stories for their audiences. Reporters, like the team at Denver's *Rocky Mountain News,* informed community members and instigated positive community change.

This chapter introduces you to several key principles of reporting. First, we discuss the nature of news values. Then we introduce the two major approaches to reporting: general assignment reporting and beat reporting.

IDENTIFYING NEWS

What makes news? You probably have a good "feel" for news already. After all, you have been watching television news and reading newspapers and news magazines, right? In other words, just by looking at the content of the news media around you, you should get a pretty good idea of what news is in your community.

That's right, *in your community.* What news is in one place might not be news in another place. Why is that? We'll try to get an answer to that as we take a look at news values and their role in determining news in the mid-1990s.

There's a variety of labels in the business that indicate a variety of approaches to news. You have likely heard someone refer to "hard news" and "soft news" or "straight news" and "features."

"Hard" or "straight" news has traditionally been event-based. That is, it has always been viewed as events such as a resignation or an election, police arrests in a drug deal or a shooting, traffic and other accidents, local government meetings, public speeches, weather disasters, and so on. Reporting about these events tends to be timely and immediate.

"Soft" or "features" news is more human interest-based and less dependent on specific events. The usual fare of soft news on television or in a newspaper includes profiles, entertainment stories, life-style stories, reviews, travel stories, social news, humor, and the like. These are much less time oriented and, thus, perhaps less important when compared with hard news.

In broadcasting, if you have ever been around a television newsroom, you begin to understand that news is not necessarily news unless there is good video to go with the story.

And most magazine editors today do not think as seriously about a potential article for their publications unless they can find some good "art" — that is, photographs or other graphics — to go with the article.

Celebrities have become a major subject in magazines in recent years. The development and success of *People* magazine are certainly evidence of the market for celebrity news. It has become such a source of news for some magazines, writer Ryan P. Murphy (1989) said, there is a "personality overkill" in U.S. magazines. Murphy noted that many U.S. magazines have taken on a "reader-friendly celebrity bent" for growth in circulation. New personalities magazines have been developed and introduced. This says much about how news is defined by some magazine editors.

Definitions of news have existed since the first reporting and news writing textbooks were written at the beginning of this century. But the definitions have not changed too much over the past three-quarters of a century except to recognize the way we "handle" news today. This means you must consider transmission and other technical factors in generating news. Furthermore, it means you have to think of news as you might think of any other product on the open market — something useful to consumers that is for sale and competing for attention.

TIM KELLY, *LEXINGTON HERALD-LEADER*
AN EDITOR DEFINES NEWS

If there's one immutable law of editing the news, it's that stories that sound too good to be true usually are.

But not always.

And for that we can be thankful, because those are the stories that make newspapers fun to read — and edit.

But what is news? And who or what ultimately determines what's news and what's not?

News is a lot of things:

- It's what our reporters tell us.
- It's what the editor says it is.
- It's what our instincts tell us.
- It's what the person at the next desk thinks.
- It's what we can get into readable form before the next deadline.
- It's what is fair and consistent given the paper's standards and previous handling of similar stories.

(continued)

TIM KELLY, *LEXINGTON HERALD-LEADER* (continued)

- It's what we fear the competing paper will report tomorrow. Or, worse yet, what it had today that we didn't have.
- It's what television plays up. (Read that: What television has the best tape of.)
- It's what the *New York Times,* the *Washington Post,* and the *Los Angeles Times* have on their front pages tomorrow morning.
- It's . . . what's that again?

Hundreds of daily newspapers subscribe to the *New York Times* News Service, the *Los Angeles Times-Washington Post* News Service, or both. Each evening those services alert their members to the page one lineups planned by the three newspapers for the next morning.

Many times I've thought to myself or heard others on the news desk say, "I wonder what the *Times* (or *Post*) has on its front."

The truth is, what the *New York Times* considers news should be, and likely will be, a whole lot more relevant to New York or a national audience than it is to your hometown – or mine.

I use it as an example of the many, many factors that influence news judgment and story play.

Critics contend that a sameness has enveloped America's newspapers. It can be traced to several trends, among them the rapid decline of two-newspaper towns, the concurrent growth of giant newspaper organizations and a newsroom work force that may be younger than any time this century.

It is an impatient work force, one that produces short tenures for editors and reporters – and even publishers – as they move from town to town in their climb up the career ladder.

I can speak with some authority on the issue. I have been one of those people.

Newsrooms are inherently insular places to begin with. And given the odd hours and intensity of the work, that extends outside the office as well.

It is common for those reporters who are far from hometowns and families to congregate together instead of making friends and getting involved in their adopted communities.

When the people who make the decisions about what's news and what's not don't know the area they serve, there's a danger that the news judgment can become skewed and not as relevant to the readership as it should be. In other words, if it worked in the last town, it'll work in this town.

But news doesn't work that way.

And that brings us to what news really *ought to be,* even if it isn't.

It *ought to be* what truly interests and affects the people for whom we produce the newspaper.

It *ought to be* what readers say it is.

If newspapers were what they *ought to be,* they would pay more attention to the way real people live and less to what their peers do or what their peers think about them.

(continued)

TIM KELLY, *LEXINGTON HERALD-LEADER (continued)*

If newspapers were what they *ought to be,* they would pay more attention to the common denominators — broad themes that cut across lots of demographic boundaries.

Start with the two biggest investments we make: housing and automobiles. Carry it through to the topics such as family, workplace, education, religion, health, leisure time, and personal finance.

Ask yourself how well your daily newspaper covers those topics. Measure that against the amount of space consumed, say, by politics and government on the local, state, and national levels.

One respected editor makes the case that the business of America really is business, not government.

Jay Ambrose of Denver's *Rocky Mountain News* put it this way: "We're a business civilization. We consume products of businesses. Our landscapes are dominated by offices and business buildings. Yet we relegate business to a little section in the back of the paper and treat it like an afterthought. Society is more dominated by business than government. . . . Then, are our newspapers really reflecting the nature of our society?"

An observation by Phillip L. Williams, vice chairman of Times Mirror Co., and its former senior executive for newspapers, is even more pointed: "There are really two kinds of journalism. There's the ASNE (American Society of Newspaper Editors) level of journalism in which you impress the other editors. And then there's the kind of journalism that impresses the readers."

The trick, of course, is to do both. That means doing the Journalism with a capital "J" that exposes wrongdoing, changes history, and wins awards as well as the journalism with a lowercase "j" that affects your readers' everyday lives.

And how do we know what's important to them? We ask them . . . in surveys, in forums, in focus groups. We get out of the office and talk to people. We listen to what they say in their letters and phone calls. And then we tailor the newspaper to their needs.

It seems so simple — just like one of those stories that sounds too good to be true.

Except this one isn't (Garrison, 1990).

Tim Kelly is the editor of the *Lexington, Ky. Herald-Leader.* Before taking that job in 1991, he was executive editor for nearly 2 years. He was managing editor of the *Orange County Register* in California when it won the 1989 Pulitzer Prize for specialized reporting. He has also worked as an editor for the *Dallas Times-Herald, Denver Post,* and the *Daily News* of Los Angeles.

NEWS VALUES

Who determines what is news today? There's a large number of people trying to do that every day. And not all of them are journalists.

Although we most often think of journalists as the persons who generate news, they are not the only ones. Reporters, photographers, and editors/producers decide what is news. These persons are called *gatekeepers*. These individuals open and close the "gates" that allow the flow of information to readers and viewers. A story judged newsworthy gets "through the gate," but one that does not get the gatekeeper's approval is, then, not aired or published and therefore is not news.

Sources, too, sometimes try to get into the act of determining what is news. Only in the past several decades, especially in the 1980s, has public relations come into its own. Specialists who were educated to assist news organizations now represent their former sources. These persons often create newsmaking situations such as press conferences or photo opportunities. What these new players in the equation decide often impacts on what journalists have on their agendas for the day to select or not select.

Much news today originates from two categories of sources. Journalists have traditionally depended on *events* to be the basis of news. You can probably think of many event-oriented news stories: city commission meetings, graduation ceremonies, shootings, concerts, football games, civil disturbances, traffic accidents, and elections. They all make news.

But in the past two or three decades, reporters have come more and more to depend on news that does not originate in an event. This may be a little harder to envision, but it includes trend and analysis stories. Trend stories include stories about changing neighborhoods, new life-styles, local buying habits, and public opinion poll-based stories such as election reports or community reaction stories. Analysis or interpretive stories attempt to explain phenomena such as community economic problems, education trends, neighborhood social troubles, and regional political conflicts.

Journalists must also consider *focus* as a principal element in their news judgment. Journalists are limited in their ability to report by either time in broadcasting or space in the print media, so their judgment must be tempered by focus. The manner in which you write your story is a form of focus. What you choose to emphasize in the lead, de-emphasize at the conclusion, or leave out entirely places focus on elements of the story.

Journalists present *point of view* in their news judgment as well. This means the vantage point taken in judging the events taking place. For example, at a football game, do you cover the game from the press box, from the sidelines, from the locker room, from the parking lot, or from the stands? Each may be a legitimate place, depending on the news judgments you make and the type of story you are writing.

If you are writing the game results story, the press box or sidelines might be the best vantage points. If you are writing a player or coach reaction sidebar, then the locker room might be your best location. But a different story, focusing on the fans, is probably best written from the parking lot, concession areas, and the stadium stands.

Certain basic characteristics of news have evolved. News consists of:

1. *Timeliness:* News is usually timely. To broadcasters, this means minutes or hours. To the print media, it means later the same day, the next day, or next week. But news does not wait much of the time. Some news,

Events involving large numbers of people, such as the U.S. Coast Guard intervention of thousands of Haitians trying to enter the United States without permission, makes big news (photo by the *Miami Herald* staff).

such as a major airline accident or a war, cannot wait for all information to be gathered. You must report it as quickly as technologically possible.

2. *Magnitude:* News frequently is broadcast and published because it has impact on many people. Decisions or events that affect only a few people may not always become news.

3. *Proximity:* Even in an era when global communication is instantaneous and of high quality, news remains largely local. We are certainly

interested in what happens halfway around the world, but most news consumers still are interested in their own communities because local events are likely to affect their lives more directly. Events halfway around the world become more newsworthy when they involve local connections.

4. *Interest:* News must be interesting. As basic as that seems, it really means that news should have a human dimension. News becomes most interesting when it consists of many of the other characteristics of this list but certainly when it involves people.

5. *Drama:* News is dramatic. Vivid news pictures of compelling resignation speeches, of social unrest, of arguments, of accident scenes, and of rescues are highly appealing to the consumer.

6. *Prominence:* News often involves those names people know. Names, as the old saying goes, do make news. Well-known names make bigger news. Local political leaders, business leaders, elected public officials, entertainers, and sports figures are examples of prominent individuals who often make news not solely because of what they do but because of who they are.

7. *Conflict:* The opposing forces of our lives often create news. Whether they are political parties, feuding neighbors or organizations, jealous lovers, or warring nations, conflict still generates some of the most important news of our time. For centuries, conflict has been a newsmaker.

8. *Balance:* In reporting news, journalists attempt to be evenhanded. When news is fair and balanced, it tells all sides of the story.

9. *Objectivity:* Although news must be balanced, it must also be neutral. Opinion-based writing such as entertainment reviews, columns and commentaries, and editorials, is an exception, but the goal of news is to be factual and not biased to one perspective or another.

10. *Unusualness:* News that is the best remembered on a given day is often the unique or most unusual. Out-of-the-ordinary events become news. Journalists often look for novelty as a factor in judging something newsworthy.

11. *Analysis:* News is becoming more and more explanatory. This "why" or "how" element of news has become particularly important to print media that try to compensate for their inherent lack of immediacy by providing depth through analysis and interpretation. Many news stories today are insufficient and incomplete if only facts are presented. Perhaps this is best illustrated by economic or medical news.

12. *Visual:* Today's news has a visual dimension. With television, and with print media graphics expanding, the visual characteristics of news take on a growing importance in deciding what is news.

13. *Audience:* When determining news, think about (a) Who is going to read, see, or hear the story? (b) Who will be affected by it? Broadcasters who know the demographics of their market on a particular day and at a particular time may be able to select news better than a competitor who does not know this information. The same applies to newspapers and magazines. Editors with knowledge of who reads their publications can more competently match stories with readers.

Broadcasters often look for even more than these factors in finding the best television news story. Emmy award-winning television investigative reporter Clarence Jones (1983) said broadcast journalists use the "FACE" formula in judging sources when putting together a story for television:

1. *Feelings:* Sources should tell the audience how they are feeling about the situation.
2. *Analysis:* Sources should provide some assessment in a sentence or two: What is the source's opinion?
3. *Compelling Cs:* One or more of these elements usually are sure-fired television news: catastrophes, crises, conflicts, crime and corruption, color/human interest.
4. *Energy:* Sources should be somewhat animated — that is, they should project energy and confidence in what they are saying.

Sociologist Herbert Gans studied the "CBS Evening News," "NBC Nightly News," *Newsweek,* and *Time* to determine the fundamental news values of some of the leading national news organizations. Gans (1979) wrote, "The news does not limit itself to reality judgments; it also contains values, or preference statements" (p. 39).

Gans found six enduring values in news that are rarely explicit — something like reading between the lines, he remarked. He listed these "enduring values" in news:

1. *Ethnocentrism:* What happens at home is more important than something happening overseas. It borders, he said, on blatant patriotism.
2. *Altruistic democracy:* With this, Gans believed "the news implies that politics should follow a course based on the public interest and public service" (p. 43).
3. *Responsible capitalism:* In looking at the economy in the news, Gans felt journalists have "an optimistic faith that in the good society, businessmen and women will compete with each other in order to create increased prosperity for all, but they will refrain from unreasonable profits and gross exploitation of workers or customers" (p. 46).
4. *Small-town pastoralism:* Even two centuries later, the rural and anti-industrial values often associated with Thomas Jefferson are often found in the news. Gans explained, "Small-town pastoralism is . . . a specification of two more general values: the desirability of both nature and of smallness per se" (p. 49).
5. *Individualism:* The news media root for the individualist. Gans noted, "One of the most important enduring news values is the preservation of the freedom of the individual against the encroachments of nation and society" (p. 50).
6. *Moderatism:* The news media, Gans also concluded, prefer news that discourages extremism or excess.

Raymond Coffey (1987), *Chicago Tribune* writer and columnist, questioned how journalists decide what is published daily by pondering the distinction between worthy news and trivial news. Coffey pointed to stories involving Judge Robert Bork, President Reagan's nominee for the Supreme Court, Kitty Dukakis, wife of then-Massachusetts governor and Democratic presidential contender Michael Dukakis, and presidential aide Lt. Col. Oliver North. Events surrounding these people lead Coffey to ask, "Is it trivia or news?" and, he added, "All of it, I'm sure, means something. But what?" Much news decision making, using values such as Gans' listed earlier, involves drawing the fine line between the trivial and the significant that Coffey emphasized.

ACCURACY IN REPORTING

We can point to many characteristics of news, but it is, *above all else,* accurate. Reporters cannot consider legitimatizing news that is not accurate. For credibility's sake, we must take extraordinary steps to assure that the content of any story, listing, screen graphic, or even pictures be precise and represent the facts and only the facts.

Although this may seem basic, it is critical to your work as a news reporter. Too many reporting errors too many times have led to eroding public trust in the news media. Once readers or viewers begin to find mistakes in the reports they see in a newspaper or on a television newscast, they may turn to another source. If enough of this happens, circulation or ratings drop and the news organization eventually fails. But before that extreme happens, careless reporters lose in their news organization's effort to protect its reputation.

Editors and news directors place accuracy as a premium attribute of news. Accuracy is the leading aspect of quality news, according to newspaper researcher Leo Bogart (1989).

The Broadcast News Services editors of United Press International (UPI; 1979) have the utmost respect for accuracy in news stories. They advised UPI staffers and beginning reporters that it is at the top of their list: "The most important ingredient of any story you move [on the wire] is accuracy. One of U-P-I's mottos is 'get it first, but get it right.' Never forget it" (p. 4). They continued, "Check and then re-check all facts, figures and names. In broadcasting, nine out of 10 corrections reach an entirely different audience. The time to make one is BEFORE the copy hits the wire" (p. 4).

THE PROCESS OF INFORMATION GATHERING

News organizations attempt to cast a news gathering blanket over their communities. Those "communities" can be vastly different. A college newspaper's community might be its campus. A rural 5,000-watt radio station's news department may serve only the county seat and surrounding area. A major market television station's news department may serve three or four densely populated counties or more. A network news department's

**PETE WEITZEL, THE *MIAMI HERALD*
A MANAGING EDITOR DISCUSSES REPORTING**

What does a reporter do?

When we asked several dozen reporters and editors that question a couple of years back as part of an effort to develop job descriptions, they offered a collection of answers that all seemed to fall into one of two tasks.

A reporter reports and a reporter writes. Brilliantly simple, but what else is there?

Last weekend, in a session at the Poynter Institute, I realized we had missed something. There's another function that is an essential part of the reporting/writing process, and it needs to be looked at as a separate step because it creates the biggest problems for both the reporter and the editor. Organizing.

The critical role of organizing in the writing process was stressed by Roy Peter Clark and Donald Fry, who make a profession of studying and teaching writing. Writer's block, Fry suggested at one point, is primarily a result of the reporter not knowing where he or she is going next—of organization.

Here are some things they said about writing that you may find helpful:

They divide the writing process into five steps: selection (the assignment, deciding what to write about); reporting; organizing; drafting; clarifying (editing/rewriting).

• Editors need to spend more time talking to reporters in the selection/ assignment process. Then, they should let the reporters develop new ideas or approaches so the assignment becomes theirs. "The writer needs to find himself in reporting. . . . The best newswriting is an egotistical venture."

• Research shows that a person who rehearses what he or she will find at an assignment will see more. "It doesn't trammel [sic] the writer at all to think about what might be found there."

• The organizing stage is too often skipped. "Five minutes of organizing can save an hour of drafting." A reporter should go through the notes, coding and marking the important things, and go back to the notes only for detail, specific quotes, etc.

• "The essence of newswriting is throwing out all but the best." Most good stories retain about 5 percent of what was gathered.

• Write out a theme statement as a guide, a point statement. Use it as a basis to throw things out. If a wonderful fact or quote doesn't fit within the theme, toss it. "Killing the babies," Fry called it, a reference to one reporter who referred to quotes she'd gathered as "my babies" because she could not bear to lose them.

• Writers know what's wrong with their writing. The editor working with a reporter should let the reporter talk it out. Editors should guide the writer through a discussion of a story, not announce what's wrong.

• Jot down a plan, a loose outline, for the story. If you try to keep that plan in your head, you'll change it. You'll keep the babies."

(continued)

PETE WEITZEL, THE *MIAMI HERALD* (continued)

• Write quickly to avoid getting tired. Most stories sag at the halfway point. Then go back and self-edit.

• Read the story aloud. "The bumps in newswriting are the little words. You don't pick up these when you read silently."

If you run into difficulty writing a story, the real problem is not where you are in the writing process; it's one step back. If you block in the writing, go back to the organizational step. If you block in trying to organize the story, go back to the reporting process. "A problem in the reporting area is rarely one of not enough material; it's not having the right material." Go back to the selection/assignment step.

• An editor can best help by asking organizing questions when the reporter comes back from an assignment.

• Clark told several marvelous anecdotes about reporters who had related rich quotes and intriguing facts on return from assignment, then left these out of their stories until the editors reminded them these had been the first things mentioned in talking about these stories.

• A quick debriefing of a reporter upon return from assignment often prevents mistakes, mistakes that take up time editors don't have on deadline.

Pete Weitzel is managing editor of the *Miami Herald*. Reprinted from the *Miami Herald* newsroom newsletter, *The Bay View*, Monday, November 17, 1986, p. 1.

Reprinted with permission of the *Miami Herald*.

---

community is the entire nation. And a few news operations, such as Cable News Network or Associated Press, view their community as the entire world.

The process of information gathering is complex. It involves many people. Most news organizations, once they have defined their "community," then must develop a plan for covering the news. Some local organizations, without many resources, must depend on outside sources such as wire services and networks for assistance. But for other news, a team of reporters, photographers, and editors or producers must be assembled. Tim Kelly (1989), editor of the Lexington, Kentucky, *Herald-Leader*, has determined the following 10 common errors made by beginning reporters:

1. They do not read newspaper or follow the competition.

2. They grant anonymity, confidentiality too readily.

3. They do not want to identify anonymous, confidential sources to editors.

4. They do not know how to search records, or even know where to look.

5. They writing is too wordy, often stiff and stilted.

6. They are too sensitive to criticism of their work.

7. They rely too much on direct quotations or partial quotations.

8. They occasionally let feelings about a controversy get in the way.

9. They do not get to know their own communities.

10. They spend too much time with other journalists.

Most news organizations cannot monitor the community like a police force or sales team of a major corporation, so alternatives must be considered. Most news organizations evolve into a combination of general assignment reporters, beat reporters, and outside sources such as "stringers," wire services, and networks.

General assignment reporters fill an important role in the day-to-day coverage. They must be ready for breaking news of the day. Beat reporters provide the foundation by contacting the most important sources of news *each day*. Stringers offer extended nonstaff coverage on stories where extra help is needed, but they also offer unsolicited news stories for potential use.

Newsgathering depends on organization. Efficient operations make the most of their resources and get the most news from their communities. Reporters must organize themselves to make certain they have effectively kept an eye on their particular segment of the community. Their supervisors take a broader view to make certain the entire subject area is well covered.

Systematic review of the community is a key. Nothing can be left out. Regular checking in person or by telephone makes certain that quick and complete reports are available to the news consumer. Reporters cannot afford to wait for news to come to them, so an aggressive, consistent approach to monitoring the events of the community is necessary to succeed. This means listening to police radios when things are quiet – just in case. It means reading public documents such as court records – just in case. It means asking questions about unusual-appearing occurrences – just in case.

There are a number of factors sometimes out of the control of reporters that affect the process of newsgathering. You will read about these factors – deadlines, space limitations, newsroom structure, technology, management, and competition – before reading about general assignment and beat reporting techniques in the remaining portions of this chapter.

REPORTING DEADLINES

There seem to be two kinds of people in journalism: those who thrive on deadlines and those who do not. Some journalists, such those working for wire services or the networks, are on deadline 24 hours a day. Other journalists, such as free-lance magazine writers, deal with deadlines on a much less stressful level. Regardless of what sort of news you wind up reporting, you will have to face deadlines. Deadlines are a fact of journalistic life.

From your beginning news writing or reporting class, where you might face your first real challenge to write a brief story in an hour or less, to a career of producing several news stories a day under pressure, this is deadline journalism. Some journalists can escape the daily rigors of deadlines by working for publications or programs with less frequent deadlines, but eventually all journalists must face deadlines.

Journalists working for the major wire services are on deadline from the moment they walk in the bureau office door until they leave at the end of their shift. This is because wire service clients are newspapers, magazines, radio, and television stations in every time zone and with widely varying deadlines. And for many journalists, the pressure follows them home because they are solely responsible for the beat at all times.

Television and radio networks, some local television stations, and all-news radio stations operate under the same constant deadline pressures.

Daily newspapers go through as many as half a dozen major deadlines a day. Weekly newspapers and magazines are less hectic, of course, but still require regular production of stories and photographs.

Deadlines are a journalistic fact of life. They are something all journalists must live with. And they affect content. M. L. Stein (1974) noted that reporters under deadline cannot always finish the story. There may be loose informational ends that cannot be tied. Errors may be made because there may not be time to confirm information. There may be imbalance because all sides to the story may not be represented. "Newsmen and women often obtain information under less than ideal conditions," he observed (p. 24). Often, when these problems are severe enough on deadline, an editor or producer may decide to hold the story until it is ready.

SPACE AND TIME LIMITATIONS

All reporters face limitations in their judgment of news. If all other factors were not considered, we must still live within physical restrictions on news. For most news days, reporters work within highly formatted presentations. That means reporters have only so much space or time to report the day's news.

For exceptional broadcast news stories, special reports enlarge the amount of time used to deliver the news. And for particularly busy news days, more and more stations are lengthening their newscasts. Years ago, this seldom occurred. But when the news demands it, stations, and networks, will preempt scheduled programs for additional news time during a given day. You probably recall this happened frequently during the Persian Gulf War coverage in 1990–1991.

Newspapers and magazines, on the other hand, often find their newshole—the average amount of space for news in a given issue—is as consistent as in broadcasting. But for extraordinary news days, most publications have budgeted additional pages throughout the year and editors can make a withdrawal from the "page bank" for extra space as needed. In anticipation of certain exceptional news days during a year, page banks are actually budgeted space set aside for big breaking news stories. Although this does not occur too often, the usual situation demands that news be written as tightly and concisely as possible. This, of course, permits more different news stories to be aired or published.

NEWSROOM STRUCTURE

Media companies produce a unique product, which can be highly perishable. This is especially true for newspapers, magazines, television stations, and radio stations. But this is not the only factor that makes the news business different from other businesses. John Lavine and Dan Wackman (1988), University of Minnesota communication professors, identified five factors that distinguish media companies: (a) the nature of the product, (b) the types of employees needed, (c) special organizational factors, (d) the media's unique role in society, and (e) the blurring lines between the traditional media (pp. 14–15). This means, in part, that the newsroom is a unique place. Its organization may be very different from other places where you have worked or visited.

In the typical newspaper newsroom and magazine office, activities are controlled by an editor. In a broadcast newsroom, a news director is in charge. As newsrooms get larger, the nature of leadership jobs becomes more specialized. At a small publication, you are likely to work side by side with the editor. The same applies to a small broadcast or cable station.

Generally, the print media have several critical roles that are filled in the organization of the newsroom. Reporters and photographers who gather information are directed by various desk editors. Copy editors process it. Graphics and layout editors organize it for presentation.

In a radio and television newsroom, reporters and photographers are the grassroots journalists directed by assignment editors. Tape editors help process the raw audio and video. Producers are responsible for packaging each show.

The newsroom is organized to expedite flow of information through the various channels to the reader or listener/viewer. Positions and procedures are set for efficiency in the flow of news. This is done to reduce the chance of error and overall cost, but at the same time, to enhance speed in reporting. One thing is certain: The news business is *not* a one-person show, even with the sophisticated technology of the mid-1990s. It really requires a *team* to get your story to its audience.

The way the newsroom is organized, in final assessment, is based on the publication or station's mission and strategy, technology, skill level of management, and resources, according to Lavine and Wackman.

TECHNOLOGY CHANGES NEWS, NEWSGATHERING

When considering news today, the discussion cannot be held without mentioning the startling developments in technology of the past quarter century. Beginning with the microchip and the transistor, things have really changed for the journalist of the mid-1990s.

Much of the change is attributable to the computer. It has revolutionized life in the newsroom. Other technology you are probably quite comfortable with has also had an impact. But for old timers around newsrooms when manual typewriters, dial telephones, teletypes, and film were used, the past three decades have been a time of adjustment. Changes have been rapid and have literally revolutionized how work is done and, to a certain extent, what work is done. Reporters can certainly cover stories today that they might not have tried to cover a decade ago.

Among recent developments that Stone (1989b, p. 9) described for radio news, the computer is at the top of the list. Included among the new capabilities are computers connected to international wire services for faster script writing, editing, and processing. Computers are used for word processing and script preparation, story notes storage, and higher speed transmission of information.

In television, cable and satellite technology has had major impact. We now not only talk about one-way cable, but in some markets two-way, or interactive, cable systems that allow viewer response and premium program selection. Microwave, laser, and satellite technologies have markedly changed both television and radio news. Reporting from greater distances is faster and clearer. Live coverage of events is now possible at all levels — from network to local cable station. Even cable has impacted on radio news. Cable-transmitted radio has developed to enhance sound quality, speed, and distribution of news programs for local stations.

Fiber optics, a technology using glass fiber that permits light to be transmitted at high speed through cable, can carry broadcast and telephone signals. As John Bittner (1989) observed, fiber optics technology "dramatically increases the amount of information that can be carried on any single cable system" (p. 267).

Laser, satellite, and microwave technology has also impacted how we print and distribute newspapers and magazines. Newspapers such as *USA Today,* the *Wall Street Journal,* and the *New York Times* use sophisticated technology to speed same-day distribution throughout the world. The laser has had an enormous impact on newspaper and magazine production techniques, for example. Development of laser technology has meant better graphics and better color printing.

Combinations of traditional news media have also resulted from the new technologies. These information systems, often called electronic newspapers and magazines, have emerged in the past decade. These electronic publications are linked by a combination of telephone lines, satellites, mainframe computers, personal computers, and broadcast/cable systems.

Teletext and videotex news and information systems combine newspaper and magazine formats with television. Teletext connects computers with home receivers such as television sets using decoders. Videotex is provided through cable systems and permits two-way service.

Database services have created on-line computer links for subscribers as well. Some of these contain reference material only, but others provide news and other current information. These are discussed in more depth in chapter 5.

New telephone services have changed reporting and writing as well. Cellular and other forms of portable telephones have made reporting and writing literally possible from anywhere. Link a cellular telephone with a laptop portable or an even smaller microportable (pocket-size) personal computer, for example, and you can write and file a story from anywhere. Although reporters have been writing stories with computers from home or remote locations for more than a decade now, these latest developments make writing and reporting easier and faster, but more demanding, than ever. Electronic messaging and call forwarding systems using telephones and computers have helped reporters communicate with sources like never before. When reporters are not at their desks, messages can be recorded, retrieved in the office or from a remote site, and calls can be forwarded to another number, such as the reporter's home.

NEWSROOM MANAGEMENT

Someone has to run the show. In a newspaper or magazine newsroom, it is an editor or executive editor. In a broadcast newsroom, the news director has final responsibility for the news operation. Editors and news directors report to publishers and general managers who rarely get involved with the daily activities of journalism. This is partly due to the tradition of autonomy of the newsroom, but it also exists because publishers and general managers have so many other responsibilities beyond the news division.

Virtually all editors and news directors started as reporters. Remember that. It means something that they have been where you are now. But from those humble beginnings, newsroom managers have mastered the basics and gone further to leadership in the newsroom.

Newsroom leaders must do three things, according to *Detroit News* publisher and editor Robert H. Giles (1988). Giles said reporters can expect (a) supervision, (b) management, and (c) leadership from their editors. Editors and news directors provide these through their intelligence, dedication, initiative, courage, and even charisma (Lavine & Wackman, 1988).

Whatever their characteristics or style, editors and news directors are in charge. They are the final newsroom authority. They set policy and direction. They set standards. If the newsroom is the center of a "quality" news operation, the leadership of the editor and news director is usually the reason.

Editors and news directors are caught in a strange middle of sorts. On the one hand, they are responsible for the quality and completeness of the news product. On the other hand, they have to provide a product that will make money. Norman Marcus (1986), a Boston University professor, suggested that news directors illustrate the conflict:

> The news director's professional orientation is to disseminate information. However, a larger influence preys upon the news director and it comes from the station's primary obligation to reap profits. Because local news programs are collectively the single greatest profit center for most affiliate stations, some TV station managers have adopted the credo that TV news is too important to be left to the journalists. (pp. 87–88)

It is an old battle often re-fought: circulation and ratings versus journalism and news judgment.

A rung or two up the ladder in most news organizations is either the publisher or the general manager. These persons oversee not only the news operations but *all* other divisions of the newspaper or magazine or radio and/or television station. For a publisher, this means responsibility for the news, production, circulation, business, advertising, promotion, and other departments. For a general manager, this means directing news, sales, production, engineering, business, promotion, public affairs, and other departments. For some publishers, it means supervision for more than one publication — A.M. and P.M. newspapers, a Sunday magazine, an electronic news service, and so on. For many general managers, it might mean supervision of more than one operation — where AM and FM radio stations and the television station are housed under one roof.

The most important impact the publisher and general manager have on their news operations is with the annual budget. Whereas editors and news directors propose budgets, their bosses approve — or reduce — them. And through the budget, the publisher and general manager have influence on the overall news product.

As mentioned earlier, publishers and general managers are rarely involved in the day-to-day activities and decision making in the newsroom. But in very small operations, they are regularly involved. Generally they are seldom seen in the newsroom. They are coordinators and planners for all the various divisions and the products of their publications and stations.

COMPETITION FACTORS

Most newspeople feel competition is a good thing. It has positive impact on their work. Journalists working in a noncompetitive situation often feel they have less to stimulate them to produce quality and to bring improvement to their writing and reporting.

This is no doubt one undesirable effect of a noncompetitive community. But competition actually remains just about everywhere. Its nature has certainly changed, however. Competition is not limited within a medium because today it cuts across media for that rare share of the free time of media consumers. Do viewers prefer to watch reruns of "Cheers" or "The Cosby Show" instead of the 6 P.M. news? Competition even cuts across news into entertainment. The effect is to force news organizations to liven up their programs and publications.

The old-fashioned image of competition is head-to-head, reporter-to-reporter competition—vying for the same information on the same assignment. These situations still exist, of course. But print reporters cannot compete with the immediacy of broadcasting, so they must compensate with depth and detail. On the other hand, broadcast reporters do not have permanency nor the luxury of more than 90 seconds to tell their story. As a result, television and radio provide the basics, and newspapers and magazines provide more depth and explanation.

Competition in television news in the 1990s is particularly intense. Former "CBS Morning News" executive producer and *Dallas Times Herald* managing editor Jon Katz (1990) proposed that broadcast journalism today is "in the midst of its greatest upheaval since Murrow stood on a rooftop in London looking for German planes" (p. 40). The growing competition from cable has completely changed how television news is approached. "In television's own perestroika, the accepted boundaries of local news are changing—*have* to change," Katz offered (p. 41).

GENERAL APPROACHES TO REPORTING

One major point to remember when considering what does and does not make news is the difference in *information* and *news*. We live in an age of information. It is everywhere. The public, not just journalists, seems to be inundated with it. There are many enterprises that originate and process information today. But the critical difference for a reporter is to be able to differentiate: When does information become news? Information is fact. News is much more, as you learned from the earlier discussions. The inability to separate information and news has drawn the concern of mass communication scholar and Gannett Center for Media Studies director Everette E. Dennis. "There is an unfortunate tendency to link information and news together so that it is difficult to distinguish them, making it all harder for us to fully understand, appreciate or comprehend our news media—especially newspapers and television—the two dominant instruments of public communication," Dennis (1990, p. 5) stated in a recent address.

The news as we know it, of course, is a report, and a report generated by people—professional people who gather information, write stories, edit them and transmit them to the public. This is the value-added aspect of news that can be distinguished from the pure information of lists and tables. Whether people generally recognize and appreciate this is another question, however. (p. 6)

The question, Dennis noted, is whether the public is satisfied by obtaining information or news. If it continues to be news, reporters will remain absolutely critical to the process. It is reporters who most often make the informed — although also often subjective — judgments that turn information into news. Reporters must be able to collect information and find the news in it. Not all information is news. But all news is information.

There are many information-gathering philosophies that guide reporters. Most journalists tend to be "pack rats" and collect more information than can be used. Tad Bartimus, a veteran general assignment reporter for the Associated Press in the Mountain States and Great Plains area and based in Denver, is one such reporter. "I tend to over-report," she said, "so part of my problem as a writer is wading through all my notebooks, being careful not to overlook a key element of the story in all the minutia. That happens more often than I care to admit, so there's more rending apart and repatching going on than is necessary" (Bartimus, 1990, p. 10). Bartimus loves reporting, however. "Reporting, for me, is the fun part: Writing is excruciating. I used to think, two decades ago when I joined the AP, it would get easier. It hasn't. Many days, I think it is harder" (p. 10).

On the other hand, some reporters only collect what information is needed for the story, culling and "editing" on the scene. There is no strict rule for the best approach. You must use the method that works best for you.

Reporters must constantly ask themselves questions about the stories they seek to cover and how these stories can be told to readers or audiences. One key is to get to the point fast. What does this story mean to the audience? Why should the news consumer care?

This is especially true of developing, or breaking, news stories. Readers and viewers will not always know what is going on. Well-written stories and scripts will achieve this goal: They will tell people what is going on early in the story. Paragraphs that fulfill this function are often called "nut grafs." Nut grafs give the essence of the story. They keep the reader or viewer interested. The *Portland (Maine) Press Herald*'s Jonathan F. Kellogg (1990), managing editor/reporting, listed three roles nut grafs can play: (a) a summary of the story; (b) context, or why you should read more, for the story; and (c) provide crucial background.

Newsweek contributing editor Robert J. Samuelson (1990) reminded reporters that they often commit a number of sins. He pointed to three serious ones:

1. *Journalists sensationalize news and have a bias toward "bad" news.* Journalists often find fault with even positive news, he maintained. He said this problem is particularly bad in the broadcast news media.

2. *Journalists, especially reporters, work in "packs."* This leads to stories that are not original, simply carbon copies of what every other news

organization is highlighting on a particular day. The "pack" principle operates in the area of daily news, but also in the area commonly called "trend news."

3. *Journalists project their own experiences on the rest of the world.* What happens in New York and Washington, or other parts of the Northeast, where most of the national news organizations have their headquarters, he said, leads journalists to frequently assume what is happening there is happening elsewhere in the nation.

GENERAL ASSIGNMENT REPORTING

General assignment (GA) reporters do just that: They take general news story assignments from the city desk at a newspaper or the assignment desk at a radio or television station. General assignment reporters often are given assignments by their editors dictated by the day's or week's news events. Many assignments are planned, or anticipated, because of advance information received. But on breaking stories, such as accidents or other emergencies, general assignment reporters must react on the spot to get the story.

General assignment reporters must have a wide range of interests and abilities. They should be able to move in and out of a variety of subjects and deal with very different types of people. They should be as comfortable covering a protest or vigil as they would be writing a story about a parade or holiday celebration.

General assignment reporters must be *curious* about all things. *Washington Post* reporter Lou Cannon (1977) pointed out that curiosity is perhaps the most important motivation for reporters. That motivation helps a general assignment reporter do any assignment well. Cannon offered, "A typical editor considers a good reporter to be a reporter who can be sent to cover any story and do a credible job" (p. 120). Cannon said good reporters should be "a mile wide and an inch deep." Reporters should know "a little about everything and nothing about anything" (p. 120).

Some general assignment reporters have part-time specializations and are really both general assignment reporters and beat reporters. This will be more the case at small news organizations, of course. In fact, many reporters start out on general assignment and gradually evolve into beat reporters. This happens because, as a general assignment reporter, a person develops an unexpected interest in a subject and takes it on as a specialization if no one else in the newsroom is writing and reporting on that subject or if another reporter who has been covering the subject leaves the staff.

General assignment reporters can generate their own assignments even though most originate with editors. Perhaps an assigned story, once completed, can lead to a related enterprise story by a reporter. The life of a general assignment reporter does not permit much free time for initiating stories. But when you get a good idea, it is always good to discuss it with your editor before investing time and energy into carrying it out.

Attending press conferences, or similar events planned on short notice, is often part of the work falling to the general assignment reporter (photo by David Walters, *Miami Herald* staff).

Although freedom to explore and try different types and subjects of stories is a positive aspect of general assignment reporting, one disadvantage is the lack of depth of assignments. Seldom do general assignment reporters get the chance to study a subject in any depth. General assignment reporters have to finish one story and move on to the next one.

Arnold Markowitz (1991), a veteran general assignment reporter for the *Miami Herald,* advised student reporters to be wary of sources and to learn as much as possible from studying working professionals. His suggestions for reporters as follows:

1. Beware of speculation from knowledgeable sources.
2. Resolve contradictions in the information you gather.
3. Learn from experienced reporters. Watch Ted Koppel and "60 Minutes."
4. Be a skeptic.
5. People will lie to you. Watch out for phonies.
6. Watch lawyers question witnesses.
7. Attend events covered by the press. Then read and watch how the pros did it.
8. Watch for technical language. It must make sense to you and your audience.
9. Learn from the mistakes of others, but don't make them yourself.
10. Read corrections. Find out what went wrong.
11. Always ask a source if there is anything else to add when you end an interview.
12. Always have extra note pads and pens.
13. Tape recorders help you to check quotations.
14. Try to learn shorthand.
15. Don't be embarrassed to ask how to spell someone's name.

BEAT REPORTING

The roots of beat reporting grow deep in newspaper journalism, but for one reason or another have yet to get well planted in broadcast journalism. Beats are systematic and routine, which is one reason some reporters prefer them. Research about journalism has consistently shown that these routines affect the type of news gathered and content produced (Bergen, 1990). Bergen found that journalists rate their best work as that which relies on routine newsgathering practices. Journalists feel comfortable with their normal institutional sources and generate their best efforts with these sources, Bergen said.

Beat reporters must assume the sole responsibility for their news organization for everything that is occurring in their area of specialization. On some large beats, such as courts and police, several reporters may share responsibility for a beat. They take responsibility for the beat on certain days or shifts. Beat reporters cannot afford to ignore events occurring on their beat. They are "on duty" 24 hours a day. If they do miss something, their news organization may be left behind by the competition covering the same story.

The most common beats are public affairs beats. These include police, fire, courts, obituaries, hospitals, city hall, education, and politics. But there are many others that have evolved during this century. Today other key beats include science and medicine, environment and weather, religion, area business and industry, sports and entertainment, and life-styles. Of course, there are others. Some unusual beats may be a function of the peculiar nature of a community. A city may have a major defense industry and local news organizations will create beats to cover it. Another city may be a significant banking and financial center, requiring beefed-up coverage on those subjects. A rural community will probably have an agriculture specialist on the news staff.

Television and radio news operations have not been as strongly committed to beat systems historically because of their smaller staffs than newspapers. Furthermore, the costs of running reporters and photographers on beats have often been prohibitive. But in recent years, more major market stations have committed money to develop specialized reporters on their staffs for investigations, health and medicine, local government, politics, entertainment, and so forth. The biggest advantage to this for

Teachers and students are two important sources on the education beat (photo by the *Miami Herald* staff).

television stations, some experts feel, is the increased ability to develop and break stories rather than to let them originate elsewhere (Katz, 1990).

Cincinnati Enquirer reporter Mike Turmell's story about an Ohio River boating accident that killed one man and injured three other persons is an example of police beat reporting diligence that turned up a breaking emergency that ended in tragedy. Turmell's story came from routine monitoring of police and marine shortwave radio channels and by contacting police and marine patrol officers. Turmell's story is reproduced at the end of this chapter.

Similarly, Atlanta's WAGA-TV, Channel 5 Eyewitness News broadcast an 11 P.M. story about a veteran doctor whose medical license was suspended. The reporting shows how diligence on state government and health-medicine beats can produce results. By regularly monitoring cases before the State Board of Medical Examiners in Atlanta, the CBS affiliate got the story and followed it through the decision announced that day. Viewers were informed of the basic facts and heard a member of the board that made the decision comment on the case. The script is reprinted at the end of this chapter.

Beat reporters not only assume responsibility for reporting about everything happening on the beat, but they must also make decisions about what to report and when to report it. Although an editor may make those decisions for general assignment reporters, they are most often delegated to beat reporters. It is an important news responsibility. This does not preclude the necessity for beat reporters to discuss their work periodically with their editors. In fact, it is part of the routine for many beat reporters. And when it is not part of the daily or weekly schedule, beat reporters should occasionally talk to their editors to advise them of stories in development, especially those that may become major news stories.

Not much has changed over the years in this respect. Willard G. Bleyer (1913), a University of Wisconsin professor, writing nearly 80 years ago in one of the first journalism textbooks, said, "As the reporter is held responsible for all the news of the places on his 'run,' he must not let anything escape his notice, because a keener, quicker-witted man on the same 'run' for a rival paper may get what he misses" (p. 31).

Most beat reporters devote full-time hours to their duties. They are assigned for a long term to a beat. Often, it takes several years to get into the news rhythm of a beat. Many events occur in cycles—annually or more frequently—thus this time is needed to get the complete feel for the news generated by the beat. It also takes time to develop sources on a beat. You cannot just march into an office and announce, "Here I am!" and expect the informational floodgates to open. Gaining the confidence of beat sources is a gradual process that beat reporters often must cultivate over months, if not years. There is the risk of going too far in developing sources. Some reporters gradually get too close to their sources on beats. This leads to conflicts in news judgment that affects coverage. Thus, some news organizations will routinely rotate beat reporters every 2 or 3 years.

Beats traditionally were created by geography. Decades ago, it was the most convenient way to divide the territory of a community. Reporters covered everything in a building — such as city hall or the police station. But with improved transportation today, combined with much faster and effective communication technology such as cellular telephones and fax machines, the old method is no longer necessary. News organizations structure beats today by more logical approaches, such as government divisions or special related interests of individual reporters.

There is no doubt experience pays in beat reporting. You can learn much from experience and the successes and failures of others. Rich Oppel (1989), editor of the *Charlotte Observer,* compiled a plan of attack for beat reporters. He offered eight tips to get started when assigned to cover a beat:

1. *Get started fast, and get out of the office.* Oppel purported that time should not be wasted at the beginning of each work day. In essence, don't spend any more time in the newsroom than necessary. "Not many stories are found in newsrooms," he advised (p. 12).

2. *Set daily goals.* Reporters should set standards, he suggested, in terms of the work they seek to accomplish. These goals can be in terms of quality, complexity, length, and number of stories.

3. *Build sources.* According to Oppel, "a critical part of beat management is cultivation of sources" (p. 12). This means an investment of time and a commitment to values. "We respect people who treat us honestly, openly and with consideration. Break a trust or confidence, and prepare for the worst," he said (p. 13).

4. *Do favors.* Help your sources with little favors such as finding old articles in the newspaper or helping the source get a newsbrief in the newspaper. Eventually, sources return the favors.

5. *Ask the sweeping questions; ask the dumb questions.* The error of some beat reporters is to focus on the specific activities related to the beat such as a burglary, a trial, or a meeting. Oppel advised reporters to take time to ask questions about the bigger picture. He also said dumb questions are often the questions reporters fail to ask.

6. *Listen carefully, watch carefully.* One-tenth of reporting is a stenographic function, noted Oppel. "The reportorial part is using your capacity for observation, selection, analysis and judgment to push beyond stenography for information that illuminates, clarifies, educates, moves, entertains" (p. 13).

7. *Look at the record.* Use original source material on your beat. Find and read minutes, calendars, reports, and other documents.

8. *Set up calls, make phone checks.* Keep a phone book, a Rolodex, or some sort of telephone list. Use it regularly. Expand it and update it. Reporters cannot always visit beat offices in person daily, so the telephone is a good substitute for contact. Oppel figures that a reporter "with a good phone system . . . can make 20 calls in 45 minutes and hit virtually every source you need to contact" (p. 13).

Two other keys for beat reporters are to be organized and be prepared. Organization helps with anticipation and completeness of reporting. Preparation permits effective work.

There are other general suggestions to enhance beat reporting. Some of these include general responsibilities, or expectations, of the beat reporter for print or broadcast journalism (Charnley, 1975):

1. Reporters must live "below the surface" to get to know people in their beat area of specialization. If it is transportation, the university scientists, engineers, and state transportation specialists would be the people to know. In just about every office you care to mention, there is a person who knows everything currently going on, and it is up to you as the reporter to meet and get to know this person.

2. Make sure that everyone in the offices on your beat knows you are a reporter. Tell them. Introduce yourself. Write down your name and office and home telephone numbers on a card or piece of paper and give it to people you meet. This makes it easier for them. Get on informal terms with them. Ask how they are doing. Small talk helps.

3. There are many ways of finding out what is happening in an office. One way is to listen to small talk and chatter. Another way is to read the bulletin boards and walls where notices and announcements are placed. A third way is to talk to support personnel in the office who might notice out-of-the-ordinary activity. You can never know too much. Don't be afraid to ask about the office activities when you talk about other things with the senior officer of the department/office/beat.

4. Spend time going through back issues of the newspaper or archives tapes of the broadcast organization for which you work. This will help you understand what the former reporter did on the beat. Study magazines on the subject. Know the literature, in other words. Always look for story ideas.

5. Establish a rapport with your news sources. If you notice that an administrator's or executive's desk is decorated with certain objects, ask about them. They usually reflect a personal or professional interest. The same applies to secretaries and receptionists. But be sincere. Don't be a phony. People can spot that a mile away.

6. As your mother used to tell you, good manners are important. Reporters are people and if they behave in a civilized manner, most people will respond the same way. But even then, some people are a real pain; they cannot help but be that way. In short, ordinary courtesies usually pay off.

7. Courteous behavior does not preclude being aggressive and stubborn when your story demands it. Know your rights and enforce them. Persistence often produces a story that would not come about.

8. You are the expert on the news. Don't let a source tell you what news might be. This is your judgment. Don't allow sources to tell you what a good story might or might not be. Don't be rude, but remind people that you make decisions on what might or might not be a news story (in consultation with your editors).

**JEFFREY L. KLEINMAN, THE *MIAMI HERALD*
HANDLING REPORTING BEATS: USING BEAT BOOKS**

"Neighbors" is the suburban section name within the *Miami Herald*. The newspaper has dozens of reporters in its Neighbors bureaus across Dade and Broward counties.

To assist new reporters going into beat assignments at Neighbors for the first time, especially reporters unfamiliar with Dade or Broward counties, editors have asked reporters to produce "Dade Beat Books" and "Broward Beat Books" containing descriptions of the beats, key sources, and potential stories.

These are a good idea for all news organizations, print or broadcast, large or small, but especially college news media where high levels of staff turnover is normal. Here's reporter Jeffrey L. Kleinman's discussion of the Dade beat book on transportation:

GENERAL BEAT DESCRIPTION

Transportation at Neighbors means you'll be covering road projects, buses, Metrorail and Metromover. There are three primary sources of information: the Highway Division of the Dade County Public Works Department, the Metro-Dade Transit Agency and the Florida Department of Transportation. All improvements in Dade are reviewed by the Metropolitan Planning Organization, the transportation arm of the Metro-Dade Commission.

The county's Highway Division is responsible for the repair, planning, and construction of county roads. The DOT is responsible for those same things on state roads. So how do you know if a road is state or county? Simple. Either agency will tell you.

The MDTA runs the county's public transportation system (buses and rail). The Kendall Area Transit (KAT shuttle buses) is a state program run by an arm of the county transit agency.

MAJOR SOURCES

Here's the cast of characters:

For county roads, speak with Pete Hernandez, the chief of the highway division (375-2092).

For Miami roads, it's Bill Mackey (579-6865).

For state roads, call 377-5800 and ask for help. The DOT is quite large and it's tough to get around, especially since the agency hasn't replaced its media spokesman yet.

For public transit, call Marc Henderson (375-5765).

The chairman of the county's Transportation Committee is Metro-Dade Commissioner Clara Oesterle (375-5123).

The assistant county manager in charge of transportation is Tony Ojeda (375-5311).

Miles Moss is head of the transportation committee of the Kendall

(continued)

JEFFREY L. KLEINMAN, THE *MIAMI HERALD* (continued)

Miles Moss is head of the transportation committee of the Kendall Federation of Homeowner Associations (386-4203).

Servando Parapar is director of planning for the DOT. Call him for long-term projects (377-5800).

Rep. Art Simon, head of the Kendall Transportation Action Committee, is at 386-4110 or 904-488-5047.

Wayne Whistler is chairman of the county's Citizen Transportation Advisory Committee (681-3026).

Cal Marsella oversees the KAT shuttle (638-6448).

POTENTIAL PROBLEMS AND WHAT TO LOOK FOR

For public hearings on road projects, do an advance explaining the project and opposition, if any. Don't forget to cover the meeting.

Keep an eye on your surroundings while you're driving the cop beat. You're guaranteed to spot a story once in awhile.

UPCOMING STORY TIPS FOR NEWCOMERS

Palmetto — The state wants to widen the Palmetto Expressway at the expense of a few businesses and 30 homes. Some of the residents have lived in the Bird Road neighborhood before the Palmetto was built. Now they have to sell, move and see their homes crushed to dirt. We've done the stories, but keep on an eye out on the process.

Busy streets — What's it like living on South Dixie Highway, Kendall Drive, Sunset Drive and other major streets where it must be hell pulling out of the driveway in the mornings and opening the house windows for some fresh air?

Runway — Bulldozers are running at Miami International. It looks like a new runway is being built on the airport's south side.

Speed traps — There are lots of them all over. A famous one is on the 878 flyover, where troopers camp out. Every municipality has a speed trap. Pretty timely story with charges that the FHP has a quota for tickets.

Reprinted with permission of the *Miami Herald*.

9. To obtain efficiency and productivity, seek cooperation from sources. If you are asked to hold a story for a short time, consider it. But use your judgment; sometimes you cannot do that even if you wanted to. You must be reasonable.

10. Reporting has traditional responsibilities. Every reporter knows that newsmen and newswomen must keep promises — they do not break release dates or embargoes, for example. They call back people. They leave messages.

11. Keep appointments for meetings and interviews. Skipping an appointment without calling will make a source angry. The same applies if you don't call when you will be late. This irresponsible behavior is a bad

reflection on you personally, your news organization, and the profession in general.

12. If you borrow something, return it. Always.

13. Follow routines with your news sources. They begin to count on your visits to the office, or calls, at the same time every day. Regular habits are easier on them to find you and get information to you. It means you must make a commitment to coming by the same place at the same time, but you should do it. It will keep you in the minds of your sources more frequently.

14. When interviewing a beat source, ask specific questions. Avoid being vague. Listen carefully. Record information accurately.

15. Organize your own beat calendar. Keep future dates and events on this calendar. A wall calendar will accomplish the same thing if you do not prefer a book. Get in the habit of writing down everything relevant to your beat. Write down these dates months in advance, just as you hear about them. Then you might not forget and miss a big story. And if you miss time on your beat, your sub can more easily fill in for you.

16. Maintain a neat and professional appearance. People respond favorably to it. They will treat you with more respect if they can see that you are trying a bit harder.

It is interesting to note that some news organizations continue to experiment with variations on the beat system. The *Orange County Register* in California has reorganized its newsroom's approach to reporting. The *Register*'s innovative approach eliminated section editors and created "topic editors" to supervise reporters. "We assigned reporters to beats, not sections, and expect them to write for all sections," explained *Register* editor Chris Anderson (1991, p. 14). In covering the Santa Ana region near Los Angeles, the newspaper added some beats. "You probably have heard about the shopping-mall beat," Anderson said. "The others we added are, like the mall beat, based on aspects of our customers' everyday lives. Among others, we have reporters writing about hobbies and pets, working, personal relationships, cars, traffic, culture and shopping (in addition to malls)," mentioned Anderson, the National Press Foundation's 1989 Newspaper Editor of the Year (p. 14). Why did the newspaper so dramatically change its approach to covering its community? "We discovered that our structure kept us from being able to change quickly and regularly and radically, if we needed to do so," Anderson explained.

REPORTING BREAKING NEWS

In the preceding section, preparation was one of the points made for successful beat reporting. On some stories, however, reporters cannot always be prepared. These stories are breaking stories. They happen without notice.

These stories are typically emergencies such as accidents, shootings, civil unrest, assaults, explosions, and natural disasters. While the best news organizations try to anticipate even the worst, such as a major plane crash at the regional airport, only general plans can be made.

Reporters have to be able to react to the specifics of a given situation.

THE MAJOR CAMPUS NEWS BEATS

College of Arts and Sciences
Dining service (cafeterias), catering, and campus vending machines
Other specialized schools and colleges such as business administration, education, engineering, communication, law, medicine, architecture, music, nursing, agriculture, international studies, government
Adult and community education programs
Student affairs
Campus police and public safety
Parking office
University health services
Handicapped services
International scholar and student services
International programs (study abroad)
Graduate school (general)
Student activities
Student government
Residence halls, housing offices
Bursar's office
Financial aid services, scholarships
Physical plant, maintenance (including contractors)
Environmental health and safety offices
Registrar's office
Provost or academic vice president's office
Faculty Senate
Enrollments/admissions office
Career planning and placement, student employment offices
University development office
Office of university relations
Office of business and finance
General university counsel (attorneys)
Library system
Campus museums (art, history, anthropology, and so forth)
Drama department/theaters
Campus intramurals and recreation programs
Debate program
Homecoming office
Sororities and fraternities
Alumni relations
Military science programs (ROTC)
Campus honoraries, service groups, and other nonsocial campus organizations
Office of the president
Board of Trustees
Campus religious organizations

WORKING WITH PHOTOGRAPHERS
AND GRAPHIC ARTISTS

For both print and broadcast/cable news reporters today, it is increasingly important to understand how to work with photographers and graphic artists. For television reporters, video has always been essential to the success of a story, but a television reporter should know as much as possible about how video journalists do their job. Similarly, newspaper and magazine reporters must have a greater appreciation for the still photographer. More and more, newspapers and magazines are depending on still photography for the extra dimension to a story. Editors want to show the story as well as write it.

A new dimension to the visual element in reporting today is the personal computer. News organizations, both print and broadcast/cable, are using computers to create visual elements to help report stories. "Exploding" diagrams, locator maps, charts, statistics tables, graphs, original artwork and other forms of graphics are part of the package to report a story today. In some news organizations, informational graphics experts will gather their own information and become reporters, but in other newsrooms, traditional news reporters must provide the information on which the graphics are based.

REPORTERS AND THEIR SOURCES

Little has been said so far about sources. Sources are perhaps the most important part of the general assignment and beat reporting formulas. Types of sources and relationships with them are discussed in more depth in chapter 3 because they are so significant to the process.

HOW PROFESSIONALS WRITE IT

SOURCE: The *Cincinnati Enquirer,* sec. B, p. 1
AUTHOR: Mike Turmell
DATE: Sunday, August 12, 1990
HEADLINE: Alcohol cited in fatal boat crash

* * *

A collision early Saturday between a 19-foot speedboat and a 32-foot cabin cruiser under the Central Bridge was the first boating fatality of the year along a 92-mile stretch of the Ohio River patrolled by the Kentucky Water Patrol.

A Cincinnati man was killed in the crash.

In the collision, the speedboat crashed through the forward portion of the cabin cruiser and ended up inside the cruiser.

The crash prompted words of caution from those who patrol and cruise the river.

One of them, Rich Cates, district supervisor of the Ohio Department of Natural Resources' Division of Watercraft, said the average boater sees a lot of speeding boats and close calls.

"The major problems are the number of boats and the speed they are traveling," Cates said. Cates said there are about 400,000 boats now registered in Ohio, up from about 150,000 in 1980.

At the same time, in defense of most boaters, fatalities have dropped the last six years across Ohio, including the Ohio River, he said.

"It's always an adventure out here," Doug Nash, 34, said. Nash, with his passenger, Barb Doran, 26, escaped serious injury when the speedboat struck his cabin cruiser.

Nash said boaters have been fighting for a no-wake zone-only idle speed after dark.

"There are close calls here every night," Nash said. "They need to slow it down because this (section of the river) has become a real center of activity."

Besides the fatality, identified as Michael Schmutte, 33, no address, of Cincinnati, three other persons in his boat were sent to the hospital.

University Hospital listed the other three in fair condition: Robert Wolfe, 27, of the 8100 block of West Mill Street, Cleves; Sharon Nadolny, 29, no address, Cincinnati; and Laurie Perkins, 33, no address, Cincinnati.

Nash, of the 5000 block of Sovereign Drive, Sharonville, suffered minor injuries. Doran, of Cincinnati, was not injured, the Kentucky Water Patrol said.

Nash said the impact pushed the dashboard into his chest and knocked the two backward.

He was among hundreds along the Ohio shore and in boats who watched Saturday as salvage crews first pulled the 1989 Checkmate speedboat from inside his $80,000 1989 Bayliner Avanti along the Public Landing, then hoisted both onto barges.

"In a boat you never turn left, you turn right," Nash said. "He just tacked right into me."

Kentucky State Water Patrol Officers Mike Fields and Doug Bryant, who are investigating the wreck, said alcohol was a factor.

Fields said he expects to interview numerous witnesses to the collision. It occurred under the bridge's second pier, about 150 feet off the Kentucky River bank, between Barleycorn's and Crockett's riverfront restaurants.

Both boats will remain on barges until they can be inspected again Monday, Fields said. One Cincinnati firefighter escaped injury when pushed backward by the cabin cruiser as it fell a short distance to the barge during removal by cranes.

"The smaller boat was moving along pretty good," Fields said he was told by some witnesses standing on the bridge. Afterward, "the smaller boat was inside the cabin cruiser, with only the outdrive sticking out."

Nash, who was above deck with his passenger, said he saw the boat coming as he was heading upriver to the Watertown Marina in Dayton, Ky. He said it was bright out because the crowd had just gotten out of Riverfront Stadium where the Beach Boys performed after the Reds–Giants game.

Police Lt. Stephen Kramer said speeding problems and near-collisions on the river aren't unusual. "It happens almost every night."

Kramer said the speedboat might have been traveling about 60 mph, but he did not have a speed on the cruiser.

When Kramer arrived at the river early Saturday, the wreckage was in the middle of the river and a small boat was coming toward the Public Landing.

"They came in and said people were injured," Kramer said. "I told them to go out and hook up to them."

Five minutes later, after the wreckage and the injured it held were towed to the bank, a barge came upriver, Kramer said.

Kramer and District Fire Chief Dallas Kelly said it took about an hour to cut through the cabin cruiser to reach the trapped passengers of the other boat.

Reprinted with permission of the Cincinnati Enquirer.

● ● ●

SOURCE: WAGA-TV, Channel 5 (CBS), Atlanta
AUTHOR: WAGA-TV news staff
DATE: Wednesday, May 9, 1990
TIME: 11 P.M. newscast

＊ ＊ ＊

BRENDA/INSERT	FOR THIRTY YEARS HE HAS SERVED THE ATLANTA AREA AS A THORACIC SURGEON . . . TONIGHT DR. TIM RAY HEATH IS SUSPENDED AFTER TWO DIE IN HIS CARE.
VTR/VOT : 00-:22	
	THE 55-YEAR OLD MARIETTA SURGEON WAS ORDERED BY THE STATE BOARD OF MEDICAL EXAMINERS TO UNDERGO PSYCHIATRIC EVALUATION AND DRUG TESTING.
	THE ALLEGATIONS AGAINST HEATH INCLUDE LEAVING AN OPERATING ROOM AT ATLANTA HOSPITAL, ALLOWING THE PATIENT TO BLEED . . . THAT PATIENT LATER DIED.
	THE SECOND EXAMPLE IN MARCH CITES HEATH'S TIMELI-

VTR/SOT :22-:30	NESS IN ARRIVING, FAILURE TO OBTAIN AN X-RAY AND HIS DE-MEANOR DURING SURGERY.
SVF/ANDREW WATRY	--------------------------------------
BOARD OF MED. EXAMINERS	:22 VTR/SOT :33
OUTCUE. . . . A SERIOUS PROBLEM	OC. . . . A SERIOUS PROBLEM.

VTR/VOT :30-:50	DR. HEATH REPORTEDLY LEFT A DRUG TREATMENT CENTER EAR-LIER THIS YEAR BEFORE COM-PLETING THE PROGRAM.
	THE HOSPITAL LICENSING BOARD IS ALSO INVESTIGATING TO SEE IF ATLANTA HOSPITAL COVERED UP THE CIRCUM-STANCES SURROUNDING THE TWO DEATHS.
	THE BOARD WILL MEET IN JULY TO DECIDE IF DR. HEATH WILL BE RECERTIFIED.
TIME: 0:53	

Reprinted with permission of WAGA-TV.

• • •

3 | Developing And Using Sources

When *Orlando Sentinel* investigative reporters Jim Leusner and Christopher Quinn (1990) began research on a series of news stories about the dangers of a local company which built and stored weapons for military use near heavily populated central Florida tourist areas, they knew they would have to depend on sources instead of firsthand observation for the majority of their stories. But Leusner and Quinn would not be able to complete their work with just a few sources. They needed dozens of people to talk to them. And they would not need just any people. These individuals had to be well informed and authoritative.

The Leusner and Quinn series, entitled "Missiles in Boomtown," was a difficult series of stories to report and write. First, the stories questioned the safety precautions taken by one of the central Florida area's largest employers and its largest industrial employer. In addition, because Martin Marietta Corp., the manufacturer, was a defense contractor, Leusner and Quinn had to deal with security barriers to much of the information on Martin Marietta's so-called "Remote Area" needed for the story. Furthermore, the company was reluctant to discuss much of the information with Leusner and Quinn. Finally, even willing sources within Martin Marietta were naturally concerned about keeping their jobs and thus were reluctant to talk to the reporters.

But there was a public service story to be done. Leusner and Quinn were concerned that the company can store 1.4 million pounds of warheads, rocket motors, and finished missiles in a company area only one-fifth of a mile from south Orange County's popular International Drive, which has developed into a tourist mecca of restaurants, hotels, and attractions. International Drive has been traveled by 30,000 tourists and local residents

---

Accessing sources on some stories can be difficult, if not impossible, because of heavy demand by news reporters (photo by David Walters, *Miami Herald* staff).

a day in the past two-plus decades. Although the area was sparsely settled 30 years earlier, development related to the tourist boom in Orlando in the 1970s and 1980s changed all of that, Leusner and Quinn reported. "Martin and its real estate subsidiary sold or developed the land around the plants — reaping in $45.5 million," Leusner (1991b) recalled. The stories reported many more detailed facts related to manufacturing and storage of the missiles and their highly flammable motors. Patriot missiles, which received much publicity during the Persian Gulf War a year after the *Sentinel* series was published, were also stored there (Bales, 1990).

To finish their series, which was published in four parts and required nine full pages for the stories and photography, Leusner and Quinn conducted *over 200 interviews* with sources. They actually did more than that, Leusner (1991a) explained, but some interviews did not wind up as part of the series. But critical to the interviewing process were interviews with five particular sources, experts in missile technology. Leusner and Quinn also found information in literally thousands of documents from more than 30 agencies of government at all levels.

Leusner and Quinn sought *independent* experts to interview for the series. The five rocket-motor authorities used in their series were the result of preliminary interviews with a group of about two dozen scientists. These persons were contacted to determine who were the foremost rocket-motor experts in the country. A list of 13 names was compiled and the final five agreed to be interviewed (Bales, 1990). Eight others declined, Leusner and Quinn said, because of "fear of losing Defense Department contracts if they spoke openly about Martin." Some did not return phone calls (Leusner & Quinn, 1990). Still, of the five persons who agreed to serve as expert sources in the series, three consented to do so only if they would not be identified. Leusner (1991b) explained:

> That was one of the worst things. The government puts money in their pockets. So, they're not likely to talk to a reporter and risk losing the funding. But lucky for us, some of them had consciences and were concerned about public safety. Some of the experts did not believe us when we told them missiles were stored less than a half mile from hotels and a retirement community. All other missile manufacturers we found in the U.S. have their plants in deserts, mountain ranges, or other isolated areas.

Martin Marietta was very "close-mouthed," Leusner (1991a) remembered. "They tried to stonewall us. Employees were threatened that they would lose their jobs if they talked to us." To get around this problem, Leusner and Quinn contacted employees away from the company facility. "We cold-called some of them, using old Martin Marietta phone books. We could tell where they worked from the phone numbers. That helped a lot. Some people there were disgusted with safety problems and had been trying to change things for years."

Among the nonhuman sources used, Leusner and Quinn found documents such as letters to government boards, production plans, building permits, and fire inspection reports. Leusner (1991a) said the two reporters also used many of the company's in-house publications such as newsletters and magazines to identify employees and where they worked as potential sources. "Building permits were very helpful for us, too," he said.

In the beginning of their work, Leusner and Quinn were forced to photograph and observe the storage facility from an aircraft and from the top of the highest building in the area, the posh 27-story Peabody Hotel, located only one-half mile from the facility. Later, after 18 months of investigation, Martin Marietta gave a controlled tour of the facility to the reporters and a photographer (Bales, 1990; Leusner, 1991a; Leusner & Quinn, 1990).

Reporting on a project this massive is not for the beginner, of course, but it does point to the need for a *variety of sources* in tackling virtually any sort of story. From the most basic obituary to the more complex series such as the one by Leusner and Quinn, reporters must have good sources. Without sources, a reporter can do little. But with well-chosen, patiently cultivated sources, a reporter can accomplish a great deal.

"I spent more than a year full-time on the project," Leusner (1991a) recalled. "I worked on it for 15 months over an 18-month period. The first 9 months I worked alone. Then it got to be too much. I was buried in paper. I could not go through it all. I got some help. That's when Chris came on to help sort through the material and develop information in new areas."

Good reporting requires good sources regardless of whether it is for a newspaper, which often can devote considerable space for in-depth stories such as the ones by Leusner and Quinn, or whether it is for television or radio, usually with limited time even for a major story.

KCBS-AM radio news in San Francisco, when confronted with covering the massive deadly earthquake in its area in 1989, produced story after story using the widest range of sources—from expert geologists to victims and witnesses—to get a comprehensive report for listeners during the emergency. When KCBS-AM was awarded a 1990 Peabody Award for its work, the judges said the reporting was comprehensive, intelligent, and useful to the audience.

WCSC-TV, Charleston, South Carolina, was given similar recognition for its emergency reporting of the aftermath of Hurricane Hugo in 1989. Using authoritative public and private sources, the station was presented a Peabody Award for getting critical information about public services to residents of the area. Peabody judges said WCSC-TV was a lifeline for viewers needing essential public services. In both the cases of the San Francisco radio station and the Charleston television station, this was not only solid reporting, but effective use of well-chosen sources under the worst possible reporting circumstances.

This chapter discusses the role of sources in reporting. From these examples, you already understand that sources are the building blocks of reporting. You will be introduced to the different types of sources; how to judge the quality of sources; how to work with human sources and how to use nonhuman sources; how to organize source lists for use and reuse; how to find sources and keep relationships on a productive level; how to avoid the problems with sources, such as hoaxes and fraud; how to use different levels of attribution and identification of sources; when to use anonymous and confidential sources; how to work with public relations sources and to develop an understanding of the basic elements of media relations policies that affect reporting.

TYPES OF SOURCES

Reporters use two broad categories of sources for their work: people and documents. This chapter focuses on human sources in reporting, whereas chapters 4 and 5 focus on using documents and other nonhuman sources for news stories.

In focusing only on human sources, you must remember there are different types to use in reporting. Some beginning reporters make the mistake in believing that *any* person is a good source, as long as the person is someone who is quotable and makes sense. Often, even experienced reporters on deadline must face the decision of whether to use a weak source or no source at all. Sometimes it is best not to use the source at all and hold the story.

The general rule is to find the *best possible* source or sources for the story. What is meant by "best"? This means the most appropriate, the best informed, and thus, the most credible. For example, if you are reporting about a small aircraft that crashed, you want a source that witnessed the accident, not someone who talked to the witness. Secondhand information is not good enough in most cases, although reporters are frequently faced with the decision about whether or not to use it. There are at least five common types of human sources commonly used in day-to-day reporting:

1. *Expert or professional sources* — These are perhaps the most common category. These are individuals who, through their experience, training, or education, have special authoritative or professional knowledge about a subject.

2. *Public sector official sources* — These are sources who may often also be expert or authoritative, but more importantly, they represent an official perspective. Officials do not have to be political officials, but often will be. Officials are appointed bureaucrats, elected individuals, civil servants, or other responsible individuals who serve the public.

3. *Private sector official sources and spokespersons* — Officials may also be private individuals representing companies or institutions, or other groups.

4. *Eyewitnesses* — These are sources who through some set of circumstances have become valuable to a story because they were present when an event occurred.

5. *"Typical" citizens* — For some stories, the perspective of the typical or average resident of an area is needed.

University of Minnesota broadcasting professor Lawrence Soley (1990) identified one increasingly important category of expert sources used today in journalism, which he called "news shapers." These individuals are not the focus of news stories but nevertheless appear in stories. "The news shapers provide background, explain events, or make predictions concerning the outcome of still unfolding stories," Soley wrote (p. 7). News shapers are often experts such as analysts, think tank spokespersons, other journalists, consultants, *former* politicians and government officials, economists, public opinion pollsters, and academics. Experts, analysts, and consultants were the most commonly used authoritative sources, Soley concluded in his study of the three broadcast networks. Former politicians and officials were the second most common sources.

Regardless of the source, two-time Pulitzer Prize-winning investigative reporter Sydney Freedberg (1991) recommended questioning everything from official sources. Freedberg, a *Miami Herald* staff member, advised students to question motives and the facts presented by news sources when she recently met with students at a journalism workshop at the University of Miami. Some of the advice she offered follows:

- The only thing that makes a story come alive is people. Go out and talk to them. Figure out what is on their minds. Smooze with them. If you rely completely on documents to do a story, you're going to have a dead story.

- People think if they read it in the newspaper, it must be true. But don't believe anything you read in the newspaper. Check to see if it is true. The truth is something which is very hard to find.

- Even the simplest little fact can be wrong. You have to ask. You have to check. I could make all different kinds of assumptions. And 90 percent of the time, the assumptions are going to be wrong. I found that conventional wisdom is usually wrong.

- You have to think about the motives a source might have for lying to the newspaper. . . . It is something to ask. Why does a source have a particular point of view on a fact?

- You go into a story with a certain perspective or mind set. Never trust your mind set. You have got to ask to figure out what the person is thinking. *Never* generalize about how people are thinking. One person is going to be completely different from the next.

In a widely cited study of reporters and public officials, researcher Leon Sigal (1973) concluded there are three major categories of sources of information. Sigal's study of the *New York Times* and *Washington Post* pointed to these major categories of sources:

1. *Routine*—Routine sources include those regularly used for typical news stories. A routine was very important to the process of reporting, he explained. Routine sources include official proceedings of meetings, press releases, and other publicity efforts, press conferences and daily press briefings, and nonspontaneous events such as speeches and ceremonies commonly called "media events."

2. *Informal*—Informal types of sources include background briefings, leaks, nongovernmental proceedings, and news from other news organizations.

3. *Enterprise*—Enterprise sources are part of stories that reporters originate, but they can also be spontaneous events that reporters witness, such as fires or accidents. These sources also include independent research from books and statistics and interpretation and conclusions by reporters from their own experiences.

Sigal's study found that leading newspapers such as the *New York Times* and *Washington Post* use routine sources the majority of the time in staff-written news stories. Enterprise sources are the second-most used channel, and informal sources were required the least. It is important to note that Sigal's findings are not unique. In research using network newscasts and other leading news organizations, studies have consistently found that public officials are the most-often cited sources. Business officials or their spokespersons are also commonly used. Expert sources such as attorneys, physicians, and university professors are frequently found in source-usage studies as a leading category also.

Journalists still have problems with broadening their base of sources in two areas, however. Research literature on sources reports that women and minority group members are not used as sources as often as their proportion of the population might suggest they should be used. Some studies show women account for only 1 in 10 sources in news stories, for instance. A recent study of ABC's "Nightline" found only 6% of the sources on the program were Blacks and 10% were women (Soley, 1990).

There is also geographical source bias in some source selection. This is likely to be more true in national or regional stories than local ones, but it is a concern when selecting sources for news stories. Research literature shows consistent bias toward sources in the northeastern United States, for instance.

JUDGING THE QUALITY AND RELIABILITY OF SOURCES

Of these many types of persons who might be appropriate for a story, how do you know which is best quality and most reliable? You do your homework first.

As Leusner and Quinn did in their series about safety hazards involving missiles in central Florida, you check people out if they are not known. Leusner and Quinn did not call any so-called expert on rocket motors. First, the two reporters called other experts for their list of names. Then they compared notes and compiled a master list of authorities on the subject. Then they checked the credentials of these persons. And only then did they call the individuals.

The process may not always be that complicated. You might be able to judge a source's quality from simpler methods.

First, you might be able to assume certain things about a source because of the institution or company with which the source is affiliated. If you think highly of a psychology department of a local college or university, then you can probably judge a professor on that faculty who is an expert on group stress to be a good source, too.

Second, you can use smaller-scale networking. References always help. If you know someone — another reliable source or another reporter in your office — who knows someone, it makes a big difference to your judgment of that source.

Third, consider the source's motives and goals. What does this source gain from talking to you? What is the source's own agenda? Did you go to the source or did the source come to you? Often these factors may become critical in judging the quality of a source for your story. If a source seems to have a great deal to gain by talking with you, does this "taint" your story's credibility? Even if this is the case, the source may still be useful.

Fourth, find a second or third independent source to back up the original source. If you do not know a source well, but the information that person can provide is valuable to the story, then find another source to back up the first source. Two or more *independent* but lesser-known sources are better than only one. And it is best if your sources are not acquainted.

Fifth, find written documentation or evidence. If your source is unknown to you but has pivotal information for your story, seek a measure of the source's reliability by asking for documentation — for proof. Many sources in the public sector can provide memos, letters, reports, and other documents to back up what they have to tell you. This will establish their quality and separate them from the crackpots fast.

Sixth, use repeated discussions with the same source for verification. If you do not have the luxury of a second or third independent source, and you do not have documentation of any substantial quality, then try several different run-throughs with your source to establish consistency. If you can, separate them over a few days. Through multiple interviews, with similar questions skillfully asked in different ways, you may be able to determine just how well the source knows the information being discussed.

FINDING AND USING HUMAN NEWS SOURCES

Finding the right sources for your story might be the hardest thing you must do on some stories. There will be occasions when you know what you want to write about, but you just do not know where to start to find the right sources for story. Sound familiar?

Here's what to do:

1. Check "clips" or file tape. Earlier stories on the same subjects may turn up names.

2. Check telephone lists and source lists in the newsroom. Many news organizations today maintain electronic telephone lists, cross listed by a person's specialization or affiliation. These lists are based on previous contacts and make good starting points.

3. Check the telephone book. It may seem obvious, but it cannot hurt.

4. Check institutional "expert" or "source" books. For public relations value, some institutions, professional organizations, and businesses publish annual directories of experts or other individuals readily available to the news media.

5. Contact government agencies appropriate to the subject of your story.

6. Talk to people you know in your newsroom and in your neighborhood to see if any networking contacts can be developed.

7. Let one source help you find another source. This is called "snowballing" and it can work well. Experts know other experts. Witnesses may know other witnesses. Once you find one person who can help you, chances are good that you can find others from that original source. After going to those sources, ask them for still others. You can repeat this process until you have an adequate number of perspectives for your story or the names repeat (indicating you have just about everyone).

Well-known or prominent sources can be a problem because of restricted access. This may be a serious barrier to your reporting. At the least, prominent sources have certain barriers such as press representatives, staff assistants, and secretaries who will stand between you and the information you need. Lesser-known sources who are just as authoritative may be preferable because they are more accessible.

News reporters must often go to the scene of a story to find the best sources (photo by the *Miami Herald* staff).

For sources in public service, you will likely have to go through a public affairs office. These offices are intermediaries set up to field news media requests for information. These individuals — often called public information officers (PIOs) — will get information for you or try to arrange for you to talk to expert sources you seek. Often, you will waste less time if you go straight to the public affairs officer if you do not know specific individuals from previous contacts.

People are most often willing to be a source in a story. Some may need to be persuaded. The problem of the reluctant source, discussed in chapters 6 and 7 about interviewing, is important because the availability of sources is a major factor in their selection and the ultimate development in a story.

Sources played the most important roles in each of the four stories reproduced at the end of this chapter. Each represents a different level of reporting: free-lance reporting for a small daily newspaper, staff reporting for another small daily, two-person team reporting for a major daily, and staff reporting for a major market television station. But sources are what make each story successful. Here's how:

Miami free-lance journalist Leanne Reifsteck, reporting for the *Key West Citizen,* wrote the lead story in a series on the high cost of living in a resort town. Her article focused on senior citizens, the largest group of individuals living on fixed incomes in the Florida island community of 30,000 persons. Reifsteck found her sources at community centers, churches, and retirement organizations. In Key West, she set up interviews by telephone and visited her sources in person at the neighborhood centers and in their apartments to establish that life in an expensive place is very difficult for persons who depend on pensions to pay their living expenses.

Muncie Star staff reporter Randy Rendfeld was on deadline for a front-page story when he wrote about a controversy surrounding fox hunting in Indiana. As with any controversy, Rendfeld went to both sides for their points of view. The story would have been incomplete without getting the arguments both for the fox hunt and against it from the leaders of each side. Proponents had the chance to explain why they thought the annual event was not the cruel event that opponents believed it to be. Rendfeld also told readers why opponents felt it unnecessary.

"This assignment was given to me at about 5:30 P.M., and my editors wanted it finished by 10:30 P.M. for page 1," Rendfeld (1991) recalled. He added:

> There was an obvious conflict: A fox hunt was about to occur and some animal lovers objected. Was there a right and wrong side of this conflict? Although that question might have been in my mind, I knew it was not my job to pass judgment. What I had to do was fairly present enough information so readers could perhaps decide for themselves.

On deadline, Rendfeld was limited in his reporting choices.

"I had just enough time to interview representatives on both sides of the argument, which I did. Then I called some expert witnesses, so to speak — a conservation officer and a professor. To find them, I asked the editors whether they knew of anyone who could shed light on the subject. I had to make several calls before I finally found and interviewed the officer and the professor," he explained. "By the time I was done, there was only about 40 minutes left to write, so I wrote this story in a great rush."

In his story, Rendfeld frequently permitted his sources to explain themselves in their own words by using effective direct quotations from interviews.

Fort Lauderdale Sun-Sentinel reporters Andrew Martin and Amy Stromberg wrote about a controversy involving public funds and management of a major public facility. The two reporters told readers about financial wheeling and dealing at the major Broward County site for international shipping, Port Everglades. The port is a $29 million-a-year publicly operated business, their story told readers. Focusing on Port Director Joel Alesi, the reporters interviewed Federal Bureau of Investigation agents and spokespersons, port commissioners, county commissioners, and even former port directors to determine whether the port's financial dealings were influenced by favors or payoffs, whether they were innocent mistakes or a conspiracy, and whether there was illegal influence or extortion taking place.

Mike Taibbi, staff reporter for WCBS-TV, Channel 2 in New York, wrote a series of stories about drugs on the streets of Brooklyn, spending several weeks inside the drug "war zone" known as Bushwick. He told—and graphically showed through compelling video—how drug-related violence savaged Bushwick and the neighborhood's spirit. Taibbi's story was made difficult by a subject that forced many timid people to shy from interviews. His challenge was to persuade residents—adults and children who were the "expert" sources in this story—to talk about their day-to-day firsthand experiences with drug-related violence. The story is told from the residents' point of view. Viewers saw and heard the resident's troubles through Taibbi's selection of the best sources for the story and his use of their own words in strong "soundbites." Taibbi's series won the Jack R. Howard Award for large market television broadcast journalism in 1989 from the Scripps Howard Foundation.

USING NONHUMAN NEWS SOURCES

California State University-Sacramento professor Shirley Biagi (1986) offered four basic questions a reporter must ask when doing research before interviewing a source:

1. What information do you want?
2. Why do you want to know that information?
3. How will you use the information?
4. How much time do you have to do your research?

If you can answer these questions, you will have a good idea just what role nonhuman sources will play in your news story.

Chapters 4 and 5, which focus on general news story research and on computer databases research in reporting, discuss in depth the wide range of choices reporters will have when it comes to use of nonhuman news sources. For now, just consider the possibilities you have, many of them practically at your fingertips:

1. Commercial reference books such as atlases, encyclopedias, dictionaries, abstracts, and handbooks
2. Government publications and reference books
3. Computer databases
4. Personal observation and experience

These are the most common nonhuman sources. Add to these the documents and reports generated by public agencies of all levels of government and suddenly you have a massive amount of information. Public sources of information must be kept available to the public by law. State laws, often called "sunshine" or freedom of information (FOI) laws, will govern city, county, regional, and state governmental bodies. Federal law, also called the federal FOI Act, will govern documents and records of national agencies and departments.

Equally available are the documents, records, and reports provided by the private sector for public consumption. Businesses, private institutions such as schools and hospitals, foundations, charities, and other organizations often produce material for public use such as promotional literature, catalogs, directories, annual reports, and so forth.

But what may be most difficult to obtain as sources for your stories will be the documents, records, and reports kept by private sector organizations not intended for public use. These materials will be the most difficult sources for you to find because they are often kept secure. Employees providing these materials to reporters may risk their job security, of course. But you can still find legitimate ways to get these if you are resourceful. Usually employees who are willing to provide such information find the information more important than any risks they must take.

ONGOING RELATIONSHIPS WITH SOURCES

It is essential for a reporter to develop a continuing relationship with sources, especially persons who the reporter feels will become frequent sources of information. As noted in chapter 2, this is an essential element of beat reporting. But it also applies to general assignment reporting. As a beat reporter, this contact will be frequent. But even for general assignment reporters, an occasional contact will keep you fresher in a potential source's mind.

Casual contacts can be sufficient. A telephone call or a brief conversation in a hallway or office might be enough to keep in touch.

Reporters should keep names, addresses, and telephone numbers of their best sources on file. ABC News television correspondent Mark Potter, who has prepared stories for the "World News Tonight" segment "American Agenda" and has done investigative reporting around the world, maintains a thick tattered notebook containing his most important names, addresses, and telephone numbers. He has not called on many of these sources for several years, but they are persons who were useful to him once or twice and he feels they might be again. His solution? He created and maintains this version of a "little black book." Potter cherishes the information in that book so much that he says he never lets it out of his sight. It goes with him everywhere he goes. As he has said on numerous occasions, his career is in that source book because he believes his success or failure as a reporter depends on the people listed there (Potter, 1990).

KEEPING SOURCE LISTS

To be an effective reporter like ABC's Mark Potter, you must learn to use your sources effectively. This requires, as you read in chapter 2, good, solid organization for both general assignment and beat reporters.

There are two levels of source lists in the newsroom. Many newsrooms keep common source lists for all reporters and editors to access at any time. But most reporters also keep their own personal source lists for their specialized work or for more individual purposes.

Most newsrooms and reporters find an efficient way to organize their sources. The traditional methods have been to keep a telephone and address book or directory and to set up and use a Rolodex-type card file.

In the age of computers, most newsrooms keep the general source list in a computer file that can be constantly updated and expanded. These files are not password protected in any special manner and are available for access through the central word processing or computer system. These source lists should be, for ideal use, cross filed by name and specialization. Often, the specialization is more important than the source's name for a reporter searching for a source on a given subject. But no matter how the list is set up, finding the right names quickly is the most important consideration.

If you are setting up your first source list while on a campus, begin with a simple system that can be expanded. If you use an address book, be sure to record the full name correctly and completely. Get the address, also; it will save time later if you write it down now. Finally, the telephone number is essential. Be sure to note area codes and extensions. But try to go beyond the office telephone number. Ask for home numbers. And do not forget to ask for the source's fax machine number if there is one.

If you want to be a little more sophisticated, develop your list on a personal computer. If you do not want to purchase an electronic "address book" program, you can still use your word processor for the same purpose. The major advantage to specially written "address book" software is the ability to search and find addresses and specialties in seconds. These programs commonly have "variable fields," which allow the user to enter descriptive information, in addition to the source's name, address, and telephone number. In these spaces you could list specializations, affiliations, and other notes about a source. This becomes more important as your list of names gets larger and larger.

Reporters who feel more comfortable with traditional methods can find a Rolodex-like device at any office supply store. Or, the low-budget approach would be to use 3×5-inch cards filed in alphabetic order and cross-listed by subject.

PROBLEMS WITH SOURCE HOAXES AND TRICKS

Sources are almost always a positive matter for reporters, but they can cause serious problems. Some sources may be media hounds and some may be overly aggressive about getting their particular story told. And some individuals want to take advantage of reporters by perpetrating hoaxes, so reporters must be careful. "Journalists have published thousands of hoaxes," wrote *Media Hoaxes* author Fred Fedler (1989, p. xii). Although the term may be hard to define or explain, journalists spot them by instinctive use of professional judgment, Fedler noted. But he added, "The media are easy to fool because they depend on other people. Reporters cannot find, investigate, and write every story by themselves. Instead, they rely on a variety of tipsters to inform them about stories that seem to be newsworthy" (p. 206).

One recent example illustrates the point. A professional hoaxster fooled New York City area news media into believing an actress he hired was the winner of a $35 million Lotto jackpot. The hoaxster sought to protest that the New York state lottery was a joke. The media prankster, Alan Abel, had played pranks on the news media many times before during the past three decades. This time he hired the actress to claim she had won the prize. When word got out that she "won" the prize, gullible reporters saw that the "story" got attention:

• The *New York Post* stopped a Sunday night press run to bump a local professional football team score in a "tease box" off the front page in favor of a similar box about the woman winner.

• WWOR-TV, Channel 9, the cable "superstation," ended its 10 P.M. Sunday newscast declaring the name of the winning ticket holder.

• WNBC-TV, Channel 4, NBC's flagship station, named the woman as the winner at the beginning of its 11 P.M. newscast.

The elaborate ruse was convincing. The prankster not only hired the actress, but he also threw a lavish party Sunday night (the lottery drawing was held late Saturday night) at a Manhattan hotel to be more believable. The actress posed as a cosmetologist. She faxed invitations to the news media to attend her celebration party. She was interviewed by television, radio, and newspaper reporters who fell for her claims. She even showed reporters a photocopy of what she said was the winning ticket.

While the prank was intended to embarrass the lottery, it was the news media that took the punishment. By not checking the source of the information, these news organizations committed one of the most severe reporting crimes—and paid a big price for it (Anon., 1991, January 9).

The best solution was to confirm the information through the New York lottery offices. But the news organizations did not do that in their competitive rush to get the information *first*.

A 3 A.M. false report of a jet airplane crash at Dallas-Fort Worth airport caused radio station KRLD to broadcast the news to listeners in the middle of the night. Monitoring emergency frequencies as a newsgathering routine, the station told listeners it was an "unconfirmed report" of a crash. The prank led the station to disrupt usual programming and to scramble reporters to the scene several miles from the major airport in the area (Anon., 1991, April 28).

These hoaxes—involving bad judgment by even experienced journalists—can occur anywhere at any time. Reporters must be on their guard with sources who are not what they seem. Jack Nelson, Washington bureau chief for the *Los Angeles Times,* remembered he was once stung by a fake. When he was a young reporter at the Biloxi, Mississippi, *Daily Herald,* Nelson got a phone call telling him that Stan Musial, the famed baseball player, was staying at a nearby hotel. After a telephone interview, Nelson's local story ran on the front page, and another story ran on the Associated Press wire, but he later found out the man was an escaped mental patient from California who had left a trail of bad checks and was driving a stolen car. His consolation? Nelson said he wound up with a better story on the second day than his original "interview" story (Kelly, 1987).

Even much simpler ruses can be embarrassing. Recently, an editor at the *Miami Herald* accepted a collect long distance telephone call from a man who said he was a public relations person. After the conversation with the editor, the man then asked to be transferred to the operator so he could arrange for his company to pay for the call. The transfer to the operator, who placed a call for the man, allowed the caller to make another long distance telephone call at the newspaper's expense. It turns out that the caller was a scam artist calling from inside a Florida prison. Needless to say, the newspaper changed its policy about accepting long distance calls from sources. Next time, the newspaper won't accept such a call (Weitzel, 1991a).

Perhaps the biggest newsroom verification problem is with information for obituaries and wedding engagement news. Problems also occur with wedding and birth news. Occasionally, sources report false sports news. To combat this, news organizations have fact verification policies and procedures for reporters to follow. The basic procedure is to call back sources. Use of alternative sources such as public records and archives is also a strong backup procedure.

LEVELS OF SOURCE ATTRIBUTION

As you have already seen, not all sources want to be identified in every story. *Orlando Sentinel* reporters Jim Leusner and Christopher Quinn had that problem with the five rocket motor experts they interviewed for their "Missiles in Boomtown" series. Only two of the experts would agree to be identified. What happens then?

Leusner and Quinn managed to use the other three sources by limiting their identification and their attribution to information contained in the stories. Although this is not a desirable alternative, it is often better than no source at all. In recent years, more and more reporters have been forced to this stance by savvy sources. It is a tough position in which to be. But most of the time, you should try to find another source that will go on the record, or be named, in your story.

There are different levels of attribution to sources. When you find yourself dealing with a source who requests to be anonymous, you must try to bargain to a higher level of identification if possible to gain a bit more credibility for your story.

In Washington, DC, where anonymous sources seem to be used in stories more than anywhere else, a tradition of four levels of attribution has evolved since World War II. Those levels, which are commonly used across the country today, are:

1. *On the record:* Sources permit you to use the information provided and to attribute it to them. Most of your reporting will be done on the record. You should always assume that reporting in an interview situation is "on the record" unless a source specifically says at the beginning of the interview that it is under a different set of conditions.

2. *Background:* If a source says a story is "on background," then you can quote the source but cannot identify the source by name. Once this condition has been set, you should arrange with the source in very specific terms just how you can identify the source. Usually identification is by affiliation such as "a city hall source" or "a parks department official."

3. *Deep background:* Under this condition, any information provided by the source can be used, but there can be no identification of the source whatsoever. This information must be written on the reporter's *own* authority without connection to the original source. This level provides a much clearer zone of protection for the source.

4. *Off the record:* When sources stipulate that information is "off the record," they are saying that it cannot be used in any form. You are being told the information for your knowledge only and you should not seek official confirmation elsewhere. However, you should always try to bargain

GENE MILLER, THE *MIAMI HERALD*
READER IS VICTIM WHEN SOURCE ISN'T NAMED

A plague of anonymity infects the print media in America, and you, gentle reader, are the victim.

Again and again, your newspapers quote someone, then fail to name him or her. How come? The alleged explanation: "He declined to be identified."

There was a time when certain concepts seemed fundamental. Every copyboy in every newsroom in America knew the bromide formula: Who, what, when, where, why and how.

Now, year after year, edition after edition, the who-declined-to-be-identified practice proliferates. Weasel Journalism, it is. Often it is sloppy and lazy reporting.

Unattributed information makes it tough for anyone to make a judgment on validity. It is damn difficult to evaluate information when you don't know where it is coming from.

So where, one might ask, do these blind quotes come from? The town drunk? The village idiot? Some crooked politician with an ax to grind? The answer is probably no.

But if you suspect the quote comes from someone who doesn't want to be held accountable, the answer is yep, usually. He may not know what he is talking about. He may be afraid he'll embarrass himself or his boss. He appreciates deniability.

Nowhere is this affliction as severe as Washington, haven for unnamed bureaucrats. There the practice is a way of life, tradition and custom, mostly unquestioned and unchallenged. It is the easy way.

Anonymity is an invitation to exaggerate, embroider, embellish, slant. Or take the cheap shot. This is true for the reporter, as well as the source. It is a bad habit and it is getting worse. . . .

Some of our critics see plot, design, method, if not conspiracy, in what they read. What they don't realize is that most newspapers run on momentum, deadlines, a touch of hysteria, and a thousand jiffy decisions every edition, some of them stupid, made by a slew of people under pressure.

We try to hire the finest journalists we can find and rely upon their good sense. We disagree among ourselves about a lot of things and some of us tolerate the unattributed source more than others.

Occasionally, it is absolutely the only way to tell an important story. But in 34 years as a newsman, I've never met a Woodward–Bernstein Deep Throat in a parking garage.

One, though, an ex-cop (Phil Thibedeau) told me homicide detectives had framed a man (Joe Shea) for murder. I persuaded the ex-cop to go public.

Most decent reporters can persuade a reluctant source to talk upfront for attribution. Too often they don't try hard enough. And too often the source reads that everyone else "declines to be identified," and figures, "hey, why not me, too?"

In the end the reader is cheated.

Gene Miller (n.d.) is a two-time Pulitzer Prize-winning investigative reporter. Miller is presently associate editor/reporting for the *Miami Herald*.

Reprinted with permission of the *Miami Herald*.

to a higher level of attribution than "off the record." When sources say they want the information "off the record," ask for "background" or "deep background" status if it is clear that an "on the record" request is out of line.

ANONYMOUS AND CONFIDENTIAL SOURCES

Anonymous and confidential sources result from conditions of attribution such as "background" and "deep background." The reason for using them, of course, is to get the information needed for a story. The reason for not using them, on the other hand, is the reduced believability of the story. Most readers or viewers will be suspicious of sources in stories who are not identified. The major problem in the use of anonymous sources in recent years has been a growth in their use on ordinary and routine stories. Reporters, in other words, have *allowed* increasingly sophisticated sources to go unnamed in a story.

Years ago, tough editors could easily decide on stories because of their unbending rule: "No attribution, no story." Veteran editor and reporter Norman E. Isaacs (1988) said the only exceptions were "tips about officeholder corruption and other hanky-panky. These needed the managing editor's okay—and the bigger the story possibilities, the more likely we had to sweet-talk the whistle-blowers into meeting the m.e. [managing editor]" (p. 12). Newsrooms of that era operated under a stricter discipline, Isaacs recalled.

Isaacs (1988) believed only editors should decide whether to grant anonymity to sources. Since being embarrassed by the Janet Cooke case in 1981—she created a fictitious source for a feature story on child drug use that won a Pulitzer Prize the newspaper returned—the *Washington Post* now requires editors to know and approve of anonymous sources before they are used.

The problem is sorting out the serious sources from those less deserving of anonymity. "To cure the sourcing problem, the top dozen papers—the role models—must draw the line separating the legitimate whistleblowers from the army of bogus leakers" (p. 13). In other words, reporters and their news organizations must work harder to protect important sources and save anonymity for very significant news stories. There are legitimate concerns— loss of jobs, seniority, and even personal danger for the sources themselves and families. But Isaacs cautioned, "That vitally important [anonymity] shield should not be wasted on political fakers and other polluters of the public wells" (p. 13).

Anonymous and confidential sources are a concern for all reporters from entry-level feature writers to veteran investigative specialists. The business of dealing with source confidentiality has become what one media law attorney called "a significant and sensitive issue for news organizations" (Sommers, 1991, p. 32). The basic issue in court is whether a reporter, once confidentiality and anonymity have been granted and the story published or broadcast, can be *forced* to disclose the source. Some states have "shield" laws to protect reporters from disclosure, but not every state, nor the federal government, has a shield law. Reporters who may need to use an anonymous source should check their state's laws before promising a source confidentiality and publishing or broadcasting the story.

Louise Sommers (1991), an attorney and communication law professor at a law school, suggested reporters take particular care to talk with a source who requests anonymity and to talk with editors or news directors to "minimize the making of promises that cannot be kept or the bungling of promises that are intended to be followed through" (p. 32). She also suggested that reporters and their newsroom supervisors avoid ambiguity. "Be clear when dealing with a source," she advised. "If possible, take the time to review with the source precisely what will or will not appear in the story. . . . If helpful, have the source articulate precisely what information would pose a threat to anonymity" (p. 32).

Most news organizations have thoughtfully written policies about confidential and anonymous sources for reporters and editors to consult. Such policies are intended to guide reporters and there may be exceptions. But reporters should always talk with their immediate supervising editor or producer when encountering situations that might call for anonymous sources and confidentiality. Exceptions to policies will normally require approval at the highest management levels of the newsroom.

In these policies, most news organizations advise reporters to avoid anonymity when possible. This is the philosophy of the *Orange County (Calif.) Register* policy on confidential and anonymous sources, written by editor Chris Anderson. The policy is included in Appendix A. In his memorandum to reporters and editors, Anderson reminded his staff that the reason to be concerned with these matters is the *credibility* of the news organization, because it is its most important asset.

News veterans John Chancellor, from NBC News, and Walter Mears (1983), from the Associated Press, agreed. They argued, "Journalism depends on credibility. If the public doesn't believe what you write, you might as well go into another business. Telling the public where you got the stuff, from government leaks to the coach on the football team, is the way to protect that credibility" (p. 169).

The *Orange County Register*'s Anderson (1988) distinguished between anonymous sources and confidential sources. "An anonymous source is one whose name we have agreed to leave out of an article, but who may later need to be identified. That need may come from legal action, for example. A confidential source is one whose identity will not be revealed," he wrote (p. 2). Because of this condition, he says granting confidentiality is an extreme case requiring support of the entire news organization, not just the reporter.

In a detailed set of guidelines for staffers, *Minneapolis Star Tribune* executive editor Joel Kramer (1988) listed three basic concerns:

1. While anonymous sources are a critical element of some important stories, frequent reliance on them in the newspaper increases the risk of inaccurate or unfair journalism and can adversely affect the newspaper's credibility with readers.

2. Anonymous statements and quotes should be published in the *Star* only when necessary to provide important information and only after both a reporter and editor are satisfied that we are meeting our standards for accuracy and fairness.

3. We will avoid making promises of confidentiality to sources that are not in the newspaper's or the reader's best interest, but we will honor the promises we make except in the most extraordinary circumstances (p. 1).

PUBLIC RELATIONS SOURCES AND USING PRESS RELEASES

Reporters find themselves working more often with public relations sources these days than ever before. It seems that just about every news-generating organization has one or more public relations staff members assigned to work directly with reporters. These individuals have two main duties in working with reporters: to assist in requests that come from reporters and to initiate story ideas for publicity purposes.

Public relations practitioners have come a long way since their early days as Hollywood movie star publicists or political machine promoters. The public relations professional today has a wide range of communication skills and responsibilities, including the duty of assisting reporters seeking sources of information.

Public relations practitioners are on duty to help you get the right source quickly. They can also become another barrier and be uncooperative; however, most public relations people try to help even in the most difficult situations.

One of the major ways they help reporters is to initiate contact by providing press releases containing information about their company or institution. These individuals also contact reporters by telephone to suggest stories.

At times it will be necessary to write stories based on information contained in press releases. How do you handle attribution? Do you attribute information to the release or not? Information taken from press releases is almost always rewritten and not published or broadcast in original form. This is not because the original is poorly written. It is because editors or producers want information from the press release combined with other information or reorganized to place focus on some other element of the story.

Attribution to public relations sources should be no different from attribution to other routine sources used in news stories. However, in press releases, company or institutional officials are often named. It is appropriate to use those individuals as primary sources, but also to note that the information comes from a prepared press release. This more complete form of disclosure is often sacrificed in the interest of space or time, however. Some reporters simply take quotations or other information and incorpo-

NEWS RELEASE

Phone (305) 591-1833   Dorothy A. Silva
Address 8685 N.W. 53 Terrace, Suite 200, Miami, Fl 33166-4611

IMMEDIATE RELEASE
MAY 9, 1991

ARMY INCREASES $ FOR COLLEGE

   The US Army now offers new recruits more money for college
than ever. New soldiers may receive up to $27,000 for college, if
they qualify, under recently signed "Desert Storm" legislation.
The legislation increases the amount new soldiers receive under
the Montgomery GI Bill. Together with the Army College Fund,
depending on length of service, new soldiers may receive $17,900 to
$27,000 for college. The total package, depending on enlistment,
looks like this:

	NEW GI BILL	+ ARMY COLLEGE FUND	= TOTAL
2 Yr. Enlistment	$ 9,900	$ 8,000	$17,900
3 Yr. Enlistment	$12,600	$12,000	$24,600
4 Yr. Enlistment	$12,600	$14,400	$27,000

   "Reserve soldiers will also benefit from the increase. A
6-year reserve enlistment will mean an additional $30 per month,
bringing the total combined Montgomery GI Bill and Army College
Fund benefits up to $19,120," said LTC Roy J. Whitehead, commander
of the Miami US Army Recruiting Battalion.

   Anyone interested in money for college through an Army
enlistment can contact their local Army recruiter for details. They
are listed in the Yellow Pages under "Recruiting."

- 30 -

Press releases, such as these sent to news organizations by the U.S.
Army and Walt Disney World (see pp. 89–90), are an important source of
news story ideas for reporters.

rate it into their stories without proper credit. Not only does full identification of the source enhance credibility, it helps readers and audiences
judge the quality and purpose of the information.

Behind most of the activity by public relations professionals is their
company's or institution's policies about publicity and public information.
In recent years, many newsmaking organizations have begun to develop
policies and procedures in dealing with the news media. This is common in

Press & Publicity Department • P.O. Box 10,000 • Lake Buena Vista, FL 32830-1000 • (407) 824-4531

ARMADILLOS AND CHILI COOKOFF
HIGHLIGHT PLEASURE ISLAND'S 'TASTE OF TEXAS'

LAKE BUENA VISTA, Fla. -- Pleasure Island's "Taste of Texas" on May 19 features entertainment as big as the state of Texas -- armadillo racing, chili cooking, bluegrass music, and the award-winning Dave Durham and the Bull Durham Band playing their hits.

Those good with a chili pot vie for the rights to represent the state of Florida this November at the National Chili Cookoff Finals in Terlingua, Texas.

Sunday afternoon, Pleasure Island will be changed into the most authentic piece of Texas real estate east of San Angelo. To commemorate the Taste of Texas, taste buds will be teased, tickled, rejuvenated and...scorched. Some fifty teams of chili cookers are expected to set up camp bright and early Sunday morning. When the call is given, "cookers, start your fires," the slicing, dicing, chopping and "pot watchin" will begin as dozens of cauldrons of bubbling chili fill the air with the robust aroma of West Texas.

Sometime later in the day, the esteemed judges start making the rounds. After tasting 50 styrofoam cups of chili, nibbling saltines and drinking cold water, the judges will announce the first, second and third place winners.

-more-

organizations that have a high sensitivity to public opinion and have developed public affairs or public relations departments. These statements often instruct management and rank-and-file employees on how to conduct themselves with the news media and specifically instruct employees on steps to take in releasing new information to reporters and the public in general.

For your understanding about the scope and depth of such policies, the

-2-

Sam "Jalapeno" Lewis is bringing his "babies." To put it more accurately, Sam Lewis is bringing his racing armadillos.

Lewis, 72, is recognized as the foremost authority on armadillos. How are armadillos raced? "Got to blow on 'em," Sam says. "It's right where the tail meets the body. Shoot, they'll run like crazy."

Sam's armor-plated little racers will run on a padded astroturf track on the streets of Pleasure Island. "Folks won't believe it 'till they see how fast armadillos can go."

For those who feel inspired, there is an open call to qualify for the Mr. and Mrs. Armadillo contest. Jalapeno Sam is expected to bring the qualifying rules for the contest upon his arrival from Texas.

In addition to Dave Durham at the West End Stage, some of the finest "pickers and grinners" in Florida are to perform. Bluegrass music at it's very best will keep the downhome beat moving to toe tapping perfection all Sunday afternoon.

Pleasure Island will look like part of a back lot in a Western movie. There will be cowboys. Rope handling. Blacksmith demonstrations. Clogging. Can't dance the Texas Two Step or the Cotton-Eye Joe? For those who are a little rusty, dance lessons are available and free. There will be awards for "Best Country Dance Couple," "Best Dressed Country," and even "Best Armadillo Caller."

Those people who have a knack with tomato sauce and other assorted ingredients, are invited to participate in the chili cookoff competition. To book space, chili cookers should call the "hotline:" (407) 828-1515.

The Taste of Texas, which begins at high noon, Sunday, May 19, is open free to the public until normal gating hours at 7 p.m.

-30-

0106T/dia/TL

Following a formal announcement, a bank executive answers reporters' questions at scheduled press conferences (photo by the *Miami Herald* staff).

University of Miami's internal policy on public information is included in Appendix B. This statement includes a general description of institutional policy and then outlines procedures for staff members to use when information is released. It is typical of such manuals, although some companies and organizations have much stricter rules than those reflected in the university policy.

HOW PROFESSIONALS WRITE IT

NEWSPAPER: *Key West Citizen,* pp. 1, 3
DATE: Friday, April 27, 1990
AUTHOR: Leanne R. Reifsteck, special to the *Citizen*
HEADLINE: Making ends meet; Senior citizens face high costs

* * *

For Ruth Brockmiller, retirement in Key West is not the rest and relaxation most people would expect.

Brockmiller will be starting work next week at McDonald's making minimum wage on the 5 to 11 A.M. shift.

Even though Brockmiller has a retirement pension from the Goodyear Tire Company, she cannot afford the high costs of living in Key West. Brockmiller makes $621 a month, but her expenses are even more. For instance:

- Rent (which has increased several times over the past eight years and is expected to go up again) and the taxes have steadily increased since she came here.
- Medical insurance, which she describes as a good plan and an absolute must for her, costs almost a third of her gross income.
- Local costs of garbage collection, electricity and water are additional large expenses in her budget.
- There is also the high costs of clothing and food.

With all of these expenses, Brockmiller had to get a job to make ends meet, despite the back problems that had forced her to retire early a few years ago.

"The cost of living here is so high, like food and gas; they say that is because they have to truck it down here," Brockmiller said, "but I don't understand that because they have to truck it everywhere."

Brockmiller is not alone, many senior citizens in Key West face the same economic hardships. Hardships that were brought on by drastic changes in the city during the past few decades.

The value of real estate has gone up, creating higher property taxes for residents. Henry Hughes, president of the local chapter of the AARP (American Association of Retired Persons), said he knew many seniors who could not afford the constantly rising costs here anymore and were forced to move.

Many Conchs that have moved have gone to Ocala in central Florida. A couple of bus loads of Key West seniors make the trip to Ocala every few years for a reunion with old friends and neighbors.

Hughes explained that many of the Conchs were born and brought up here. When they have to leave, it is really wrenching.

Hughes said that everything has gone up; insurance, for example, keeps increasing every year.

Hughes said he knows seniors that pay upwards of $3,000 and $4,000 a year for insurance coverage. He also said that even though you make more money, you can't buy what you used to with it.

There are several programs that are available to senior citizens that need economic assistance making ends meet.

The SCSEP (Senior Community Service Employment Program) has 40 positions available to seniors who need to earn additional money to supplement their pensions.

The SCSEP jobs are in the community services or county offices. The senior workers receive minimum wage and work on polishing old skills or learning new ones. The object of the program is to prepare seniors to re-enter the work force. The SCSEP then assists the senior in finding a job in the private sector.

The program is sponsored by National Council on the Aging and the Board of County Commissioners. Seniors who want to participate in the program must meet set financial criteria to be eligible.

The county has a transportation program headed by Cecil Bain, the program director, that provides transportation for seniors who need it.

The program takes seniors to the armory for the hot meal program, to shopping, and to doctor's appointments.

The hot meals program provides two services for Key West seniors. A hot lunch program provides lunch Monday through Friday at the armory and a hot meals delivery program to homebound seniors. The service is free, however, a $1.25 donation is recommended to assist in paying for the cost of the meal.

Mary Bain of the nutrition program said, "It is very difficult for some senior citizens to make ends meet on a limited income like social security, especially with the high cost of living in Key West."

These programs do have limits. A combination of economics and a larger older population has created a greater demand. There are waiting lists for some programs and more are expected as the high cost of living in Key West increases.

Reprinted with permission of the *Key West Citizen*.

• • •

SOURCE: *The Muncie Star,* sec. A, pp. 1, 13
AUTHOR: Randy Rendfeld, staff reporter
DATE: Friday, January 6, 1989
HEADLINE: Fox hunt: It's legal, but is it humane?

* * *

LOSANTVILLE, Ind.—It's bound to be an enjoyable day of scaring up foxes, deer and coy dogs when the Losantville Fire Department hosts its foxhunt starting at 9 A.M. Saturday.

But that's not Marjorie McConnell's idea of a humane morning. McConnell, president of the Society for the Prevention of Cruelty to Animals, remembers foxhunts as a group of men, women and children wielding bludgeons, converging on a helpless animal and clubbing it to death.

Conservation Officer Ed Townsend, whose jurisdiction includes Randolph County, explained, "It amounts to a bunch of guys getting together, chewing the fat and having a bean supper."

Townsend, who's been a conservation officer since 1960, says foxhunts have been around as long as he can remember.

"It's pretty simple," said Willard Fisher, secretary-treasurer of the Losantville Fire Department. "We just take the guys out and scatter around a square mile. They circle cautiously. Most of these guys have done this before. The word is slow. When they get that fox up, you'll hear three or four shots from shooting into the circle.

"We're concerned with getting everybody fed, counting the money and getting through the day without anyone getting hurt."

Fisher said coffee and donuts will be served at the fire department beginning about 6 A.M., and the hunt will begin about 9 A.M. When the hunting's over, all the deerburgers, cornbread and beans you can eat for $3.50 will be served. Door prizes will be awarded to participants.

McConnell says she's found the foxhunt to be legal as long as participants have valid hunting licenses. "But it's very, very unnecessary," she said. "We have no overpopulation of foxes, and they're necessary in keeping down rats and rodent populations. Instead of killing them, we should be helping them."

If the foxhunters use guns instead of clubs, it'll be less brutal, she said. "But I still don't like it. It's unnecessary."

McConnell said she referred the Losantville foxhunt to the Humane Society of the United States in Bowling Green, Ohio. HSUS officials told her radio journalist Paul Harvey once aired details of a foxhunt which was about to occur in Illinois. Harvey's broadcast caused the foxhunt to be cancelled. She said the HSUS told her they would contact Harvey again, but there wasn't much else they could do.

About a decade ago, Indiana counties paid a bounty for the fox. Townsend said hunters pursued them in a variety of ways, sometimes with backhoes, and sometimes by throwing sticks of dynamite from passing airplanes.

"People'd shoot them and throw them in ditches. You didn't need a license to hunt them," he said. Now foxes may only be hunted in Indiana between October and February.

"I've got mixed feelings," Townsend said of foxhunts. "It's not detrimental to anything—of course it is to the poor fox. But probably wild dog packs are more detrimental. There'll probably be more coy dogs shot that day than fox."

The "coy dog" is a cross between a coyote and a dog, Townsend explained. He said coy dogs and coyotes were becoming more and more prevalent each year in surrounding counties.

Townsend recalled a Paul Harvey story about a man who refused to mow his lawn because he claimed he could hear grass and weeds scream each time he cut it. He says ironically many of the people he meets who are anti-hunting are also pro-abortion.

Red and gray foxes, the most common variety in east central Indiana, are valuable to the ecosystem, according to Thad Godish, Ball State University professor in the Department of Natural Resources. But they're not rare. Foxes are nocturnal animals, so they're not often seen, he said.

"The question is, 'What is acceptable?' " Godish said of the opposing views of the foxhunt. "If they shoot them, I suppose it's not much different than other types of hunting."

Reprinted with the *Muncie Star*.

• • •

SOURCE: *Fort Lauderdale Sun-Sentinel*, pp. 1B, 10B
AUTHORS: Andrew Martin and Amy Stromberg, staff writers
DATE: Friday, June 15, 1990, final ed.
HEADLINE: Port's past coming to surface: Inquiry seeks truth about influential group, financial dealings

* * *

When Port Everglades Director Joel Alesi arrived in New York to court business people at the port's annual stone crab luncheon in 1989, a black limousine picked up Alesi and his closest advisers at the airport.

Three other port staffers had to hail a cab.

The limo ride was a gift from Bill Glynn, former head of the Broward County Republican Party, a friend of port commissioners and, until last year, part owner of a North Carolina mountain cabin with Alesi.

Glynn had reason to keep in Alesi's favor: Glynn has earned $4.84 million in fees for his employers as the underwriter for $272 million in bonds the port has issued since 1986.

Now Glynn is enmeshed in a massive inquiry by the FBI and other law-enforcement agencies trying to untangle a web of lucrative financial deals at the port.

Investigators are focusing on the actions of a small group of people who have exercised a large amount of control at the port since the mid-1980s.

Investigators want to answer questions that have hung over the port for months: Were the port's financial dealings influenced by favors or payoffs? Innocent mistakes or conspiracy? Influence or extortion?

Investigators soon will begin poring over five years of documents—contracts, bond deals, leases and purchases—and present them to a federal grand jury, which could spend months reviewing evidence before deciding whether criminal charges are warranted.

"The purpose of the task force is to ferret out any activity of a criminal nature that might have been going on," FBI spokesman Paul Miller said.

The port is a $29 million-a-year public operated business that serves hundreds of petroleum tankers, cruise ships and container-cargo ships.

It is presided over by a seven-member commission, five of them elected and two appointed by the County Commission. One appointee represents labor, the other, business.

The port commission and its staff have been accused of mis-spending millions of dollars on everything from gold rings to expensive luncheons and awarding contracts and leases to politicians and friends.

Port officials say investigators will come up empty-handed.

"There's nothing there," said Walter Browne, the appointed labor representative on the port commission. "There have been some mistakes down at Port Everglades, but I genuinely believe that there has not been any kind of criminal activity."

Many of the port's problems, Browne and others say, result from its unusual status: a public agency that must operate like a business to be successful.

"We're running a business, and you need to promote a business," Port Commissioner Joseph DeLillo said.

They point out that the port has experienced unprecedented growth during the past five years. Now the world's second-largest cruise passenger port, its revenues have jumped from $9 million in 1981 to $28 million in 1989.

Even before the inquiries began, port officials were blasted for mismanaging port money.

For instance, for parts of 1988 and 1989, commissioners paid former Port Director C. Thomas Burke $80,000 a year as a consultant, although he did little more than write a monthly memo.

Criticism intensified in September, when commissioners levied the port's first property tax in six years to finance construction projects.

Newspaper articles detailed how the port bought nearly $3,500 in tickets for Democratic fundraisers, $9,984 for tickets and parking for Miami Dolphins and Miami Heat games, and expensive office furnishings such as a $2,250 painting.

Top executives were earning some of the nation's highest salaries for port officials and rewarding themselves with port-provided cars, car phones, fancy lunches and first-class hotel rooms.

But problems are nothing new at the 62-year-old port, long plagued by ethics violations, organized crime allegations, cozy deals and drunken antics.

As recently as the early 1980s, the port went through four directors in as many years and was regularly decried as a circus.

At the helm of the port for the past two years has been Alesi, 48, a soft-spoken man who rarely raises his voice or debates in public. These days he avoids the news media whenever possible.

Alesi is a Chicago native who was hired as a firefighter/security guard when he landed at the port after a semester in college, two years in the Army, and a stint as a short-order cook and apartment manager.

Alesi became involved in union and Democratic politics, moving quickly to the forefront of the port's firefighter union. He also was active in the AFL-CIO.

In the Democratic Party, Alesi went from campaign worker to second vice chairman under then-Chairman George Platt. The two remain close allies.

Another important figure is Port Commissioner Browne.

His brash style and tough Brooklynese reflect his New York City upbringing and the personality of his late father Charles Browne, a powerful union leader in Broward for many years.

Browne and Alesi met in about 1980, when Alesi sought Browne's help to organize the port's supervisors.

As divisional director of the Federation of Public Employees, Browne boasted he built the union into one of the county's most powerful.

Browne solidified his political base with thousands of dollars in contributions to political candidates. In 1984, Browne's union contributed about $12,000, including $1,000 donations to state Sen. Jim Scott, R-Fort Lauderdale, and then-County Commissioner Howard Forman, now a state senator.

When the port commission was restructured in 1984 to include a labor appointment, Browne pushed hard to get the job.

"He took over immediately," said Jim Connolly, a former port director who frequently clashed with Browne. "He was running the port from the commission standpoint from that point forward."

Browne forged a solid majority with DeLillo, Michael Marinelli and then-Commissioner Stan Harris, mostly because of their mutual dislike of Connolly.

With Platt's help, Browne pushed through a proposal to locate the county convention center, at the port, Connolly and other port officials said.

Browne, along with DeLillo, was also instrumental in persuading other commissioners to approve a $104 million bond issue in 1986 to finance a port expansion, port documents show.

As chairman of a charter review committee, Browne oversaw recommendations that gave the port more power. The Broward delegation pushed them through the Legislature in 1989.

Still, Browne said he has no more authority than any other commissioner.

"I do not control Port Everglades," Browne said. "I have never gone to Joel Alesi and said, 'I want you to do this or hire this person.'"

Browne blames people who have been fired from the port and members of the Federation of Public Employees, which he left amid controversy in 1988 to work for the Teamsters Union.

Two former port directors, Connolly and C. Thomas Burke, said Browne and Alesi engineered their ousters by feeding negative stories to newspapers.

Meanwhile, Browne and other commissioners were doling out contracts to friends and allies.

For instance:

• Every bond issued since 1988 — $272 million worth — has been underwritten by firms employing Glynn. The firms were chosen without competitive bids.

• Without seeking competitive bids, the commission voted 4–3 in 1987 to hire the law firm of House Speaker Tom Gustafson, D-Fort Lauderdale — Ruden Barnett McClosky Smith Schuster and Russell — as its outside legal adviser.

• Frederic R. Harris Inc., an engineering consultant, has been selected for at least six contracts since 1987. Since January 1988, the port has paid the firm $6.2 million. Harris employs the daughter of Port Commissioner Herb Myers.

• The port awarded its contract for third-party administrative services in 1989 to a friend of Browne's, Anthony Lapiana. The port bid the contract three times before awarding it to Lapiana's firm, Automated Benefit Services.

• The port's staff swelled with new hires, many of them friends and allies of Alesi and commissioners. For instance, the port hired Browne's former aide at the Federation of Public Employees to be director of human resources. Port salary: $39,224, $10,428 more than his union salary. Alesi also hired a member of the Democratic Executive Committee as the port's $47,807-a-year special projects coordinator. Her former salary: $36,000.

• Spending became even more extravagant. The port's tab at Burt & Jack's restaurant — once called "the port's restaurant" by Alesi — totalled $12,315 in 1988 and $18,716.19 in 1989.

But the port's most ridiculed expenditure was for rings.

Alesi authorized the purchase of seven $478 gold rings for commissioners shortly after becoming interim director in August 1988. The rings were discarded because a port aide thought them unacceptable.

A second set of diamond-studded gold rings, costing $1,263 apiece, was then purchased.

Commission Chairman Betsy Krant has been pushing to eliminate the port's property tax and working on a tougher ethics code.

Regardless, Browne said he is fed up with the controversy and criticism.

"When my appointment expires, I could care less what happens to Port Everglades," he said.

Reprinted with permission of the *Fort Lauderdale Sun-Sentinel.*

• • •

SOURCE: WCBS-TV, Channel 2, New York, *The Scripps Howard Foundation National Journalism Awards,* p. 16
REPORTER: Mike Taibbi, staff reporter
DATE: 1989
TITLE: The stranglehold drugs have on the Bushwick neighborhood of Brooklyn

* * *

Anchor: It is an urban battleground where no one is claiming victory—the city streets that have become ravaged by drugs. Channel 2's Mike Taibbi spent several weeks inside this war zone in Brooklyn and tonight he continues his series on life and death in Bushwick and we must warn you— the pictures that we have chosen to show you will shock you, but we feel that they must be shown.

Music from an ice cream truck.

Mike Taibbi: Sometimes in quick glances it can look just like any normal city neighborhood on a warm late summer afternoon. Kids on the stoop— a man reads the paper. But look closer, scan your vision, and you can see how drug related violence has savaged Bushwick and Bushwick's spirit.

On Irving Avenue where that ice cream truck pulled to a stop the residents of one building were not surprised at all that a crack gang had smashed through a window and just taken a vacant apartment.

Woman: "But then he came in here and he bring all these people in here and they do all their stuff in here."

Taibbi: "All of what stuff?"

Woman: "All their drugs."

Taibbi: They're not surprised because even the kids can point to the crack den that used to be livable apartments in buildings all around them.

Boy on the street: "On the fourth floor, brother, it's worse than that."

Taibbi: "Oh, there's crack dens up there?"

Boy: "Yeah."

Taibbi: They're not surprised any more because the arrogance of the drug people and their purposeful or casual violence are almost taken for granted.

Sirens in background

Taibbi: "Do you ever hear any gun shots?"

Boy on the street: "Just last night."

Another boy: "Everyday."

Taibbi interviews another group of youths on the street.

Young man: Camera focuses on his bandaged hand. "It was a little gun, though, a .25."

Taibbi: "A .25-caliber gun. How do you live with it? You're laughing about it now."

Young man: "Cause it's nothing."

Taibbi: "Nothing."

Young man: "Well, it's something, but it's nothing big. Things like that happen."

Another boy: "It be that way in the ghetto."

Another street scene, where a crowd has gathered to watch two young women fight.

Taibbi: At a drug nest on Melrose Street a fight breaks out between two women addicts. The cops have been watching this scene for an hour—just watching. The drug use goes on openly. A woman who knows the two combatants gives a blow by blow and this is how it goes.

Taibbi: "We're not pointing the camera now. Tell me what they're fighting about."

Woman: "Because one got one high. No, she gave her some money to get her some drugs. Right. And she took the money and smoked it with someone else. So, the girl is over there waiting for her to bring her stuff and she didn't bring it. You should have never smoked."

Crowd noises. Police breaking up fight and questioning people.

Taibbi: What was amazing about this was that in a minute and thirty seconds—no more than that—two TNT detectives showed up, an EMS truck showed up and two other foot patrol cops showed up. All within a minute and thirty seconds and the two cops have been standing here all along. It had been a fight in earnest and Melrose Street is no stranger to deliberate or accidental violent death. But the onlookers cheered and laughed, a 12-year-old shouting in excitement that "this is the best street in the city, the best."

They fight and die in Bushwick's war zone—the dealers in their battles over turf—the addicts in their battle just to live another day—the addicted hookers when they pull in the wrong trick. You can see it all over Bushwick—the exhortations to rest in peace for all the victims of the commerce in drugs. They're so young, most of the dead. The seamless mosaic of mourning is a terrible emblem for the rule of narcotics.

Resident: "It's chaos out there you know—the drugs are killing everybody, you know."

And they do kill themselves with drugs. In this horrific scene in the shooting gallery known as the Jefferson Street Condos—we watched a man come close. We show you this scene because if you can watch it you will know how desperate the needs that feed the drug suppliers, that give them their power.

This man tries eleven times to find a vein from which he can draw blood. He calls on a friend to help but he's getting sicker by the minute. He tries again to do it himself—his arm is full of blood but only from the stabs of the needle. He can't draw blood into the needle—he can't empty the heroin into a vein. Finally after five minutes of this he begins going into convulsions—we don't know why exactly, but later after he staggered out of the range of our camera lens I would watch him struggle down Jefferson Street. He would fall once, hard, but he would pull himself to his feet and make it around the corner—still alive, barely.

There was a lot of discussion in our newsroom about whether to broadcast that sequence as it happened, as you just saw it. I can tell you that a lot of seasoned journalists had a lot of trouble watching it. But while the decision to run it was not unanimous, for we're not showing you gratuitous brutality. We're showing you the way things are. And if the drug plague has now escalated to the status of war, then all of us who will pay for that war—with dollars if not with our children and our lives—need to know exactly what it is like in the trenches.

• • •

II | REPORTING TECHNIQUES

4 | Background: Researching News Stories

From November 12, 1989 through December 15, 1989, residents of central Kentucky were shocked by revelations that their property tax system that was the lifeblood of the schools was not working. It was in effect cheating the children of the state.

That's what the *Lexington Herald-Leader* found in its award-winning series of articles on political abuses in the Kentucky state public school system. Once the importance of the stories and what the stories revealed began to sink in, readers provided overwhelming response. They wrote 1,800 letters. They complained to their elected officials. The complaints expressed outrage at the system that put politics and back-scratching ahead of the development of good, strong public schools.

But the response did not stop with reaction of the readers. It hit a nerve like seldom before in the state. The state legislature began a revolutionary series of reforms for state school system funding and allocation of those funds. A 1,000-page reform bill was passed and signed by the governor in 1990, setting the stage to raise $1 billion over the following 2 years for state schools. Just about everyone in Kentucky traces the reforms to the series of stories. The series told readers in 12 daily parts what had been happening to put things in such bad condition:

Day 1: A study of a county tax assessor who kept millions of dollars off the tax rolls by failing to assess property. This story is reprinted at the end of this chapter.

Day 2: How the governor of the state avoided paying taxes on property he owned in the state capital.

Research about the activities of frequent newsmakers such as former President Richard Nixon and his Miami businessman friend Bebe Rebozo should be easy compared to other news sources (photo by David Walters, *Miami Herald* staff).

Day 3: Child "tax collectors" who, in one rural county, resorted to selling candy door-to-door to raise money for basic school supplies. The story told of one student who raised more money in a year than his county seat's mayor paid in property taxes.

Day 4: An analysis of undervalued property statewide, and how it robbed education.

Day 5: An analysis of delinquency lists in some rural countries and the inaction that occurs when a tax bill is thrown away.

Day 6: A look at a poor rural county that refused to help itself by increasing taxes. Instead, the county lowered its property taxes.

Day 7: A look at teachers who work in fear of losing jobs. The article reported that school superintendents often punish teachers who do not support the "right" candidates at local levels.

Day 8: By studying one county, this installment focused on the political and educational roles of school system superintendents in some counties in the state. The story concluded their roles were more political than educational.

Day 9: Nepotism is widespread, readers learned on this day of the series. Because of the practice, there is little discipline of employees, nor is there quality control.

Day 10: This part described how unnecessary employees wind up working for school systems as part of a political spoils system. Jobs awarded for political support are provided through the school system at taxpayer expense.

Day 11: One eastern Kentucky county was analyzed because its school board was "paralyzed" by political warring over jobs.

Day 12: This wrap-up portion of the series listed problems and their possible solutions—in addition to the problem caused by funding troubles.

The success of the series was a result of hard, time-consuming research. Much of the documentation was later supplemented by interviews, but the team of 10 reporters—Kit Wagar, John Winn Miller, Bill Estep, Bob Geiger, Jack Brammer, Mary Ann Roser, Lee Mueller, Valarie Honeycutt, Jamie Lucke, and Joseph S. Stroud—did its homework first, said *Herald-Leader* Special Projects editor David Green (1991). "Our reporters prepared themselves before they went into the field," Green explained. The reporting team did research for its stories first in the library, with background checking, and then did research in the field. Then the reporters checked property documents in about two dozen county offices, looked at property in person, and interviewed their sources. "Research was a huge amount of this series," explained *Herald-Leader* editor Tim Kelly (1991), who joined the newspaper as the series was being prepared.

The series won the national Society of Professional Journalists' Sigma Delta Chi Public Service in Newspaper Journalism Award for large newspapers in 1990. It also won the University of Southern California's Selden Ring Award, an investigative reporters and editors award, and was a finalist for the Pulitzer Prize. John S. Carroll, editor of the newspaper at that time but who later became editor of the *Baltimore Sun,* said his staff was prepared to write the series. "We had been covering education as Kentucky's Number One problem for about seven years, so we had a pretty good grasp of things," he said (Nelson, 1990, p. 19).

It all began with an idea. In the *Herald-Leader's* case, a state Supreme Court ruling induced the staff to look into the support for the state's school system. The team of Kentucky reporters used 2 years of computerized property tax records from the state revenue department. The reporters read property deeds, assessment records, property transfer affidavits, mortgages, lawsuits, school board minutes, education department records, social worker reports, and much more (Wagar, 1991). You cannot take the research step for granted in the process of reporting.

For example, when *Lexington Herald-Leader* reporter Kit Wagar requested tax records for the series, he was punched in the face by the son of a county official. "Kit's pretty persistent when it comes to getting information for a story," Kelly (1991) said. The newspaper had to get a state attorney general ruling to force the county — and all others — to open its files for research.

This chapter helps you understand how background research can strengthen news stories and it reviews the most common public and private sources used by journalists. It also gives some ideas about how to contend with limitations of restricted public and private information that you might need for a story.

Background research for news stories is a complex process that, if done well, can be productive. Such research work has its pitfalls, too. Scholars have found in their analysis of newsgathering processes that biases such as stereotypes may influence newsgathering (Horvath-Neimeyer & Kent, 1990).

This chapter discusses two general categories of written sources for background research: (a) those open and available to you and (b) those not generally available to the public.

NEWS MEDIA LIBRARIES

Until recently, at least, the role of the news library in journalism has been virtually ignored. Newspapers and, more recently, broadcast stations, have always had some form of library or "morgue" for filing background information needed for future stories. But that has been changing in the past decade. "Professionalization of the library staff and the acquisition of new technologies that enhance information gathering have contributed to the increased importance of the library," wrote University of Minnesota journalism researchers Jean Ward, Kathleen Hansen, and Douglas McLeod (1988b, p. 143).

News libraries centralize resources for reporters. They provide access to the more traditional and newer information collection skills of librarians, provide background for working stories, enhance accuracy in reporting, save time, and even "recycle" information purchased by the news organization previously (Hansen, Ward, & McLeod, 1987; Ward, Hansen, & McLeod, 1988b).

Most news organizations will have libraries or story clipping/video-audiotape file systems for you to use. A larger newspaper or magazine library will be staffed by professionals who assist with fact checking, locating previous articles or video-audiotapes, conducting electronic database searches, and finding graphics. Smaller newspapers and magazines, as well as remote bureaus of larger news organizations, usually are not as well equipped, forcing reporters to be more resourceful in finding information.

News media libraries, like the rest of the newsroom, are being revolutionized by the personal computer (Mooney & Trivedi, 1983; Paul, 1991c). As is detailed in the next chapter, which focuses solely on computer databases and computer document searching, the computer has made your library work faster and less expensive (Aumente, 1989). There is an indepth discussion of computerized library work in the next chapter, so the discussion here focuses on more traditional, non-database-oriented research for news story reporting.

Many television and radio stations, especially larger ones, have tape, film, and slide libraries as well as small reference book libraries. The value of these, of course, depends on how well they are catalogued and maintained on a daily basis.

One recent study of news library usage shows that experienced reporters know the value of research (Hansen, Ward, & McLeod, 1987). The study shows news libraries are now significant sources of information for reporters. The study found reporters use reference books (84% of inquiries), current newspapers and magazines (59%), and electronic databases (38%). Journalists with 5 to 10 years' experience use libraries most often, being more information-oriented than others. Thus, beginners should take advantage of the suggestion from their more experienced colleagues and make the library their first stop for backgrounding.

If you are fortunate enough to have a good library or news research center serving your newsroom, it can help you in two ways. First, the research center's primary resource is previously published or broadcast material, thus it is usually filed in "hard copy" form in two ways: by personal name and by subject matter.

Second, as more and more news organizations become computer-based in story and script preparation, this information is being transferred to permanent storage databases for easy access and use. This is the continuation of a computer transformation that began in the 1980s and continues today. But the electronic library is just beginning to take shape.

The next revolution in news media libraries will be in electronic storage of visual images, pointed out Nora Paul (1991a), library director at the Poynter Institute in St. Petersburg, Florida. "When the storage and retrieval quality problems are resolved, it will happen in a major way," she suggested.

For the basics today, just about all libraries will have a standard set of

---

FINDING INFORMATION FOR YOUR STORY

Although this chapter's discussion on research for news reporting might introduce you to the general procedures and sources, there are four excellent books that take the subject into greater depth and detail:

1. Horowitz, L. (1986). *A writer's guide to research.* Cincinnati, OH: Writer's Digest Books.
2. Kessler, L., & McDonald, D. (1987). *Uncovering the news: A journalist's search for information.* Belmont, CA: Wadsworth.
3. Ullman, J., & Colbert, J. (Eds.). (1991). *The reporter's handbook: An investigative guide to documents and techniques* (2nd ed.). New York: St. Martins Press.
4. Ward, J., & Hansen, K. A. (1987). *Search strategies in mass communication.* White Plains, NY: Longman.

---

atlases, abstracts, directories, handbooks, encyclopedias, almanacs, and other general reference books. Libraries should update their holdings as often as new editions are published. The standard tools for finding information in these sources are card and on-line catalogs, as well as published indexes.

PUBLIC AND PRIVATE LIBRARIES

Public and private libraries will be your next options for conducting research for your story. If you cannot find what you seek in your own newsroom's library, then go to your local public library. In most major communities, there will also be university and college libraries, but these are sometimes restricted. Many state universities and college libraries are open to the public, but some private schools allow access only to faculty, students, staff, and alumni. If you need to use a private library, contact the director of the library to request permission to use it.

Public libraries often contain very useful sources, particularly for local and regional subjects. If you reside in a metropolitan area, then the wealth of library resources should be great. The only restrictions by public libraries will be hours of operation and demand on resources. Some special collections will be accessible only by advance arrangement, but the reference materials you need most likely will be available for your use during normal library hours.

Besides your office library, public libraries, and academic facilities, there are three other types of special libraries to remember. First, you can often use area historical society libraries. Many communities have these, and in state capitals there may be several that are usually open to the public. In addition, there are museum libraries. Presidential libraries and science museums are examples of this type of facility. Moreover, there are company and corporate libraries. Large corporations, such as those on the Fortune 500 list, maintain these for employee use but the facilities may be available to you if you request permission. If you are not permitted on site, you may possibly receive special permission from the public relations or public affairs department of the company. Or, if you are resourceful, you may be able to persuade a company employee to find the information for you. All three of these types of libraries may require notice in advance for access.

Most libraries have open stacks. That is, the shelves are open for you to browse and to find your own materials. However, some libraries do not open their stacks because of theft or other loss of materials. Closed stacks are a hardship because you must list the books you want and request a clerk to get them for you. Needless to say, this takes time and you have to know exactly what you want. You might want to talk to the director of the library for permission to use the stacks for browsing if your research project is complex.

Your ability to take advantage of whatever library you use will depend on you and one other person: an experienced reference librarian who specializes in the subject you are writing about. Subject specialists are on staff to assist you, so call on them as you need assistance.

Another service to remember is the networking that libraries use to multiply their resources. Many libraries link together in national, state, or regional networks to lend and exchange materials needed by borrowers. These interlibrary loan services may be fee-based and may take time to use, but they can save you a lot of travel expense to find materials not locally available if you can wait for it.

Finally, check the facility's hours of operation. Hours can change and a telephone call may save you valuable time.

USING CITY AND "CRISS-CROSS" DIRECTORIES

There are three major publishers of city or "criss-cross" directories: R. L. Polk and Company is headquartered in Detroit; Cole Publications, Inc., is headquartered in Lincoln, NE; and Bresser's is also based in Detroit. Polk is by far the largest, preparing directories for over 1,400 cities in the United States and Canada. The books are published by city or metropolitan area in most cases.

Polk Directories

These books have three types of listings:

1. White pages—Alphabetical listings of people and businesses in a city, including information about occupation and employer of the head of the household.
2. Green pages—A list of every address in the city in alphabetic or numerical order, including the name and telephone number of the current resident or business.

(continued)

USING CITY AND "CRISS-CROSS" DIRECTORIES *(continued)*

3. Blue pages—A numerical list of all telephone numbers indicating whose number it is. Nonpublished numbers exclude the person's name. This is also known as a reverse telephone directory.

Cole Directories

There are six parts to Cole Directories and the following four sections are of most interest to reporters:

1. Street address directory—The white pages, this is the street address directory, comparable to Polk's green pages.
2. City, county, state, and federal directory—These pink pages list elected officials by name, address, and telephone number for all government bodies and units in the metropolitan area.
3. Office building directory—More pink pages that list the major buildings in a metropolitan area and all tenants in each office or suite by name and telephone number.
4. Numerical telephone directory—These yellow pages are the reverse telephone directory, comparable to Polk's blue pages.

Bresser's Directories

There are five main sections in Bresser's directories of value to reporters:

1. Trading zone map section—This contains buying power information and how to use it effectively (yellow pages).
2. Zip code section—This is a marketing section (green pages).
3. Street address directory—Listings of streets in alphabetical order (green pages).
4. Office building directory—Lists the main office buildings and inhabitants in the area covered by the book (yellow pages).
5. Numerical telephone directory—A reverse telephone directory (green pages).

THE MOST USEFUL REFERENCE BOOKS

For a news story, you might need to know, for example, the combined enrollment and the cost of tuition of Harvard and Radcliffe Colleges. Go to a reference book such as an almanac. (The answers to these questions are 6,587 students and $14,560 a year, according to *The 1991 Information Please Almanac;* Johnson, 1991.) Even a common reference book such as this, available at just about any neighborhood drug store, can be a boon when you are researching the facts for a story. These general reference volumes are inexpensive enough to permit you to keep one at your desk. It is not difficult to build a small reference library of your own. To get started, you might want to use the *Orlando Sentinel*'s guide to reference materials included in Appendix C as a check list.

If you take news story background research a step further, you will find your local library's reference section to be one of the most useful sections of any library for a reporter. You'll find many types of books and periodicals.

For starters, *directories* are specialized books that list wide-ranging content such as membership lists and statistics. City directories are one useful example. These can be extremely helpful for finding names, addresses, telephone numbers, and building occupants. Reporters find them particularly helpful in locating sources. There are directories for several thousand cities in the United States that are published annually by private companies such as R. L. Polk or Bressler's.

These books contain traditional white pages (alphabetic listings by last name), as well as color pages that list (a) addresses in alphanumeric order; (b) telephone listings in numeric order (often called reverse telephone listings); and (c) directories of major buildings and occupants. Some even include (d) directories of government officials, addresses, and telephone numbers.

There also are *almanacs*. As mentioned previously, many of these basic references are inexpensive and easy to find. These books, often sponsored by news organizations such as the Associated Press or *Time,* are updated and published annually, and list facts and figures on a wide range of subjects. But there are other types of almanacs, too, some of which focus on only one subject, such as politics or business, or a state. The *Texas Almanac,* published by the parent company of the *Dallas Morning News,* is an example of a statewide general-purpose reference book.

Atlases and gazetteers include a great deal more than just geography. For starters, though, you can learn a great deal by simply studying a map of an area. When geography is the subject you need to study, atlases and gazetteers will likely contain the answers. You can use them to check locations, distances, spellings, population, trade, industry, available natural resources, economic development, politics, and distribution systems. An inexpensive starting point might be to collect local, state, and regional maps from a local automobile association if you or someone you know holds a membership.

Encyclopedias should not be overlooked either, because these books can often give you an authoritative introduction to a subject. Encyclopedias are often thought of as general sets of books that are updated every 1 to 3 years and have a universal application. However, these books are often much more useful as specialized volumes devoted to limited information on subjects such as world history, physical science, and music. Yearbooks are usually supplements that update existing editions of books or series of books such as encyclopedias.

Abstracts are valuable because they take sets of statistics and other data and condense the data into useful form for the user. Abstracts can also list bibliographic information and offer annotations or summaries of books, articles, theses, or dissertations.

Chronologies are reference books that list events in chronological order over a period of time. Many of these are limited to certain periods of time, such as a decade or century, or are limited to the duration of a historic period such as World War II or the depression.

Dictionaries and thesauri are critical to research and writing. Many general dictionaries and thesauri are available, some at very inexpensive paperback edition price ranges. Yet there are many dictionaries within particular disciplines, such as law or the physical sciences, that can help when you are working with technical subjects that require explanation in your story for your audience.

Biographical dictionaries are extremely helpful in researching well-known persons. There are different types of biographical dictionaries, many focused on specific disciplines, so you need to know where to go to find information about the person you are researching. Good examples are *Current Biography* or *Who's Who*. There are biographical master indexes to these reference books that are kept in most major libraries.

Books of quotations are another valuable category of reference books to reporters. When you need an authoritative quotation or a familiar quotation to make your point, these books are the source to use. The leading example is *Bartlett's Familiar Quotations*.

USING GOVERNMENT PUBLICATIONS AND DOCUMENTS

Thousands of federal, state, and local government publications and documents can help you research a story. As has been often said about Washington, DC, most of the time the information you need is there but you just have to know how to find it. This applies to government publications and documents. Virtually all departments of government produce publications and documents. Although most are public records, a few are classified and unavailable to the public.

REPORTER'S AND WRITER'S REFERENCE BOOKSHELF

Here is a list of commonly used reference books in newsrooms. These are the traditional favorites of reporters, copy editors, editors, and free-lance writers. This is not a comprehensive list, but it can be used in building a personal library.

ENCYCLOPEDIAS

An encyclopedia of world history. (1973). (5th ed., W. L. Langer, Ed.). Boston: Houghton Mifflin.

Encyclopedia Americana. (1989). (international ed., 30 Vols. D. Holland, Ed.). Danbury, CT: Americana Corp.

(continued)

REPORTER'S AND WRITER'S REFERENCE BOOKSHELF *(continued)*

Encyclopedia Britannica. (1969, updated annually). Chicago: Encyclopedia Britannica Inc.

The new Columbia encyclopedia. (1975). (4th ed.). New York: Columbia University Press.

World Book encyclopedia. (annual). (22 Vols.). Chicago: World Book, Field Enterprises Educational Corp.

Encyclopedia of associations. (annual). (4 Vols. plus supplements, M. Fisk, Ed.). Detroit: Gale Research Co.

ATLASES/MAPS

The National Geographic atlas of the world. (1981). (5th ed.). Washington, DC: National Geographic Society.

Shepherd's historical atlas. (1980). (9th ed., W. R. Shepherd, Ed.). Totowa, NJ: Barnes and Noble.

Commercial atlas and marketing guide. (annual; 1876 to date). (D. Zapenski, Ed.). Chicago: Rand McNally.

DICTIONARIES/THESAURI

Roget's international thesaurus. (1977). (4th ed.). New York: T. Y. Crowell.

The American heritage dictionary of the English language. (1983). (2nd ed., W. Morris, Ed.). Boston: Houghton Mifflin.

Webster's ninth new collegiate dictionary. (1985). (8th ed.). Springfield, MA: Merriam-Webster.

Webster's new world dictionary of the American language. (1987). (rev. ed., D. B. Guralnik, Ed.). New York: Simon & Schuster.

Webster's third new international dictionary. (1981). (unabridged ed.). Springfield, MA: Merriam-Webster.

DIRECTORIES

"Yellow Books" series, published semiannually, including the *Corporate Yellow Book, State 1000 Yellow Book, Federal Yellow Book,* and *Congressional Yellow Book.* New York: Monitor Publishing Co.

Congressional Directory, new edition each Congress, U.S. Government Printing Office, Washington, DC (Hint: some home district congresspersons and senators will send a free copy on written request, but supplies are limited).

Congressional staff directory. (annual). C. B. Brownson & A. L. Brownson, Eds.). Mount Vernon, VA: Congressional Staff Directory, Ltd.

Lesko, M. (1990). *Lesko's info-power.* Chevy Chase, MD: Information U.S.A., Inc.

Washington information directory. (annual). Washington, DC: Congressional Quarterly Publications, Congressional Quarterly, Inc.

City and county directories, R. L. Polk, Bresser, and Cole are among companies that annually produce these directories.

(continued)

REPORTER'S AND WRITER'S REFERENCE BOOKSHELF *(continued)*

ABSTRACTS

Statistical abstract of the United States. (annual). Washington, DC: U.S. Government Printing Office.
    Various state statistical abstracts are produced by public and private publishers.

READY REFERENCE/GENERAL TRIVIA

Guinness book of world records. (1990). (D. McFarlan, Ed.). New York: Bantam Books.
    The information please almanac, atlas, and yearbook. (annual). (O. Johnson, Ed.). Boston: Houghton Mifflin.
    The official Associated Press almanac. (annual). New York: Associated Press, Almanac Publishing Co.
    World almanac and book of facts. (annual). New York: Grossett & Dunlap.
    Various state almanacs are printed by public and private publishers.

STYLEBOOKS

French, C. W., & Goldstein, N. (1987). *The Associated Press stylebook and libel manual.* Boston: Addison-Wesley.
    Hood, J. R. & Kalbfeld, B. (1982). *AP broadcast news handbook.* New York: Associated Press.
    Papper, R. A. (1987). *Broadcast news writing stylebook.* Columbus, OH: Publishing Horizons.
    United Press International Broadcast Services. (1979). *United Press International broadcast stylebook.* New York: United Press International.

To help find the information you want, there are indexes — especially at the federal level. General indexes, such as the *Monthly Catalog of U.S. Government Publications,* can help. This contains a subject index of new materials that are issued.

Congressional sources provide us with hearings documents on specialized topics such as medical care, defense, banking, agriculture, and even the routine daily activities of Congress. These documents are available at local libraries that are designated U.S. Government document depository libraries or from the bookstores of the U.S. Government Printing Office.

Executive branch sources cover subjects as broad as the various departments that help the White House carry out the laws of the land. *The Federal Register* and *Code of Federal Regulations* are good sources for orders, proclamations, and regulations that are announced by the White House. A reporter interested in the words of the president may check the *Weekly Compilation of Presidential Documents.*

For the judicial branch and other legal subjects, two good sources are *Black's Law Dictionary* and the *Martindale–Hubbell Law Directory*. The *Index to Legal Periodicals* is also a good starting point. For court decisions, the West Publishing Co. of St. Paul privately publishes reports from many federal courts, all state appellate courts, and some state courts in its National Reporter System. The West reports are often found in county and city libraries, law school libraries, and law offices.

You can also find reports by the Federal Bureau of Investigation (such as the *Uniform Crime Report* issued annually), by the Food and Drug Administration, and by the Federal Communications Commission in libraries or obtain them from the agencies directly.

At the state level, there are many good publications. Look for handbooks, directories, guidebooks, and other volumes produced by official and private sources. One good example of an official reference book is the *Blue Book* produced by the state of Wisconsin each year.

Other general reference books include works produced state by state. These books can be excellent regional sources and are published by both public and private sources. These books are published annually or biannually. There are also general indexes of state publications. One such book is the *Monthly Checklist of State Publications,* which is produced by the Library of Congress. Some states, such as Virginia and Kentucky, produce their own similar lists. For most state documents, start with the secretary of state's office. This person is the state's official record keeper.

Local government publications vary in quantity and quality. Most metropolitan areas will produce a substantial number of publications and local reference materials. But small cities and towns will not always have the resources to do so. In this case, go to the county or parish as your main regional source. Some private sources can be helpful. For example, the International City Management Association produces the *Municipal Year Book.*

A good example of use of government records for a news story is the award-winning investigation by Dan Wadlington for KWTO-AM/FM News in Springfield, a city of 150,000 in southwest Missouri. Wadlington, news director for the small market station, investigated a Greene County sheriff who failed to report an alleged molestation of a boy by a sheriff's deputy. Wadlington conducted "extensive research" for over a month to get information for the three-part series of stories that ran a total of 19 minutes and 40 seconds. Wadlington interviewed key individuals on tape after completing his research.

Wadlington (1991), looking back over his project, concluded, "I got lucky in my research on these stories." First, he got a tip. Second, he found a "smoking gun" memorandum in a juvenile file that he got court permission to review under limited conditions.

"I was walking up the courthouse steps when I ran into Perry Epperly, chief juvenile officer for the county. He said to me, 'Do you know what the sheriff did?' I said, 'No.' He told me and that was my tip," Wadlington explained. "I then went down the hall in the courthouse to talk to a friend in the Missouri State Highway Patrol office who was a distant relative of the victim it turns out." Wadlington's source directed him to documents that he got permission to review. In the process, Wadlington checked sheriff's office incident reports, memoranda, Greene County Circuit Court case files, Missouri State Highway Patrol reports, County Prosecutor's Office files, and juvenile authorities' records in preparing his series. In the juvenile file, he found key documents. "It was a bit of luck," Wadlington admitted. His first report, which ran an exceptional 8 minutes in the three-part series, is reproduced at the end of this chapter. Such background research is hard work. "I found it hard to find time with everything else I do. At that time, there was only one other news person on our staff," Wadlington explained. "There's literally reams of material out there if you have the time to look at it."

FEDERAL STATISTICS AND CENSUS DATA

Want to know how U.S. population trends are changing or, for example, how many teenage females reside in your state or county? Use government census data. There are lengthy census reports and shorter, more accessible abstracts of 1990 census data available. The most popular book form of census data is the *Statistical Abstract of the United States,* which is published annually. However, there are several other statistical abstract publications produced either annually or at other regular intervals such as the *City and County Data Book,* issued every 5 years.

As you may have guessed, a growing area of reference materials for reporters is federal statistics, primarily statistics generated by the Bureau of the Census. Census data tell us much about our communities, of course, and many federal and other levels of funding are based on formulas computed with census information.

Census statistics originate from the Bureau of the Census, a part of the U.S. Department of Commerce in Washington, DC. But they are available for public consumption and many private, commercial interests purchase decennial census statistics and reprocess the data for resale or simply reproduce the data "as is" for sale. In fact, as more news organizations become capable of doing their own analyses, they have increasingly purchased the information directly from the Census Bureau for research and story development.

Most university and college libraries have rather complete census data reports as produced by the U.S. Government Printing Office. These are also found in major public libraries that are government repository libraries. Some census data are "on-line" through a computer-based service known as CENDATA. To use CENDATA, users must access the system through CompuServe, Dialog, or other database services. The Census Bureau also maintains a dozen regional centers for convenience. But be careful, sometimes getting telephone help is often difficult.

Census data are not limited to national statistics. The bureau provides

---

BASIC REFERENCE SOURCES FOR REPORTERS AND WRITERS

1. *Access: The Supplementary Index to Periodicals.* (annual). Evanston, IL: John Gordon Burke Publishers. Covers 1979–present.
2. *Editorial research reports.* (2 Vols.). Washington DC: Congressional Quarterly. Weekly.
3. *Editorials on file.* New York: Facts on File. Semi-monthly and annual cumulation.
4. *Europa year book.* (annual). (2 Vols.). London: Europa Publications.
5. *Facts on file.* New York: Facts on File. Annual cumulation and regular updates.
6. *Guide to reference books.* (1986). (E. P. Sheehy, 10th ed.). Chicago: American Library Association.
7. *McGraw-Hill concise encyclopedia of science & technology.* (1989). (2nd ed., 15 Vols.). New York: McGraw-Hill.
8. *New York Times cumulative subject & personal name index.* (annual). (E. A. Reno, Series Ed.). Glen Rock, NJ: Microfilming Corp. of America. Covers 1913–present.
9. *NewsBank index.* New Canaan, CT: NewsBank, Inc. Updated monthly. Covers 1982–present.
10. *NewsNet,* Bryn Mawr, PA: NewsNet, Inc. Covers content of several hundred specialized organizational newsletters.
11. *Wall Street Journal index.* (annual). New York: Dow Jones. Covers 1958–present.
12. *World of learning.* (annual). (2 Vols.). London: Europa Publications, Ltd. Issued since 1947.
13. *The magazine index: Hot topics.* Los Altos, CA: Information Access Co. Updated monthly.

---

reports tailored to very localized levels. In addition to national and regional data, reporters can use state, metropolitan area, county, "urbanized" areas, towns and villages, and even blocks within the communities as breakdowns of the census statistics.

What exactly can you expect to find by rolling up your sleeves and diving into some census statistics at the local library? To start, you get population numbers. You can learn about group demographic characteristics of your community such as gender, income, education level, employment, marital status, health disabilities, immigration, age, racial and ethnic origins, languages spoken, transportation methods, where people live, how they live (housing), and children.

From all this information come potentially fascinating stories about how our nation lives. The *Orange County Register*'s Stephanie Craft (1990) said there are significant stories to be written from the 1990 census. For instance:

- Aging of the American population
- Surge in minority group population growth
- The changing workforce

- The new, redesigned American family
- Changing apportionment of political districts
- Wealthy-poor gap growth
- Movement to the suburbs
- Homeless and working poor

The Census Bureau is only 1 of about 70 federal agencies that perform statistical work. Research is conducted to gather statistics on banking, manufacturing, education, health, labor, wholesale and retail businesses, transportation, and construction—just to name a few examples—on a regular basis. The best sources for these are the departments and agencies responsible for collecting the information (Craft, 1990).

PRIVATE SOURCES OF INFORMATION

It is important to remember that with private sources you have no guaranteed right to the information. You have to obtain permission to access the information. Most commonly, this can be done by purchasing the information in published or other form, or by obtaining oral or written permission to access and use it. But this is an important step and should not be overlooked, especially if access and use of the information do not require payment of a fee.

Many enterprises are in the business of gathering and publishing information for profit. Most of the reference books you will use are privately produced, of course, and many are quite expensive. But beyond commercially published books, look to other private sources for useful published and unpublished information. This information may come in many forms. In addition to books, there are periodicals such as newsletters and magazines. Private information is also released on videotape, in unpublished but photocopied reports, memoranda, letters, and so forth.

Businesses and corporations provide much information. Groups of businesses, such as professional and trade organizations, also provide information. In fact, these groups are often the best business sources because the information they distribute is in aggregate form. And do not overlook the annual meetings of these groups as sources of important information being released for the first time to the public and the news media.

Special interest groups also can be good sources of information. Special interest groups can be associations, federations, boards, clubs, societies, committees, foundations, institutes, unions, task forces, and so forth. Keep in mind that although these groups often have a purpose or motive for providing the information, it may still be useful to you in preparing a story. But do not assume that a group will always provide neutral or balanced points of view. In the area of legislation and public policy, a few of these

Private citizens such as the Rev. Jesse Jackson live very public lives, but often private individuals present a challenge when conducting background research because information is not always easy to find (photo by Pete Cross, *Miami Herald* staff).

groups would include political parties, political action committees, lobbyists, foundations, and so forth.

Religious organizations can also be good sources of information. Churches and church groups keep information that can often be useful in stories about the spiritual and family life-styles in your community. Similarly, private colleges and universities, as well as other levels of schools, may be enormous sources of information for a reporter.

CURRENT LEGAL AND ETHICAL ISSUES

There are some important legal and ethical considerations that involve research. In conducting research for a news story, you may not have access to restricted information. The reasons are many, but these restrictions arise in both the public and private sectors. Public limitations come in the form of closed records for security reasons, personnel reasons, and other reasons, and are imposed in local ordinances as well as state and federal laws. Private limitations are imposed by those holding the information you wish

Religious leaders such as Yahweh Ben Yahweh are among the most sought after newsmakers in the private sector, especially when those individuals or their groups are investigated for illegal activities. However, private religious organizations are often very resistant to divulging information (photo by Albert Coya, *Miami Herald* staff).

to use. You may risk legal penalties if you use information obtained without permission, although at times there is public debate about what information should and should not be classified by the government, for example. Private information may not only require purchase or payment of a "rights" fee, but it may also require written permission. You must check with each vendor of this information.

Ethically, you must consider whether or not information you have obtained is better used or not used, even when you have legally obtained the information. When NBC's "Nightly News with Tom Brokaw" reported the identity of the woman victim in the alleged rape at the Kennedy family winter estate in Palm Beach, Florida, other competing news organizations at first refused to use the name because the news business traditionally does not name sexual assault crime victims. The network's story also showed photographs of the woman and her stepfather. NBC argued that the name was important to the story and that it was well known in Palm Beach County. Perhaps NBC also considered that a supermarket tabloid, *The Globe,* had identified the woman a day earlier (Donnelly & Coto, 1991). It is interesting to note that after NBC news revealed the individual's identity, several other news organizations, including the *New York Times,* followed suit by revealing the woman's name the next day.

The *Miami Herald*'s investigation of the personal activities of 1988 presidential aspirant Gary Hart is another example. Whereas the newspaper's reporters were not violating any law in observing and interviewing sources for the story, many persons, from both the public and news media as well, felt the story constituted an invasion of privacy of the senator, his family, and friends.

Information such as this is routinely available in police investigations. But whether or not to use the information is an ethical matter. Most news organizations attempt to be sensitive to the privacy of crime victims. As a news reporter, you must first be careful of the accuracy of the information you find in your research. Then you must decide, perhaps with the guidance of your editors and news directors, whether it is necessary to use the questionable information in your story.

On another level, computerization of government records has created still another research problem. Many persons who once could inspect public records freely, using the actual documents, can no longer do so as easily because the records are stored in electronic databases that often require clerical assistance to access. More and more libraries computerize their holdings to save precious storage space.

Remember that whatever barriers you encounter and regardless of how you hurdle them, you must remain accurate in your research for any story you write. Authors Patricia Kubis and Robert Howland (1985) advised:

> If you are inaccurate in your research, and your article or book is published, you will have every specialist writing to your publisher and pointing out all your discrepancies. If you write stories, inaccuracy will not have a favorable effect on your career—because truthfulness is a major part of being a journalist. . . . Being inaccurate destroys your credibility as an authority figure. (p. 145)

HOW PROFESSIONALS WRITE IT

NEWSPAPER: *Lexington Herald-Leader*
DATE: November 12, 1989, p. 1
AUTHORS: Kit Wagar, John Winn Miller, and Lee Mueller, staff writers
HEADLINE: This tax man gives away the store—and the schools

* * *

If you enjoy watching magicians make handkerchiefs, rabbits or even people disappear, come to Pike County and watch tax assessor Reo Johns put on a different kind of magic show.

With the thump of a rubber stamp or the stroke of a pen, Johns and his assistants have made tens of millions of dollars in property assessments vanish.

Assessments are haphazard and unfair across Kentucky, but Reo Johns' operation in many ways stands out.

Here are some of the ways he works his magic:

• Larry Belcher, Johns' chief appraiser, was given $200,000 worth of rental property by his sister. The next year, Johns' office issued an order that removed the property from the tax rolls. No taxes were paid on it. When the property reappeared on the tax rolls a year later, it was assessed at $22,100.

• Thomas "Webby" Huffman, a Pikeville city commissioner, received repeated tax breaks on the Landmark Inn, the city's largest hotel. With the magic of the rubber stamp and a lowered assessment, Johns made $51,000 in back taxes on the hotel disappear from Huffman's bill.

• Krishna Malempati, a factory owner, has a massive two-story brick-and-stucco house in the middle of the city's nicest subdivision. It has never appeared on the tax rolls.

Malempati, who built the house and estimated it would cost $350,000 to duplicate, said it was not his fault that Johns never assessed it.

"If you're speeding, going 80 miles per hour somewhere, and you don't get caught, do you go in to the police and say, 'I was speeding. I want to pay a fine?' " Malempati asked. "Of course not."

Schools pay the price

While Johns quietly has reduced assessments for friends, business partners and even casual acquaintances, schools and local government have lost millions of tax dollars.

The effects are easy to see. In recent years, Pike County schools have operated in the red. The district had to get rid of its full-time kindergarten and eliminate teaching positions.

"I think anybody who asks will get a tax cut," said Phil Stalnaker, the attorney for Pikeville schools. "But people with connections know to ask for it. A widow out in the country struggling to pay her taxes doesn't know she can come in and get her taxes lowered."

It starts close to home

Some of the people with the best connections don't need to ask for a break. They work in Johns' office.

Assessment Clerk Helen Newsome bought her house near Virgie for $40,000 in 1980. It is assessed at $2,700—the cost of a modest used car. As a result, she paid $5.72 in school taxes on the house in 1988.

Although her office is responsible for assessing property in the county, Newsome said it was up to the state Revenue Cabinet to determine whether her assessment was fair.

"I'm not trying to defraud the state about it," she said. "But I feel like that is their duty. If they feel like I've got a $50,000 home sitting out there, why don't they go out there and find it and put it on" the tax rolls?

Toni Canterbury, a field assessor, owns a home that a jury in a lawsuit said was worth $46,000 in 1979. Since then, the Canterburys have enlarged their yard by purchasing an empty lot next door, but the total assessment is $18,300.

Velva Ray, Johns' chief deputy, bought a house in Mullins for $65,000 in 1987. It was put on the tax rolls at $30,000.

Johns explained the assessment by saying the $65,000 price included a houseful of furniture and other property not subject to property taxes. But a property transfer affidavit signed by Ray says the price included no such personal property.

Johns even underassessed his car, an Excalibur roadster. He valued it at $5,000 for 1988. The state overrode the assessment in 1989 and set it at $31,500.

Criticism, but no crackdown

Like all other property valuation administrators, Johns serves two masters, the voters of his county and the state Revenue Cabinet and theoretically is subject to its oversight.

After studying Johns' operation in 1989, the state concluded he broke the law.

"We have not seen more significant problems in the operation of the PVA office in any other county," said Property Tax Commissioner James Coffman.

Yet the state has done little, if anything, to discipline Johns, even though it has the power to withhold his paycheck or seek his removal from office.

Coffman said the state had made several suggestions after completing the study and was giving Johns time to carry them out rather than cracking down on him.

But Johns dismissed the state's criticisms.

"That's their opinion, and they don't have the final say in this county. I do."

Johns insisted that his assessments were accurate and that he did not give tax breaks to his friends. But he said his job does allow him to help people.

"Anybody that gets down and out, if I can give them a break and help them over the hump, then I do that," Johns said. "The business people know that in this town."

The classic self-made man

John, a rugged, beefy man with an easygoing manner, has become popular in his eight years as property valuation administrator of Kentucky's seventh most populous county. He had no opposition when he ran for re-election this month.

His father, a coal-camp doctor, died when Johns was 4 months old. Johns was raised mostly by his grandparents.

He put himself through Pikeville College and eventually became a principal and assistant superintendent for Pike County schools and a regional director for the state Department of Education.

Earlier in 1989, he was a serious candidate for Pike County school superintendent. He has become a wealthy man with interests in coal and oil.

County Attorney Gary Johnson, a friend, business partner and legal adviser, said Johns couldn't bear to be unpopular.

"The only thing wrong with Reo is poor judgment with a big heart," Johnson said. "If he's done anything he shouldn't have done, it's not because he's dishonest.

"It's not his nature to have somebody mad at him. Reo's uncomfortable if he thinks somebody out there dislikes him."

A little help for his friends

One person helped by Johns' big heart is T. T. Colley—coal operator, land developer and former county campaign chairman for Gov. Wallace Wilkinson.

He also is a political ally of Johns and has received several breaks from his office.

One was on a Pikeville house that Colley owned, which was assessed at $40,300. Its true value became apparent when it sold in 1988 for $150,000.

A house Colley and his mother own in Bowles Addition is assessed at $54,300—about the same as the going price of a lot in the subdivision, home to some of Pikeville's richest residents.

His company, Colley Block, is one of the largest concrete block manufacturers in Eastern Kentucky. Its three-building plant is assessed at $23,300.

Colley, who was Pike County PVA for 16 years before Johns, acknowledged that the assessment on the plant was too low.

He said he had never asked for favors and wouldn't comment on the other properties because he never paid attention to assessments.

How Johns makes the cuts

One of the most powerful weapons in Johns' tax-cutting arsenal has been a rubber stamp.

The stamp was imprinted with the signature of Pike County Judge-Executive Paul Patton, who is required to approve special tax—changing orders called exonerations.

Patton gave his signature stamp to Johns years ago and acknowledged that he didn't keep track of how Johns was using it.

Exonerations allow PVAs to step outside normal procedures and reduce or eliminate assessments to correct clerical errors. But the state found that Johns was using the stamp to hand out improper breaks left and right.

In June, after the *Herald-Leader* reported that Johns' office had removed property valued at $186 million from the tax rolls in the last two years, Patton revamped the way exonerations were handled and retrieved the stamp.

Johns can't explain

Johns said his exonerations were justified, but he couldn't explain many of them.

He said he did not realize that his own company, Wilgar Land, had received an exoneration cutting its 1986 assessment by $70,000 — more than half.

He also could not explain the tax cut given to Malempati. In addition to not being taxed on his house, Malempati gets a big tax break on his business, Kris Electrical Manufacturing Co. Inc.

Malempati's case illustrates how, through exonerations, property values just evaporate.

Malempati paid $350,000 for the plant in 1985. When property changes hands, it usually is assessed at the sale price.

But Malempati's attorney argued that Malempati should not pay more taxes than the previous owner.

So Johns cut the assessment to $240,000 for 1986.

The next year, Malempati complained again. Johns' office dropped the assessment to $160,000, where it remains.

In two years, $190,000 worth of property was gone.

"Am I happy with my property taxes?" Malempati asked. "Yes, because I'm paying what I think I should."

Stamping out back taxes

The rubber stamp has another use — it helps people out of trouble with back taxes.

One such person was Michael Epling, owner of Skyline Coal Co. of Huddy. Epling never paid the commercial tax bills he got from 1982 through 1987.

The bills mounted to $4,901. But Johns' staff went back and reduced assessments that had been put on the property beginning in 1982.

That reduced the tax debt to $858, which Epling paid last April. Epling did not return phone calls to discuss his taxes.

Under state law, it is improper to reassess property after the fact, but the practice is common in Pike County. Records of such reassessments fill a double drawer in the Pike County clerk's office.

One of the largest examples involves the Landmark Inn and its owner, Huffman, the city commissioner who routinely fails to pay his taxes.

Huffman bought the 103-room hotel in 1984 for $2.97 million and quickly began a five-year campaign to avoid paying taxes on it.

He filed a deed incorrectly listing the sale price as $2.5 million. Johns' office set the assessment at that amount.

Even with that break, Huffman didn't pay his taxes.

In 1986, he went to Johns' office and got his assessment cut even more— to $2 million.

But he didn't pay his taxes for that year, either. Or the next.

In 1989 he got Johns' office to go back and reduce the 1985–87 assessments to $1.5 million. The change effectively cut Huffman's back taxes.

But Huffman still didn't pay the bill.

Pikeville city schools sued Huffman in May for three years' worth of back taxes, interest and penalties. Huffman quickly gave $79,701 to the schools and county. But school and county officials say he still owes $51,122.

In an interview, Huffman said he had not paid the bills because business had dropped.

But an appraiser who saw the hotel's financial statements as part of another lawsuit testifies that the hotel's business has increased after Huffman bought it.

And while Johns was cutting the assessment on the hotel to $1.5 million, two appraisers Huffman had hired to testify in the same case placed its value at $2.3 million to $2.475 million.

Johns said he reduced the back taxes because Huffman was on the ropes financially.

"He hires a lot of people up there, and I swear to God to you that when I adjusted his assessment, I was not only thinking of Webby, I was thinking of the jobs," Johns said.

"It's the only decent place we've got to eat in this town."

Huffman said there was nothing wrong with getting his taxes lowered.

"Everyone in the community does it," he said.

Reprinted with permission of the *Lexington Herald-Leader*

• • •

SOURCE: KWTO-AM/FM Radio, Springfield, Missouri, *Scripps Howard Foundation National Journalism Awards,* p. 12

REPORTER: Dan Wadlington, news director

DATE: Wednesday, July 19, 1989

TITLE: KWTO investigated a Greene County Sheriff's failure to report a deputy's alleged molestation of a boy

* * *

Dan Wadlington: Did Greene County Sheriff John Pierpont fail to adequately investigate a child molestation charge against a former deputy sheriff? Was there an attempted cover-up? In mid-June 1988, Sheriff Pierpont reported the case to Prosecutor Tom Mountjoy. Juvenile and Highway Patrol investigators say that it is unusual, and they also point to some other irregularities in the handling of the case. Over the last month, KWTO News has completed extensive research into the Shaw case and found some questionable practices.

Thirty-eight year-old Donald Shaw is accused of molesting one young

Willard boy in late 1987, and exposing himself to a 10-year-old boy early June of 1988.

It was the latter incident that was reported by the boy to his mother, who is an employee in the records office of the Greene County Sheriff's Department. She reported the incident to Willard Police Chief Dwayne Davis. Davis sent the report to the sheriff's chief deputy on June 13th. It was on June 17th that Sheriff John Pierpont returned to town from a trip and was notified of the incident.

Pierpont called Davis, now a Springfield policeman, for more details. While Davis refuses to discuss the phone call with KWTO News, a confidential memo he prepared does provide some details about the phone conversation.

Unidentified voice: "Sheriff Pierpont expressed great displeasure with the person who went to someone outside the sheriff's office to report incident. The sheriff said that by going outside of his department, could cost the person their job. Sheriff Pierpont was also informed there may be a second case of child-molestation involving Shaw, but that there had been no contact with that second victim. Sheriff Pierpont told me to drop my investigation and added that the person who reported the incident had caused problems in the past by disclosing confidential information and telling lies about the department. The sheriff requested I not tell anyone about the incident. I was not invited to participate in an investigation of the allegation."

Wadlington: Sheriff Pierpont admits he ordered David to drop his investigation.

Pierpont: "It was a Greene County Sheriff's Department . . . when I talked to him . . . a personnel problem within this department involving two employees. And all I know is what the chief told me he had heard. This happened to be on that weekend when I returned. And I thought — John Pierpont is the sheriff of this county and my background as far as experience, ah, I thought I was capable of taking it under my hands and trying to do the investigation as best I could."

Wadlington: But Pierpont's investigation never materialized. The sheriff says the victim's mother rejected his advice to bring juvenile authorities into the case.

Pierpont: "I told her I thought we should go to juvenile authorities because there was a juvenile involved. Ah, she did not, at that time, want to proceed that way . . . the employee did not."

Wadlington: The woman later told her ex-husband and others, that she feared being fired by Pierpont for reporting the incident to outside agencies. Pierpont's own notes on the case say, and we quote: "She was very much out of line to get other people involved in any personnel matter regarding the Greene County Sheriff's office." But the sheriff denies threatening to fire the woman. The sheriff says the woman did not want to broaden the investigation due to a close personal relationship with Shaw. And according to the sheriff's notes on the case . . . he pursued as a personnel inquiry rather than a criminal investigation.

Pierpont: "On personnel, to start with, in both, really. We've looked into both phases of it because it involved personnel in this department."

Wadlington: On June 27th, Sheriff Pierpont summoned Shaw, the victim's mother who worked in his department, and two top commanders. The meeting lasted an hour. According to the sheriff's summary of that meeting, Shaw apologized for the incident. The female co-worker approved dropping the incident since there were no life threatening matters and her son had not been touched. Shaw allegedly masturbated in front of the ten year old.

The sheriff's conclusion, and we quote: "All the parties left my office with the understanding the matter would be dropped at this time. And no further action was needed by me as sheriff." During that same personnel hearing, Shaw admitted there had been an "accidental circumstance" with the boy. Despite that admission to the sheriff, Pierpont never disciplined Shaw and never checked with the victim about that story.

Pierpont: "The reason I didn't talk to the boy . . . he was a juvenile. I'm a little strict on that . . . I think there should be juvenile people involved when there's anything taken to juvenile. It is not required . . . but here we had a personnel matter . . . two people in my department involved, and I thought that was a proper procedure."

Wadlington: Pierpont never reported that incident to juvenile authorities. In fact a search of files in Greene County Circuit Court on this case finds no criminal or incidental reports about the incident involving Shaw and the boy from the Sheriff. Perry Epperly is the chief juvenile officer for Greene County.

Epperly: "I have never received any reports from the Greene County Sheriff's office pertaining to the investigation of the report involving Don Shaw.

Wadlington: Even Greene County Prosecutor Tom Mountjoy, who's prosecuting Shaw, finds no Greene County Sheriff's reports in the case files.

Mountjoy: "We don't have any Greene County Sheriff's reports *per se,* the reason for that being that it was investigated by the Missouri State Highway Patrol. And, they conducted the investigation. As far as I know, the sheriff's department did not generate any reports concerning it."

Wadlington: But the Highway Patrol entered the case a month after it came to the attention of Sheriff Pierpont and almost three weeks after his personnel inquiry had been resolved. Sheriff Pierpont says he continued to work on the Shaw case after June 27th, in what he terms a "personal" investigation. . . .

Pierpont: "As my investigation went on, then I thought that there was more to it and at that time, that's when I contacted the prosecutor to request an outside agency."

Wadlington: But there are no reports on his follow-up inquiry, and still the victim of the incident was never contacted. And Sheriff Pierpont never reported the cases to juvenile authorities or to the County Prosecutor's office. Veteran investigators in the Missouri Highway Patrol and juvenile investigators familiar with the Shaw case say it appears that the criminal misdemeanor allegations against the deputy sheriff, were allowed to die as a personnel item by the Greene County Sheriff John Pierpont.

Could it be that Sheriff Pierpont believed he could contain the incident ... keep it a secret and spare his department defaming publicity in an election year? Sheriff Pierpont admits the case against Shaw was shocking and embarrassed both he and his department. But he staunchly insists the case was handled properly.

Pierpont: "I pride myself on being a professional. And I think the two chiefs and I both felt that we did the right thing and handled it the proper way."

Wadlington: It is clear the sheriff ordered the six people who knew about the incident in his department to keep quiet about it by June 27th. It is also clear that the sheriff undertook no effort to report the case to an outside agency for a follow-up investigation after June 27th. There are no notes, files, or records on any criminal investigation in the Shaw case by Sheriff Pierpont. And his detectives were not allowed to work on the case, either.

Tomorrow, we'll explain how the case resurfaced after it was apparently buried, and how the second investigation led to a broadened probe against former deputy sheriff Don Shaw who was still working for John Pierpont at the end of June, 1988.

• • •

5 | Computer Databases And Document Searching

When Iraq invaded Kuwait and war broke out months later between Iraq and the allied forces in the Persian Gulf, news organizations scrambled for information to assist in educating readers and audiences about the conflict and that distant region of the world. There were many questions about many subjects to answer: geography, military-defense, health and medicine, psychology, history, economics, politics, and much more. News organizations sought to inform audiences about the action on the "war front" and on the "home front." There was much to research and much to prepare.

Background research took an increasingly important role in covering this year-long developing news story. And with the assistance of *computers,* greater amounts of information were found faster than ever before. "As the crisis in the Gulf heated up to all-out war, news organizations made preparations to cover the events," said Nora Paul (1991c, p. 1), library director at the Poynter Institute for Media Studies in St. Petersburg, Florida. Paul added, "News librarians did their part by ensuring they had the resources available to answer questions on a wide range of war-related topics" (p. 1).

Much of the work came from reference books and other similar resources discussed in the preceding chapter. However, for this long-term story, reporters found computer databases to be an extremely fast and important source of background information. For example, here are some of the computer databases Paul and her colleagues at the *Miami Herald* used in their research on the Persian Gulf crisis:

Linda Urhmann, a staff member of *The Press* in Atlantic City, New Jersey (left) and Vu/Text SAVE Support Manager Lora Davis discuss using the on-line computer database for news story research (photo courtesy of Vu/Text Information Services, Inc.)

• *Geopolitical background:* National reports compiled by the U.S. Department of Commerce, Bank of America, Political Risk Services, and the *Economist*. Kaleidoscope — Current World Data was also used. Each of these was found in a service called Nexis/Lexis.

• *Military history:* Everything from troop size to "Navajo code-talkers" in World War II was researched. Databases in a service called Dialog provided much information. Historical Abstracts and America: History and Life, two Dialog databases, provided military history background. Another database service known as Periscope provided key naval information.

• *Weapons:* On weapons systems of the United States, its allies, and Iraq, Nexis/Lexis and Dialog offered access to such databases as weapons patents in the Patents database. Using this database, Paul said the editors got lucky. "This is how we found the patent for the Fuel-Air Explosive. The public library faxed a copy of the patent, which included 2 pages of detailed diagrams," she explained (p. 2).

• *Experts:* Answering a wide range of specific questions, databases also helped reporters identify and locate expert sources. Among the databases used by the *Herald* were the Dissertation Abstracts database in Dialog, the Forensic Services Directory in Nexis/Lexis, and specialty "forums" (electronic special interest groups) in a service known as CompuServe.

• *Maps:* Even computer databases can provide geographic research assistance. "A good way to check on the availability of certain maps is the Government Printing Office database [in Dialog]," Paul explained (p. 2). Paul also used CompuServe's forums to check regional political maps and daily weather maps.

Computers have revolutionized the newsroom in a number of ways. Television stations, for instance, now use them for news video graphic design just as the print media have done in recent years (Casey, 1989; Schmerler, 1989). One of the latest developments has been computer information searching, also called electronic libraries (Aumente, 1989). With news breaking at any time, the instant long distance reach provided by "on-line" computer-based research is increasingly important for newsgatherers. "On-line" means your computer is linked to a second computer by a telephone line. The information you transfer is known as "datum" (singular) or "data" (plural). The link is completed by use of "modems" in each computer. "Modem" is an acronym for "modular-demodulator," the process that data go through to be transferred over a telephone line. Technically, the data in the computer of an "on-line" information provider are converted into analog wave form by the modem to be transferred to your computer's modem, where the analog wave version of the data is transferred back into data (Davis, 1991).

For some reporters and librarians, electronic information gathering is the single most important change in news story background research since clip files were first developed. Reporters need only compare the cost of collecting the same information firsthand and it becomes apparent that on-line research is much faster and less expensive. This argument alone convinced many publishers and general managers to invest in on-line hardware and software and to budget for on-line user time each year (Martin, 1986).

Information is usually not free. Valuable information is rarely inexpensive. Vendors, the companies providing the services, understand this. Certainly the on-line services most commonly used today can be very expensive, but still worthwhile for reporters. Reporting has entered the era of "on-line database research." Databases are collections of related information. One computer expert defines a database as "an integrated, centralized collection of an organization's data" (Davis, 1991, p. 180).

Editors and news directors see the light. This is the fastest-growing information-gathering field in journalism in the mid-1990s. Some editors and news directors call it the best research innovation since encyclopedias. "Computer searches are not just for big stories and big stations with big budgets," wrote Ohio Wesleyan professor Michael Murrie (1987, p. 36). "With the right controls, smaller radio and television stations can benefit."

As the use of database searching grows, so does the amount of information available (Murrie, 1987; Rambo, 1987). For example, at least 115 newspapers in 33 states and the District of Columbia have their contents on-line for public access (Wall, 1991). There are literally hundreds of databases available to check today—Dialog lists about 320 databases through its "boutique" system, for example. The number grows larger each month.

One of the reasons these newspaper and other periodical full-text databases have caught on is economics. Publishers and other managers have found these materials have a public market value. In addition to being tools for their reporters, these services, when sold publicly, are a big new source of revenue for news media companies (Donovan & Schalit, 1989; Miller, 1988a). Many major newspapers today will conduct literature or news story database searches for the public for a fee. And the major networks news divisions are now on-line. Some searches can be costly, depending on the effort involved (Donovan & Schalit, 1989).

However, reporters have been the newsroom reason this method of research has accelerated in recent years (Chichioco, 1989; Weinberg, 1991b). Yet most reporters have not allowed this new high-powered research tool to substitute for their regular background research for a story. Instead, it has become a supplement for research on a news story (Jennings, 1989). University of Missouri computer-assisted reporting expert Elliot Jaspin, a Pulitzer Prize-winning reporter, believes personal computers help good reporters to "become better because they have a new tool for analyzing and building pieces of information into a complete story" (Jennings, 1989, p. 14).

According to the Poynter Institute's Nora Paul (1991d), it is high time reporters became aware of the capabilities of their news library professionals. "For too long, librarians have been going to library conferences and talking only to other librarians. We've been writing articles for other librarians. . . . We know what we can do, but we need to do a better job telling our customers (you all) what we can do for you" (p. 3).

Paul (1991d) acknowledged that good librarians are an important part of an investigative team and this fact is increasingly recognized by wise reporters and editors. "We can lead you through the forest of available databases and efficiently mine the resources that will help give you the background, the statistics and the source documents you need for thorough reporting of your story," she explained (p. 3).

For those who have toiled long hours in libraries searching for literature on a subject, the computer is the best thing that has come along since movable type. Investigative reporter Bruce Maxwell, WTOL-TV, Toledo, admitted computer-hunting has saved him "hundreds or even thousands of hours of work" (Murrie, 1987, p. 36). Computer databases have been available for public use for more than a decade now. But to take full advantage of this tool, you have to be able use a computer. In the early days of computer database searching, the search had to be made from a library or other special facility. But with a modem, just about any computer and, therefore, any location, can be used to access a computer database.

The assignment editor for WRC-TV in Washington, DC, Jody Beck, said on-line searching of databases such as Nexis is important for reporters at her station, but she has to be careful to limit costs. "Not everyone in the building can use Nexis," she explained. "It's limited to the seven or eight people on the assignment desk" (Blankenhorn, 1991, p. 18). Some television stations such as WRC-TV can spend from $500 to $2,000 a month on searches (Murrie, 1988).

Cable News Network (CNN) also uses databases extensively. But all on-line searching is conducted by trained librarians to keep costs manageable. CNN library director Kathy Christensen says on-line research has increased each year since CNN began service in 1980. CNN's librarians usually field requests from reporters by telephone. "When a reporter calls with a question, we talk to them to find out what they really want to know" (Blankenhorn, 1991, p. 18).

These new databases have also extended the range and life of local newspapers and network broadcasts. Users can now read stories in newspapers from cities at the opposite end of the country. Network telecasts are now available in full-text for use a day or years later instead of the usual one-time viewing (Miller, 1988a, 1988b).

Commercial computer databases are "read-only" files that allow you to look at information, but not modify it in any way. Users can "download" information into their computers to be printed or stored for later use.

Usage fees are not inexpensive. Some run as little as $5 to $10 per hour during off hours, but others reach as high as $200 per hour for more exclusive systems at corporate, prime usage time rates. Most searches cost $10 to $25 an hour, however, especially if they are done in "off-hour periods." "Prime-time" premium database searches cost an average of $50–$150 per hour. But these rates may be well worth the investment in terms of time and travel expenses saved. *IRE Journal* editor Steve Weinberg (1991b) pointed out that computer and databases are "yielding projects that would have taken years instead of months" (p. 21).

Popular newsroom database providers are CompuServe, Nexis/Lexis, Dialog/Knowledge Index, Vu/Text, Dow Jones News/Retrieval, Data-Times, and Burrelle's Broadcast Database. At CNN, the favorite databases of librarians and reporters seem to be Nexis, Dialog, DataTimes, and Vu/Text. These are national commercial services and users pay for the time they are "logged on," although some services such as Prodigy and Compu-Serve offer a fixed unlimited-use monthly fee.

"The most popular newspaper databases are Vu/Text and Nexis," said reporter Brock Meeks (1991, p. 9). "Between these two databases, one can find the full text of hundreds of newspapers, large and small. It's the small, regional newspapers that often contain the real gems."

But don't despair about costs. Many colleges and universities have libraries with access to these and other databases. Some schools completely subsidize searches or at least sell access at a reduced rate to students. You should check with your professors or reference librarians. Most searches that your library can do for you are through a central computer system somewhere else. Your library simply links its computer to the larger "mainframe" computer and requests a particular database for you. The database you request will, of course, depend on the subject of your search. Some databases have become available on compact disk. Compact discs are not on-line, so there are no connect charges. Many libraries, to save money, have installed compact disc, read-only memory (CD-ROM) systems for student use.

Some current databases used for literature searches are electronic versions of indexes traditionally published in hardbound form. The convenience is obvious, if you are willing to pay for the time to do a broad search. Other databases are full-text or abstracts of articles in other publications or newscasts. These may be most helpful for reporters working on stories.

Many large libraries are beginning to computerize their card catalogs for easier remote and on-site searching. But the scope of the databases is often limited to the last few years, primarily because of the high cost of entering older acquisitions. Yet these databases are helpful in finding the most recent editions of books, or at least the most recent acquisitions by libraries. These searches work on the same principle as the database searches: You search for the author, the title, or a subject in key words. Terminals set up in the card catalog room or elsewhere make the work convenient. If you can get the access codes and telephone number, you can search the catalog of your local or university library with your personal computer in your office or home. Some libraries, to encourage use of such resources, provide this information access to appropriate individuals, such as students.

Through computers you can access the articles of most major daily newspapers published since the early 1980s. Some larger magazines and magazine groups are following suit. It is easy to find an article through a service such as Knight–Ridder Inc.'s Vu/Text, which allows access to more than 70 newspapers such as the *Philadelphia Inquirer, Charlotte Observer, Detroit Free-Press, Miami Herald,* and the *Washington Post.*

A computer database of periodicals called Info Trac is now available in many libraries but it is not on-line. It includes newspapers and magazines and is comprehensive in scope. The service includes recent reviews and uses the Library of Congress subject headings. The service is provided by Information Access Company and encompasses its Magazine Index.

Searches can turn routine stories into highly effective stories. J. Craig Crawford, Washington correspondent for the *Orlando Sentinel,* was assigned to write a story about the judicial record of President Bush's relatively unknown U.S. Supreme Court nominee David Souter. Part of his research was to find Souter's opinions as a judge in his native New Hampshire. Crawford went immediately to check Souter's 74 opinions – his interpretations of the state constitution – that were written while he served on the New Hampshire State Supreme Court. A search of the Lexis legal database service was critical to the immediate completion of his assignment. After locating the opinions, the database provided full-text of the opinions, which were printed out while on-line and then read and analyzed by Crawford as he prepared his story. Crawford's story is reprinted in full at the end of this chapter.

ELECTRONIC LIBRARIES
AND COMPUTER SEARCHES

Most major U.S. daily newspapers, NBC news, ABC news, CBS news, National Public Radio, and Financial News Network have gone electronic for public consumption. These sources of information have created electronic news libraries for reporters and for the public. In 1980, this was only a dream. But this dream came true at a majority of larger newspapers and broadcast news operations a decade later. "New predictions [in 1990] abound that soon reporters and editors will have unlimited access to commercial and public records databases via their PC-equipped workstations," wrote University of Minnesota journalism professors Jean Ward and Kathleen Hansen (1990, p. 34).

With these developments, the size of the newsroom library is shrinking. Although it is still a large room stocked with books, file cabinets, and computers, it need be only the size of your personal computer and desk. Moreover, electronic libraries never, or seldom, close. Reporters are no longer restricted to "normal business hours" for their research (Paul, 1991b).

The electronic library, using databases such as Nexis/Lexis, Vu/Text, DataTimes, Knowledge Index, BRS, or Burrelle's Broadcast Database, permits reporters to check clips quickly on breaking stories by asking librarians to do searches for them or by conducting their own searches for information. As noted earlier, Vu/Text and Nexis are the most popular databases used by journalists today. Studies show that Vu/Text is the dominant database (Ward & Hansen, 1990).

One study found that reporters use electronic libraries for the following reasons: to develop compilations and lists of information for crime story investigations, for business stories, for political stories, for local government stories, for trend stories, and for stories about public figures (Splichal, 1991).

The director of specialized reporting for WBNS-TV in Columbus, Ohio, Jim Mentel, said he used computers to prepare for backgrounding important interviews. "The prime minister of Slabovia comes in and you've got to go out and interview him" (Murrie, 1987, p. 36). Some television stations even use newspapers to help find file tape in video archives. By finding the date an event occurred in a newspaper database, it makes searching videotape archives by date easier and faster.

The proficiency of journalists in using these systems is reminiscent of some fears expressed when computers used for writing and editing first arrived in newsrooms in the mid-1970s. Some veteran journalists, as well as beginners, have fears about using computers for something besides writing. Some newspapers even prohibit it until after users are trained to control costs (Ward & Hansen, 1990). Some journalists ignore computer-based research, *St. Petersburg Times* news researcher Deborah Pam Wolfe (1989b) said, because the access procedures are too cumbersome, they lack the time to learn how to do it, computer searches actually increase research time, computer searches decrease the local perspective on a story, searches discourage original work, and searches increase errors in stories when reporters use uncorrected files (Jacobson & Ullman, 1989). Some reporters prefer someone else to use databases for them if they use them at all, Wolfe (1989a) concluded.

Whereas it is often best to learn to "search-it-yourself," most news organizations prefer that librarians or a newsroom computer "guru" do the searches to control costs. Conducting searches is not difficult, however, when you find yourself in a situation when you must work alone.

MARY ANN SKINNER, *NEWSDAY*
CHOOSING THE RIGHT RESEARCH DATABASE

Mary Ann Skinner, library director for *Newsday,* the Long Island, New York, daily, suggests asking these five useful questions for persons or news departments operating on a limited budget when selecting which of the major full-text news services to subscribe to:

1. When did the newspapers you want to see go on-line?
2. What actually is in the database offered by each vendor?
3. Which vendor will give you the best deal?
4. Which vendor provides the best customer support?
5. Does the service provide other databases? Source: Paul (1991).

The most difficult problems in computer searching are selecting the best database and deciding on the most appropriate "key words," which the computer uses to make its search. A "key word" or series of key words define what the computer searches for in the database. Many index or full-text databases are bibliographic—that is, they contain bibliographic information such author, title, and subject—consequently you have to have an idea who the authors are or what specific words might appear in titles. Full-text database searches will also search the text for key words. For example, a search of "animals" or "pets" would work if you wanted to find previously published or broadcast stories on domestic housecats, but the search would turn up far too much information. The search would be better executed by requesting "cats" or even a specific breed.

Research shows that local beat reporters tend to use electronic news libraries more than other reporters. They use database information for background before starting on a story, to find names for interviews or contacts, to verify information, and for general education about specialized subjects. The most obvious advantages to using electronic libraries are greater perspective, more detail, time savings, identification of new sources, and wider geographic coverage (Jacobson & Ullman, 1989; Wolfe, 1989a).

One thing is clear regarding electronic libraries: The nature of news work is changing because of new storage and retrieval procedures. (Ward, Hansen, & McLeod, 1988a). It may never be the same.

FREEDOM OF INFORMATION ACTS

In the 1960s and 1970s, commercial databases were developing primarily in the medical and science fields. In the 1980s, the new growth area was in newspapers and magazines. The 1990s are the decade of growth for on-line access to *public* records (Paul, 1991b). And this growth has raised freedom of information (FOI) and privacy concerns about public records (Dean, 1986).

State and federal laws ensure public access to most government records in the United States. These laws benefit all citizens in the country, not just journalists. Journalists have no more or no fewer rights to public records just because they are news media representatives. There are exceptions to access to some public records, of course. For example, personnel files and national security records are excluded.

Most freedom of information laws were written before the onslaught of electronic database storage. Thus, there may not be provisions for availability of this form of public records. For example, Florida, a state that has for nearly a century been a national leader in government access legislation, has recently begun to develop policies for access to the state's computerized public records. Most states and local governments across the nation are in similar situations. Finding most of the records being placed into computers has required re-thinking FOI laws and policies. But whereas laws have not yet completely resolved access and other freedom of information issues,

---

LEADING ON-LINE RESEARCH DATABASES FOR REPORTERS

Database Name	Summary of Content
Burelle's Broadcast	Full-text of ABC, CBS, NBC news programs, Financial News Network, National Public Radio
CompuServe	General interactive service including news such as full-text AP, UPI, some newspapers
DataTimes	Full-text newspapers, magazines, wire services, newsletters, international databases; a total of 640 database sources
Dialog	Over 320 bibliographic databases including full-text newspapers
Dow Jones News/Retrieval	*Wall Street Journal* and other Dow Jones information
Government bulletin board services (BBSs)	Specific information from individual agencies such as announcements, statistics, press releases
Knowledge Index	Over 100 bibliographic databases, including full-text daily newspapers
Lexis	Lexis is a set of full-text legal/law databases;
Nexis	Nexis is a set of full-text daily newspapers, magazines, wire services, newsletters
NewsNet	Business information through over 300 newsletter databases
Prodigy	General interactive service, includes AP
U.S. Datalink	Public records data
Vu/Text	Full-text of more than 70 daily newspapers, newswires, magazines, and business publications
Westlaw	Legal citations, full-text opinions of major courts

---

some state courts have interpreted the issue in civil cases. One Florida court, for example, ruled that all data in a state computer are public records, not just data accessible through a particular program. But the agency does not have to provide data in the format requested by a citizen (Splichal, 1991). Although courts are resolving some of the FOI issues, state attorneys general are also interpreting existing laws when problems arise. Interested persons can request opinions by a particular state's attorney general by contacting that office.

With the wide range of computerized public records, rules for access are a necessity. Dade County, Florida, for instance, had at least 33 different government databases in 1990 (Splichal, 1991). The content of such massive sets of information is wide ranging.

Despite freedom of information laws, reporters seeking to use public records on computers may find their access delayed or even denied. The most common argument given by officials to reporters to deny or delay access is because there is no mechanical means to complete the request. Other reasons include unwillingness to take time to make the search, lack of familiarity with the information in the request, requested data are being processed at the time of the inquiry, concerns about privacy, interpretations of existing state laws, and uncertainty over access fees (Dean, 1986; Splichal, 1991).

GOVERNMENT DATABASES

There is an enormous amount of federal and state data being collected today. This does not even include such information as census data. There are other types of information being collected, compiled, and released to the public. Yet some of that information is just collected and sits in a warehouse somewhere, never released to the public.

There are at least eight different types of government information available on-line. Records are kept on all aspects of our lives. The major types of government records include:

- Corporate records (state level)
- Uniform commercial code filings of debtors and secured parties (state level)
- Motor vehicle and driver's license records (state level)
- Bankruptcy filings (state and federal level)
- Official Records Index, a locator for documents (state and local level)
- Real estate records (local level)
- Tax liens (state and federal level)
- Lawsuits (local, state, and federal levels) (Paul, 1991b).

On-line access to available information has changed what it means to use sources from Washington, DC or in state capitals. Craig Webb (1989), correspondent for McGraw-Hill News and a former United Press International reporter in Washington, wrote that "proliferating computer links to federal agencies are redefining what it means for a reporter to cover Washington, DC. The links enable anyone with a personal computer or office computer, communications equipment and the requisite software to hook-up to government-run information banks" (p. 18).

Access is achieved in several ways:

- Direct access to a host computer through a commercial "gateway" computer
- Copies of data sold to an information provider
- Direct access to the host computer provided by the government
- Records collected and processed by a commercial information provider
- Synthesized voice databases (Paul, 1991b).

There are still other methods. Some news organizations purchase raw data tapes for original analysis or reanalysis by the news organization. A second, more common, method is to access information that has already been processed, analyzed, and prepared for public release. This is done on-line in one of the most popular trends in the 1990s to access government information: electronic computer-based bulletin board services (BBSs). A BBS is linked in a fashion similar to commercial databases through telephone lines. It is a concept that originated with a community center bulletin board that citizens would visit regularly to get current information tacked onto the board. Most electronic BBSs have menu-driven commands to guide unfamiliar users through the system. The first step is to "log on" and identify yourself. Then a menu offers options for the user. BBSs usually provide references, announcements, message services, questions-answer files, press releases, report abstracts or full-text files, and general background information about the agency.

Many individual federal or state agencies have set up their own BBSs. One popular example is the U.S. Commerce Department's economic BBS. This is not a free service, but it is inexpensive compared to fees charged by commercial data providers. The federal departments of Agriculture and Labor have public-access BBSs and the Federal Communications Commission also has a BBS for public use (Webb, 1989).

A fast-growing application of computers is to conduct secondary analysis of raw data. This is much more sophisticated, may require high cost processing, and may be beyond the skills of most reporters. Nevertheless, many reporters are learning these procedures and moving to use a new investigative tool.

NORA PAUL, THE POYNTER INSTITUTE
HOW TO SEARCH A MURDERER'S PAST
USING ELECTRONIC PUBLIC RECORDS

Eric Dubins wounded his girlfriend, killed her sister, then shot himself.

A *Miami Herald* reporter called the paper's library director to see if there were any stories on Dubins. In the course of checking out his background, she found:

The killer left a paper trail.

It's amazing how much information reporters now can find through computers, without having to talk to anyone.

Our computer search on Eric Dubins did not result in a big story, but did turn up a number of leads and sources. Although the information was interesting, it did not automatically make a story.

Newsrooms of the 1990s more and more will gather their information through computers. That information requires interpretation, common sense, knowledge of sources and restraint.

(continued)

NORA PAUL, THE POYNTER INSTITUTE *(continued)*

We got the following on Dubins in less than an hour, for about $100.
(An important note—it is possible to pull up credit reports when using the National Address Identifier database, but it also is illegal.)

Real estate microfiche
Records on Dubins' and his victims' homes. The microfiche is a product of Red-Real Estate, a company that pulls county property records nationwide and puts them on microfiche, by either property owner or address. They are now on line.

Lexis legal database
Record of a lawsuit he had filed against a former fellow corporate officer which had gone to the state appeals court. This gave us his lawyer's name.

Fort Lauderdale Sun-Sentinel
Available through Vu-Text
A society column story from 1985 about Dubins and an ex-girlfriend smooching at a charity auction.

The National Address Identifier database
Available through W.D.I.A. Credit Information Network—all you need is a name and an address
Dubins' previous addresses (one in California), employers and years of employment, ex-wife's name, date of birth and social security number.

Florida driver's license records
Available through CompuServe—since we now had date of birth
Dubins' height, eye color and the fact that he had to wear glasses.

Prentice-Hall's public records database
Record of Dubins' notice of default on his California mortgage in 1987, and an ex-girlfriend's personal bankruptcy filing last year.

Florida secretary of state listing of corporate officers
Available through CompuServe
Ten corporations in which Dubins was an officer—three of them with former girlfriends.
Source: Paul (1990).

Reprinted with permission of Nora Paul.

However, some government agencies simply do not have information in computers that reporters need for their stories. "We're at a funny juncture right now. While there is a lot that is computerized, not everything is computerized," said former investigative reporter Elliot Jaspin (Chichioco, 1989).

One example of this problem involved the federal Bureau of Alcohol, Tobacco, and Firearms (ATF) in Washington, DC. Reporters James Stewart and Andrew Alexander, Cox Newspapers national correspondents based in Washington, DC, found this out the hard way. The two reporters sought to learn about the use of assault weapons in crime for a series of articles they planned for their newspaper group. The most important information they needed was not available from local metropolitan police-departments, private groups, or even the Federal Bureau of Investigation. Turning to ATF, they found boxes of noncomputerized records at ATF's massive warehouses in Maryland, but the agency would not permit the records to be taken from the warehouse. ATF had stopped computerizing its records because of budget cuts. Did this stop Stewart and Alexander? No. The two got funding from their editors to set up six rented personal computers in the warehouse with six temporary clerks and keypunchers and entered the 15 months of data on their own. The process took more than a month, but resulted in a package of stories that was sent to all Cox Newspapers and published weeks later. Their findings have been cited in numerous publications and used by members of Congress. "If they (government officials) tell you that the information is not available, find a way to make it available. Eventually it will pay off," Stewart said (Chichioco, 1989, pp. 20PC–21PC).

There are limitations to government databases, according to Paul (1991b). Paul listed three problem areas:

1. *The purpose of the database.* Some databases simply do not provide the information you seek. These types of databases are not designed for archival purposes and have short electronic lives such as 1, 2, or 5 years.

2. *How data are entered in the database.* Most data are keypunched from hard copy forms by clerks. These naturally contain keypunch errors and other inconsistencies.

3. *How (or if) searching is monitored.* Some systems monitor how they are being used. This can reveal to individuals being searched, especially public officials, that an investigation is being conducted.

MAJOR NATIONAL NEWS DATABASES

Throughout this chapter mention has been made of the major databases used by reporters and library personnel today. This section describes in more detail the nature of these databases and how they can be useful. Although not all databases or database services are described — there are far too many — the major ones used in news organization libraries are discussed here.

Burrelle's Broadcast Database

Headquartered in Livingston, New Jersey, Burrelle's Broadcast Database is one of few on-line sources for television and radio news stories. Burrelle's

Broadcast "Database" is actually a collection of many databases. Burrelle's records and transcribes a wide range of television and radio news programs from national sources, but not from local sources. These full-text news and public affairs program transcripts are from ABC News, CBS News, NBC News, Financial News Network, and National Public Radio. Users can also access transcripts of some press conferences, speeches, and interviews. Most of Burrelle's databases were started in late 1989 or early 1990, so they are new by news database standards.

Burrelle's databases include the most-watched nightly newscasts, as well as morning news, weekend public affairs programs, and late night news network programming. Burrelle's updates the databases by 9 A.M. of the day following the broadcast, and text files remain in the databases indefinitely.

There is a more comprehensive discussion of Burrelle's and other on-line broadcast news later in this chapter.

CompuServe

CompuServe, located in Columbus, Ohio, provides a very wide range of on-line services from electronic mail to mail-order shopping to news and other information. One of the oldest "boutique" services, CompuServe charges fees based on usage or a standard monthly rate. Perhaps the most helpful CompuServe services for reporters are access to the major wire services, AP and UPI, through its "executive news service" (ENS). ENS also includes McGraw-Hill business news, the *Washington Post,* and other news databases. In addition, ENS also provides an electronic clip file service for users wanting the computer to "read" all news wires for a particular subject preidentified by key words. The items are then saved until the user requests them. Beyond ENS, CompuServe also provides search capabilities through newspaper archives using Vu/Text. Fees are on a per-search basis. Other research resources such as CENDATA, public relations press releases, encyclopedias, abstracts, and indexes are available on the service for a premium additional charge beyond the basic service fee.

CompuServe also offers "phonefile," a service that permits users to find telephone numbers of individuals on a national level. It is a helpful means for finding "lost" individuals with unusual names, for example.

Other useful information includes complete National Weather Service forecasts and maps, travel information such as airline schedules and ticket prices, business information, and stock market background and current price quotations.

CompuServe also serves as a "gateway" computer to other systems and databases. For example, users interested in Florida Department of Motor Vehicles registration information, driver's license information, or Secretary of State corporation records can assess them through CompuServe.

The system is completely menu driven to aid beginners.

DataTimes

DataTimes is an Oklahoma City company that provides full-text newspaper files from across the country.

DataTimes provides access to the text files of more than 640 information sources including national publications such as *U. S. News & World Report, American Banker,* and *Christian Science Monitor.*

Newspapers are part of the DataTimes system. Just about all regions of the country are represented coast to coast. Newspapers include the Gannett newspapers such as *USA Today* and the *Louisville Courier-Journal.* Also on-line are the *San Francisco Chronicle, Dallas Morning News, Orange County Register, St. Petersburg Times,* and the *Minneapolis Star* and *Tribune.*

DataTimes also provides current stock market quotes and statistics. There is a wide range of wire services on DataTimes such as the Gannett News Service, Associated Press, Business Wire, and Government Economic Data wire. There are other specialty newswires as well.

Dow Jones news and financial services are included. The *Wall Street Journal* and other Dow Jones statistics are on-line. Public relations press release wires include the PR Newswire, Press Release Wires, and the BPI Entertainment Newswire.

Business reports, company/industry information, business and economic magazines, special industry magazines and newsletters are also databases on-line. Researchers needing to read international newspapers from the United Kingdom and other parts of the world will find publications from England, Canada, and Australia.

There are also several international news services such as Agence France-Presse, the European Associated Press, and Xinhua (China). Financial "profile" information from Europe, Asia, and the Middle East is on-line in databases.

The system is particularly expensive for international databases, but users are billed by the minute after paying a monthly maintenance fee that depends on the price option plan selected.

Dialog/Knowledge Index

Dialog and Knowledge Index are Knight–Ridder information services containing hundreds of databases for users. Dialog is the more complete and more expensive version of the two systems, offering over 320 databases. Knowledge Index offers a trimmed-down range of databases to search, but still provides over 100 sets of data available during nonbusiness hours at about one third to one quarter of the hourly fees charged to Dialog users.

Both services provide databases in agriculture, the arts, the physical sciences, the business and corporate world, computers, drugs, food, and medicine, economics, education, engineering, the environment, government publications, law, magazines and newspapers, reference source data such as quotations, book lists, and dissertations, religion, sociology and psychology, and travel.

The system is menu driven and easy for users to learn.

Dow Jones News/Retrieval

Located in South Brunswick, New Jersey, Dow Jones News/Retrieval features information about business and the financial world. The most useful databases, perhaps, are the full-text files of the *Wall Street Journal* and the Dow Jones News Service. The *Washington Post* is also on-line in this system. Dow Jones News/Retrieval also features texts of national business magazines such as *Barron's, Fortune, Forbes, Money,* and *BusinessWeek.*

Clearly, one of the other strengths of this database "boutique" is access to current stock information as well as background research reports and other information on stocks and companies listed on the stock exchanges. Generally, this information is the same data that stock brokerage houses use on a daily basis.

Other features include a press release wire, Japanese business news, national and world news summaries, sports reports, and weather forecasts. Certain business services are also a part of the package, including airline schedules and prices, electronic mail, and on-line shopping. The PBS program, "Wall Street Week," is also transcribed and kept in full-text files for access.

Lexis/Nexis

Lexis and Nexis are full-text Mead Data Central services originating from Dayton, Ohio. These are actually two separate services from the same company. Nexis/Lexis are two of the most popular and most widely used databases in news libraries today.

Lexis is focused on the legal world. From it, users can find full-texts of court opinions from many of the states and the federal court system. Lexis offers access to general legal "libraries" or databases that cover federal codes, state statutes, law reviews, and state legal libraries. There are also over two dozen specialized legal libraries in Lexis. These include databases on admiralty law, corporate law, military justice, tax law, and federal securities, to name only a few examples. Lexis also provides legal library databases from the United Kingdom and France. Citation services are also available in this system.

Nexis, on the other hand, provides complete text files of national publications such as newspapers and magazines. It is the only on-line source for the *New York Times.* Also available are the *Los Angeles Times* and many regional business publications. Nexis also includes numerous wire services and specialized newsletters. Within the Nexis "boutique" are also databases covering advertising and public relations, patents and trademarks, government and political news, energy news, transportation news, and insurance. Lexis offers a financial information service, a country information service, and Associated Press political service. There is also a National Automated Accounting Research Service.

Vu/Text

Vu/Text is another Knight–Ridder information services company based in Philadelphia that offers full-text access to more than 70 major U.S. daily newspapers in 29 states. It is the largest newspaper database provider.

Vu/Text is perhaps the most popular database used by news libraries today. But Vu/Text covers more than just newspapers.

Vu/Text includes over five news and business wires, eight magazines, and eight business publications. News wires include AP, *Fortune,* Knight–Ridder, and the PR Newswire. Magazines include Time Inc. publications such as *Time, Sports Illustrated, Money, Life, Time* international edition, and *People.* Profile databases are files that provide international news, marketing, advertising, business, and finance through the *Financial Times* in London. "Business Dateline" databases include the full-text files of more than 60 regional and local business periodicals.

Vu/Text files are usually updated within 24 hours. The depth of the newspaper archive files vary, of course, but many date back to the early to mid-1980s. The *Boston Globe* database is the oldest, dating back to January 1980.

Other Useful Database Services

There are many other databases and database services not discussed here. New services are continually being created. There are many useful sources outside the United States, for instance. Most commonly used, of course, because of the native English-language text, are databases from Canada and the United Kingdom.

The Canadian Press database contains articles from the Canadian Press news cooperative. InfoGlobe lists full-text articles from the *Toronto Globe and Mail.* It also contains directory information from a variety of Canadian reference sources such as *Who's Who in Canadian Business and Finance* and the *Canadian Periodical Index.*

DataCall provides full-text files of wire stories within the past 24 hours from the *Los Angeles Times* and *Washington Post* News Service. It also includes Deutsche Presse Agentur (DPA), the German news agency, and Agence France-Presse (AFP), the French news agency.

Baseline is an entertainment-oriented database that provides information

---

JIM LEUSNER, *ORLANDO SENTINEL*
GIVE ME YOUR TAG NUMBER AND
I'LL TELL YOU YOUR LIFE STORY

That may sound strange, but it's often an automobile license tag number that begins the process behind many of the in-depth stories you read in newspaper.

Investigative reporting is something all reporters practice. It's reporting taken to its extreme—to find out the trend, pattern or story-behind-the-story. In short, it's just good old detective work and many times it starts with the complaint from a concerned citizen.

Did a public official vote to approve government funding for a project he had an interest in?

(continued)

JIM LEUSNER, *ORLANDO SENTINEL (continued)*

Was a controversial rezoning approved by a governmental board because the developer was a major contributor to a powerful board member's election campaign?

How did a group of criminals get close enough to a congressman to plan being business partners with him?

What caused a seemingly harmless drifter to walk into a courthouse and kill a bailiff and wound two other officers?

Through public records, you can follow the "imprint" most of us leave on society during our lifetime.

By examining public records at the county courthouse, you can find out if someone owns a home, how much they paid for it and how much they pay each year in property taxes. You can also determine if someone has a real estate or electrical contractor's license or what kind of driving record they have.

Along the way, you can discover associations, former employers, classmates, friends or maybe a police source who can help fill in the gaps.

The process is similar when checking out a business.

In the case of Thomas Provenzano, the man convicted of the shootings at the Orange County Courthouse in January 1984, a team of *Sentinel* reporters started from the bottom. Beginning with his license tag number on his car and date of birth, we reconstructed his life—all within two weeks of the shooting.

We checked his criminal and driver's records in state computers and at the courthouse, and we were able to document previous encounters with the law, prior addresses where he lived and neighbors who knew him.

Next, we traced his employment record with the help of neighbors, state workers' compensation files, lawsuits and divorce records, and applications on file with the Florida agency that licenses electrical contractors. Eventually, we obtained his military records and were granted interviews by him and his sister, which helped to answer the few remaining unanswered questions.

What we found was a paranoid man with a dislike for police and a history of mental problems that went ignored. Two weeks after the shooting, we reconstructed the crime and gave the police a motive.

At times during the investigation, a reporter stumbles across some information unrelated or not relevant to the story, such as the identity of a mistress or the fact that an innocent victim of a crime has a criminal record.

Though tempting to use, reporters and editors must carefully decide what is news-worthy. Many times, this "dirt" would be unfair if put in the story.

But with luck, documentation and well-placed sources, a story can solve a mystery, a crime or point out loopholes in the law or abuse in government.

And that's our job.

Source: Leusner (1985). Reprinted with permission of the *Orlando Sentinel.*

about more than 330,000 entertainment industry personnel and contact information leading to over 10,000 celebrities. It also provides financial information on films and television programming and has files containing awards and company/corporate data.

CQ/Washington Alert is a Congressional Quarterly service that updates users on legislation, provides text of bills and resolutions, lists abstracts and text of the *Congressional Record,* member and district profiles, and other information related to the activities of the Congress.

U.S. Datalink, based in Baytown, Texas, is an on-line gateway to public records using a national network of hundreds of local vendors of public information. Its databases include driver's license information, employment reports, motor vehicle registrations, property records, and more. This database service is frequently used by private investigators.

BROADCAST NEWS DATABASES

One of the more recent developments in electronic databases has been the application of full-text storage and retrieval to broadcast news writing and reporting. Newspapers and magazines, which were first to use computers in typesetting and production, simply stored their words in electronic form for later retrieval. But most radio and television stations, the networks, and other broadcast news organizations did not begin to apply computers for these purposes until later. But by 1990, three of the major news networks and several other broadcast news organizations had made their broadcast story transcripts available for permanent storage and retrieval by the public for a fee.

At present, the major database service providing broadcast news program transcript retrieval is Burrelle's Broadcast Database in New Jersey. For over 100 years, Burrelle's has offered a press clipping service to the public. Its on-line service is relatively new to the electronic library world, but this full-text service will become more and more useful to broadcast journalists interested in national television and radio reporting about a subject (Ojala, 1991). Burrelle's offers the full range of network news programs from ABC, CBS, and NBC. Not only are the nightly newscasts available, but so are the public affairs programs such as "Meet the Press," "60 Minutes," "48 Hours," and "This Week with David Brinkley." Furthermore, morning news programs and late night news programs such as "Nightline" are included. However, Burrelle's does not include CNN programs. Burrelle's also provides specialized transcripts of programs by National Public Radio (NPR; e.g., "All Things Considered") and the Financial News Network (FNN; e.g., "MarketWrap"). The television news text is available a day after it is aired. Seventeen different news programs from ABC have been available since July 1, 1990. CBS has the transcripts of 11 different programs in the database since February 1, 1990. NBC has seven of its daily or weekly programs included since November 1, 1989. The FNN database began October 1, 1990. The NPR database began on September 1, 1990 (Ojala, 1991).

There are other on-line sources of broadcast news. Nexis also offers full-text transcripts of ABC news and full-text transcripts of the "MacNeill/Lehrer Newshour" from the Public Broadcasting System (PBS). Another service known as Delphi offers full-text transcripts of PBS's "Nova" and "Frontline." Another on-line service, CompuServe, provides on-line access to transcripts of major programs produced by Journal Graphics, but the actual full-text is not on the system. Instead, on-line users place an order for a transcript and it is faxed or mailed to the user. The advantage is a wider range of information sources, and the "Transcripts" service through CompuServe also includes CNN newscasts. Dow Jones News/Retrieval on-line includes transcripts of its latest "Wall Street Week" programs. And NewsNet's Hotline provides abstracts of political news from the previous day that features a database known as "TV Monitor." It summarizes television news reporting (Ojala, 1991).

There are problems unique to broadcast news databases. Marydee Ojala (1991), an information consultant based in Overland Park, Kansas, proposed that the foremost problem is the visual component of television news. It is seldom represented, and when it is, users find brief parenthetical material supplied. She also said live interviews are a search challenge. "People interrupt each other. They talk over each other. A sentence might begin far away from where it ends," she warned (p. 40). The shorter, more conversational writing style might also cause search problems not encountered in print-oriented databases, she suggested. Repeated stories in newscasts are also a minor concern.

The major area for future development of these broadcast news databases will be major market local news stations. Whereas Burrelle's does not presently offer these stations' stories, it may later in this decade.

ON-LINE CREDIT RECORDS

Another major source of on-line information are private commercial credit reporting services. Credit records are maintained for a variety of reasons on just about every adult individual in the country. Credit records, because of the personal nature of their information, are highly restricted databases.

The federal Fair Credit Reporting Act sets the rules for disclosure of this information. Usually a user must submit specific legitimate reasons for using this sort of information such as employment, loan applications, and other credit situations. Credit services do provide limited forms of their credit reports for more general public consumption that do not violate the federal credit information reporting law. Even in stripped form, these files can be a tremendous asset for reporters searching for information about individuals for a story. The most common information available to the general user will be addresses, birth information, social security numbers, spouses, and employment history.

The major national on-line credit network services are TRW Information Services in Dallas, CBI-Equifax in Atlanta, and Trans Union Credit Information in Chicago (Naylor, 1991; Paul, 1991b).

But as with other on-line databases, caution is necessary in using the credit databases because of errors. Consumers Union, publisher of the national magazine, *Consumer Reports,* says there are numerous and serious errors in these reports (Naylor, 1991). Using this type of information for facts for a story may be dangerous. Instead, as many reporters and news librarians do, use the information to locate other information and people. Then verify it through other reporting strategies such as interviewing and firsthand observation (Naylor, 1991).

HOW PROFESSIONALS WRITE IT

SOURCE: The *Orlando Sentinel,* pp. A-1, A-9
DATE: Tuesday, July 24, 1990
AUTHOR: J. Craig Crawford, Washington Bureau
HEADLINE: Nominee has record of firm law

* * *

President Bush's nominee for the U.S. Supreme Court toed the conservative line for more than 20 years in the courts of New Hampshire.

David Souter served as New Hampshire attorney general from 1976 to 1978, when he was named as a trial judge. In 1983 he was appointed to the New Hampshire Supreme Court, where he served until his recent appointment to the federal appeals court in Boston.

While on the state Supreme Court, Souter wrote 74 opinions interpreting the Constitution. In nearly two-thirds, he sided against criminal suspects, according to computer research by the *Orlando Sentinel.*

Souter has not voted on any cases directly involving abortion, research shows. The issue is expected to be a major question at the Senate's upcoming confirmation hearings.

Yet Souter did offer a hint of his views on abortion in a 1986 written opinion. He joined the New Hampshire Supreme Court decision that said government has no business deciding whether a child saddled with birth defects would have been better off aborted. The court refused to let the parents sue their doctor for negligently allowing the child to be born.

In his concurring opinion, Souter said that to allow such suits could force doctors to perform abortions against their will. He questioned how a doctor "with conscientious scruples against abortion, and the testing and counseling that may inform an abortion decision, can discharge his professional obligation without engaging in procedures that his religious or moral principles condemn."

On other social matters, Souter's judicial views have followed a conservative bent. During his seven years on the bench of New Hampshire's highest court, Souter:

• Was the lone dissenter in a 1985 decision that struck down the use of police sobriety checkpoints. The U.S. Supreme Court this year upheld such police tactics.

• Joined a 1987 decision that said homosexuals may be barred from becoming adoptive or foster parents. But the court ruled that homosexuals may not be barred from running day-care centers.

• Wrote the majority opinion in a 1988 ruling that denied unemployment compensation to two elderly janitors who were laid off. Souter disagreed with the men's claim that they were too frail to seek full-time jobs, as state law required. "A weak back, poor eyesight or angina do not necessarily prevent an individual who can work four hours a day from working eight," Souter wrote.

Two powerful patrons have guided Souter's career — Republican Sen. Warren Rudman and White House chief of staff John Sununu. As state attorney general, Rudman gave Souter his start in state government.

It was Sununu, while governor of New Hampshire, who appointed Souter to the state's highest court. In January Sununu persuaded President Bush to appoint Souter to the federal bench in Boston, where the Rhodes scholar has not yet written a court opinion.

Rudman once said Souter, who was considered a potential Supreme Court nominee by the Reagan administration before Anthony M. Kennedy's appointment in 1988, has "the most brilliant legal mind" he had ever encountered.

Souter first proved his conservative mettle as attorney general. In 1977 he made a special trip to ask a judge not to give suspended sentences to more than 1,400 protesters arrested at the Seabrook nuclear power plant. Souter said he found it offensive that people could conduct criminal acts and go without punishment.

During a "sickout" by the New Hampshire State Employees Association in June 1983, Gov. Sununu asked Souter, then trial judge, to hold a hearing — which he did at 3:45 A.M.

Souter ordered the workers to return to their jobs or face possible fines. He also threatened the union and its leaders with fines.

Among New Hampshire lawyers, Souter has a reputation for conservative decisions.

"He does not pay any attention to the emotional, political aspects" of cases before him, said Stanley M. Brown, a Manchester, N. H., lawyer and a former American Bar Association officer. "He doesn't go out blazing new pathways. That's not his forte."

Reprinted with permission of the *Orlando Sentinel.*

• • •

6 Interviewing Basics

For many journalists, *interviewing* seems to be the essence of reporting.

For Sheryl James, 39-year-old news features writer for the *St. Petersburg Times,* the subtle art of persuading a source to be interviewed resulted in an excellent feature series about a mother who abandoned her child. James wanted to explain how the mother's decision affected the mother's life as well as the lives of the people around her. Although the story idea might have been obvious, James said, interviewing the right person and gaining access to that person were not so easy (Gersh & Case, 1991; James, 1991).

The toughest part of James' series was *persuading* the mother to trust her as a journalist and then talk to her. Once the woman's trial had ended, James talked to the woman and her attorney and persuaded the source to be interviewed. James took particular care not to be aggressive or pushy, remaining sensitive and yet persistent. "She was a million emotions going on. It was like handling live dynamite," James said (Gersh & Case, 1991, p. 33). James' stories hinged on the trust built between the reporter and her key source. "I simply tried to be straightforward about what I was doing, and get her to trust me, to know that I would keep my word to her," she explained (James, 1991). Aside from that, when I finally did interview her, I felt as I do with many people I interview—I try to establish a relaxed rapport, to be human myself so that they know I'm not a media monster." James also used court files, transcripts from the trial, and recollections of conversations and thoughts obtained during interviews. The series impacted the community and her professional peers by winning the 1991 Pulitzer Prize for feature writing. She described how her series developed:

Interviews are not always what you expect. Here *Dayton Daily News* sportswriter Tom Archdeacon found that out when he interviewed the "San Diego Chicken" mascot at a baseball game (photo by Michael Carlebach).

This [series] definitely evolved, which is part of the reason it was so exciting. At first, I thought it would be a Sunday front, a compelling story (if we were lucky) of a woman who granted us an interview, along with various background and scene-setting. But little by little, it grew as I realized the material I had was very rich and the story was complex and involved. I kept going back to Sandra [Thompson, her editor] saying, "Well, this may be a two-day story," then "three days," and finally, it stretched to four days. It was a matter of the stories growing out of the material, not the other way around. (James, 1991)

James revealed she easily spent 10 times the amount of time on interviews than she did on other reporting. Although she was able to interview the woman who abandoned her baby, it was not an easy project. "I was a basket case about the interview with Judy, the mother. She was volatile, belligerent, and unpredictable. She had stood me up twice. In fact, I had given up and was prepared to write the series without the interview with her when she called me. I about fainted" (James, 1991). James also faced a tough decision, she said, about journalistic ethics of interviewing: "From an ethical point of view, I was dealing with a good but somewhat unsophisticated source who would have been easy to manipulate. It was a challenge to be sure they understood what I was doing and to keep promises made during the reporting process that I could have broken with impunity" (James, 1991).

Interviewing large numbers of people for a variety of opinions and verifying information were keys to an investigation by KQED-TV, San Francisco, into brutality in the San Francisco Police Department. The story required patience in collecting information, said producers Scott Pearson and Lewis Cohen. The producers said it is important in conducting interviews for such a story to "know who you are talking to and their local political ties and influences. Develop inside police and internal affairs sources," Pearson and Cohen advised (1990, p. 11). What did the interviews and their research reveal? The city paid over $3 million in settlements in brutality cases over a 10-year period.

Sources interviewed were wide-ranging in experience and expertise. KQED-TV reporters interviewed attorneys, community activists, police officers, victims, "street people," court officials, federal law enforcement personnel, clerks, public defenders, and prosecuting attorneys.

Three examples of the importance of interviewing to reporting are outlined here; each story is reprinted at the end of the chapter.

Mike Christensen, feature writer for the *Atlanta Constitution,* picked up on a nostalgia theme underlying what might seem to be an ordinary event and turned the event into an entertaining story about crayons. Christensen learned that the makers of Crayola crayons—a school supply that most children used in elementary or grammar school—were "retiring" eight of its standard colors for new ones. Whereas this might not seem to be a major development in today's world, Christensen artfully set the tone for the entertaining story by looking at how these particular colors were important enough to a small group of people that they light-heartedly protested the decision at the manufacturer's offices in Pennsylvania. Christensen used interviews with the concerned people to present the nostalgic look at crayons. Yet, his tongue-in-cheek feature maintains an informational level because it explains why, through the words of a company vice president, the colors were "retired." But Christensen did not stop there. He also talked to a major department store spokesperson for the store's point of view. He also interviewed individuals present at the ceremony revealing individuals present at the ceremony revealing the new colors at the company's headquarters. Direct quotations from interviews with these individuals add a large amount of personal flavor and mood to the story. Interviews with carefully selected individuals resulting in strong direct quotations brought success to the feature.

Muncie, Indiana, *Star* beat reporter Randy Rendfeld took a feature story approach in his amusing story about a nearby rural community with two time zones, Union City, Indiana and Union City, Ohio. Rendfeld recognized the strong feature potential in the story and went to the eastern Indiana–western Ohio location that straddles the state border to find out how residents cope. It was an interview-dependent story published on the day when the summer daylight savings time change took effect. Ohio observes the summer change to daylight savings time and much of Indiana does not, so Rendfeld wanted to find out what residents thought of the predicament. He interviewed the two mayors for explanations. He interviewed long-time residents for reaction comments. He interviewed business owners and major industry managers about how the change affected their work. He interviewed school and other government officials.

"Because I was trying for a colorful and entertaining story, I joked around quite a bit during the interviews," Rendfeld (1991) explained. Rendfeld elaborated:

> I suggested to a couple of the interview subjects that they consider building a revolving restaurant on a tower located on the state line, so people from Indiana, who are subject to blue laws, could pickup a six-pack and some lottery tickets when the restaurant revolves to the Ohio side. This kind of joking around seemed to open up the interviewees, particularly Mayor John Ford. You can see from his comments, Ford had some jokes of his own.

The uniqueness of the situation, highlighted through the quotations from community residents, was not easy for Rendfeld to report. "I wasn't too familiar with Union City when I wrote this story. I had covered the Indiana-side city council and school board, so I knew a few people. I called a Union City English teacher I had befriended. I told him what I was working on, and specifically asked whether he knew any colorful characters. He suggested Leroy Stentzil and he turned out to be a colorful senior citizen with some humorous anecdotes to share.

Rendfeld's effort paid off. The story was unusual and widely read. "One thing that distinguishes this article for me is that I had fun writing it. It's rare when a beat journalist gets an entertaining assignment like this. I played it for as many laughs as I could without alienating the sources," Rendfeld recalled. His extra effort paid off—it was picked up and given national distribution by the Associated Press.

Tom Coakley and John Aloysius Farrell, reporters for the *Boston Globe,* and Christopher Boyd, a *Globe* correspondent, needed interviews to get their story about the developments in the alleged sexual assault at the winter home of the Kennedy family in Palm Beach. Their interviews were conducted in difficult circumstances because of the group reporting environment of a major breaking story involving a prominent U.S. political family. Coakley, Farrell, and Boyd interviewed officials such as the police chief. They conducted interviews with many sources who would talk only if they were not identified. Because of the nature of the story—an alleged sexual assault—Coakley and Farrell faced decisions about attribution. Should they identify the sources of their information? Their story has numerous passages where information is not attributed to a named source. Use of ambiguous terms such as "sources" or "sources close to the case" do not identify the individuals providing information in interviews. There is a price to pay for such interview information—readers do not always know whether to believe the information offered. The story's credibility may be reduced with anonymous sources who refuse to be identified as a condition to be interviewed.

Interviewing, as these three examples show, can be exciting and productive. It is the most significant reason some reporters choose journalism for a career. Most reporters like working with people. Most reporters are fascinated by the different individuals they encounter on their daily assignments. The interaction with famous, unusual, average, and even undesirable people makes the work appealing. Perhaps an interview's best aspect is the exchange that provides reporters—hopefully—with the information they are seeking for the story.

After you have done your background research and you have learned what you can, you still have to consider the special demands of interviews. Each interview, if done well, should have its own preparation effort, customized for the source.

DEFINING THE JOURNALISTIC INTERVIEW

What exactly is a journalistic interview? First, it is important to realize there are many kinds of interviews that extend beyond news gathering. There are job interviews. There are public opinion survey and poll interviews. There are job performance and appraisal interviews. There are persuasive interviews. There are medical care interviews. There are legal interviews known as interrogations, investigations, and cross-examinations. You can probably think of other types and purposes of interviews.

Second, it is important to analyze journalistic interviewing. What is it? Bleyer (1913) said interviewing boiled down to "conversations" in which reporters focused more on what was said than how it was said. But Bleyer noted that some interviewing required getting what was said verbatim. "Interviewing of this type requires great skill and tact, and successful interviewers are highly valued" (pp. 44–45).

Bleyer considered the meaning of the interview early in this century, and since then journalism has changed dramatically. Today, good interviews are conversational in nature. They certainly must involve an exchange of information, but that exchange does not have to be one way. In fact, some of the best interview experiences are two-way exchanges of information. A source's confidence in you as a reporter grows if you provide information to the source as well. That information can be about you personally or about your story. But you are there to gather information. A definition of the journalistic interview must focus on information gathering. Because you are gathering accurate and complete information with a purpose, the conversation becomes an interview.

Another key element is *control.* Shirley Biagi (1986), in her book *Interviews that Work,* underlined the importance of control. "In an interview . . . the interviewer causes the discussion to happen and determines the direction of the questioning" (p. 6).

University of Oregon journalism professor Ken Metzler (1989) reshaped the definition, saying *creative* interviewing is "a two-person conversational *exchange* of information on behalf of an audience to produce a level of intelligence neither participant could produce alone" (pp. 13–14).

MAJOR TYPES OF NEWS INTERVIEWS

There are at least seven different kinds of news reporting interviews. You will probably find these are not mutually exclusive categories, with some

---

BOOKS ABOUT JOURNALISTIC INTERVIEWING

In the past two decades, a number of strong books have been written about interviewing. Here is a list of eight leading titles:

Biagi, S. (1992). *Interviews that work* (2nd ed.). Belmont, CA: Wadsworth.

Brady, J. (1977). *The craft of interviewing.* New York: Vintage Books.

Downs, C. W., Smeyak, G. P., & Martin, E. (1980). *Professional interviewing.* New York: Harper & Row.

Gottlieb, M. (1986). *Interview.* New York: Longman.

Killenberg, G. M., & Anderson, R. (1989). *Before the story: Interviewing and communication skills for journalists.* New York: St. Martin's Press.

Metzler, K. (1989). *Creative interviewing.* (2nd ed.). Englewood Cliffs, NJ: Prentice-Hall.

Sherwood, H. C. (1972). *The journalistic interview.* (rev. ed.). New York: Harper & Row.

Stewart, C. J. & Cash, Jr., W. B. (1985). *Interviewing: Principles and practices.* (4th ed.). Dubuque, IA: Wm. C. Brown.

interviews taking on characteristics of two or more of these types of interviews:

1. *Spot interviews:* These are interviews that occur without any advance preparation on the part of the reporter. There are many assignments when you will not have enough time, or only a very short time, to prepare questions for a source.

2. *Advance preparation interviews:* These interviews are set up in advance and allow the reporter (and source) to prepare for the session. The major advantage to this form of interviewing over spot interviewing is time for research and development of questions and overall strategy for the interview.

3. *Live broadcast interviews:* Many times television and radio reporters on the scene of a breaking news story must conduct a live on-the-air interview. This type of interviewing is likely also a spot interview, but regardless of whether or not there is preparation, the pressure is great on the reporter to ask strong, meaningful questions in an extremely short time period.

4. *Background interviews:* For many stories, some interviews must be conducted to collect information to prepare for still other interviews. These

Spot interviews are often conducted in uncontrolled environments. *Miami Herald* reporter Michael Browning, taking notes on a pad balanced on his knee, talked to this homeless Florida man in the lobby of a library (photo by Michael Carlebach).

interviews may never be aired or published, but they play an important role by providing a first layer of information for the story.

5. *Telephone interviews:* There is great dependence on the telephone for interviews by all reporters. Newspaper, magazine, and radio interviewers use the telephone for time and travel savings on less important interviews. Even television reporters use telephone interviews on spot stories for background purposes. These interviews might be used to qualify a source for a story or to obtain background information for another interview. Of course, some sources may be unwilling to be interviewed on camera and prefer only to assist the reporter by telephone.

6. *"Q & A" interviews:* Question-and-answer interviews, often called Q & A interviews, are published or broadcast as the full text or full interview. Often these are edited for length and time but generally follow the chronological plan of the original interview. Magazines have often used Q & A interviews, but they are rarely used in newspapers today. Q & A interviews on radio and television news programs are seldom used because they often take more time than can be afforded with the additional time given to questioning. In broadcasting, Q & A interviews are more popular in "electronic magazine" format or weekend public affairs news programs.

7. *Panel and group interviews:* Interviews are sometimes conducted in panel or even larger group situations. This is not always desirable but may occur by request of the source or sources. There can be one reporter and several sources or, of course, several reporters and only one source. These may differ from press conferences only in size, because press conferences usually permit a restricted form of interviewing to occur. These are not much different in terms of exchanges between a single reporter and the source in group situations.

George Killenberg and Rob Anderson (1989) also listed four main purposes of interviews: (a) Routine news gathering, (b) Investigations, (c) features, and (d) profiles.

STEPS IN THE INTERVIEW PROCESS

Distinctive steps in the interviewing process have evolved as experienced journalists have tried techniques, refined them, and passed them along to their younger colleagues. There are a dozen important steps to the complete journalistic interview:

1. Determine the reason and purpose of the interview in the context of the story assigned.
2. Research the interview subject and source.
3. Set up the interview with the source.
4. Set the interview strategy and develop key questions to ask the source.

5. Meet the interview source and set the atmosphere of the interview by breaking the social "ice."
6. Establish your source's confidence in you as a journalist and measure your source's credibility and reliability.
7. Ask opening questions.
8. Ask basic information questions.
9. Ask tough and sensitive questions.
10. Conclude the interview.
11. Assess the interview and review notes or tapes.
12. Decide whether there is need to re-interview this source.

CONTROLLING THE INTERVIEW

A few pages earlier, you read that *control* was a critical element of interviewing that distinguished it from normal human conversation. Now you should consider how to establish control of the interview. There are four types of control to consider:

1. *Environment:* Often where the interview occurs can make a significant difference in the success of the interview. A reporter may prefer a neutral location for some interviews, if only because it reduces interruptions and other distractions.

2. *Subject:* Some sources will attempt to direct the interview away from the original subject when it becomes apparent that the subject is embarrassing or otherwise disagreeable.

3. *Direction of questioning:* If you have prepared questions in advance, this may reduce the likelihood that you will drift from the original purpose of your interview into some other appealing subject. Your source may try to change the line of questioning, also.

4. *Form of answers received:* Reporters must retain control of responses gathered in an interview. This means listening carefully to answers, asking for clarifications if needed, and following up with second and third questions if answers are unsatisfactory for any reason. Some expert sources used for television news stories will talk in difficult-to-understand terms that require explanation. Follow-up questions may elicit better responses that can be aired.

PREPARATION FOR AN INTERVIEW

Columnist Art Spikol (1987) told *Writer's Digest* readers the two words all reporters need to remember are "be prepared." He argues that "there's no excuse for sounding ill-prepared" (p. 10). Without the right preparation or focus, an interview may waste both your time and your source's time. Biagi

(1986) wrote, "Well-documented research gives you the background you need to ask good questions, to match your interviewee's answers with what your research tells you. To be a truly good researcher, you can't be satisfied with just *an* answer. You must always look until you find *the best* answer" (p. 44).

When you get that best answer, you can then set up the interview. Most of the time, your research will tell you what direction to take. You should write down or type your questions in advance, each one based on the research you have done. These question lists can serve as a "crutch" during the interview. They also show that you took the time to prepare for the time you have with the source. But you must remain flexible during the interview to move into other subjects and concerns beyond what your research told you if opportunities arise. There are times when your well-researched questions will wind up only as a jumping-off point for an interview.

In many cases, the story you are writing will require that you do some detective work to get the information you need. A few subjects will give you the luxury to get by without significant research. Your best approach, regardless, is to know where to find answers when you need to get them *before* you go into an interview.

After you have done your preinterview homework, the time arrives to go to the telephone or into the field. Once you have found authoritative sources for your story, your next step is to set up the interview meeting.

DYNAMICS OF CONVERSATION

Your interpersonal communication skills are put to test during a news interview. You should try to relax the person you are talking to and make the experience seem less like an interview and more like a purposeful conversation between two people who just met.

How is this done? If you can, start by chatting about something neutral and nonthreatening. Take a moment to get to know the person. Tell the person a little about yourself. Let the source get to know you and become more comfortable—and confident—with you. But you have to judge how much casual conversation is enough. It is obvious that a busy banker would be less interested in casual conversation than a relaxed grandfatherly craftsman might be. Always use time wisely. That busy banker might agree to the interview if it takes only 15 minutes. The craftsman might not care how much time is needed.

Shirley Biagi (1986) recommended that during the interview you should also relax and let your source do the talking. Simply bite your tongue if you are inclined to talk too much or interrupt before someone finishes answering your question. Biagi said reporters should display empathy and concentrate on what the source is saying. She also mentioned it helps your story if you note gestures and expressions by sources, as well as their physical characteristics.

It is also helpful during in-person interviews to look around the room when you get the chance — to learn more about the person if the interview is on your subject's "turf" such as a home or office. Biagi also cautioned beginning reporters to watch for sudden shifts in direction of the interview. This is the control factor. And, she suggested, be prepared to get away from the questions you developed if something more interesting arises.

Remember when you are winding down the interview to make certain you know how to find the person if you need to conduct a follow-up interview. Get a telephone number. It may not always be in the same place as the first interview. And double check critical information before you leave the first interview.

This is how just one interview might take place. Most stories require that you repeat this process in preparing a story. Seldom can you get a complete picture of a situation by depending on one interview and one source. Unfortunately, this is the error of many beginning reporters. There are always more than one point of view and one side to a news story. It is your job to find and report about the others.

What else should you do? Treat your source as you would like to be treated. Dress professionally. Be polite and considerate. Identify yourself. Explain your purpose and how much time you want.

Getting information is your goal, so always be certain of the information you are collecting during your interview, regardless of whether it is gathered in person or on the telephone. Verify spellings and the meaning of technical terms. Ask a second time if necessary. Follow the responses with questions designed to clarify, such as "Why?" Don't be afraid to show you don't know something.

HOW YOUR SOURCE SEES IT

What's it like to be a source? Few journalists have undergone the experience themselves. They do not realize the perspective of the source. It is a rude awakening to the impact that journalists have on people when a journalist must become a source for a story. Journalists must be particularly sensitive to their sources and how they react to having a reporter present, taking down their words on paper or on tape.

First, remember there are two kinds of sources. One type of source has never dealt with a reporter before. These are victims or eyewitnesses, for example. The other type of source has experience in dealing with reporters on previous occasions. It might be helpful to know whether your source has been interviewed by a journalist before. Ask. There will be anxieties and fears in inexperienced sources that you must calm. For some sources, being interviewed by a reporter is about as appealing as a trip to the dentist.

Sources will be concerned about your abilities as a journalist. They will want to be reassured that you can do the job well. This means getting the information right. You can give them clues that you will do it well by writing down information, recording it, and asking clarification questions.

You can also help ease the uncomfortable source's anxiety by telling the source a little about your own background and professional experience.

Another helpful technique is to tell your sources what you are doing and why they are important to the story. For some assignments, this may "tip your hand," but for most stories it does not matter and helps by allowing the source to learn about your goals and motivations for the interview.

For interviews with experienced sources, you have a different set of concerns. Sources who have dealt with reporters on previous occasions may have a preconceived notion about you, based on those experiences. If the earlier experiences have generally been positive, this helps you. But if they have been negative, you have ground to be made up. How can you tell? Usually, you will get clues during the early moments of the interview. Sources may even caution you of their wariness. Some skeptical sources may actually tape record the interview and keep it in an effort to intimidate you.

If you encounter a source who does not trust you, the job becomes more challenging. You have to establish your own professional abilities and skills with this source, perhaps by reviewing your own experience or by reminding your sources of a recent story you did that they may have seen.

Sources worry about several things in the interview process. Sources worry, first of all, about being made to look bad. They worry they will not be treated fairly. They also worry about whether the information you are given will be accurate when it becomes part of the story. They worry about being misquoted—that is, they worry about being quoted incorrectly. Sources worry about bias and unfairness in stories in which they will appear. And, finally, they worry about complications at work or at home that may occur from the story. You must be sensitive to all of these concerns and do your best to alleviate any fears that are expressed or otherwise perceived.

WRITING AND SEQUENCING QUESTIONS

Once you have selected your subject and source and have done your research homework, then you are ready to develop questions for the interview. There are two stages in this step to consider: writing and asking the questions, and sequencing the questions.

Writing and Asking Interview Questions

Writing and asking questions is an art form. The truly skillful interviewers in journalism today can develop the right questions to ask sources. Your first consideration in this portion of the interview process is to *decide what you want to ask.* This process can be a form of "brain storming" in which you just write an outline or list of topics to cover. Then turn each item on the outline or list into a question or series of questions. When this is completed, go back and decide the order of your questions.

"You have to have a clear idea of what you are doing when you prepare

News sources frequently have their own informational agenda during an interview and will work hard to get that point of view across to a reporter (photo by the *Miami Herald* staff).

questions for an interview," said *Miami Herald* city desk general assignment reporter Kimberly Crockett (1991). "You have to start with research. And do not assume anything. One plus one does not always equal two."

Question formulation is very important. Getting these questions on paper is more important. The better prepared you are, the more positively a source will respond to you. Question preparation enhances your credibility as an interviewer.

Questioning should be done with some self-control. One book (Balinsky & Burger, 1959) on interviewing skills wisely advised:

Probe, but do not cross-examine.
Inquire, but do not challenge.
Suggest, but do not demand.
Uncover, but do not trap.
Draw out, but do not pump.
Guide, but do not dominate.

There are different ways to ask questions. You can ask what are commonly called "open-ended" questions and you can ask "closed-ended" questions:

Open-Ended Questions.   These questions are not limited in any form or fashion and do not lead your source toward a particular response. These questions are typically very general in the type of information they probably will elicit from the source. Example: "What do you think about construction of the new condominiums on the environmentally sensitive land near Jackson Corners?"

Closed-Ended Questions.   These questions most often propose a possible range of answers for your source. Thus, these questions are more specific in the type of information they will elicit from the source. Example: "What do you think should be done about construction of the new condominiums on the environmentally sensitive land near Jackson Corners? Should the county allow the developer to build the condominiums, require the developer to conduct an impact study, or should the county ban all construction?"

While preparing questions, do not overlook the need for questions that gather the most basic facts: How do sources spell their names? Address? Age? There are other basic questions that follow the general who, what, when, where, why, and how model (Metzler, 1989). Perhaps, however, the most important questions from the five *W*s and *H* model are *how* and *why.* You might remember being around a 3-year-old child. The child's natural curiosity—they are always asking, "Why?"—provides a lesson for reporters. Ask why! Ask how! You will often find the most revealing responses come from sources when you have pushed them to the depths of their knowledge of a subject by asking those two very simple questions.

Sequencing the Questions

Question sequencing is a serious consideration for an interview. Most journalists begin interviews with softer, *ice-breaker questions,* which ease tension and get both persons comfortable. These questions should be given full effort to be timely and useful. Ken Metzler (1989), author of *Creative Interviewing,* recommended using good-natured kidding and conversational banter to start. Tough and sensitive questions should come near the end of your interview if there is no more logical place. This allows you to get as much information from the source as possible before circumstances of the interview change because of the more difficult questions.

Metzler also urged interviewers to use *filter questions,* which permit you to determine the qualifications of the source to answer certain questions. These can be simple questions about professional or educational background or about whether the individual was present when an event occurred, or other general experience a person has related to a subject.

Good interview question sequencing, like a good news story, needs to be connected. Use transitions to cue your source that you are changing subjects or topics within a subject. This gives the interview a sense of continuity. These transitions can be casually conversational in nature, but they alert your source to a change in direction of the material being covered. Simple statements or phrases can do the job: "Now I want to talk to you about . . ." or "Now let's turn our attention to a related subject."

Often it is necessary to preface a question with background. For unusual subjects, very recent developments, which your source may or may not know about, or for explanation of your purpose, it is often helpful to your source to begin a question with an explanatory statement. In this example, a reporter interviews a criminologist and illustrates the point: "There was another murder this morning in the East Side Dutch Heights neighborhood. That is the third shooting death of a known drug dealer in a week. Do you think there is a vigilante-type killer stalking the streets?"

At the same time, with your more detailed questions prepared, you have to be able to probe into the source's answers. Thus, when writing questions, reporters need to write follow-up questions—or, at least, need to be prepared to ask them extemporaneously—to get the needed information. You can follow up and probe by asking to clarify information, by withholding response and waiting to force the source to continue the answer, or by responding with natural excitement that encourages further discussion.

Remember your ultimate audience for your story. What will readers and viewers want to know and hear? Can you persuade a source to explain a complicated subject in better terms for your audience? Mary Ellen Conway, health and medicine reporter for KTRK-TV, Channel 13, in Houston, said this is essential for her interviews. She routinely interviews doctors and scientists about complicated subjects. Yet she keeps her audience in mind: "If an interview gets too technical, I will stop it and ask the person I'm working with to think of simpler words" (Garrison, 1990).

There are problem areas in interview questioning. You should try to avoid *leading questions* and *loaded questions.* Leading questions strongly suggest answers to questions and many sources accept the suggestions. Loaded questions are even more dangerous because they often contain the reporter's opinion or point of view, suggest responses, and take an accusatory tone. Both types of questions should be avoided, of course. University of Miami journalism professor Alan Prince (1991), a former

Miami Herald editor, pointed to another source of loaded questions: "I think the 'guts' of a loaded question has less to do with these elements (dealing with the questioner's motive) than with an inherent difficulty or logic flaw in the question."

There are also *double-barreled questions.* These questions are really two questions built into one and often confuse your source. At best, your source might answer both, but most often the source answers only the second one.

The Final Questions to Ask

There are effective and ineffective ways to wrap up an interview. Perhaps the most effective manner is to give the source a chance to speak without a question. Veteran *Miami Herald* city desk reporter Kimberly Crockett (1991) revealed that this is essential to her interviewing style.

"I always ask, when an interview is about to end, 'Is there something you'd like to tell me that I failed to ask you about?' This will shed a new light on the information you are trying to get," she explained.

"You have to have your questions in mind, but you also have to be open minded enough to let the source speak," she said.

Arnold Markowitz (1991), a *Miami Herald* general assignment reporter and a newspaper reporter for nearly 30 years, also asks this closing question: "What's your schedule, in case I have to get back to you?"

ASKING TOUGH AND SENSITIVE QUESTIONS

There will be interviews that require you to ask tough or difficult questions. These can be tough because you feel awkward asking the questions or they can be tough because your source will not want to answer the questions. They may involve sensitive subjects.

These situations often occur when you must discuss sensitive or controversial matters with sources. But you must be willing and able to ask the tough questions, regardless of whether they are planned in advance or are asked on the spot. These questions can cause the most problems in an interview situation. Veteran journalist Hugh Sherwood (1972) wrote, "It should be obvious that, when you ask tough questions, you may run up against a stone wall. . . . Persistence can sometimes help greatly in coping with [refusal to answer]" (pp. 85–86). Sherwood also distinguished between tough questions and "dirty" questions; tough questions are necessary, but "dirty" questions have no purpose other than embarrassing a source.

Metzler (1989) called these questions "bombs." When you have to ask a threatening or sensitive question, you must be concerned about emotional reactions to the questions. What helps most, he explained, is the *trust* and *rapport* you have built with your source before asking the question. This is a big reason for holding the "bomb" questions for the latter stages of your interview.

LISTENING SKILLS

Biagi (1986) pinpointed listening as one of the most important skills a journalist can develop toward becoming a strong interviewer. "Every person wants an active listener, and the interviewer plays this role, as well as many others, during an interview. Listening well is your most important responsibility" (p. 86).

Good listening requires concentration. You must pay attention. You must focus on what is being said. You must forget other things on your mind, no matter how important they might be. As you listen, maintain as much eye contact with your source as possible.

Many reporters take notes during interviews, thus it is important to pause in note-taking from time to time to reestablish eye contact with your source. Let the person know you are paying attention. Tape recorders have reduced the note-taking pressure, of course, and this permits more focused attention and listening effort.

Most experienced reporters will tell beginners that listening is a tough discipline to learn because there is a great temptation to talk and get involved in the "conversation." But these experienced reporters have learned how not to fill silent moments, how not to interrupt, and how to provide nonverbal cues that they are paying attention.

TAKING NOTES DURING AN INTERVIEW

Another difficult interviewing skill to learn is how and when to take notes. Most reporters prefer the special pocket-size 4-inch by 8-inch spiral notebooks with wide lines (they also come with narrow lines) for taking notes during an interview. These can be found in most stationery stores or can be ordered. The notebooks easily fit into a purse or a jacket or pants pocket. They are hand-sized and work well for interviews conducted on the move or standing up. Not all interviews afford you the luxury of sitting in a chair or at a desk. Some reporters prefer the 8½-inch by 14-inch yellow legal pads for notetaking. Some reporters, when conducting interviews by telephone, will type their notes on their personal computers (PC) because they type faster than they can write. Beginners should try a variety of notebooks to see which is most comfortable to them.

What you write down is more important than the material on which you write, however. Taking complete, accurate notes requires using a form of shorthand. Most sources will speak much more quickly than you can write, so a short-cut system is needed to get the information down on paper. Formal shorthand courses, such as those offered in secretarial programs, are ideal.

But for most journalists, a variation will work as well. A common trick is to drop vowels when you write words. Another trick is to use abbreviations. As you become more experienced, you develop your own system that will be a combination of both methods.

When preparing for your interview, you can either type out your questions on a single page or handwrite them in advance in your notebook, one question to a page, leaving space to write down the answers from your source.

Note-taking practice helps. Beginners can work on their note-taking skills while in classes or by taking notes while watching speeches or press conferences on television. It is clear, though, that the more you work at this skill, the better you get. Speed and accuracy are essential to be a good note taker. They will improve with repetition. Practice is a no-lose situation in interviewing.

USING TAPE RECORDERS

An interview can be vital to your story, thus it is often wise to take a tape recorder with you. For electronic media reporters, this is an absolute necessity, but taping should not preempt paper-and-pencil note taking as a backup and as an fast "index" to your tape. For print reporters, tape recorders have become valuable in the past two decades. As you record the interview, you should continue to take notes as you would normally. Your notes will help you in finding quotations and other information on the tape during the writing process.

For all reporters, tape recordings assure greater accuracy in information gathering. The fact that there are many small and inexpensive recorders on the market today that require little or no technical expertise to operate makes the tape recorder a tool that reporters can seldom choose to ignore.

Tape recorders may also help you develop a level of trust with your source. If a source knows you are making the effort to tape, it may provide reassurance because of your concern for accuracy.

Perhaps the biggest problem with tape recorders is the growing dependence a reporter feels toward the recorder. There is a danger of taking fewer notes. And when a machine fails, it can be a big problem. In fact, some reporters use two recorders to guard against failure of one of the machines in their most important interviews.

Another problem with tape recorders is a potential to intimidate a source. Taping can cause a source to refuse to talk or be less candid when the tape is rolling. Always let your source know you are taping the interview. In some states, in fact, it is illegal to tape a conversation without notifying all individuals involved. In other states, at least one party must know about the taping to avoid violation of "wiretapping" and "bugging" laws. Always check your state's laws — a local state attorney general's office can help — for the most recent rulings and laws affecting tape recording conversations both in person and on the telephone.

Tape recordings can be very time consuming after the interview has ended. Listening to an interview requires a great amount of time, more than you might have on deadline. Tape transcription is perhaps the most time consuming of all, and it should not be done unless absolutely necessary. This underlines the value of written notes during a taped interview.

Experienced reporters will also remember to check their recorders for fresh batteries before beginning a session. You should keep a few new batteries nearby at all times to guard against such failures. Another tip is to keep spare blank tapes nearby for unexpected interview situations that develop. Longer length tapes will help you avoid those awkward moments when tapes run out. Always remember to label your tapes, too. List the source's name and the date of the interview. Unlabeled tapes can become lost or misplaced when mixed with other tapes. It is always wise to test your recorder prior to leaving for an interview.

TELEPHONE INTERVIEWING SKILLS

In-person interviews are almost always going to yield better information, but there are times when you cannot conduct your interview in person. You will have different interview experiences, depending on whether the interview is conducted in person or on the telephone. If you are like most reporters today, many of your interviews will be conducted by telephone.

Although the telephone saves time and money, you lose the familiarity of being there with the source. You lose detail from firsthand observation. You cannot watch facial expressions as your source responds. You cannot observe the environment or what the source is wearing. Your source has greater control of the situation with the simple ability to put you on "hold" or to hang up on you. Journalist Hugh Sherwood (1972) pointed out still other drawbacks to using the telephone. "There is a much greater danger that the interview will be superficial and touch only on the highlights," he wrote. "This is primarily because the telephone interview tends to be much shorter" (p. 99).

Sherwood offered a check list that may help you determine whether to interview in person or by telephone when you have a choice:

1. How many questions do you need to ask?
2. How long and how important is the article you plan to write?
3. How many other people do you plan to interview?
4. How complex is the information you wish to obtain?

Telephone interviewers should consider a few guidelines to make the interview go smoothly. Here's some time-tested advice:

1. Identify yourself at the very beginning of the telephone conversation. Be sure your source knows you are a reporter. Give your news organization's name.

2. Speak loudly and clearly. Do not talk too fast. Make sure you have a good, clear connection. If not, end the call and call back immediately.

3. If you are calling long distance, tell that to your source or the person answering the telephone for the source. This may bump your call into a "priority" status.

4. Explain the purpose of your call. Estimate how much time you will need from your source if it is more than 5 minutes.

5. Cut down "ice breaker" time to get to the point. This is conventional for business conversations by telephone in U.S. culture, so it will not be offensive in most circumstances. For business persons, it will be appreciated.

6. If you plan to tape the conversation, always inform your source.

7. As your interview proceeds, give verbal cues to let the source know you are paying attention.

8. If you plan to type your notes on a typewriter or computer while on the line, tell your source. Otherwise, select a place where you can write by hand comfortably. A telephone with a shoulder cradle or headset will free both hands for typing or writing.

9. Always ask for a call-back number—such as a home number—for later if you need it while preparing your story.

10. Repeat questions if needed. This helps your source understand what you want.

11. Ask your source to repeat answers if needed. This helps you to understand and to get it right. Also, ask for spellings on all important information such as names for technical or foreign terms. Ask sources to repeat numbers for accuracy, also. This is especially wise for getting statistics and telephone numbers.

12. Use the telephone interview to ask sensitive and tough questions. Some people will prefer to answer difficult questions with the artificial barrier of a telephone "protecting" them.

13. Use fax machines. This new reporting tool complements telephone interviewing. When a source mentions a document or report, ask if you can get a copy faxed to your office or a nearby public fax service such as a copy center or office supply store (always have a fax-receiving telephone number handy).

14. Be courteous and polite. Treat people the way you would like to be treated during a telephone conversation. Don't talk to someone else at the same time, for example. Don't do something else while you conduct the interview. Don't permit interruptions—for example, try not to use a telephone line with "call waiting" because many people view that as an annoyance and intrusive.

15. At the conclusion of your telephone interview, immediately go over your notes carefully to fill in gaps to be sure you have noted all relevant details.

QUOTATIONS AND SOUNDBITES/ACTUALITIES

A person's exact words make stories come to life. They add credibility to a story. Someone's actual words provide readers and audiences with an exciting dimension not available through a paraphrase or summary of what was said.

Rene J. Cappon (1982), a veteran Associated Press editor in New York, noted that exact words are vital to the process of reporting news: "News, to a remarkable degree, is what people say and how they say it—as actors in events, kibitzers, witnesses, informants, as movers and shakers and as the moved and shaken. The chatter is incessant. So are the news writer's efforts to distill quotes from it" (p. 70).

Soundbites and actualities are the electronic forms of direct quotations. Soundbites are the words of a source commenting on a subject for your story. This term is often used for television stories. Actualities are the radio form, which uses natural sound such as voices in a news story.

As a reporter, you have to have a good sense of when to quote and when not to quote. A few editors still believe direct quotations should never be used. This is extreme and somewhat old-fashioned, but they will argue a good writer can always restate something better than it was said in a direct quotation. Cappon (1982, p. 71) said direct quotations should be used in these circumstances:

1. To document and support third-person statements in the lead and elsewhere.
2. To set off controversial material, in which the wording can be the issue (such as legal situations).
3. To catch distinctions and nuances in important passages of speeches and to convey the flavor of the speaker's use of language.
4. To highlight exchanges and testimony in trials, hearings, meetings, and other newsworthy situations.

Using Direct Quotations

As helpful as quotations can be to a reporter, there are some basic rules about quotations that you should remember.

First, in much of your story writing, you will find that quotations help back up generalizations made about a person, place, or thing. Quotations give the story an element of specificity and of reality beyond the perspective of the reporter. It means you can let someone else speak in the story, using that person's exact words.

Many experienced reporters use quotations in dialogue to recreate situations to provide for the reader the effect of being there—getting to watch history occur, for example, through the exact words of the persons who were present.

There are some helpful guidelines in using quotations in your stories:

1. Make certain it is clear in the flow of your story just who is speaking. This is especially true if you change the person being quoted.

2. Vary verbs of attribution. At times, you should rely on the standard verb, "said," but there are more precise verbs. Print news writing employs the past-tense verb, "said," instead of the present tense verb, "says." Radio and television news attributions use the present tense "says." Remember that verbs and verb tenses have specific meanings when used, so take care in selecting just the right word.

3. Vary placement of attribution verbs. It will be necessary to place them at the beginning of a sentence on some occasions; avoid using the verbs only at the end of sentences.

4. Be careful in using long quotations or long segments of natural sound. If you must use a lengthy quotation from a person or text from a document, make certain you have introduced it to the reader or viewer to explain what you are doing and why.

5. Dialogue adds a great deal. Use it. But be clear about who is saying what. Break up long passages of dialogue with some description of action by the speakers.

6. Quote exact words and do not change the words in the quotation. Incorrect grammar will give the reader insight into the personality of the individual speaking.

Chicago Tribune writer John Camper was assigned to write a story about growing racial tension at Loyola University caused by offensive comments made by an award-winning philosophy professor during an ethics class. Camper went to the urban campus to talk to individuals involved. He interviewed the professor. He interviewed the student who had been shocked and scared by what the professor said to the class. He interviewed other witnesses to the classroom incident for their reaction. He questioned university officials, including the vice president in charge of academic affairs. He talked to officials from the U.S. Department of Education for background information such as minority faculty statistics from across the nation. He interviewed Black student leaders at Loyola for their reaction to the developing problem. The story wound up painting a picture of the situation at the school that developed in the time between the incident and publication of his story 3 months later. But this story would have never succeeded without interviews with the principals of the story. That's what made it work. *Here's how his story began:*

Unlike many college faculty members, who would rather be doing research than teaching students, Loyola University philosophy professor Al Gini still creates excitement in the classroom, even after 22 years on the job.

But Gini, who has won several Loyola teaching awards, made things a little too exciting one day, unintentionally sparking the same sort of racial unrest that has gripped many college campuses in recent years.

At other schools, racial fires have been ignited by overt racists: the student who told racially demeaning jokes on the University of Michigan radio station, for example, or the person who drew thick lips on a Beethoven poster at Stanford.

Gini, on the other hand, is an avowed liberal on racial matters. But by using a racially demeaning epithet in class, he brought so many resentments to the surface that black students and community leaders are demanding his resignation and using the incident to push their own agendas.

The controversy, now almost three months old, has forced people at Loyola to deal with difficult questions that have vexed their counterparts across the country:

- Does academic freedom include the freedom to offend minority groups?
- How can a university respect the sensitivities of students and protect freedom of speech at the same time?
- Can people talk openly about racial issues without sparking polarizing controversies?
- Are minority groups overreacting to some racial incidents, or exploiting them to advance campus agendas?
- Are "liberals" as enlightened on racial matters as they think they are?

It all began Jan. 22, as Gini was telling his business ethics class that people often do unethical things out of habit. For instance, he said, they might use racist language unthinkingly.

Then, to provide a more vivid example, he turned to the lone black student in the class and said, "We have a nigger student in our class."

Gini, who had used that technique in previous classes, made it clear that this kind of language was unacceptable. But the student, Sandra Westmoreland, was mortified.

"I couldn't move," said Westmoreland, a 20-year-old sophomore from the West Side. "I wanted to run out but was afraid I didn't have the strength to make it to the door." (Camper, 1990, p. 2)

The Debate Over Using Exact Words

There are two schools of thought about use of exact words in quotations (Leslie, 1986; McManus, 1990). For broadcast journalists using taped natural sound, the problem seldom comes up but creative tape editing can change an electronic "quotation." For print journalists, the issue often arises: Should you change quotations to provide intended meaning or to improve grammar? Some editors are absolutists about quotations and say this should not be done. Others are more flexible and practical, permitting quotations to be changed within specific limits.

In fact, as you gain more experience, you will come across some media-savvy sources who will expect reporters to "clean up" the source's words by taking out extraneous words and occasional "uhs" and "ahs" (Leslie, 1986; McManus, 1990). Broadcast journalists can do this also, to a limited extent, with good editing. This problem is not too serious for radio editing, but it may be for television. When it is done for television news stories, you must be aware of problems such as "jump cuts." When a tape editor edits out a section of a soundbite for television, the source's face or head and shoulders might suddenly jump from one position to another if the two pieces are butted together without an intervening shot, such as a quick cut to the reporter or another scene.

Regardless of the medium, exact words are *exact* words. This is an absolute. You should not change the words in an effort to "clean them up" or get to the "real meaning."

This is part of the trust between reporter and reader, reporter and audience. The symbols for direct quotation in print on or a television screen— " " —mean these are a person's *exact* words.

There are some journalists who do not subscribe to such an absolutist view when it comes to direct quotations, however. Some reporters, in a fit of practicality, argue that minor changes are acceptable as long as the meaning is not changed. According to Associated Press editor Rene Cappon, "The furthest you can go is to fix minor grammatical errors and omit pure padding or meaningless repetition" (p. 71).

In the end, you will have to decide if you will clean up a direct quotation. But the safest approach is to not change it at all or use a paraphrase without quotation marks.

Using Soundbites and Actualities

The broadcast news forms of direct quotations are the soundbite and actuality. Just as print reporters use direct quotations to back up generalizations made about a situation with specific comments from an authoritative source, broadcast journalists use soundbites and actualities in the same fashion.

Soundbites and actualities provide the natural sound and pictures of the individuals making the news. They are often used to illuminate main points made in stories. The spoken word of authoritative sources, the experts in a given subject, adds a strong, but necessary, dimension to your story.

"Short bites prove the story you are showing," said NBC correspondent Bob Dotson (1988). However, Dotson advised beginning broadcast journalists: "Don't use soundbites as substitutes for more effective story telling."

Soundbites and actualities are extraordinarily important to the success of a broadcast news story. You must write to make these key parts of the story fit smoothly with the rest of the story. This involves, as broadcasting professor Robert Papper (1987) said, framing the actuality or soundbite in the script. Just as the print reporter will set up a quotation with a generalization before the quotation, this is necessary in a script. Weak introductions can hurt the story, in fact.

All set-ups and exits from soundbites and actualities need to provide useful information to the listener. Flat set-ups such as "Here's the union chief's comments:" will hurt the story. A smooth flow in and out of the soundbite does this effectively, telling viewers before the soundbite background about the organization's position and also telling viewers there is opposition to the position as the writer exits from it into another segment of the story.

Soundbites and actualities should not run very long as a rule. Certain exceptions will occur, of course, but most soundbites and actualities are less than 15 seconds—even as short as a sentence of only a very few words. When a longer exchange occurs, such as testimony in court or questioning at a hearing, you might consider using longer soundbites and actualities. But, remember, these can kill a story if they run too long. If you have just 1½ or 2 minutes for a story, a long soundbite or actuality will reduce what you might be able to say.

The quality of sound will also become a factor in your decision whether or not to use it. Severe background noise can ruin an actuality or soundbite. If it is poor quality, you might choose not to use it. Yet, highly newsworthy content can often overrule the usual inclination not to use bad sound or pictures/sound.

SOURCE ATTRIBUTION

In the earlier discussion in this chapter about the *Boston Globe*'s news article on the alleged sexual assault at the Kennedy compound in Florida, you read that some stories can have source attribution problems. Put simply, some sources just do not want to be identified. In the story by *Globe* reporters Tom Coakley and John Aloysius Farrell, there were sources who wanted to talk to reporters but they just did not want to be named. In their story at the end of this chapter, there are numerous paragraphs where sources interviewed are not identified. In this example, the story is filled with paragraphs with unnamed attribution or no attribution at all, using the words "source" and "sources" throughout.

There are a variety of ways to identify sources in a news story. Many are described in chapter 2. The most preferred manner is on the record with full identification. Normally, this means full name, address, and age. But more and more, yielding to privacy concerns, many news organizations are dropping precise address identifications or using informal names (Terrell, 1990).

The way you identify your source will depend on the individual. Different types of persons will require different identifications, depending on how and why the person is named in the story. For victims and suspects in police stories, there is special consideration. Many editors and producers believe victims deserve privacy, especially those involved in sexual assault cases. Most other crime victims are not fully identified. About persons suspected of committing a crime, reporters must be careful of incorrect information. Police records are not always correct because the information often comes from the suspect.

The main point is to reduce the chance of misidentification. There are other ways to identify people than just using name, address, and age. For example, affiliation, school, or place of employment is a good way to differentiate among John Smiths. A thoughtful reporter can clearly identify an individual as a source in the story without invading privacy.

• • •

HOW PROFESSIONALS WRITE IT

SOURCE: *Atlanta Constitution*, p. B1
AUTHOR: Mike Christensen, staff writer
DATE: Wednesday, August 8, 1990
HEADLINE: Waxing nostalgic: Crayola retires a colorful octet

* * *

EASTON, Pa. — Karen Latinik and two college friends registered their protest at the National Committee to Save Lemon Yellow.

"Lemon yellow is a classic. You can make bright suns and yellow flowers," said Ms. Latinik of Alexandria, Va.

She was among about a dozen fans of maize, raw umber, lemon yellow, blue gray, violet blue, green blue, orange red and orange yellow who came to protest the retirement of the colors in favor of eight new, brighter ones. Five-foot replicas of the old colors were enshrined Tuesday in a "Crayola Hall of Fame" in the factory's visitors center.

"Binney & Smith, America takes umbrage," said one protest sign. "Indians call it maize, we call it gone," said another.

"This is the original box of 64," said out-of-work disc jockey Robert Paganini, holding up a green-and-yellow flip-top Crayola box.

"They've arbitrarily taken eight of them out of there," he complained.

But there was nothing arbitrary about the decision by Binney & Smith, which has been making Crayolas in the Lehigh Valley since 1903. Children are wearing brighter colors, and they want to color with them.

Fans of the new colors outnumbered protesters at the ceremony.

The mayor brought a proclamation, and a congressman sent a speech. Miss Pennsylvania was there with her feathery puppet, Oscar, and the Pen Argyl High School Green Knights marched solemnly in bearing flags, trumpets and sabers.

There were balloons, a folk singer, cake and juice, a children's fashion show by Bloomingdale's and, of course, crayons. Lots of crayons.

The company, now owned by Hallmark Cards, expanded its line from 48 to 64 colors in 1958 and for the first time offered eight fluorescent shades in a separate box in 1972.

"The kids love these colors. I see it when the kids come through here every day," said Tom Mullins, vice president and general manager for crayons. "They're all wearing bright colors nowadays."

Carol Gies, public relations director for Bloomingdale's, didn't have to look far to match the colors Crayola adopted. The clothes were already in production.

Tuesday, her eight young models showed them off on an improvised runway in the visitors center, while tour groups of youngsters who were sprawled about the floor gaped and nudged each other.

Even in the era of new Coke and Coca Cola classic, executives at Crayola were flabbergasted by the attention their decision, announced earlier this summer, generated.

"We didn't expect this kind of reaction," Mr. Mullins said.

The promotions department came up with the idea for a hall of fame. Ms. Gies who had read about the changes, got in touch to make a deal — Bloomingdale's will feature the new colors in its back-to-school fashions this month.

"Then we got the idea — it's the 90s, so we've got to recycle," she said. So each store will have a crayon collection bin. When all of the bits and pieces of color are melted down, they will make the most-used hue — basic black.

Marla Wynne, Miss Pennsylvania, chose a fuchsia dress for the occasion, although she said it was closer to wild strawberry.

She grew up in Easton, using crayons in elementary school and Crayola markers for posters as a high school cheerleader.

It was Miss Wynne, aided by several executives, who drew the royal-blue curtain to reveal the row of retired Crayola colors, each encased in plastic on a wooden pedestal. Wall plaques describe the history of each.

Maize, for instance, was often used for autumn leaves and is one of the University of Michigan's colors. Orange red was popular for tabby cats, green blue was handy for peacock feathers and blue gray was a favorite for the uniforms of Confederate soldiers.

Basic red remains the most popular color and was the uniform for "Tip" the giant crayon, who, aside from smiling and waving to the children, was designated to cut the multilayer retirement cake. Tip managed to hack off one slice onto a paper plate, then had to leave it behind — his flannel tongue was no good for tasting.

Meanwhile, the serious work had begun. Seated on red stools, their elbows on a long table, a row of youngsters colored paper masks with the new crayons. They picked out the sticks with some deliberation.

"My dad was an artist," said 7-year-old Jeannine Perna of Egypt, Pa., intently coloring a rainbow between two fleecy clouds.

"He wasn't really an artist," her 10-year-old brother Brian corrected. "He just went to art school." His mask had brown cheeks and a wild-strawberry nose. Jeannine said she liked the new colors "a little bit," but to Brian they made little difference.

He will miss blue gray, though. It was good for "airplanes and ships and stuff like that."

Reprinted with permission of the *Atlanta Constitution*.

• • •

SOURCE: *Muncie, Ind., Star,* p. A10
REPORTER: Randy Rendfeld
DATE: Sunday, April 2, 1989
HEADLINE: A time for two cities: Sometimes you're early; sometimes you're late

* * *

UNION CITY, Ind. — Union City offers jet lag without the muss and fuss of long-distance travel.

That's how John Ford, mayor of Union City, Ind., describes it. He's referring to the peculiar time change that annually splits Union City into what residents call "slow and fast time." That time change took effect at 2 A.M. this morning.

Citizens on "fast time," or Daylight Saving Time, live east of State Line Road in Union City, Ohio. However, most of Indiana remains on Eastern Standard Time year-round.

"Most people have adjusted to it, but there's still confusion," said Scott Stahl, mayor of Union City, Ohio.

Both mayors seem to enjoy the attention the time split brings to their cities, which total about 6,000 in population. Stahl says the time split has been reported by CNN and media as far away as Cleveland.

"It's a nuisance until you get used to it," said Leroy Stentzil, a native of the Buckeye State. He has lived in Union City, Ind., since 1930. But he prefers to stay in synch with Ohio time.

Stentzil said a few years ago he had clocks in his house labelled "Indiana Time" and "Ohio Time."

"I don't do that anymore," he said. "But it does cause confusion. I've been late lots of times. Now if I'm invited to something in Indiana and I don't think about it, I'm there an hour early. I keep reading material in my side pocket all the time."

Most Union City residents will experience the anxiety of being an hour late for an event during the coming months, Ford said. "But they'll make up for it by being early for something else."

"When we're on fast time, we don't gossip," joked Betsy Jefferis, co-owner of J&J Vending Inc., on the Indiana side of Union City.

Her company's service department wants to be on fast time, she said, but the rest of the company stays on Indiana time. She says it just takes a few mental notes to yourself to remember which times are which.

Jefferis said the town's big August festival, Farmer Merchant Days set for Aug. 2–5, would do well to capitalize on the peculiar split between the towns.

On that premise, Ford suggested this attention-getting promotion: "You could start a marathon race in Ohio. Start them at 2 o'clock, run them about 3 miles, and have them arrive before they started."

Stahl explained how Union City stores would deal with slow and fast time:

"In some instances there are stores that stay on slow time no matter what. The Ohio stores go on fast time. There are some stores that might split it down the middle. It just gets confusing.

"If they're normally open till 5 o'clock fast time, that would be 4 o'clock slow time. So maybe they'll move it a half hour and close at 5:30. That way it would be 4:30 slow time."

Ford said most of the larger industries in Union City, Ind., run on fast time despite their location. This includes Union City Body Co., which produces step vans, and Sheller-Globe Corp., which manufacturers auto trim.

"Most of the businesses in cities such as Detroit and New York expect them to be following those hours," Ford said.

However, Union City, Ind., schools and government stay on slow time.

In some cases, this creates a situation where parents are leaving for work while their children are just starting to prepare for school. Instead of viewing that as an interesting variation of the latchkey kids phenomenon, Ford points out families have more time to spend together at day's end.

"Part of the people in Indiana go on the Ohio time, just like I do. And part of them don't," Stentzil said. "I used to laughingly say, 'I don't care if they put ABC's on the clock. I'll get along.' But I'm an old man now, and it just isn't so easy to adjust.

"Back in the old days we used to laugh and say, 'Well, the businessmen who get out early and play golf, they were the ones who changed it.' "

But Stentzil said if Indiana legislators lived in Union City, they'd think again about the wisdom of exempting Indiana from Daylight Saving Time.

Exemptions from Daylight Saving Time are Arizona, Hawaii, Puerto Rico, the Virgin Islands, American Samoa and parts of Indiana, according to *The World Almanac*. DST starts the first Sunday in April and ends the last Sunday in October.

"It puts us on the map, so to speak," Stahl said of the time split. "People know you, or at least they've heard of you. They say, 'Isn't that the town on the border?' "

[NOTE: This story was distributed nationally by The Associated Press.]

• • •

SOURCE: *Boston Globe,* p. 7
DATE: Wednesday, April 10, 1991
AUTHOR: Tom Coakley and John Aloysius Farrell, staff writers
HEADLINE: Palm Beach police say it's likely a crime occurred at Kennedy villa

* * *

PALM BEACH, Fla. — Police Chief Joseph L. Terlizzese said yesterday that he has "reasonable suspicion" that a crime occurred at the Kennedy villa here on the night a 29-year-old Florida woman says she was raped.

In saying that he was virtually sure a crime had been committed that night, Terlizzese gave his first public evaluation of the strength of his department's case against William Kennedy Smith — endorsing the alleged victim's story in a week in which Kennedy loyalists have challenged her version of events and suggested she concocted a tale of rape to cover up the theft of a valuable vase.

But Terlizzese said his detectives have not yet reached the legal standard of "probable cause" needed to make an arrest.

"If I did," he said, "I'd make the arrest."

Terlizzese said he hoped the department did not have to wait for the conclusion of genetic testing of forensic samples, including hair and blood. That could take two months. "I don't know if I need it; I hope not," he said.

Also yesterday, sources confirmed that the alleged victim had told authorities that she took an urn from the Kennedy mansion the night of the alleged rape so that she could prove that she had been there—and thus support her charge.

A question of timing

Meanwhile, as detectives, lawyers and newspaper reporters try to construct a logical chronology of what took place in the early morning of March 30, it has become clear that the alleged victim called the authorities much earlier than had previously been reported.

The Palm Beach County Sheriff's office said yesterday that the victim of the alleged rape arrived at the sheriff's department before noon that Saturday. Another source said she may have contacted the authorities as early as midmorning.

That would cut in half the 10-hour span that Palm Beach police previously said had passed between the time of the alleged assault — around 4 A.M. — and the time the city police were alerted to the allegation, at around 2 P.M.

Smith, 30, a fourth-year medical student at Georgetown University, has been named as the suspect in the case, and has provided hair and blood samples to the police.

Smith's uncle, Sen. Edward M. Kennedy, and Smith's cousin, Patrick Kennedy, the senator's son, have been interviewed by the police as possible witnesses but are not, at this time, considered suspects.

From interviews with sources close to the case, a review of public records and published reports that have been confirmed by knowledgeable public officials, it is possible to construct the following scenario:

The woman in question and Smith are believed to have met at Au Bar, a trendy pub along Royal Poinciana Way, where they arrived with separate groups of friends or relatives.

Smith is said to have gone to Au Bar with the two Kennedys, while witnesses say the alleged victim was part of a group that included a friend named Anne Mercer, Mercer's boyfriend and her father, released in 1989 from federal prison.

The Mercers have told friends that they left Au Bar sometime before Sen. and Patrick Kennedy left with Michele Cassone, a 27-year-old waitress, in a white convertible driven by Patrick Kennedy.

Sometime around 3 A.M., the alleged victim drove Smith to the Kennedy oceanfront mansion, some two miles away, in her small foreign car. On the beach below the villa, Smith took off his clothes to go swimming; the woman did not.

A confusing episode

By one source's account, the alleged victim has told police she was grabbed by the ankle as she tried to return to the mansion and then was raped by Smith, suffering bruises on her ankle and pain in her ribs.

The police report says that the extent of her injuries are "minor." Smith has denied that "any offense" took place.

Paul Donovan, a spokesman for Sen. Kennedy, declined to say if the senator witnessed the couple together at the house or on the beach that night.

Cassone, who socialized until almost dawn with Patrick Kennedy, said she never saw the alleged victim, though she did say she saw another woman going skinny-dipping in the ocean, and an unidentified man talking with a woman in a small foreign car in the compound parking lot shortly before 5 A.M.

In one of the night's most confusing sequences of events, the alleged victim is next known to have phoned the home of Anne Mercer, in nearby West Palm Beach, and to have left after Mercer and her boyfriend arrived to escort her from the Kennedy villa, at around 4:30 A.M. to 5 A.M.

The stolen urn

At about this time, the woman is said to have taken an urn—part of a matched set of china—worth about $1,100, a notepad and some sort of picture collection.

The woman has told police, who acknowledge that they have recovered the urn, that she took the items to prove she was at the Kennedy household. Kennedy defenders suggest the opposite: that the rape allegation was concocted to a cover up a theft.

There are persistent reports that the woman left the compound at least once and then returned before finally leaving for good. Anne Mercer's sister lives within three blocks of the Kennedy home, but her sister's husband, Donald Leas, said that "nobody came here" that morning.

Apparently, the woman first contacted law enforcement officials five to seven hours later from an address in Palm Beach County. She was interviewed at the sheriff's department, where officers determined that the alleged assault took place within the Palm Beach city limits, and turned the case over to the Palm Beach police, who took her statement, drove her to Humana Hospital and stopped by the Mercer house to conduct further interviews.

Constructing a chronology of the night's events is difficult, since members of the Kennedy and Mercer parties have refused to discuss the case in detail, and the police decline to release an official version.

Christopher Boyd, a *Globe* correspondent, contributed to this report.

Reprinted with permission of the *Boston Globe*.

• • •

7 | Interviewing For Television And Radio

Tulsa television news reporter Scott Gordon's series of feature stories on the Oklahoma Panhandle region told viewers about the isolation of the rugged people who live in the western-most portion of the state. His stories focused on the *people* there. His series of news packages—a pre-produced news segment complete with introduction by an anchor, soundbites, and close—succeeded on the strength of his *interviews* with many of these residents. Gordon, who works for KTUL-TV, Channel 8, in Tulsa, went to the Panhandle to interview the most interesting and typical residents of the area he could find. In Guymon, a tiny Oklahoma town where there are more animals than people, Gordon tells viewers that residents can drive for miles without seeing someone else. In Guymon, he interviewed the editor of the town's newspaper. Gordon talked to an 82-year-old cowboy who called himself a loner. Other residents became a part of the series as he talked to as many people as he could to get the spirit of the region. The script of Gordon's first installment of this series, which ran a long 2:37, is reprinted at the end of this chapter.

When Miami reporter Bonnie Anderson was in Saudi Arabia to cover the troop buildup during the Persian Gulf crisis, she naturally focused much of her coverage on activities of the troops from south Florida. Her station, WTVJ-TV, the NBC affiliate in south Florida, assigned her to provide the local dimension to that major international story. Day after day, Anderson gathered information and conducted interviews for stories that she wrote when she returned to Miami. She put much of her attention on south Florida National Guard units deployed in Saudi Arabia to defend the region against Iraq's threat, at that time, against Saudi Arabia and Israel. Anderson's work typified the work of countless reporters and photographers assigned to cover troop movements and exercises at that point in the crisis.

Newsmakers often find themselves literally surrounded by radio and television journalists (photo by the *Miami Herald* staff).

Anderson conducted dozens of interviews. One of her stories focused on a group of Vietnam war veterans still serving in the reserves. Her story depended on interviews with these soldiers to express in their words how they felt to be back in a foreign land, fighting a war to stop aggression against a peaceful nation.

In Anderson's script, reprinted at the end of this chapter, you see how she artfully wove the words of these unusual soldiers into a story about patriotism and service to their country. Anderson did not rely on only one or two veterans, but she used seven different sources in the 4:16 package. She let the soldiers tell their own story in their own words. Nearly half of the package is sound on tape (SOT) of the soldiers speaking. She merged their words with pictures to show the soldiers on duty, relaxing, and reflecting on their commitment to be there. Her story used a wide variety of sources for a compelling sense of what is happening with this unit's most experienced soldiers (Anderson, 1991).

Personal, on-air interviews like these are the heart of many television and radio news stories. These stories are so short, however, that rarely can much of an interview be used in a 90- to 100-second package. But good interviews are as critical to television features as are pictures. The best television and radio reporters know how to find and interview the right people for their stories, just as Scott Gordon and Bonnie Anderson did in their stories.

In addition to feature stories, most other broadcast news is interview dependent. The interview is the most basic of broadcast news reporting skills (Yoakam & Cremer, 1989). Spot news stories such as accidents, shootings, trials, protest marches, and speeches require strong interviewing skills. Television and radio news offer the immediacy that other news media cannot provide. Audiences expect broadcast news to place them at the scene of the spot news event (Finn, 1991). There are occasions, of course, when reporters cannot get to the scene as an event occurs. Interviews help to "reconstruct" the event through eyewitnesses. Interviews get story participants to speak pointedly on the issues. Interviews provide balanced perspective on these issues as well (Goedkoop, 1988). "It is quite common for a news reporter to arrive at the scene of a story and try to interview eyewitnesses or people involved in the incident," said Cal Downs, Paul Smeyak, and Ernest Martin (1980, p. 299).

ABC news correspondent and anchor Sam Donaldson (1987) believed that interviews, especially on political subjects, are critical to our society today. Because so many people depend on television for their political information in the "television age," Donaldson said, "a reporter's job in a campaign is to challenge the candidate to explain and defend his views and to answer charges leveled against him by his opponent" (p. 217).

There are times, research studies about television news have shown, when some interviews are assigned and broadcast for their visual or aural value, rather than their strict news value. "Broadcast interviews have a production value whether or not they have a news value," according to Downs, Smeyak, and Martin (1980, p. 299). "A 30-minute television newscast would

```
SLUG                    SHOW     WRITER    DATE                          TIMING  LC
BAKER SCRIPT/BONNIE              BANDERSO  FRI APR 12 04:47 1991 READY  1:44    60
```

THIS IS BONNIE ANDERSON SCRIPT ON BAKER VISIT TO DAMASCUS - FOR WTVJ AND OTHER
O & O'S.

SUPER: BONNIE ANDERSON REPORTING - DAMASCUS

(SHOW BAKER AND PRESIDENT ASSAD)

SECRETARY OF STATE JAMES BAKER'S EFFORTS TO WIN ARAB SUPPORT FOR A REGIONAL
PEACE CONFERENCE GAINED MOMENTUM TODAY AS SYRIA JOINED A GROWING LIST OF
COUNTRIES WILLING TO SIT AT A TABLE WITH ISRAEL.

(SOT: SYRIAN FOREIGN MINISTER FAROUK A'SHARAA, 5:44)

"THE ULTMATE OBJECTIVE IS TO REACH A COMPREHENSIVE AND JUST SETTLEMENT OF
ARAB-ISRAELI CONFLICT AND THE PALESTINIAN QUESTION."

(SHOW PRESSER)

BUT BAKER WARNED THE FACE-TO-FACE DISCUSSIONS WOULD BE BUT A PRELIMINARY STEP
TOWARD STEP - ONE HE HOPES WILL LEAD TO DIRECT, ONE-ON-ONE NEGOTIATIONS BETWEEN
ISRAEL AND ARAB NATIONS.

(SOT BAKER   6:15)

"ANY CONFERENCE THAT MIGHT BE CONVENED WOULDNOT BE FOR THE PURPOSE OF IMPOSING
A SOLUTION, TAKING VOTES AND THAT SORT OF THING."

BUT BAKER AND SYRIAN FOREIGN MINISTER FAROUK A'SHARAA AGREED THE PROCESS SHOULD
BE TIED TO ISRAELI COMPLIANCE WITH UNITED NATIONS' RESOLUTIONS THAT CALL FOR
THE JEWISH STATE TO TRADE OCCUPIED TERRITORY FOR PEACE.

(SHOW GOLAN)

DESPITE THE OPTIMISM, BAKER AND A'SHARAA WARNED SEVERAL ISSUES REMAIN
UNRESOLVED... SYRIA'S DEMAND THAT ISRAEL RETURN THE GOLAN HEIGHTS CAPTURED
DURING THE 1967 6-DAY WAR... AND WHETHER THE PLO WILL BE REPRESENTED AT THE
CONFERENCE, WHICH ISRAEL OPPOSES.

(BONNIE ANDERSON STANDUP BRIDGE)

SENIOR STATE DEPARTMENT OFFICIALS SAY WHAT IS DIFFERENT ABOUT THIS LATEST ROUND
OF SHUTTLE DIPLOMACY IS THAT ALL SIDES APPEAR TO GENUINELY WANT THE PEACE
PROCESS TO CONTINUE.

(SHOW BAKER AND ASSAD OR A'SHARAA LEAVING)

BUT THEY ADMIT IT'S ALONG ROAD TO A SETTLEMENT ACCEPTABLE TO ALL - AND THAT AT
ANY POINT, THE SMALLEST DISAGREEMENT COULD THROW THE PROCESS OFF COURSE.

IN DAMASCUS,
BONNIE ANDERSON,
CHANNEL 4 NEWS.
CHANNEL 5 NEWS.
NEWS 4 NEW YORK
NBC NEWS

HER THE PLO WILL BE REPRESENTED AT THE CONFERENCE, WHICH
OPPOSES...

Original scripts (see also pp. 190–191) written and filed by WTVJ-TV reporter Bonnie
Anderson from the Middle East (courtesy of Bonnie Anderson).

```
   nolan     Fri Jan 18 14:31   page    1

Page   Slug               Show    Date    Anchor    APVLS   Status  TOTAL   Writer
3-07P  IRAQ/CENSORSHIP    530P    01/18/91                  READY   0:40 anderson
Written                Changed      By       TAPE ##     TIMECODE   Copy  SOT's
Fri Jan 18 12:55 1991  Jan 18 14:30 nolan                           0:40   1:19
```

===

                                          {Live: Saddam Hussein has remained in
                                          power over the years largely due to his
                                          ruthlessness and the fact he skillfully
                                          manipulates public opinion within Iraq
                                          with misinformation and out-and-out
                                          censorship. The people there only know
                                          what they're told... and they believe
                                          it.
                                          He uses the same tactics with foreign
                                          reporters, hoping to fool the world,
                                          but with less success... in part,
                                          because we have other sources for
                                          information.
                                          --}
#s/Bonnie Anderson reporting
                                          The day after the American attack, the
                                          only pictures the world saw from Iraq
show saddam visiting   were of a jovial, unconcerned leader...
                                          images aimed at calming his people
people in the streets   while allowing him to simultaneously
                                          thumb his nose at Washington.

                                          While the Pentagon reported only a
                                          handful of coalition planes downed by
                                          the Iraqis, Saddam Hussein announced
                                          his heroic forces shot down more than
                                          70...

                                          Misinformation foreign reporters there
                                          are often unable to clear up.

today show stuff   "This is Tom Aspell from NBC News in
2:16:48 (:10)   Baghdad. I'm filing this report under
                                          conditions of censorship. There is a
                                          government official standing beside
                                          me."

                                          While Americans are unaccustomed to
                                          this sort of manipulation, it has been
                                          standard procedure in Iraq for nearly a
                                          decade.

                                          This is an excerpt of a report I did
                                          from Baghdad six years ago at the
                                          height of the Iran-Iraq war:

#s/March 1985   An early morning explosion in Baghdad.
#s/Baghdad   A blast so strong it shook buildings
:36 on file tape   miles away, broke windows and woke up
                                          residents throughout the city. Foreign
                                          military experts immediately said it
                                          was an Iranian missile. Iraqi officials
                                          at first said nothing, then conceded it
                                          might have been a small car bomb.
```
```

nolan,   Fri Jan 18 14:31   page   2

```
                              {nat sound}

                              The city's attention was quickly
                              shifted to military celebrations
                              honoring the Iraqi forces' battlefront
                              victory over Iranian troops. Iraqi
                              civilians and journalists from other
                              countries are rarely shown anything
                              else.

#S/BONNIE ANDERSON             Foreign journalists are forbidden to go
#S/BAGHDAD-1985                anywhere without a government escort,
                              who decides what can and cannot be
                              photographed. And as a backup measure,
                              Iraqi censors thoroughly screen all
                              television stories before transmitting
                              them by satellite.

                              Iraqi officials want the world and
                              their citizens here to only see
                              positive Iraqi actions. Day after day,
                              television newscasts and newspapers
                              highlight successful Iraqi military
                              missions, rarely if ever mentioning
                              Iranian attacks. These stories
                              emphasize that all Iraqi jet fighters
                              and helicopter gunships always return
                              safely to base.

                              {------------------------------------------
                              Live out: As a matter of fact, at no
                              time during the Iran-Iraq war did
                              Baghdad admit they lost any aircraft at
                              all.
                              Back to you.}

                                 {HOW DID YOU GET THAT REPORT ABOUT
                              CENSORSHIP OUT OF THERE??}
```

be awfully dull if there were no visuals other than the news announcer
reading the news."

BROADCAST INTERVIEWING IS DIFFERENT

Broadcast journalists have a different sort of job to do. There is a
"performance" element in television and radio interviewing. Print journalists seldom consider this factor when they plan and conduct interviews.
Interviewing experts Charles Stewart and William Cash (1985) called this
the "showtime" dimension to interviewing.

Journalism professors George Killenberg and Rob Anderson (1989)
noted:

> When the red light of the camera appears, they [reporters] are on stage, and
> their "performance" may be watched by an audience that numbers in the
> millions—an audience, too, that undoubtedly includes the boss. Every
> blunder, stammer and blemish is noticeable. If the broadcast is live, there are
> no retakes or opportunity to edit. (p. 182)

The performance factor is not just limited to broadcast journalists. Sources will perform, too. They will play to the microphones and cameras. Some will even experience a remarkable change of personality when they realize the tape is "rolling." Attendant with this are the nervousness, timidity, and anxiety of appearing on radio and television—that is, being aware of the large audiences who hear what is said and see who is saying it. Beginning radio and television reporters go through it. Most sources experience it.

The pressure to perform with perfection in a short period of time is another reason broadcast interviewing is vastly different from print interviewing. An audience will be hearing or seeing the interview, or portions of the interview, thus concern for its presentation as well as its content becomes important.

There is still another important difference. *You,* the reporter, play a much more involved role in the interviewing process for radio and television. You become part of the news story in the electronic news media. Viewers see you. Listeners hear you. This does not happen in print interviewing. Audiences hear and see you as a participant in a broadcast news interview in a way they rarely witness for their print news media. This means your appearance and behavior become considerations. It means your personality takes on a magnified role in the process, too.

The time element is another consideration. Print interviewers have much less concern for the length of an interview. Although this is true to a limited degree for broadcast journalists in terms of background interviewing, an on-air interview frequently has severe restrictions regardless of whether it is live or taped. Long-time Chicago radio interviewer and author Studs Turkel (1974) once wrote that the hardware of electronic newsgathering has an impact on interviewing. Turkel, in his classic book, *Working,* said,

> The camera, the tape recorder [are] misused, well-used. . . . [A recorder] can be, tiny and well-concealed, a means of blackmail, an instrument of the police state or, as is most often the case, a transmitter of the banal. Yet, a tape recorder, with microphone in hand, on the table or on the arm of the chair or on the grass, can transform both the visitor and the host. On one occasion, during the play-back, my companion murmured in wonder, "I never realized I felt that way." (p. xxiii)

People simply seem to be themselves more often when there is no camera facing them or a microphone a few inches away. Metzler (1989), who wrote *Creative Interviewing,* offered "Freed of the need to perform in front of a camera, people are more likely to be themselves. Skilled, sensitive broadcast interviewers, however, can reach that level of candor despite the camera" (pp. 144–145). Metzler likened broadcast interviewing to "living room conversation" whereas print interviewing is more comparable to "kitchen-family room–bedroom discussion."

There are technological factors as well. Electronic news gathering (ENG) depends on tape and recording equipment. Television news, which has used

ENG equipment for over a decade, and radio news are especially vulnerable to equipment failure. Batteries, recording heads, tape cartridges, lighting, microphone cables and connectors, extraneous sound, and other problems can interfere with the audio and video quality of an interview. If ENG equipment fails, you start over. This is one reason stations spend so much money on equipment maintenance. Rarely will an interview be broadcast with "production" flaws. Most producers will demand second interviews. You never hear about a newspaper's city editor sending a reporter back to retake an interview because of hard-to-read notes.

Considerable effort goes into broadcast interviewing. Whereas a print or radio reporter can get a quick interview completed in a few seconds on the telephone if necessary, this is rarely acceptable for television news stories. Television reporters, even if they need just a short soundbite for a story, must pack up the equipment, drive to the location of the source, set up the equipment, conduct the interview, take down the equipment, and drive to another interview or back to the station. It is time consuming and people intense. Some small stations in small markets use one-person crews in the field for interviews. It is possible, of course, but not usually done. Instead, most television stations use two-person crews with a photographer and reporter-field producer. Some stations use three-person crews for an interview if an engineer is needed (for a live remote interview, for instance) or if a separate field producer is involved. But this seems to be changing as more and more stations use two-person crews with the photographer assuming engineering duties. Networks usually work with four-person crews including a reporter who conducts the interview, a field producer, a photographer, and a sound person.

Naturally, there are many skills required in broadcast interviewing that are similar to other news media interviewing. From reading the preceding chapter, you know about many of them. This chapter focuses on techniques unique to broadcast interviewing.

INTERVIEWING SOURCES FOR RADIO NEWS

Without the need for video, radio interviewing is a little more flexible than television interviewing. The major difference is that it does not have to be done in person. Of course, television reporters are not always at the location of an interview either, but someone must be there to operate the equipment. For radio, there is no need. Radio journalists depend on extensive telephone interviewing in small one- or two-person operations. Increased quality of telephone equipment has meant that radio journalists can do their work by telephone for fast actualities for a story.

Radio interviews are almost always taped. Some are live. But as you have already read in the previous chapter, taping raises legal concerns. You must be aware of the laws in your state. It is always wise to tell your source that the interview will be taped. In fact, to eliminate any doubt that you asked

Some news sources seeking to reach the public with their message, such as U.S. Rep. Ileana Ros-Lehtinin from Miami, will agree to interviews with journalists in a radio station studio (photo by Al Diaz, *Miami Herald* staff).

and received permission, tape the request to tape and the response. This may avoid legal problems later. Most radio stations possess sophisticated recording equipment that is ready to tape at the push of a button because it is wired into a specific telephone line or set of lines. Check the equipment before you call to begin an interview. It is always wise to determine voice levels on the recorder's sound level meters for each call because levels can vary wildly depending on the quality of the connection. Sound checks are usually easy to learn to do. Having things ready in advance helps you with your source, because the source does not have to wait. Once an interview is taped, you can select the best actualities for your story. Most of the time, actualities are chosen because they have substance related to the story, but radio reporters must also be concerned that the actuality is of good technical quality. If possible the actuality should be as clean as possible in terms of "ahs" and "uhs" that clutter our everyday conversation. In order to attain this, some reporters will ask a source to "clarify" an answer in hopes that the second "take" will be clearer and more understandable.

Radio interviews tend to be quite brief because usually you will not need much information for a radio news story. Running the tape for a long interview has its advantages, of course, but it also means you have to spend additional time hunting for one or two actualities when the interview ends.

Radio reporters usually identify the actualities on note paper or by memory and mark down the tape counter numbers (counters record revolutions of the tape cassette).

Radio, like television, is an instant news medium. But unlike television, which may have five or six newscast deadlines in a single day, some radio news operations have one, two, or even more deadlines in 1 hour. All-news radio stations in major markets have what are essentially news deadlines each half hour. Most AM stations offer regular news briefs each hour. Radio news departments are typically very small in size. Stations rarely have more than a few full-time news reporters. Some are even one-person operations and some stations have cut news so much the stations have lost their news identities completely (Rodman, 1991). Small staffs mean demands on those who remain to produce fast and in large quantities. This pressure to get information, including actualities, on the air promptly often forces radio reporters to interview exclusively by telephone.

Radio interviewing has been aided in recent years by improved technology. High quality cellular telephones and other radio technology mean reporters can provide live remote interviews anywhere at any time. This only enhances radio news' role in covering fast-breaking news from the scene. But radio reporters must remember when interviewing, either in person or by telephone, to be careful about extraneous sound. Background noise can ruin sound quality in an interview actuality even if you are using the best equipment.

INTERVIEWING SOURCES
FOR TELEVISION NEWS

Donaldson (1987) rated sources as absolutely critical to success in television journalism. Interviewing is particularly dependent on good source selection by the television reporter. Good sources will lead to successful stories. Bad sources can cause both short- and long-term problems for the reporter. It can be short-term trouble because the story suffers. Long-term problems can damage a reporter's credibility and career prospects. Donaldson cautioned:

> In the end, it's the reporter's reputation on the line when background sources are wrong. Why should the public have to sort through the "who struck John?" of the source chain any more than I want to hear excuses from the plumber when the drain continues to stop up? Sometimes, of course, we get it wrong because we just don't know as much as we should about a subject. . . .
> Occasionally, reporters are wrong because they learn things too quickly. (pp. 263–264)

Along with the problem of selecting the right sources for their interviews, television reporters must contend with a problem few other journalists have—heavy, cumbersome, and intrusive equipment. Clearly, as equipment has become smaller, lighter, and more sophisticated in the past decade, the problem is not nearly as severe as it once was. But television reporting crews still have cameras, microphones, cables, battery packs, extension cords, and lights to move around on assignments.

Most television interviews are conducted in person because of the need to record audio and video. Increasingly, however, reporters and anchors are conducting live or taped interviews with sources miles from the station. In these cases, only a production team goes to the site and the reporter or anchor interviews using a monitor. Ted Koppel made this technique popular by using it routinely on "Nightline." This technique eliminates influences of body language during an interview, which is one advantage to the interviewer.

Television interviewers must be concerned about sound and video quality. Reporters should try to conduct interviews where sound quality will be good. This means checking for loud air conditioners, constantly ringing telephones, traffic noise, crowd noise, and other similar distractions. These same types of problems can also destroy the video portion of the interview. If you are interviewing a source outdoors, for example, try to avoid situations in which other people can interfere. Excessive movement in the background of the video or bad weather conditions can be trouble (unless it needs to be part of the story, of course). Selection of the location for an interview is an important decision, because it can lend to the visual element of the story. For example, an office is acceptable, but to conduct the interview with your source standing in front of the building with the company name or logo in view might be more appropriate.

Television interviews are usually short. Reporters are wise to conduct a "preinterview" interview once they sit down with a source. When you feel you are ready to get to the point, then signal your photographer to start rolling the tape. This will cut down the amount of tape you will have to review when you return to the station to find the right soundbites for the story. This helps photographers, too, because they might be hand-holding the camera and other heavy equipment. In most cases, of course, tripods should be used for interviews.

There are several aspects of television interviewing that are important for beginning reporters to understand. These are the need to screen sources, the art of putting nervous sources at ease prior to the interview, and the usefulness of rehearsing some interviews.

Screening Sources

You must be sure your source is the right person for the assignment. At larger radio and television stations this duty is handled by an assignment editor or a production assistant but, if it is your responsibility, try to determine qualifications of your source before you leave the station for the interview. The worst scenario is to arrive at the scene of the interview and decide the source does not know enough to be useful to you or your story.

"Screening" is an important step in broadcast interviewing because of the

ROBIN DAY, BRITISH BROADCASTING CORP.
BRITAIN'S LEGENDARY TV JOURNALIST ON INTERVIEWING

Sir Robin Day, probably the foremost interviewer in British television history, developed a reputation for his hard-hitting questioning during his 34 years on Great Britain's Independent Television News and the British Broadcasting Corporation. He developed a "code" for television interviewers over 30 years ago. "The idea was to set down the principles which could help to achieve that balance between satisfying a critical public interest and enabling the people interviewed, be they statesmen or strikers, to make their case," he explained (Day, 1989).

Here are Day's 10 rules for television interviewing:

1. The television interviewer must do his [or her] duty as a journalist, probing for facts and opinions.

2. He should set his own prejudices aside and put [ask] questions which reflect various opinions, disregarding probable accusations of bias.

3. He should not allow himself to be overawed in the presence of a powerful person.

4. He should not compromise the honesty of the interview by omitting awkward topics or by rigging questions in advance.

5. He should resist any inclination in those employing him to soften or rig an interview so as to secure a "prestige" appearance, or to please Authority; if after making his protest, the interviewer cannot honestly accept the arrangements, he should withdraw.

6. He should not submit his questions in advance, but it is reasonable to state the main areas of questioning. If he submits specific questions beforehand, he is powerless to put any supplementary questions which may be vitally needed to clarify or challenge an answer.

7. He should give fair opportunity to answer questions, subject to time-limits imposed by television.

8. He should never take advantage of his professional experience to trap or embarrass someone unused to television appearances.

9. He should press his questions firmly and persistently, but not tediously, offensively, or merely in order to sound tough.

10. He should remember that a television interviewer is not employed as a debater, prosecutor, inquisitor, psychiatrist, or third-degree expert, but as a journalist seeking information on behalf of the viewer.

Source: Day (1989). *Grand Inquisitor,* London: Pan Books.

effort and time involved in conducting on-location interviews. This is certainly most important when it comes to live interviews and interviews conducted near deadlines.

Screening can occur in several ways. If you are interviewing an expert, determine the level of expertise. Many experts are so specialized that their authoritativeness is really restricted to only certain narrow subjects. If you are interviewing a victim, make certain the person really experienced the incident for which you need comment for your story. If the person is an eyewitness, make sure the person actually saw the event and is not relaying secondhand information to you.

Putting Your Source At Ease

After learning as much as you can about your source, you should have a good idea whether your source will experience any on-air anxiety or nervousness. If you feel this may be the case, it might be a good idea to put your source at ease. This is most commonly done by talking off camera with your source about the interview.

One option is to tell your source about how you are approaching the story. Tell your source about other sources and what you think the story might say. You should always tell the source when the story will be broadcast—if you know—because most sources want to watch.

Often, simple conversation such as small-talk will do the job. This allows sources to become more familiar with you as a reporter and it enhances their trust in you. The small-talk subject really does not matter. If you notice something unusual in your source's home, or office, then ask about it. Or talk about the weather (if it is worthwhile to do so). Or get the photographer involved in the discussion while the equipment is being set up. Another technique to get the source's mind off the subject is to ask for a cup of coffee or a soft drink if it is convenient. And, of course, you could also offer some instructions to your inexperienced source about looking at you or at the camera.

Rehearsing the Interview

Many television and radio reporters like to practice parts of an interview with sources before the tape begins to roll. This has the advantage of permitting a source to think about what to say when the light goes on.

You can tell your source the topic if you have not already done so. Give the source a general idea of the question, or even ask the key question or two before you record. You can expect a stronger answer when you provide questions in a rehearsal circumstance. It also eases the tension and anxiety of inexperienced sources. This might have a greater impact on the source's sense of relaxation and comfort than any small talk, in fact. It will allow the source to feel more confident, and this strengthens your story in the long run.

There are certain situations—such as investigations or emergency reporting—when you do not want to rehearse, but in many stories, it can do no harm. When reaction and spontaneity are critical to your story, rehearsal should not be considered.

George Killenberg and Rob Anderson (1989) cautioned reporters about rehearsing one question or subject and then asking about something different or unexpected when the tape is rolling. "Beyond the ethical questions such behavior raises, you may leave an inexperienced interviewee speechless. You're left with dead air" (p. 184).

TAPE IS ROLLING!
BUT YOUR SOURCE REFUSES . . .

What happens when you find the seemingly perfect source, get that source on the telephone or in front of your camera with tape rolling, and the source refuses to talk? This can happen for several reasons. First, sources can be intimidated and scared by the prospect of being on the air. Second, sources may not feel they have anything significant to say. Third, sources can be angered by a "tough" question you ask.

The best method to deal with the first two situations is to spend time in advance of the interview to make sources feel comfortable with you and with the camera and microphone. Try to strengthen the sources' feelings that they have something important to add to the story, that they can enlighten or educate the audience, and that the interview is an opportunity to discuss their particular position on the subject.

The third possibility, sources who are asked tough questions on controversial or sensitive subjects, poses special problems. British television journalist Robin Day (1989) said a "tough" question is often determined

> not by the content of the question, but by the tone and manner of the answer. I have spent hours in hopeful preparation of penetrating and incisive questions, only to find they are deflected and blunted by a calm or emollient answer on the lines of "I'm so glad you asked me that, Robin." Conversely, the most innocent and unprovocative question can become "tough" or "abrasive" if the interviewee chooses to blow his top in reply. (p. 275)

When a source chooses to avoid answering a question in a television or radio interview, the strategy falls into several general categories. A sharp television or radio interviewer will be better able to respond to the evasion by understanding these "nonanswer" strategies. The most common approaches used by skilled sources include the following 10 methods (Day, 1989):

1. *Ignoring the question* — Some sources will simply start talking about whatever is on their mind regardless of the question you ask.

2. *Acknowledging the question without answering it* — More experienced question evaders will acknowledge the question, even repeat it, but then talk about something different.

3. *Challenging the question* — Confident sources will not answer your question and instead will challenge the premise on which your question may be based. In this way, the sources feel they are not obligated to answer a "flawed" question and avoid it.

4. *Criticizing the question* — Experienced and expert sources may also attack the question for its quality or its content as a means of avoiding an answer to a "flawed" question.

5. *Criticizing the interviewer* — Some sources choose to criticize interviewers for their personal attitudes instead of answering the question.

6. *Refusing to answer the question*—Less creative sources may choose not to answer by simply refusing to do so without offering a reason.

7. *Answering, but on a different subject*—Crafty sources will provide a nonanswer by discussing a related subject to the question, but not the exact subject of the question. So, you get what may seem to be an appropriate answer when it is not.

8. *Providing a partial response*—Sly sources often select a part of an answer that they are willing to offer and then avoid the rest. This partial response may seem adequate to the source.

9. *Repeating a previous answer*—This common technique allows the source to use information already provided by a response to an earlier question. Reporters often ask questions in several forms to get at an answer. Sources, alert to this technique, just give the same answer over and over.

10. *Claiming to have previously answered that particular question*—Again, sources may avoid answering a question by arguing that they have already done so earlier in the interview or even in other interviews.

SETTING UP INTERVIEWS

A good interview has much invested in it long before the interview begins. You know about research. That sort of preparation is critical when time allows. But setting up broadcast interviews often requires as much effort as research and conducting the interview itself.

At the networks and at large stations, reporters are assisted by field producers and by assignment editors. Field producers are the field generals on stories. These individuals report to the program's executive producer, but field producers often have most of the responsibility in shaping a story as it develops. One of their critical duties is finding sources and setting up interviews with them. Assignment managers/editors do much the same kind of duty, especially when reporters are already in the field and are working on more than one story or are conducting an interview for the same story on deadline.

But at many stations and small bureaus for networks, reporters often must double up as field producers and serve as their own assignment managers/editors. It becomes their responsibility to set up and conduct interviews.

To set up an interview first means that you have to find the source. For broadcast reporters covering fast-breaking news such as accidents, unexpected resignations, or crimes, it often means using contacts to find the right witnesses, victims, and experts for the story. It means going to the scene.

Once you have the person in mind, you must "sell" them on the prospect of being interviewed live or on tape. Not everyone will readily agree. Some will say they do not have the time; others will claim they don't know enough. "Getting the interview sometimes is more work than doing the interview," advised Biagi (1986, p. 109).

SAM DONALDSON, ABC NEWS
HANDLING THE STAND-UP CLOSE FOR YOUR STORY

A broadcast story, such as one using interviews with sources, should end with the reporter's *stand-up close*. This is a short summary, from 10 to 15 seconds, which literally "closes" the story. The reporter stands in a location pertinent to the story such as outside of a building at the scene, or in the foreground of an event as it occurs.

ABC news correspondent and anchor Sam Donaldson (1987) pointed out that the stand-up close is critical to the story.

"I often try to round out the story and answer the question 'What's really going on here?' " he said (p. 105).

Finding the "right" source might be most challenging part of the effort. Screening, as you read earlier, helps determine whether you truly have that right person. Biagi recommended: "Talk with the person for a while to test what they know. Look for someone who is articulate, outspoken and willing. Beware of an exuberant volunteer who waves both arms in the air when you are looking for someone to be interviewed on camera" (p. 110).

PRESENTING YOURSELF ON THE AIR

Interviewing for radio and television, you read earlier in this chapter, is different from other interviewing because of the *performance* nature of broadcast news. Because of this direct involvement in the story by the reporter, you must be especially concerned about how you dress, how you speak, your general body language, and how you present yourself within the story.

Your appearance is most important for television. Viewers will see you, so it is essential to dress appropriately for the situation. For spot news stories or interviews in business and government settings, professional clothing such as a suit is right. But a suit is not always best for interviews for a beach feature or a sports story. Use your judgment, but dress right for the story. For some reporters, this means carrying several sets of clothes in the car or keeping them at the station. It means keeping personal grooming aids handy. And it might also mean helping a source with the same cosmetic concerns when you can, such as fixing a turned up collar, or lending a mirror for straightening tousled hair.

Radio and television reporters must be more concerned about how they ask questions than print reporters. This does not refer to the content of the question so much as it means the smooth manner in which the question is asked. Killenberg and Anderson (1989) called these "on-air sacrifices," because these trade-offs may limit interviewing style. "The typical passive probes that help encourage responsiveness ('I see,' 'Tell me more,' 'Uh-huh,'

'Really?') may be distracting to the audience. If you're off camera, you can still use nonverbal encouragement, like nodding, smiling, or raising an eyebrow. But it's better to augment nonverbal messages with verbal ones" (p. 186).

Body language is another form of nonverbal communication called *kinesics*. Body language includes your posture, facial expressions and eye movement, touching, perspiration, gestures, and use of arms and legs. It is a complete means of sending and receiving messages. We learn to interpret it from childhood. In interviews, your body language, just as you "read" your source's body language, will reveal much to the source and your audience. You must be conscious of what you are communicating through your body language so you do not send a confusing message to your source or the audience and spoil the interview. Slouching posture, for example, can unintentionally signal your fatigue or boredom.

It is essential to show through your body language that you are alert, attentive, and interested, whether or not you are on camera. This encourages your source. But also be careful not to send the wrong message. If you are on camera, for instance, you must be aware of what you may be communicating. Even subtle facial expressions may signal agreement or disagreement with what your source is saying. Unnecessary gestures can be distracting to your source and the audience.

WORKING WITH THE TIMID AND THE FAMOUS

Certain types of news sources create special broadcast interviewing problems. The two most difficult are timid sources and famous or celebrity sources. These individuals force you into two different sets of interviewing strategies.

Timid Sources

Timid sources are unfamiliar with broadcast journalism and are quietly frightened by the attention, cameras, microphones, and lights.

You must make these individuals feel at ease. Tell them about the story. Discuss how television (or radio) works. Give some hints concerning which direction to look when the interview begins. Convince the sources of their appropriateness as a source. Talk about the news of the day. This should help build confidence.

Start an interview with a timid source by asking easy-to-answer questions. Basic factual questions are easiest. Ask for observations if needed. Then gradually move into questions requiring the source's opinions.

Famous and Celebrity Sources

Famous or celebrity sources are often the most experienced interview sources. These individuals are rarely influenced by the trappings of radio and television newsgathering. They have done it before, probably dozens of times.

These sources are sometimes called "media heavyweights." This is because of their power, influence, and importance. You know the type: chief executive officer of a big corporation, a governor or senator, a visiting foreign leader, a former president or presidential candidate, a miracle-worker physician, a major Hollywood movie star, a championship-level professional athlete, or a billionaire business leader.

Sometimes, even an experienced reporter is challenged by such an individual. Reporters are frequently awed by the real, or imagined, stature of the individual. But these sources are coming into interviews with ammunition. Often they are surrounded by aides and public relations executives. Many of these sources have taken courses and seminars on acting in front of the camera, on projecting a proper television image, and on answering questions from reporters. These individuals are quite sophisticated even if they do not seem so. New York University broadcast journalism professors Mitchell Stephens and Eliot Frankel (1983) suggested that reporters can be overmatched by these individuals: "Reporters who interview graduates of these workshops and coaching sessions appear seriously outgunned by executives who have learned at the feet of moon-

Celebrities such as National Hockey League star Wayne Gretsky are accustomed to television interviews. This interview was on the arena ice during the Los Angeles Kings' media day (photo by Wen Roberts, *Photo Ink*, courtesy of the Los Angeles Kings).

lighting and lapsed journalists how to obfuscate, evade questions, refuse comment, and gobble up gobs of air time with their slogans and puffery" (p. 38).

But interviewing these heavyweight sources does not have to be conflictive. Stephens and Frankel (1983) recommended these steps to keep pace with sophisticated sources:

1. Don't get trapped in a love-in with your source. Your source wants to be liked, even loved, by the audience. You do not have to contribute to that.

2. Bone up. Do your homework to be as prepared as your source will be. If the interview is important, the celebrity source will be ready for you with a message of some sort.

3. Burn their bridges. Do not let your source change, or "bridge," to another subject. Keep the interview under control.

4. Listen for news judgments. Be alert for sources who try to judge news for you. Some sources will attach value statements to what they say to influence you and the audience about the merits of the information.

5. Watch for turning tables. Do not give up control of the interview to your source. The source will try to take it from you.

Similarly concerned about heavyweight sources, Chicago-area journalism professors and free-lance writers Connie Fletcher and Jon Ziomek (1986) learned a great deal from interviewing celebrity sources. They recommended seven tips:

1. Don't rush into the interview. Do some research. Stop to figure out what is going on with the celebrity source. Find things the celebrity would like to talk about if you want full participation. What do you really want to know about this person?

2. Do not go into an interview unprepared. And do not try to fake your preparation.

3. Reinforce your sources. Let them know you are interested. This will probably keep your source from becoming bored, especially if this person is on a promotion tour of some sort. Let the celebrity talk about the reason for the visit to town. Then take your turn at the information you want to gather.

4. When you find you are interviewing a tired, hostile, or unfriendly celebrity, avoid showing your frustration and anger. Sometimes an interviewer can bring the celebrity out of the mood with a direct approach: Tell the person you are not getting the information you need.

5. When you are working with a severe time limit, such as 10 or 15 minutes, make the most of it. Go straight to the provocative and sensitive questions. Perhaps the celebrity will enjoy it and permit the time to expand.

6. Go into unexplored territory if you have a problem with celebrities telling old stories and repeating the same soundbites over and over.

7. Keep the interview on track if your celebrity source tries to ramble off course.

GOING LIVE

There is nothing more thrilling in television and radio news than "going live" with your news story. For many stories, this means conducting interviews as part of your live report. Much "live" reporting is actually prepackaged with the live interview at the end. In these cases, the anchor will lead into the reporter live at a scene, the reporter introduces a prepackaged story that sets up the viewer with background information about the story. When the package ends, the reporter then has a minute or less to ask several questions live to a source.

In some breaking story situations, you do not have time to prepackage your story. At the scene of a double murder, you might gather as much information about the crime as you can before the newscast begins. But if you have only a few minutes on this breaking story, you get the essentials and try to find a knowledgeable source such as a police department public information officer to discuss the case with you on camera. When your director gives the cue, you may have just 90 to 100 seconds to report what happened. The story begins with the basics that you know. What happened? Where? When? How? You know that much. After a half minute of setting the scene for viewers, you then ask the PIO to step into the camera shot with you to answer one or two questions. You are live, so it is wise to remind your source before the interview begins that answers must be concise and to the point. After you ask your question about who was shot, you perhaps ask a follow-up about why the shooting occurred. Then you must wrap up the story. The live shot is finished in what seems a blur of time. You are done. That's live television.

As a radio reporter on the same scene, you might have even less time. If your station has a 5-minute, or even a 10-minute, newscast at the top of the hour, you must keep your story very short—45 to 60 seconds—and you might be able to ask only one or two key questions of your source. Live radio can be even more pressure-filled than live television because of the greater frequency of deadlines.

Live interviews are part of what makes television news stimulating to audiences. The spontaneity of the news can make it most appealing. Viewers who saw CBS anchor Dan Rather spar with presidential candidate George Bush in 1988 remember how electrifying television news can be. Bush had agreed to a rare *live* interview on the network's nightly newscast. Rather wanted to ask the then-vice president about his role in the controversial Iran–Contra arms sales investigation. Bush wanted to discuss his plans for domestic programs such as education. The two men would not budge from their respective positions. The interview stretched to 4, 5, then 6 minutes as the two men debated the purpose of the interview and why the vice president would not discuss the Iran–Contra case. And Bush raised the issue of Rather's professionalism by recalling the incident when Rather walked off the set in Miami, resulting in a 6-minute blackout on the network. Audiences and people in the news business discussed the interview for weeks after it aired.

Live interviews may provide this type of excitement and may be necessary because of time constraints under deadline, but reporters give up some of the editorial control of the final story when the interview goes live. There is no opportunity to edit—only to "pull the plug." But that Rather–Bush confrontation signaled a change in television interviewing. Sources began to stand up to reporters and they seemed to have the audience's support. Reporters realized they would possibly lose their direction in producing the story.

Anchor Robin Day (1989) remarked that live television interviews play a critical role, particularly in the political process:

> When politicians or powerful public figures have access to the platform of television, they should be open to questions of a critical, informed and challenging nature. When a TV interviewer questions a politician, this is one of the rare occasions . . . when a politician's performance cannot be completely manipulated or packaged or artificially hyped. (p. 160)

Day, who conducted television and radio interviews for the British Broadcasting Corporation for three decades and earned the reputation as Britain's foremost news interviewer, felt live television interviews fill an important void:

> It seemed to me that if politicians or other public figures were to have access, as they should have, to the powerful platform of television, they should pay a reasonable price for that access. That price should be the obligation to answer fair and challenging questions in a TV interview or debate. In other words, they should be accountable on TV. (p. 162)

WHAT SOURCES HATE MOST

Some sources will react with fear or hostility to broadcast interview situations they do not like or do not expect. Some will be less obvious with their reaction, but still be less cooperative if you let things get out of control. Reporters must be careful because such reactions may cause interviews to end abruptly.

During the peak of public interest in the alleged sexual assault at the Kennedy family compound in Palm Beach, Florida, Michele Cassone, who was at the estate on the night the alleged rape of Patricia Joyce Bowman occurred, became a major source in the national news media. She was in great demand by television programs to tell what she knew. Producers of Fox Television's "A Current Affair," a syndicated news–entertainment interview program, persuaded the woman to be interviewed for the program. Steve Dunleavy, who was assigned to interview her, saw his interview suddenly end when the woman became angered by one of his questions. The woman's hostile reaction was caused when Dunleavy indirectly questioned her integrity as a witness to events at the estate. The interview, being taped in advance in a New York studio, turned sour when Dunleavy asked the woman if she had ever posed nude prior to the night of the assault and she said she had not. Dunleavy then produced four photographs of the woman nude, including one in which she was involved in a sex act. The woman screamed at her interviewer, attacked him with a microphone cord, and even bit him (Anon., 1991, April 24).

The lesson is not lost on beginning reporters. People do not like to be surprised or trapped even if it is justified or necessary. The Florida woman no doubt felt betrayed and embarrassed by the interviewer. This type of interviewing strategy does make entertaining television. People like to watch it. However, the degree of news value involved in the incident is questionable.

There are four special concerns that reporters must guard against, noted free-lance journalists Connie Fletcher and Jon Ziomek (1986). First, reporters should not arrive to interview a source unprepared. Sources can tell even if the reporter does not confess to a lack of preparation. In addition, reporters should not arrive to interview a source with preconceived notions about the source and the story and then proceed to ignore everything else. Fletcher and Ziomek said sources sense this and do not like it. Moreover, reporters should not talk more about themselves than about the source. This will chill a source very fast. And finally, reporters should not act bored or distracted. Each of these factors will ruin an interview by "turning off" a source.

NATURAL SOUND FROM INTERVIEWS

Some television interview stories do not need a great deal of reporter or source sound from the subject of the story. And on some occasions, a source for a television story will decline to be interviewed. Television reporters have an option for those stories. Some stories will tell themselves if structured properly. Good photography and natural sound captured with the camera running may do well enough alone.

ABC news correspondent and anchor Sam Donaldson (1987) credited his "good sense" to do this on some stories. On stories when he "let the pictures and natural sound speak for themselves, it has always worked out well," he said (p. 209).

NBC news correspondent Bob Dotson (1988) agreed. Dotson pointed out that moments of silence can be eloquent. "Stop writing occasionally and let two or three seconds or more of compelling action occur without voiceover. For a writer, nothing is more difficult to write than silence. For viewers, sometimes nothing is more eloquent" (p. 1).

Dotson also said natural sound boosts a story. Natural sound is important "to heighten realism, authenticity, believability; to heighten the viewer's sense of vicarious participation in the events you're showing. Some reports merely let you watch what happened. The best reports let you experience what happened" (p. 1).

It is imperative that reporters conducting interviews keep natural sound in mind for production of their story. While in the field, take the time to record natural sound. It will add much to the story when it is produced in the editing room. Tell the photographer (or sound engineer) what you want in very precise terms. Sometimes this means using sound and pictures alone. On other occasions, it will mean using sound, pictures, and voice-over together.

OTHER PROBLEM AREAS TO AVOID

There are a few trouble spots in broadcast interviewing. Experienced reporters know how to avoid them. Some involve judgment and some involve techniques used to conduct broadcast interviews.

Jerry Jacobs (1990), author of *Changing Channels,* suggested that one of the biggest recent ethical problems in broadcast news is staging or enhancing news interviews. "Although real journalists don't, or rather aren't supposed to, reenact or *stage* news, the problem has never been completely eliminated from broadcasting," he said (p. 84). One concern Jacobs expressed is with "reverse questions." The tactic usually involves reshooting a reporter's question after a source has left, ostensibly to "clean up" a flaw. Jacobs added that "phony reactions" are another problem. Often these camera shot "cutaways" are used to bridge two soundbites, but are not always shot with the source present. They make the interview appear to have been photographed and taped with two or more cameras when only one was actually used.

A technique tried by some network and locally produced news programs involves staging reenactments of events and situations. Fortunately, most of the broadcast news industry opposes such techniques, even if labeled, because it is not presenting reality to audiences (Jacobs, 1990).

Another problem is a technique called the "ambush interview." In this type of interview, reporters wait for sources at predetermined locations to catch and force a source to answer questions. On some occasions, these interviews are impossible to avoid. Essential sources in a story may be reluctant to comment and will try to avoid you. But in some cases, these types of interviews are not necessary and only contribute to lower reporter and station credibility with the audience and source.

Jacobs (1990), a professor at California State University at Northridge, criticized broadcast journalists for taking "cheap shots" at sources in interviews. When people are suddenly involved in tragedy as a victim or family member of a victim, some reporters needlessly badger these individuals. "In the classic case, the distraught man sits on the curb in shock, his burned-up house the backdrop. The young, aggressive TV reporter, looking for on-camera emotion, preferably tears, asks him, 'How does it feel, losing your wife, three kids, house, and all your belongings in that fire?' It happens" (p. 86).

Incidents such as these are often perceived by audiences as grossly invading the privacy of people. Reporters must weigh their need for the information against the privacy needs of the individual. It is not always an easy decision.

Another problem involves using soundbite tape from other sources without credit. Often reporters use material from network feeds, other reporters in a pool, or from free-lancers or home video enthusiasts, but fail to give credit for it. Usually it is acceptable to provide credit on the screen in small letters while the tape is on screen. On more important material, it may be better to integrate the credit into the text of the script as well.

HOW PROFESSIONALS WRITE IT

SOURCE: KTUL-TV, Channel 8, Tulsa, Oklahoma
AUTHOR: Scott Gordon
DATE: Monday, May 14, 1990
TIME: 6 P.M. newscast

* * *

FORGOTTEN LAND PART ONE	5–14–90
6	SDG
	70 + 1

2-SHOT	(ELY) IMAGINE LIVING MILES FROM YOUR NEAREST NEIGHBOR . . .
	(CAROLE) THE GROCERY STORE IS AN HOUR AWAY.
CAROLE GRAPHIC	(CAROLE) LIFE IN THE OKLAHOMA PAN-HANDLE . . .
	FOR YEARS, IT WAS A NO MAN'S LAND. AND TODAY, IN MANY WAYS, IT STILL IS.
	IN THE FIRST PART OF HIS SE-RIES, "THE FORGOTTEN LAND," NEWS 8'S SCOTT GORDON SHOWS US JUST HOW FORGOTTEN IT IS.

PEEL GRAPHIC VTR/PKG ----------------------PKG ----------------------

(NATS-BIRDS)

(NATS-FADE UP RADIO TAPE 7)

1413 "WELL GOOD MORN-ING. . . .")

DAYBREAK IN THE OKLAHOMA PANHANDLE. A BEAUTIFUL PLACE OF VIRTUAL ISOLATION. WHERE HIGHWAYS LEAD TO NO-WHERE. WHERE EVEN THE BIRDS SEEM FAR AWAY AND LONELY.

120

IN: IT'S A NICE FRIENDLY PLACE . . .

OUT: I'VE EVER LIVED

CG_____MAURINE DUNKERSON
GUYMON HERALD EDITOR

141
IN: YOU GO ANYPLACE ELSE . . .

OUT: STRANGE PERSON

HERE, PEOPLE WHO DON'T WAVE ARE STRANGE.

OUTSIDE THE SMALL TOWN OF GUYMON, PLENTY OF ANIMALS ROAM THE COUNTRYSIDE, BUT NOT MANY PEOPLE.

----

209 TAPE 7

CG_____SCOTT GORDON SU

SU: DRIVING IN THE PANHAN-DLE, YOU CAN GO FOR MILES WITHOUT SEEING A SOUL. TO SAY THIS IS ISOLATED DOESN'T START TO DESCRIBE IT. TRUTH IS, A TORNADO COULD TOUCH DOWN AND NO ONE WOULD EVER KNOW.

(NATS-FRED AT FENCE)

24422 (B-ROLL BITE)

IN: WE'RE ABOUT AS FAR AS . . .

OUT: YOU CAN GET

WE WENT WAY OUT OF OUR WAY TO FIND FRED TUCKER, 82, AND STILL A COWBOY.

TAPE 3 749

IN: (SQUALL . . .)

OUT: MY LUNGS AT IT

TUCKER REFLECTS THE SPIRIT THAT MAKES UP TODAY'S PAN-HANDLE.

24917

CG____FRED TUCKER
PANHANDLE RESIDENT

IN: I CONSIDER MYSELF A LONER . . .

OUT: BARELY SEEN ANYBODY

24042

IN: I TELL EVERYONE. . . .

OUT: PEOPLE OUT HERE

(PICKUP DRIVES AWAY)

24310

IN: IF A FELLOW CAME IN HERE . . .

OUT: I WOULDN'T GO

THAT'S THE FEELING OF MOST EVERYONE HERE . . .

(DISSOLVE TO SUNSET SHOT)

A LIFE MONEY CAN'T BUY . . . AN-OTHER DAY IN THE HIGH PLAINS . . . ONE PLACE WHERE THE ROU-

TINE HASN'T CHANGED IN GEN-
ERATIONS.

(NATS-FRED COW CALL . . .)

(NATS-RADIO AG REPORT)

SCOTT GORDON, NEWS 8, IN THE
OKLAHOMA PANHANDLE.

VTR ENDS ---

TAG TAG
                6   SDG

                                                        70 + 4

CAROLE GRAPHIC   (CAROLE)

                                 SCOTT HAS PART TWO OF "THE
                                 FORGOTTEN LAND" TOMORROW
                                 ON NEWS 8 AT 6.

                                 TOMORROW, A LOOK AT THE
                                 PANHANDLE'S UNIQUE HISTORY.

Reprinted with permission of KTUL-TV.

• • •

SOURCE: WTVJ-TV, Channel 4, Miami
REPORTER: Bonnie Anderson
DATE: Wednesday, December 19, 1990
TIME: 6 P.M. newscast

* * *

Page Slug   Show   Date   Anchor   APVLS Status TOTAL   Writer
  MIDEAST/VIET VETS   600P 12/19/90   READY   4:16 anderson
Written   Changed   by   TAPE ##   TIMECODE Copy SOT's
Tue Dec 18 14:43 1990   Dec 19 10:27 anderson   2:16 2:00

#S/Bonnie Anderson reporting

#s/Viet Nam and date   (music and video montage of Viet Nam)

                                    It was a time when our nation's youth
                                    were forced to grow up quickly, often
                                    brutally . . . when boys and girls became
                                    soldiers in a strange land . . . and all too
                                    often came home in pine boxes. It was
                                    an era that tore the country apart . . .
                                    and somehow changed all of us.

Spc. Arthur Head
tape 12 at 13:39 (:06) b-roll

"I know that when I went over there I was scared to death and I'm not afraid to admit it. I was a kid."

Sgt. Bob Bradford
tape #4 at 1:45 (:11) b-roll

"Maybe it's the adrenaline rush that you get. When I was in Viet Nam, it was hard to get back to normal life after being so high on it all the time, so aware of life."

Sgt. Rafael Pacheco on camera
tape #12 at 11:37 (:05)

"And I never thought that I'd find myself in another war. None of us did."

three shot. CW3 Jim Ives
speaking
tape ##12 at 11:45 (:04)

"No. Didn't really think it would happen, but it happened."

They are the Viet Nam vets of the South Florida National Guard unit in Saudi Arabia. Men who joined the Marines or Army as teenagers. For the 743-rd Maintenance Unit, the voices of experience.

#s/Sgt. Terrence Rutter
tape #12 at 14:43ish

"I feel real good about who I am. I'm 43. I've seen a little bit of this before and it helps me to understand that it's OK to be scared. It makes you sharper."

Sharp enough to know Saudi Arabia is not Viet Nam.

#s/1Sgt. Hank Obester
tape #13 at 5:22

"This is a completely different situation from what we had in Viet Nam. Climate's different. Everything's different."

show dunes desert shots
tape #10
NG tape #10 at 8:57 is
scorpion gas masks
bradford reading etc lots
of shots on tape #4 at 3:00

"Instead of jungle, sand dunes and scorpions. And the specter of chemical warfare."

Sgt. Bob Bradford, a platoon leader in Viet Nam, still wears a bracelet remembering a prisoner of war. Today, he is the South Florida unit's chemical warfare expert.

3:34 pow on tape #4

flag on helmet 3:58 on
tape #4
#s/Sgt. Bob Bradford
tape #12 at 16:45 (:15)

"I was down in the Delta. It was hot and wet so I never saw a protective mask. It just didn't exist. Chemical warfare was defoliants. That was it. And when we flew through that we were just told to hold our breath. That was it."

These men — in their late 30's and 40's — are known as the old-timers to the young troops . . . a nickname they embrace with pride.

Rutter tape 12 at 14:24 (:10)

"It makes me feel pretty good because I know that they're going to be coming to me at times saying, hey, what do you think about this? Why do they do this? I can say, well, this is the reason. It's to save you."

#s/Bonnie Anderson standup bridge
tape #1 at 14:16, 14:35, 16:17
16:36, 17:15, and 17:47

While the veterans understand the enthusiasm of the young troops, they add they wouldn't be here today had they not learned to temper it with caution and common sense.

#s/Sgt. James Berry
tape #13 at 2:19 (:08)

"It scares me to see all these young fellas running around like this. They're borderline crazies right now. But they'll all settle down. They have to."

berry (butt)
tape 12 at 13:26 (:07)

"And it helps for them to talk to some of the olders who've been through this and I guess that's one reason I'm still here."

What words of caution do these vets have for the young troops?

obester tape 13 at 7:12 (:07)

"Follow the advice of the senior NCO's. The people with the experience. They're the ones that got to pull them through this."

1Sgt. Obester at formation (brooks tape) tape NG #8 at 15:30 and more shots of obester on ng#1 at 2:02 talking with officers on bunk. and at 6:01 digging into briefcase. also at 10:19 putting papers away.

"Sgt. Steele! Sgt. DiDonna!

As the unit's first sergeant, Obester is the hands-on leader. He says his job has caused him many restless nights.

obester tape #13 at 5:45 (:07)

"That's probably the thing that's worrying me more than anything, is my responsibility to bring these people back."

Why do these men still serve their country . . . these soldiers so unappreciated the last time they answered the call to duty?

berry tape 13 at 3:04 (:13)

"I'm not all that bitter. I have to forgive my country and some of the people in this country for their thoughts. And we have to put that behind us and just go on with what's in front."

ives tape #13 at 4:44 (:09)

"And I'm proud to be part of what has to be done. And if I'm still able at 70 and God forbid there should be another one, I'll go then, too."

Specialist Head sums up his reason in one word.

head tape #13 at 1:13 (:13)

"Pride, I guess. That's all I can say." (Pride in yourself and your country?) "And the country. Myself and the country." (Is there anything you wouldn't do for this country?) "No, nothing at all."

Rutter ng tape 16 at 14:22
emotion on face and squints

These vets have seen the worst this world has to offer. But like Sgt. Rutter, whose eyes tear when he sees his seven-month old baby on videotape, they've also seen the best . . . and THAT, they say, renews their dedication.

rutter tape #12 at around
12:40

"And I'm hoping he doesn't ever have to do anything like this. And if I can stand in these 200-man lines and if I can eat malaria pills and if I can eat this chow, which isn't so bad, then I feel maybe he won't have to do the same thing 20 years from now."

Pacheco, a Merrill Lynch employee, agrees.

pacheco tape 12 at 15:49 (:10)
b-roll last part of it

"I'm losing a lot of money, but it's worth it. Because I know down the road sometime, this won't happen again. This world has got to become a peaceful world. And united."

From Saudi Arabia,
Bonnie Anderson,
Channel 4 News

• • •

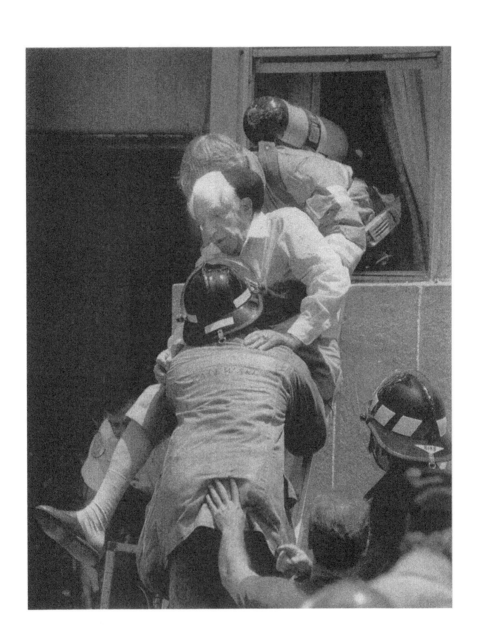

8 | Observation Skills

Television news anchor and reporter Giselle Fernandez became a homeless person to find out what it was like to live on the streets. Fernandez worked for WCIX-TV, Channel 6, the CBS owned-and-operated station in south Florida, when she did the undercover work for a five-part series on people who live on the streets of downtown Miami. For a part of her series, she spent 24 hours under an interstate highway overpass dressed as a homeless person.

Her stories gave viewers a closer look at the lives of individuals who spend the winter in south Florida's more tolerant outdoor climate. Instead of just taking her camera and microphone to simply interview and photograph these withdrawn and private individuals, she went beyond that more conventional form of reporting. Fernandez, who left WCIX-TV to become a correspondent for the CBS Evening News, became less intrusive by becoming a participant observer, watching and talking to homeless people about their lives and troubles.

Fernandez, an Emmy Award-winning journalist, was followed by a production crew in an unmarked van to watch and protect her, but also with hidden equipment to record sound and videotape of her. "I always knew that I was getting out, that I had a crew watching me, so I could never know what it's like to be as vulnerable as they [the homeless] are," she said. "But it's a terrible feeling when strangers come up and put their arms around you, sometimes under the guise of being your protector" (Loudis, 1991).

Fernandez met many different people, including men who said they would protect and take care of her. Those individuals were actually more threatening than helpful, she recalled. She was able to talk with an 86-year-old homeless woman and a 50ish veteran who took care of his

---

Emergencies such as a fire rescue require sharp observation skills with an eye for detail. (Did you notice the yarmulke—a skull cap worn by Jewish men—on the man's head?) (Photo by the *Miami Herald* staff.)

homeless family, even sending his children to school every day. Through these contacts, she built the series of stories. But she got dimensions of the story through first-person observation that she could not get using other reporting techniques. Even direct observation from a distance, which she used, could not generate the richness of detail she found by going onto the streets herself (Loudis, 1991).

WCCO-TV's Alan Cox used a different form of observation for his assignment to cover the trial of three former Northwest Airlines pilots who had been accused of flying their jet aircraft while under the influence of alcohol. Going into the assignment, the Minneapolis-based reporter knew he would be at the federal courthouse daily, quietly observing the court proceedings as an important part of his story. But his work had to be supplemented by interviewing the principals in the case as they entered and left the courthouse. On the day the defense began its portion of the trial, Cox described the testimony of expert witnesses and the attempts by the prosecution to undermine the credibility of those witnesses. Much of his package — a preproduced news segment complete with introduction, sound-bites, and close — summarized the testimony. His script for the story, which is reprinted at the end of this chapter, shows the important role of routine observation and listening to events as they unfold. By paying attention to key testimony and by watching the attorneys and defendants, Cox got his story.

These examples show the power of observation in reporting. This chapter introduces you to methods that will enhance your information-gathering abilities through different forms of observation. Observation is one of the major information-gathering skills a reporter must master. Interviewing and observation form your most important journalistic "one–two punch."

HOW REPORTERS USE OBSERVATION

Do you notice small details? Colors? Smells? Sounds? Even the most ordinary things? What is the breed of the dog next door? Did you look at a license plate number of a car ahead of you when you were last out for a drive? Do you remember the clothing that people wear? How was the last person you interviewed for an assignment dressed? Do you remember how a room, such as an office or a kitchen, was decorated? Did you notice the title of the book on the desk of the person you interviewed? Consciously noting (and often recording on paper or tape) details such as these are part of observing. These details can make or break a story.

Observation must become a routine part of your reporting. As a reporter you must learn not to assume anything and, instead, use your observational powers to confirm or refute facts gathered from other techniques such as interviewing or document searching.

The following is an example of what observing small details can do for a story:

Miami Herald city desk reporters Lisa Getter and Joe Starita were working on a major story about a Dade County man who was suspected of using a social service agency's funds improperly. The funds supported Miami's oldest inner-city social service agency, the James E. Scott Community Association (JESCA). At the time the reporters worked on the story, JESCA had laid off nearly one third of its 300 employees to contend with a growing budget deficit. In her research into JESCA's records, including cancelled checks and memos from the agency, Getter found several 1990 memos that the director of the agency had submitted to explain more than $100,000 in agency checks he and a second agency executive had written to themselves and cashed during the year. In checking the dates on the memos with a calendar, she found that two of the dates fell on Sundays. Starita then noticed that the typeface of the suspicious memos matched the typeface of recent letters the man had sent to *Herald* editors. Starita dug more and found out that the laser printer used for the memos and letters had been purchased *after* the dates on the memos.

But the reporters were not finished. Each memo, the reporters noticed, had initials of the typist at the bottom of the page in the conventional business document form. The reporters tracked down the typist and interviewed her. She said she did not work for the organization when the memos were prepared.

The reporters confronted the director in a 2-hour tape-recorded interview and he conceded the memos had only recently been prepared and that one memo contained reference to an amount of money that was incorrect. The official said the memos were "reconstructions" from his memory of missing documents. When the two reporters prepared their story, the backdated memos and the taped interview concession were an important portion of the account of the man's problems at the agency. The man took leave, with pay, while the state attorney's office investigated his use of the funds. A big breakthrough in the story occurred because of their observational skills, and their desire to not miss checking the smallest detail or their determination to not assume anything (Hancock, 1991; Weitzel, 1991b).

MAJOR TYPES OF OBSERVATION

For journalists, there are two circumstances for observing. As a reporter, you can (a) observe with your sources knowing you are observing or (b) you can observe without your sources knowing that you are observing. There are also three types of observation. Figure 8.1 displays the types of journalistic observation and their usage by reporters. The three types of observation are: Conventional, unobtrusive, and participant.

Conventional Observation

This type of observation is also known as nonparticipant observation to social scientists who use the technique to conduct research. In a way, reporters are social scientists when they observe because reporters also study

	Reporter is Known to Source	Reporter Not Known to Source
Conventional Observation	Frequently	Occasionally
Unobtrusive Observation	Very Rarely	Frequently
Participant Observation	Frequently	Frequently

FIG. 8.1. Types of Journalistic Observation.

human behavior. Journalists watch meetings take place. They watch speeches. They watch football games. They watch concerts. They watch parades. They witness rocket launches, drug busts, and even executions. This type of observation is so frequently used that it is often taken for granted by those using it. But think for a moment what a story might be like if you could not observe as an information-gathering technique. The story would not be as complete. Observation is required activity. And most of the time, conventional observation is done with sources aware that a reporter is present.

Unobtrusive Observation

This special form of observation is similar to conventional observation. It is most common when reporters want to gather information about something that is happening but they do not want to intrude on what they are watching. In some reporting situations, if individuals know a reporter is watching, the behavior you wish to observe might change. This is a serious problem for television reporters who wish to observe an event in an unobtrusive fashion. When cameras, lights, and microphones arrive, subtle and not-so-subtle changes in the behavior of those present can occur. Unobtrusive observation can also be a problem for radio reporters who also need to use recording equipment. For print reporters, observing without affecting behavior may become a problem when photographs are needed. Thus, unobtrusive forms of observation have been adopted. The techniques include working unannounced as an average person instead of as a reporter, hiding in a hard-to-see location, and getting "lost" in a crowd (or simply blending-in). Examples? Attend a professor's class lecture to help prepare a profile of the professor. Watch a campus police officer make a traffic arrest at a dangerous intersection. Watch people park in handicapped-only spaces on campus. Or watch men and women interact in a campus nightclub.

Participant Observation

In this type of "do-it-yourself" observation, reporters get directly involved in the story, gathering information by becoming participants. In participant observation, sources may or may not know whether the reporter is a reporter. When the reporter is not known to sources, the observation is called "undercover." Although disclosure is preferred as a means to avoid deception, it can interfere with the natural order of things and prevent you as a reporter from observing and experiencing behavior necessary to include in your story. Fernandez's segment described at the beginning of this chapter shows how participant reporting can produce a unique edge to a story that might not be found using conventional observation or even unobtrusive techniques.

OBSERVING DETAILS

Seeing is observing. But in a journalistic sense, observing should be much more than just seeing. It is *sensing*. Observation includes using all your senses to gather information for your story. For some stories, details and description will play a greater role than it will in others. But detail can be an important dimension for all stories you do.

Miami Herald police beat reporter Edna Buchanan, winner of a Pulitzer Prize for local reporting, is a firm believer in observation and detail in reporting. For instance, her ability to notice abnormalities at a crime scene is legendary. Buchanan's stories jolt readers with the bizarre side of life in a large city. She focuses on depicting aberrations that make her stories extraordinary and fascinating studies of human behavior. She built her reputation by working long hours and asking unusual questions, but also by noticing things no one else would see. She often observed things even detectives originally missed. And when she observed something interesting or odd, it usually found its way into the lead of her stories. Police reporting with Buchanan, because of her fine-tuned observation and interviewing skills, is anything but ordinary. Here is a typical Buchanan lead as an example of mixing her observations with facts from the police department sources:

> The dead man left a nickel, three pennies, and a mystery that baffles Miami Beach police.
> "It's a lonely way to die," detective Paul Scrimshaw said. "It bothers us."
> Ten days of investigation led detectives to a dead end. They are still unable to identify the child-like man who was apparently retarded, a victim of Down's Syndrome. He was found alone, an apparent suicide, in an oceanfront room on the second floor of a closed and shuttered Miami Beach hotel.

About age 30, he wore extremely strong prescription eyeglasses, a gray wool pinstripe suit and a down jacket. Detectives Scrimshaw and Phil Kromsky believe he came from out of town.

Perhaps, they theorize, he left a cold, Northern city after a parent died. He may have come here to try life on his own. Or he may have come to die.

Speculation is all they have. Leads are few.

Here are the facts. (Buchanan, 1988)

Buchanan's lead to the 17-column inch story—about average length for a newspaper story on an unusual crime—is rich with description and details. Buchanan artfully wove information gathered from police reports, interviews, and her own observations. She showed you details such as how the man was dressed (most reporters would notice this), how much money he left behind (fewer reporters would probably notice that), and even how strong his eyeglasses were (how many reporters would think to check that?). The details she observed make the story work by piquing your interest as a reader. You want to know more, to solve the unsolved mystery.

Seeing is a major part of observation. How does an accident scene look when you arrive? Is there confusion? Is there control? Was the collision violent? Are people hurt? Dying? You must get a visual sense. Television reporters must be concerned with getting what is seen onto tape and into the script. This means working closely with photographers assigned to the story. For print and radio reporters it is essential to ask questions of yourself that help you to notice what you see in a more systematic manner: What shade of blue is the water? What texture is the material of the chair? How short is that person's haircut? What model car is that? These are details of ordinary objects that can become a part of a story.

Listening is also part of observation. What sounds do you hear? Background noises? Conversations? Music? Traffic? How does noise become a part of the story?

Smelling is part of observation. Not everything will have the aroma of a bakery. At a toxic waste dump site that is being cleaned up by the government, can you smell the chemicals? Should this be part of your story to help drive home the point about the contamination? You must decide.

We learn much about objects by *touching* them. The ability to feel an object is an important sense that is sometimes overlooked by reporters as a means of gathering information for a story. How rough is a surface? What does a bullet hole in a car fender feel like? How does a new hair product you tried as part of a story feel to you?

University of Oregon journalism professor Ken Metzler (1989) recommended that reporters remember four categories of routine observation when on assignments. These categories take the form of Metzler's "SCAM" formula and parallel the basic five *W*s and *H* of reporting:

1. *(S)cene or setting:* Representing "where" and "when," this is simply description of the environment to establish a sense of place.

2. *(C)haracter:* representing "who," this gives the people in your story personality and depth.

Arrests at crime scenes always require keen observation skills to enhance accuracy (photo by the *Miami Herald* staff).

3. *(A)ction:* representing "what" and "how," this element shows what happened as it is relevant to the story.

4. *(M)eaning:* representing "why," this element brings together scene, character, and action. What do your observations mean? What's the point? Here you help the reader when the meaning, or theme, of other observations is not obvious.

BILL ROSE, THE *MIAMI HERALD*
HOW TO AVOID "NEWSPAPER DISEASE"

If you talk to a reporter who has just covered a nice feature or has been through some dramatic news event, he or she often tells you the most wonderful, colorful, attention-grabbing kind of story. But when you see that story in print, you have to work to get through the first few graphs.

It happens the other way, too: You go out for a drink after work and say to a reporter, "Hey, that was a nice story." Whereupon the reporter begins to tell you all sorts of neat things that weren't in the story. Often, they are better than the story that appeared in print.

I call it *Newspaper Disease.* The symptoms: self-importance, stuffiness about the written word, a tight rear end, a fear of experimentation, an

(continued)

BILL ROSE, THE *MIAMI HERALD* (continued)

exaggerated sense of moral responsibility (to the point where the reporter thinks his/her moral compass is the only one working in the newsroom and therefore he/she is the sole fit arbiter of what is appropriate to put in the paper on a given subject). There are other symptoms, of course. These are just the primary ones.

But what happens? Why don't these people write their stories the way they tell them?

Like [former *Herald* assistant managing editor/metro, now at the *Wall Street Journal*] John Brecher used to say, I think the formality of sitting down and writing things inhibits many reporters. Instead of just telling the story, there's somehow this feeling that you have to mold the story, put it in some sort of acceptable, formal language, make it somehow CORRECT.

Thankfully, The *Herald* is less at fault here than most other newspapers. When I was covering the South from Atlanta, the correspondents for the other big newspapers would tell me the most interesting, colorful stories of what was really going on in the civil rights movement, in the coal fields of Kentucky, in the governor's mansion in Louisiana. But when I read their stories, that material was inevitably not part of it. During the Mariel inmates' takeover of the Atlanta Federal Penitentiary, reporters for the local newspapers told me great stuff about what was going on in the prison and I gritted my teeth, thinking we were getting badly beaten. Then I saw the papers. The coverage was good, yes, but it didn't have the wonderful stories they had told me.

Frequently, during big news stories, our own anchor will get lots of files from reporters quoting this person or that saying how things were at the scene. But the reporters themselves often don't tell the anchor anything — except on the phone, talking to the anchor personally. Often, an anchor like Arnie Markowitz or Marty Merzer will finally have to say to them: "Look, in your file, give me three graphs just from your own eyes. I want to know, from you, what the hell is it like there?"

As Brecher used to say, don't save your best copy for the 1800 Club. Don't come into my office and tell me neat facts that you're not going to put in the story. Don't see things with your eyes and fail to tell our readers. If you go to a Madonna concert, don't be shy to tell me: If I had been there, what would it have been like?

Some people, eaten up with the awesome responsibility of being a journalist, develop the crazy notion that what we see and think and feel shouldn't be passed on to readers. That is absolutely insane. You cannot and should not be a serious journalist if your attitude is, "I don't do first person." Sorry, that's just silly. Part of your job is first person.

If it makes you feel better, let me put it this way: To a great extent, you should write like you talk. (You don't SAY "persons" or "approximately five miles" or "developable land" or "contiguous boundary," do you?)

Long ago, when I was a reporter, editors would sometimes suggest that I sit down at the typewriter (I told you it was a long time ago!) and write my

(continued)

BILL ROSE, THE *MIAMI HERALD (continued)*

stories without looking at my notes. Then I would have to go back through my notes and correct facts and quotes and add in things I might have forgotten. What that meant, in effect, was that I was forced to TELL a story rather than REPORT it.

The point is simply this: With many of the stories you write, you can sit down at the terminal and pretend that I'm on the other end, having just said, "Hey, what's this story all about?" Your story will be more readable, more interesting, move along more quickly and seem more exciting.

Bill Rose (1991) is the editor of Tropic magazine, the Sunday supplement of the *Miami Herald*. Rose was formerly the *Herald*'s southeastern U.S. correspondent based in Atlanta. He is originally from Mississippi.

Reprinted with permission of the *Miami Herald*.

AVOIDING THE PITFALLS OF OBSERVING

Observation can be an essential tool in your reporting if it is done well. But it can also cause problems and errors. First and foremost, do not rely on your memory when you observe. Take notes. The notes will help your recall of facts and descriptive details. What you later thought was a blue dress might have been a different shade. This is how accuracy errors creep into your story.

Second, take another look. If you are not sure, look again. This way you are more confident of what you saw, especially if it was unusual, illegal, or otherwise troubling.

Stanford University journalism professor William Rivers (1975) recommended these guidelines to avoid problems related to observing:

1. *Remember the process of distortion.* People tend to mentally change what they see to become consistent with their own previous experiences. There is also distortion of perspective. Point of view can give you a different look at matters from someone else's position.

2. *Recall emotional states.* Your emotional response to a situation can affect what you see and later recall.

3. *Concentrate on important details.* You cannot remember everything, so focus on what is most important.

4. *Seek other evidence.* Consider the perspectives of others. In other words, get a second opinion.

5. *Observe unobtrusively.* If people know you are intentionally watching, it may affect their normal behavior. This does not preclude observation that is known to the source, but do not interfere with what you are observing. Also remember that it is sometimes impossible to observe without intruding.

6. *Become a participant if you can.* Get involved only if you want this special point of view. You are certain to distort behavior of those around you if your purpose is known, but often the experience is still worth it for your story and the distortion may be insignificant.

7. *Watch for nonverbal communication.* This includes body language, which was discussed in the chapters on interviewing. What a person says is not all that the person communicates.

SYSTEMATIC OBSERVATION

Some observation is episodic. Some of it is more systematic. This means we observe in pieces or incidents, or we can observe in more formal and organized fashion at a series of episodes to get a greater perspective. *Advanced Reporting* authors Gerry Keir, Maxwell McCombs, and Donald Shaw (1991) purported that systematic observation is an important part of the observation process of journalists.

Systematic observation comes from social science research. Sociologists, anthropologists, and psychologists use it. Reporters have begun to apply some of its approaches to studying sources and social behavior for news stories. Systematic observing includes five different advanced reporting techniques:

1. *Polls and surveys:* Observing public opinion on issues and other matters has become a very important means of learning about the community.

2. *Content analysis:* This procedure involves systematic analysis of documents and records.

3. *Social indicators:* This technique requires study and analysis of vital statistics and other data about your community.

4. *Field experiments:* These are behavior tests in the field where a reporter observes behavior resulting from certain conditions set up and controlled by the reporter.

5. *Participant observation:* Discussed in detail later in this chapter, this involves becoming a participant in the story to get an inside view.

THE STORY'S ENVIRONMENT

Each story has an environment. This is the physical space where the story takes place. Some people call it a setting, but it is the location of the action. You should give the environment of each story you cover adequate attention so you can construct it for your audience or readers if it is necessary for the story. If you are routinely observing the story's environ-

Outdoor event-based stories occur in an environment that tests observation skills to the fullest (photo by the *Miami Herald* staff).

ment, your work will be more complete and your story writing will be easier.

There will be times when a story can be improved simply by going to its primary location and looking around. You might be writing a story on flood damage from heavy rains. A tour of the flooded area can tell you much more than telephone interviewing, reading books, or talking to people who had previously experienced floods.

Most of the time, however, you will be combining observation with interviewing and other research skills. You do not need to be a detective, but you cannot be oblivious to what is going on, either. If you find yourself dependent on other persons for detail and description, you must contend with their potential distortions. Thus, the more you see of that environment for yourself, the richer your story will be. Most people are simply not accustomed to noting detail such as a detective does, and you have to train yourself through practice to do it well.

Author Jacqueline Briskin (1979) recommended one rather unusual technique that will lend a guiding hand to your observational talents. She suggested that when you are out looking around—touring a new police station, for example, to research a story—sometimes your camera can help you with your notetaking. Use the camera to record some of your observations. The photos you take do not have to be publishable. Yet the approach makes good sense. The detail contained in a picture might just jog your memory or provide an image for a description needed in your story.

Television reporters can do the same thing. Ask your photographer to record certain scenes or objects. As you begin to write your script, review

---

MARYLN SCHWARTZ, *DALLAS MORNING NEWS*
USING OBSERVATIONAL SKILLS FOR FEATURE STORIES

When I'm writing my newspaper column, I look for the small details that give readers a clear view of the big picture.

For instance, when Prince Charles visited New Mexico, I wanted to give an example of what it means to be royalty. I didn't want to just write that people were bowing, because we already know that people bow to royalty. So I just watched for a little while. Then I noticed that Prince Charles was the only person at the party who wasn't wearing a name tag. And this wasn't a "B" Party. Cary Grant was there and he wore a name tag.

This is the kind of touch that separates real royalty from mere legend. I did the same thing recently when I was watching the Miss America contestants give their predictable pre-pageant TV interviews. They were all insisting they weren't beauty queens; they had a message to give the world. They didn't want to discuss sex appeal. They wanted to talk about nuclear disarmament.

Then I would flip channels to interviews of the presidential candidates. The political analysts kept trying to talk about Michael Dukakis' charisma or George Bush's sex appeal.

I knew I had my column when I began to realize that politics and beauty pageants have somehow become confused with each other: "Would someone please tell me what's going on? Why is it that Miss Montana can't wait to discuss Manuel Noriega and George Bush only seems to want to discuss his grandchildren?"

To write a good feature story requires as much observing as it does writing. You can have a beautifully crafted story, but no one will really care unless you have something to say. Information is the most important aspect. There will always be an editor who can help you turn a better phrase. But all the editing in the world isn't going to help if your information isn't interesting.

You don't have to have been at a major news event to find a good feature story. And you just have to train yourself to see details that other people overlook.

Actress Farrah Fawcett was the most interviewed actress in the country when she was starring in the "Charlie's Angels" TV show. My editor asked me to do a story and to be sure to mention that the actress had been named one of the "10 Most Beautiful" on campus when she attended the University of Texas.

The story had been done again and again. I didn't think anyone would even want to read it. Instead, I decided to find out what had happened to the other nine most beautiful. The story went on the wire and was used in about 40 newspapers.

I got my information by phone. It took only two days.

Maryln Schwartz (Garrison, 1989, pp. 132–133) is an award-winning feature writer and columnist for the *Dallas Morning News*.

the field tape taken on the assignment. Although most of the video will not get on the air, of course, the tape can help you in preparing your story by prompting memory and helping you recall details in the same way Briskin uses a still camera.

But do not look for an environment for every story. Some stories just do not have them. Trend stories, analyses, and other nonevent stories have other elements on which you should focus. An environment may be insignificant.

STUDYING A PERSON

When you interview someone, what can you learn just by observing that person? There often is much to be learned if you study the individual.

You might recall the discussion on body language, or kinesics, from the chapter on interviewing. This is one way to study people. Watch how they conduct themselves. Study actions. Study reactions. Study interactions. Study expressions. How do they express themselves?

Also study the physical appearance of the person. How is the person dressed? (For instance, formal or casual? Expensive or inexpensive clothing?) How does the person appear? (For instance, thin or overweight? Ruffled or neat? Tanned or pale?) What is this person's individual *style?*

What are the details of this individual's behavior? Does the person move slowly or is the person hurried? Is this individual emotional or nonemotional? Is the person relaxed or nervous?

Also take time to notice the environment of this person, regardless of whether it is a business or home environment, or even somewhere else. What can you learn from the decor? From the mementos on the walls? From the workstyle or playstyle evident in this place?

CONVENTIONAL OBSERVATION

This is perhaps the most common and most basic form of observation for reporters. You know the assignment. Direct observation is used when important newsworthy events occur. Reporters watch sports events, parades, meetings, speeches, festivals, and civil disturbances. On observational assignments such as these, richness of detail is important in your story. You must capture the people, places, and objects of the event. You must take little pieces of many activities and put them together to form a larger portrait of that event.

There are many events set up today just for the news media to observe. Public relations professionals are well-schooled in orchestrating the most visual and newsworthy elements of these events for television cameras and for print photographers. They also know how to get the right sources ready with the right soundbites and most quotable quotations. "Media events" such as a victory celebration, a celebrity appearance, or a tour by a government official are often created just for the news media's observational needs.

But there are more routine events that require routine direct observational skills of journalists. A sportswriter, for instance, observes and then describes many different plays in a game to create the game story. A political writer observes a political party's leadership seminar to gather information about the decision-making activities taking place. This builds a foundation for the story about the direction that party may take or perhaps for projecting which candidates are front-runners for nominations in the next round of campaigns and elections.

There is also postevent direct observation. Reporters often arrive on the scene after an event has occurred. Unexpected events such as an automobile accident, an airplane crash, a violent crime, or a natural disaster require aftermath observation of the event's effects. Reporters put their observational skills to the test when they must report what has happened, especially when no photographs or video can be part of the story.

UNOBTRUSIVE OBSERVATION

In unobtrusive observation reporters are not directly involved in the story. As is pointed out in the next section of this chapter, some observation requires more direct involvement in the story.

Nonparticipant unobtrusive observation requires an "invisible" approach. That means that, as a reporter, you cannot interfere in the normal course of action taken by those in which you are interested. One type of nonparticipant unobtrusive observation is stakeout reporting, discussed later. Another indirect form is to observe what is happening in the community by using certain "social indicators" such as population data, crime statistics, or professional license summaries.

You can learn a great deal by looking at the modern "artifacts" of people. Their neighborhoods tell you how they live. So do their cars, homes, and even garbage. Their businesses tell you how they work. Their parks and playgrounds tell you how they play. By visiting these places and observing in some detail, you may find revealing information that could develop into a trend-oriented story.

For example, a simple tour of on-campus housing may tell you a lot about how noncommuter students live their lives. Walking down the hallways and looking into rooms with opened doors might provide hints about decorating trends. Or that same walk might tell you a lot about current music interests as you listen to sound systems in use.

Observing long lines at the campus cafeterias may tell you something else. It might suggest a problem. If you see these lines every day over a period of time, the lines might suggest that most students eat at the same time, overloading the facility, or it might suggest management or labor troubles for the food service.

Stakeout Reporting

Reporters might need to spend a large amount of time on stakeouts. When reporters must stake out a location, they are often waiting and watching for a newsmaker to appear.

For example, when a royal family member visits a community, reporters wait for a chance to see what the special visitor will do. When an individual accused of a serious crime is taken to the courthouse for arraignment, reporters wait for a chance to see and photograph the person, or perhaps to ask a question if it is allowed by authorities.

But reporting stakeouts also include quiet, and perhaps covert, observation of individuals. There is nothing illegal about this form of observation as long as it takes place in a public place or on private property with permission of the owner of the property. For example, you may have a tip that a local public official is using public property improperly. You get an anonymous telephone call that the county executive is using police helicopters for personal trips to visit a relative in a county about 50 miles away. To confirm this, you go to the county's airport where the police helicopters are kept and wait for the county manager to appear. At the same time, another reporter is at the location where you believe the county executive lands to determine if this is what occurs.

Stakeout reporting is not a very efficient form of observation because it can involve large amounts of time and money, and it is often not productive. It often requires advance information from a reliable source, also, because you must have some knowledge of the event occurring so you can be set up to observe when it happens again.

PARTICIPANT OBSERVATION

Participant observation, or "do-it-yourself" reporting, comes in two major forms. In this third major type of observation, you directly participate in the story rather than observe in a detached manner. Participant observation reporting can be overt or covert, a special type of participant observation called "undercover" reporting. In these two forms of participant observation, reporters become part of the story to gather information.

Overt Participant Observation

Participant observation has its roots in the social sciences. Sociologists and anthropologists have used this technique to study human behavior for over a century. In journalism, participant observation is also called first-person reporting. In this type of reporting, you actually become a participating member of the group that is part of your story. For many decades, reporters have become involved in stories, but this form of reporting has become popular in the past quarter century as a means to get an unusual perspective for stories.

Overt participant observation is different from undercover observation

Veteran journalist Hunter S. Thompson built his reputation with fearless unconventional reporting techniques, including first-person participant observation reporting (photo by Bill Andrews, *Miami Herald* staff).

because reporters make no attempt to conceal their identity as a reporter. But there are some stories requiring the reporter to remain unidentified as a journalist.

Newspapers, magazines, and television files are full of examples of reporters participating in stories for a unique angle. Examples? A television reporter flies a new A-320 Airbus, or so it seems to viewers from the opening video. But it turns out that the reporter is really sitting at the controls of a sophisticated multimillion-dollar training simulator, which offers the same flight experience. A Milwaukee sports writer works as a beer vendor at a professional baseball game. A middle-aged San Diego features reporter "joins the circus" to become part of a trapeze aerial act (with a net). A national business magazine's writer takes a private course in currency trading from a major international bank to learn the ins and outs of international currency trading. A reporter writes about the experience of being stranded 2,000 miles from home in an airline strike.

Overt participant reporting is common in feature stories. Reporters perform stand-up comedy, drive fast race cars, parachute from airplanes, work as disk jockeys, and do all sorts of things to learn firsthand about unusual activities of people in their communities. They participate in an activity to learn more about how the people of the community live their lives.

But overt participant stories can be serious news stories also. For example, student reporters have examined handicapped access on their campuses by using wheelchairs or by going to class blindfolded. Sportswriters and sportscasters work out with teams at practices and play "one-on-one" with star athletes. Entertainment reporters go on the road with musicians and dance troupes. Each of these first-person situations offers insight not gained through conventional observation, unobtrusive observation, or interviewing.

Undercover Reporting

After more than a decade of debate, this form of covert observation reporting remains controversial. Advocates feel it is a tool for reporting to gather information for stories that otherwise cannot legally be obtained. But some editors feel covert participant observation reporting is just not ethical, arguing it is a form of entrapment and that it unfairly uses deception.

These techniques are sometimes called undercover "sting" operations. They are designed to catch someone in the act of committing a crime or some other undesirable act that cannot be detected in any other conclusive way. This technique provides documentation and evidence needed when accusations must be made in a story.

There are examples of undercover reporting successes as well as examples of decisions not to do this type of reporting. The *Chicago Sun-Times* once bought and operated a bar called the "Mirage" to document payoffs and other forms of graft and corruption in city government (Hoge, 1978). *Newsday,* New York's daily newspaper based on Long Island, decided after a long internal debate, not to carry out what would have been an expensive, elaborate undercover observation operation to document racial discrimination in the real estate industry on Long Island (Dufresne, 1991).

The controversy surrounding undercover reporting concentrates on the propriety of deceptive reporting to gather information. The *Sun-Times,* when its Mirage payoffs series was judged for a Pulitzer Prize, was not selected because some judges disapproved of the deception used to document the bribing. This was one of the reasons offered by some editors at *Newsday* who opposed the proposal to send test Black and White couples posing as home buyers into the community to find housing.

There are other problems with undercover stories. Such covert reporting operations almost always involve great expense. The *Newsday* project might have cost as much as $50,000. The *Sun-Times* spent even more. Secrecy was another difficulty that concerned *Newsday* editors. With so many people involved, keeping the test secret would have been difficult. Another matter, called by one editor the "threshold," involved assuming guilt. In planning an undercover project, you must have sufficient reason to believe wrongdoing is occurring (Dufresne, 1991).

Such complicated stories are not often attempted by student journalists. But the same ideas can be applied to other subjects. Undercover student journalists can test quality of instruction in classrooms. They can observe cheating problems. They can examine ID-checking policies at local clubs. They can go undercover to work in local restaurants near campus or cafeterias on campus to check food handling and preparation. Or, as patrons, they can observe violations of occupancy limits of the most popular campus area nightclubs on weekends.

But such reporting is a very tough call. It involves extensive use of valuable resources such as people, time, and money. And it is a significant ethical issue still unresolved in debates about reporting techniques. There is no doubt such undercover reporting is valuable, but it is still unclear if using this particular observational tool is worthwhile.

HOW PROFESSIONALS WRITE IT

SOURCE: *Sioux Falls Argus Leader,* Associated Press A wire.
AUTHOR: Ward Bushee, executive editor
DATE: Thursday, May 31, 1990, APn 05/31 1156 Jets Collide-Account

* * *

EDITOR'S NOTE — Ward Bushee, executive editor of the *Sioux Falls Argus Leader,* was in a South Dakota Air National Guard A-7 fighter jet when it collided Wednesday with another A-7 over northwest Iowa. He gave his newspaper this account of his flight with Maj. Duncan Keirnes, of Sioux Falls, and of the crash.

SIOUX FALLS, S.D. (AP) — It was a great day for flying. My wife, my 5-year-old son and young daughter watched from the runway as we took off.

I've always been scared to fly. But the plane takeoff was so smooth. I was feeling very comfortable and was talking to Duncan much of the way.

We flew in formation to the tanker and practiced fueling in air. Everything was going so smoothly. . . .

I handled the plane for a couple of minutes. Then Duncan took control for good. We took it for a roll. We went up and did some G-force testing to see how I would react. . . .

Then he brought the squadron back together and began setting up for combat exercises. . . .

We did the first exercise. It was pure Top Gun. . . . We were moving so fast I saw Duncan's head swinging around looking at the other planes. It was very aggressive. . . .

We were engaged in a dogfight with another plane and we were the aggressor. Suddenly, it got turned around and another pilot was the aggressor. Duncan told me on his radio, "Now we're on defense." We began going around with Greg Gore, the other pilot, in pursuit of us. . . .

I noticed way down to the left of what I could see that Gore's plane was coming up in an arch towards us. Duncan suddenly pointed the nose higher and seemed to be backing off the fight. That is when I fixed on Gore coming at us. The pilots later said they were trying to exercise a scissor maneuver.

Those planes go so fast, a mere second makes such a difference. I said to myself, "There isn't any danger. These guys are too good of pilots. We won't collide." Then it became obvious he was going to hit us.

I saw the whites of the other pilot's eyes.

We went up, but I think we took the hit low. He hit us from underneath towards the tail section.

Gore said later he thought he was going to take it right in his canopy and he would have died instantly. . . .

Duncan hit the ejector button as soon as we hit, sending me exploding through the canopy and him following a second later. Then everything came apart. It was just a ball of flame. Duncan later told me that if he had waited a couple of seconds longer to eject, we would have been crispy critters.

It was just a surreal scene. I was floating up in the air and my flight suit was burning like a torch. My first thought was, "I'll never see my wife and kids again. This is it."

Pieces of the plane were going by. Flames were all over me. I couldn't remember where the cord was to open the parachute, but it went open automatically.

It was like one of those movies. The plane and debris were spiraling down below me in flames. It was completely silent up there.

The parachute was swinging me around. I thought, "Oh my God. I'm alive."

Then I noticed blood was dripping from my head. The only thing I could think was, "I wonder if I'm really seriously hurt." I didn't know if half my head was blown off. I looked down at my feet and saw my shoes were completely singed, but they were both there.

I saw the other guys were alive. Duncan gave me the thumbs up. I gave him the thumbs up. It was very peaceful floating down. But I kept smelling this smell and finally figured out it was my own skin that had burned.

I was trying to remember everything they told me about landing—how to avoid trees, power lines. It seemed like five minutes to get down. It was very, very slow. The whole world was sitting out there.

I saw people gathering in cars below us. There were a lot of farmers there with the wreckage off in the distance. . . .

I just sort of floated down and hit kind of awkwardly. I thought I'd broken my leg. I couldn't get out of the chute right away and it was blowing me across the field. A farmer came out and grabbed the chute and helped me. . . .

Duncan came along and asked me if I was all right. He said he was sorry it had to happen.

• • •

SOURCE: WCCO-TV, Channel 4, Minneapolis
AUTHOR: Alan Cox, reporter
DATE: Friday, August 10, 1990
TIME: 6 P.M. newscast

* * *

NWA PILOTS KS A, CU (DAVE)	(DAVE/_____) THE DEFENSE BEGAN ITS CASE TODAY IN THE TRIAL OF THREE FORMER NORTHWEST AIRLINES PILOTS ACCUSED OF FLYING WHILE UNDER THE INFLUENCE OF ALCOHOL. HERE'S ALAN COX.
TAKE VT/ 10 SOT TAKE VT SOUND FULL ON_____ title :mpls IN:_____ OUT:_____	OC: ". . . Captain Lyle Prouse was in charge of Flight-650. But like any jetliner crew . . . Prouse and the other 2 pilots had to follow the orders of air traffic controllers.
title: Artist: IN: Martin Harris OUT:	Prouse's defense opened with a reconstruction on the flight as controllers at Fargo, Farmington, and Twin Cities International guided it in. Retired controller Robert Collette . . . called as an expert witness by the defense . . . described the twists and turns Flight-650 had to make . . . changing altitude, direction, and speed . . . following several orders to change course as it came in for an instrument landing

PILOTS TRIAL/2

on a day with 1-mile visibility.

Collette testified, "There were no instances of noncompliance. The crew did not act confused on the tape. They were able to respond to several unplanned events in a professional manner."

But prosecutor Elizabeth de la Vega challenged Collette's ability as a non-pilot to judge how well the crew worked . . . and how hard their job was that day.

The prosecutor said, "It sounds complicated if you break it down and use all these numbers, doesn't it? It sounds complicated to a lay person, but it's not to a pilot, is it?"

PILOTS/P3

Late in the day, a veteran Northwest pilot said he found the crew's communications "prompt and accurate . . . clear and concise.

ALAN READS – LIVE/
CONTROL ROOM

The last witnesses of the day was a psychiatrist associated with the Hazelden Foundation . . . who began to describe alcoholism.

TITLE: ALAN

Prouse's attorney seemed to be close to asking him whether problems in the family the captain grew up in could have predisposed him toward alcohol dependency. But the judge cut that questioning off because the psychiatrist had examined him for only a few minutes.

It's expected Prouse will discuss his disease when he takes the stand . . . possibly tomorrow.

TAKE 2BOX (NEWSROOM)

(DAVE/2BOX/ALAN)

Reprinted with permission of WCCO-TV.

• • •

9 | Press Conferences, Hearings, Meetings, Conventions

One of your first reporting assignments will probably require you to cover an announcement at a press conference, a decision made at a meeting, or a speaker at a convention. Public presentations at press conferences, meetings, hearings, and conventions are the bread-and-butter assignments of reporting. Mastery of these assignments is basic to your existence as a local news gatherer. Most editors and news directors will assume you have a solid background in writing stories about announcements at press conferences, hearings on public issues, developments at conventions, or decisions at meetings.

Take a look at today's news. In the newspaper, you probably see reports about speeches made by prominent politicians, bankers, or educators. On television newscasts, you may see soundbites from a press conference that happened earlier in the day when a developer announced plans for a new high-rise office building or an accused individual denied wrong-doing. Driving home, you might hear a story on your favorite radio station's newscast that reports a tax rate decision made by the city council. The current issue of your favorite journalism magazine might contain a story reporting developments at a recent national convention or seminar.

These types of stories are very common. Because of their frequent occurrence, they are important story forms to learn. This chapter gives you the basic elements of these types of stories involving public presentations to groups of people. You will learn how to cover a presentation with one or more speakers. You will also learn the best way to report and write a story based on press conferences, public hearings, and conventions and seminars

Press conferences are often well-orchestrated "media events" at which major announcements are made. Business executive Wayne Huizenga uses a press conference to reveal that his bid for a new professional baseball franchise, the Florida Marlins, has been approved by Major League Baseball (photo by the *Miami Herald* staff).

featuring both individual presentations and panel discussions. This chapter concludes with an important section devoted to covering both public and private organization meetings.

PRESS CONFERENCE STORIES

Press conferences are held by news sources for a variety of reasons, but the most common purposes are (a) to save time and (b) to gain maximum media exposure. Instead of conducting numerous one-on-one interviews with reporters, news sources often use press conferences as faster and easier ways to deal with the news media. Of course, reporters may gain access to a source through press conferences, but they pay a price by giving up story exclusivity.

Typically, press conferences are organized on short notice. Usually a press conference is held by busy and important news sources who have announcements they believe to be newsworthy. But some press conferences wind up not being very newsworthy at all. *Always* remember you and your editors or producers are the final judges of news value — not the people who call the press conference.

Press conferences are held to announce just about anything — major decisions, reactions to major decisions made elsewhere, appointments and promotions, retirements or resignations, proposals, mergers, and many other similar developments. Press conferences are also held to provide updated information in ongoing stories such as labor strikes, medical condition reports, criminal investigations, or missing person searches. Press conferences are held after major events — such as sports contests and tournaments, trials, or lottery drawings — to give participants a chance to provide reactions.

A press conference may be formal and directed by tradition, such as those held at the White House, or quite casual and informal, such as one called by a first-time candidate for city council. Many press conferences are planned, but some are impromptu. During the Persian Gulf War, for example, reporters in Saudi Arabia found that major sources, such as allied forces military leaders, frequently held press conferences at the spur of the moment. Thus, reporters have to be prepared at all times for opportunities to quiz key sources.

Press conferences are news media events. That is, these are events orchestrated by sources and their aides to produce publicity in the news media. Most organizers will have materials prepared to distribute to reporters such as videotapes, audiotapes, still photographs, copies of prepared statements, biographies of the key individuals, chronologies of key events, and graphics like slides and camera-ready logos.

Press conferences may be the only way information is disseminated on a breaking story when many reporters need information from few sources. Sources may be completely unavailable and inaccessible through other channels. Thus, the situation will be highly competitive.

The competitive nature of press conferences seems to bring out the best and worst in reporters, remarked *Miami Herald* general assignment reporter Kimberly Crockett (1991). Crockett said press conferences can get nasty:

> I've been to some press conferences where I've been embarrassed. Reporters claw at each other and at the sources. Reporters are not on the same team and must get information. If I need something unique for a story, I will save the question for later if I can ask it in some private situation with a source.

Most news reporters combine information they obtain at a press conference with other sources of information in preparing their story for the day.

A typical press conference begins with a statement by one or more principals in the announcement. The statement can be a few sentences (perfect for television and radio soundbites, of course) or much longer and elaborate. Following the announcement portion of the press conference, the source or sources usually open up for questions by reporters. There may be a time limit set on the press conference—typically it is 30 to 60 minutes. Formal White House press conferences held by the president rarely last more than 30 to 40 minutes, for example.

Press conferences can be advanced also. When a Miami police chief resigned, *Miami Herald* city hall beat reporter Ronnie Ramos had the story a day in advance. His lead focused on the press conference at which the announcement was expected to occur:

> Miami Police Chief Clarence Dickson is expected to resign today at a press conference at Miami City Hall.
>
> The press conference was called late Thursday [Ramos' story appeared on Friday] by City Manager Cesar Odio's office. Media representatives were told only that Dickson and Odio would be present for a major announcement.
>
> Several sources confirmed that Dickson, the city's first black chief, will resign today and said if news of his resignation appeared in the media before the press conference, he would not go through with the announcement.
>
> Mayor Xavier Suarez, Odio, and the four city commissioners refused to comment Thursday night. Dickson, who has been on vacation for the past two weeks and wasn't scheduled to return until Monday, could not be reached for comment. (Ramos, 1988)

The chief did quit, despite his threats not to do so if advance word leaked. He had been angry about internal meddling by the city commission and budget problems. Ramos attended the press conference at which the chief announced his resignation and his reasons for the decision. There was a bonus to the press conference: Ramos also got the official announcement of the name of the new chief in his Saturday story.

Although most press conferences are held on the record, some are not. This will occur when an official or some other individual wants to disseminate information to the news media but not be held accountable for it. As a reporter, you have to decide how to handle the information. Do you use it in the restricted form? Or do you try to find another source who will go on the record with it? Most of the time, reporters cannot find a second source who will go on the record and the information must be used without complete attribution.

Another restriction is an "embargo." An embargo is a sometimes arbitrary time restriction on release of information. The release time and date are set by the source for reasons that the source believes important. Embargoes assure the universal simultaneous release of information and are thus appealing to sources who wish not to show favoritism to a particular news organization.

Typically, embargoes are set for a specific release time and date. Embargoes are usually listed on news releases distributed at the press conference or they are announced one or more times during the press conference. Most journalists honor embargoes, but some reporters break them. It is not a legal issue, of course. But there are ethical issues and other consequences to consider. There are two groups you must answer to if you break an embargo to use information in your story. First, you may have to answer to your colleagues who honor the embargo. Peer pressure can be significant. In addition, your sources will be aware of the broken embargo and may not include you in the release of information the next time it occurs. You may become *persona non grata*.

Here are the most basic steps to covering a press conference:

1. *Get there on time.* It might not start on time—some don't—but you cannot afford to risk missing an opening statement or announcement. There may be a shortage of press kits and handouts if the media turnout is large. You will learn from experience which organizations will or will not start press conferences on time. But, as a beginner, you cannot afford to guess.

2. *Contact the right person once you get there.* Find the organizer or media relations contact. If you don't know who is running things, ask. Someone will know. The media relations person might have additional information for you.

3. *Allow time to set up.* If you are working in radio or television, arrive in time to set up your equipment. This means an extra 15 minutes or so for cameras and possibly lights, depending on the location. Print reporters need less time, but it helps to be prepared with your tape recorder set up and your pen and notebook ready. Broadcast news reporters should remember to check if there is a central sound source to use.

4. *Listen for the opening statement.* The statement opening the press conference will probably contain the key news of the day. The person holding the conference may be introduced by an aide or media representative. Opening statements are normally allowed to run until they are finished without interruption.

5. *Be ready to ask questions.* When the formal statement is finished, you can ask questions for more information not covered in the statement. There may be a time limit on questioning and, depending on the number of

reporters present, you may need to be selective in questioning. And remember, if you have a chance to ask a question, always identify yourself by name and media organization if you are not known to your source.

6. *Be aggressive in questioning.* You may not be called upon if you are not aggressive. If there are not many reporters present, wait your turn and you will get a chance. If it is crowded, you must attract attention—by standing, waving your hand, or even shouting.

7. *Listen carefully to questions of other reporters and the answers they bring.* Just because other reporters ask a question, the response is not just their material. You have the right to use it as well.

8. *Rephrase questions if necessary.* This may get an answer to the second question if the first was evaded. It may also clarify if the original question was not well stated.

9. *Wrap ups are important.* Fill in the information gaps by asking questions at the end (either in the group or alone with the source if given the opportunity). You may find press aides to help you fill in holes if the primary source is not available.

10. *Leave yourself an out.* In the event you must recontact persons involved in calling the press conference, take down a telephone number that you can use to call later in the day.

11. *Write the story.* Usually press conference stories are written in one of three ways. The inverted pyramid remains most popular. Chronological approaches are sometimes useful, but be careful not to bury key news if you use this plan. A third approach would integrate information from the press conference with additional information from other sources in roundup-style organization.

12. *Remember to exercise your news judgment.* Keep in mind that you might not write anything about information you obtain at a press conference. Some press conferences are only for background purposes and some are purely promotional.

One newspaper story reprinted at the end of this chapter shows how press conferences can generate solid, informative news stories.

The story was based on a Washington press conference and was written by States News Service reporter Michael M. Phillips. Phillips attended a press conference conducted by the U.S. Department of Health and Human Services. At the session, Secretary Louis Sullivan released a report about a national study of drug use by teenagers. Typical of these news events, Phillips was given a package of materials that included the report and a Health and Human Services public information office press release summarizing the report and providing comments from department officials. But most important, he had the opportunity to question the story's key sources, Sullivan and John P. Waters, acting director of the Office of National Drug Control Policy, and their aides about the study and its significance. Phillips' story summarizes the findings of the national study but also gives readers direct quotations from Sullivan's comments at the press conference that help interpret and explain the study's findings.

CHUCK CROUSE, WEEI-AM, BOSTON
A LITTLE SECRET TO SAVE THE DAY

Chuck Crouse (1991), reporter for WEEI-AM radio in Boston, never permits himself to be at city hall, in an auditorium, or at other story locations without his best friend.

Oh, you mean his tape recorder, right?

No.

Chuck Crouse's friend is *gaffer's tape.* If you don't know what it is, take a look around the next time you go to a press conference. The gray cloth tape is very sticky and useful in many ways. Here's a list of 11 ways a roll of gaffer's tape, secreted away in your briefcase or duffle bag, can help:

1. Mount a microphone on a lectern.
2. Mount a microphone on a light stand where there is no lectern — such as impromptu press conferences in the open.
3. Attach a microphone to a public address speaker to capture sound.
4. Attach a cassette recorder to a microphone stand (when you forget your microphone cable).
5. Safety protection for long extension cords. Tape them to the ground for safety and to assure the cable does not get pulled loose.
6. Hold equipment such as batteries together or to serve as a temporary strap.
7. Tape your notebook to the wall when you need an extra hand free for using the telephone and so forth.
8. Mark workspace boundaries. This is similar to setting up a fence when several stations cover the same event.
9. Label tapes, writing temporary telephone numbers and so forth. The tape will usually take ink from a ballpoint pen.
10. Make friends. Lend it to help colleagues.
11. Keeps the news car going. It is waterproof and can even be used to patch things such as broken automobile radiator hoses in an emergency.

Where can you find the tape? Just about any hardware store, Crouse said.

After you look at how this story was structured and written, think about what you would do if you were assigned to cover a press conference involving a prominent individual. How would you begin the assignment?

PUBLIC HEARINGS STORIES

In places where governmental bodies convene — everywhere from a village, city, or county seat to Washington, DC, policy- and law-making groups hold public hearings. Usually public hearings are information-gathering exercises by the governing bodies during the process of policy-making or lawmaking or other formal decision making.

Some press conferences are spur-of-the-moment events that take place when a news-maker such as Miami Mayor Xavier Suarez stops to answer questions by a group of radio and television journalists (photo by the *Miami Herald* staff).

Hearings can be held for dozens of reasons by a wide range of sponsoring groups. Most hearings that are covered by news organizations are those involved in the lawmaking process. Other types of hearings are also conducted and covered for their news potential. Some hearings are held to confirm or even remove appointments of officials. Others are held to guarantee rights to individuals before disciplinary decisions are made.

You may have the chance to cover a hearing and, whereas it is similar to a speech or press conference in some ways, it is quite different on other levels.

Public hearings are seldom conducted by a single individual. Most of the time, hearings are conducted by an inquiring body such as a legislature, a legislative committee, or a council or board. Members of the group are present during the information-gathering process.

Panel members invite speakers and listen to the statements, or testimony, of these interested parties. Much of the time, these interested persons are *experts* in the area of concern. For a legislative hearing on a new bill on gun control, for instance, opponents and proponents (within the legislature) of the bill will request experts to appear. Opponents, such as gun-owners' associations, and proponents, such as law enforcement groups, will be given a chance to appear and state their cases.

This is often significant in the newsmaking process because it may be the

Union leaders use a press conference at their union hall to respond to questions from reporters during a labor strike (photo by Al Diaz, *Miami Herald* staff).

first official opportunity for the two opposing forces to come together in spirited public debate of a new issue. Remember, hearings are fact-finding efforts and, at this point, the process should offer reporters a rich source of information from all sides.

Procedures at hearings vary, but most hearings begin with opening statements from the members of the group holding the hearing. Experts are then asked to come forward to speak. Following each statement, often prepared in advance by these individuals, members of the group usually ask questions of the persons testifying.

Confirmation hearings work the same way. At a hearing to confirm a public office nominee, the "star" of the show is the nominee. However, other individuals may testify about the activities of the nominee and their comments may be just as newsworthy as those of the nominee.

Here are the basic steps to covering public hearings:

1. *Research the topic.* It may be voting rights, pollution, or housing. Whatever it is, the more you know, the better the testimony will make sense to you as a listener and observer. Know what is going on and why. Find out why the hearing was scheduled. Is it routine? Your readers and viewers will want to know.

2. *Get there early.* Arrive with sufficient time to get handouts and other background material. Often there will be an agenda of speakers. Give yourself enough time to meet the principals of the hearing—the chair, other members of the panel, their aides, witnesses, and attorneys.

3. *Give time for set up.* Give yourself time to set up for any recording or photographing you might want to do. You may have to ask permission in advance. Always check this out.

4. *Find sources for after the hearing.* Find out who will be available for further comment after the hearing. Prepare a recontact list if you find the material complex and likely to raise questions when you write.

5. *Listen for opening statements.* During the hearing itself, record key statements of the officials in charge. Listen for testimony from key witnesses. Remember to get full identification of each speaker because there will be several speakers in the course of a hearing session.

6. *Ask questions.* Be prepared to ask follow-up questions for clarification after a speaker leaves the hearing or when the hearing ends.

7. *Save the materials you collect.* Reports and other documents may be useful to you at a later date or they may be useful to another reporter/editor in your office. Put them in the newsroom library if you no longer need them.

The 310-word public hearing story written by *San Jose Mercury News* reporter Laura Kurtzman, which is reprinted at the end of this chapter, focuses on deliberations over whether to rename a major civic facility for a former mayor of the city. The city's historic landmarks commission held a 4-hour hearing to decide the matter but, as Kurtzman's story says, the decision was made not to decide. She tells readers that this body was unfamiliar with controversy and that fact led to a delay of 1 month in making the decision. Kurtzman's story summarizes the issues and presents both pro and con sides through leading spokespersons of each side. The story is strengthened by direct quotations from the proponents and opponents who testified before the commission. She also adds important background on the issue, tracing the proposal to a press conference a month earlier.

MEETING STORIES

Meetings have always been a major source of news. At *public* meetings, the major decisions are made. A community's fiscal policies, for instance, for a year or longer are decided. Reporters cover meetings because most citizens cannot be there. You, as a reporter, become the public's representative. It is, therefore, an important social responsibility. And you have a *right* to be present at public meetings, with certain exceptions specified in each state's law.

Private organizations may hold meetings that are of public interest. You

---

PUBLIC MEETING AGENDAS

When you get your first assignment to cover a public meeting, the action on the floor may intimidate and confuse you. It helps if you understand the flow of the meeting. Whereas the order and names of the agenda items may vary, most county and city meetings have some or all of the following elements on their agendas:

1. Roll call, invocation, and pledge of allegiance
2. Approval of previous meeting's minutes
3. Requests to add, defer, or withdraw items from the agenda
4. Recognition of, and presentations by, visitors
5. Proclamations and other honors
6. Discussions of the "committee of the whole" or reports by district and constituency representatives
7. Standing committee recommendations and reports
8. Presentation and discussion of proposed ordinances or resolutions
9. Public hearings on ordinances and resolutions
10. Appearances, requests, and pleas by citizens
11. Recommendations and reports by members
12. Recommendations and reports by the group's attorney
13. Recommendations and reports by the group's executive officer—for instance, a mayor or manager
14. Recommendations and reports by other special committees and boards
15. Bid discussions
16. New business and special emergency items

---

may be *invited* or allowed to attend these as well, but you attend only as a guest of the hosts.

Some public agencies' meetings will not be open to reporters. Each state has its own open meetings laws, so the exemptions will vary slightly from state to state. But generally, the public cannot be present at a public body's meeting when certain personnel matters or national security issues are discussed.

Probably the most important aspect of writing a news story about a meeting is to determine the news value of business conducted at the meeting. This might not be easy to do in advance, so you must make this judgment at the meeting itself. The key element is to judge the *impact* of the decisions made at the meeting. How many people are affected? What is the cost? There are other concerns, of course. Is there controversy surrounding the issues discussed? What is the level of community interest? Of your audience's interest? Most public policy meetings are routine. Some will generate high levels of interest. You have to be prepared for both the routine and the extraordinary.

Most organizations have a set format for meetings. Agendas are prepared in advance. Records (called minutes or proceedings) of previous

Often at public meetings and hearings, citizens are given an opportunity to speak out (photo by Al Diaz, *Miami Herald* staff).

meetings are kept. An individual, such as a clerk or secretary, is usually required by law to keep these records—if they are public records.

Many organizations conduct meetings following explicit parliamentary procedures. It is helpful to understand these rules. Other organizations, especially private groups, may be much less formal. If you are confused about the business being conducted, you must ask questions.

Here are some tips to make things go easier on your meeting assignments:

1. *Get oriented.* When you get the assignment, find out what you can about the organization that has called the meeting. Who is in charge? When and where will the meeting be held? *Why* is the meeting being held?

2. *Get to the point.* Why are you going to the meeting? Do you need to attend the entire meeting or just part of it? What action by this group will be newsworthy?

3. *Do your homework.* Do some research in advance. Get an agenda. If this is a public body, most states require through their open meetings laws that an agenda be available in advance. Most private groups prepare agendas for formal meetings, so ask the secretary, or even the chair of the group, for a copy in advance.

WAYNE GODSEY, KOAT-TV, ALBUQUERQUE, NM.
IF YOU ARE ASKED TO LEAVE A MEETING

When a reporter is asked to leave a public meeting, there is usually a good, valid reason. But there are times when there is no apparent legal reason. If you have reason to believe you are being asked to leave, but feel you should not be, there are three steps to take, according to Wayne Godsey, vice president and general manager of KOAT-TV, Channel 7, in Albuquerque, New Mexico. Godsey worked with attorneys when he was news director at WTMJ-TV in Milwaukee to provide these guidelines:

1. *"Stand your ground until physical removal is imminent.* If you guess wrong about leaving a meeting, you may be criminally punished, so it is wise to leave at the last possible moment. Resisting a police officer is also an offense, so you must leave when an officer says so.

2. *"Demand that the chair state a specific reason for removal.* If the wrong reasons are given, it becomes an illegally closed meeting even if the meeting could have been legally closed.

3. *"Demand that the matter of closing the meeting be voted upon by the body before you leave or are removed.* The vote must be public. Members voting are accountable for the decision when the vote is taken. The group's members are also subject to fines or other forfeitures if they improperly close a meeting. You should remind group members of this fact."

Wayne Godsey (1980) is former president of the Radio-Television News Directors Association and a former reporter in New York, North Carolina, and Virginia.

---

4. *Get briefed.* Some organizations will hold news media briefing sessions in advance of a major meeting. Attend this if you can. At least make some telephone calls in advance to key individuals to get an idea of what may occur.

5. *Arrive early.* After you know what to expect, go to the meeting with some time to spare. Good seats, the best camera locations, and even parking may be at a premium. Not every organization has the media savvy to save seats for reporters.

6. *Look around.* Check for available telephones, sound or lighting problems, standup locations, and photo-visual prospects.

7. *Find the official sources.* The members of the organization holding the meeting are your key sources. What these persons say during the meeting may be central to your story. However, do not forget these sources are sometimes available before and after the meeting. Some sources may be available during the meeting, too, especially if individuals frequently enter and leave the room — just be sure you do not disrupt the proceedings.

8. *Find alternative sources.* Although members of the organization are good sources, they are not the only sources. Look for the legal counsel,

staff assistants/aides, secretaries, and "regulars" (interested people who always seem to be at the meetings). These persons can often provide you with documentation or background when other sources cannot.

9. *Take good notes.* Don't rely on a tape. This is one type of assignment in which you will find tapes to be tedious or even a waste of time. If you think you might get confused when you are covering a large group of people, draw a diagram of the room and the seating arrangements. Then write numbers, from left to right, and take notes with the numbers. Just be careful to note who is what number!

10. *Listen for quotations.* A meeting story can be very dull, so try to enliven it with quotations and soundbites from debate and discussion among the main players. Quotations and soundbites will help your story get specific when you might be writing mostly generalizations about what occurred.

11. *Focus on action.* In the end, your story will focus on *action* such as voting that is or is not taken. The decisions that lead to policy are those that your audience is interested in. Then focus on how and why the action occurred.

12. *Decide how to write it.* In writing your story, consider that most meeting stories use a summary lead with inverted pyramid organization.

13. *Roundup approaches also work.* Some meetings, with many different decisions made, are best written by using roundup-style organization. The story can employ a multielement lead with the focus on one or two major decisions and itemization (or "bullets") on the remaining decisions.

14. *Remember to get contact numbers.* Before you leave the meeting, find one or two people whom you can call later in the day for additional information if you need it.

Three stories reprinted at the end of this chapter illustrate how different kinds of meeting stories could be reported and written. Kelly Turner, a reporter for the Ocala, Florida, *Star-Banner,* tells readers about a protest about crime problems by city residents during a city commission meeting. Turner described the scope of the concern while summarizing what happened in the crowded commission chambers. But Turner went beyond the events at the meeting. Turner also discussed events before and after the meeting, including reaction comments in the form of direct quotations from the police chief.

WPLG-TV political editor Michael Putney focused his story on a growing controversy that originated from comments made during a city commission meeting in Miami. Putney highlighted odd remarks made by a city commissioner over the appointment of a Black Hispanic man to a park management trust. The commissioner was concerned about the nominee's ethnic, racial, and national background. Putney used videotape of the meeting, held several days earlier, containing the exchange between the commissioner and others present. Putney supplemented the commissioner's comments on the floor of the chambers with soundbites from interviews with other commission members and the nominee. The commissioner at the center of the controversy refused to talk on camera about his comments at the meeting that led to the applicant's hurt feelings.

The third example was written by Idris M. Diaz, staff reporter for the *Philadelphia Inquirer*. Diaz covered a Philadelphia city council meeting at which senior citizens sought discounted fares for public transportation during peak-usage periods. Early in her story, Diaz was clear about the central financial issue. The city did not spend more money, but instead approved a resolution promising to search for alternative funding sources. Diaz also offered direct quotations from the resolution's sponsor and from the leader of the opposition.

CONVENTIONS AND SEMINARS

Covering newsmakers at a convention or seminar is often an interesting assignment because these are not everyday events for most reporters. Because covering conventions in most communities is not routine, it is an assignment that can be both challenging and stimulating.

Conventions are usually organized around a theme or common interest. Some meetings focus on an issue or subject, such as the homeless, child hunger, labor problems, women's rights, AIDS, environmental awareness, or violent crime. Some focus on interests of specialists or collectors. Whether it is a meeting of heart specialists, parents of handicapped children, insurance agents, Elvis fans, politicians, or even journalists, conventions often generate news.

TSITSI WAKHISI, UNIVERSITY OF MIAMI
ADVICE FOR BEGINNERS

Beginning reporters are a lot like Dorothy, the Tin Man, and the Scarecrow in the "Wizard of Oz." Remember their chant as they made their way through the forest en route to Oz?

"Lions and tigers and bears.

"Oh, my!"

Student reporters face speeches, press conferences and civic meetings with much the same fear the Oz trio had on their way to the Emerald City. Somehow, they can make its way through interviews (one-on-ones), do pretty well on a profile, and can cover breaking news (fires, accidents, and police chases). But speeches, press conferences, and meetings?

Oh, my!

Think of these assignments as the mainstays of your journalism career. No matter where you go in journalism, be it broadcast or print, there's going to be a meeting to cover, a speech to hear, and a press conference to record.

(continued)

TSITSI WAKHISI, UNIVERSITY OF MIAMI *(continued)*

But relax. You already have some of the necessary skills it takes to be a good reporter—whether the forum is the White House, the state house, or your house.

Let's start with the latter.

In your own house, probably around the age of 12, you learned and perfected the art of *listening, filtering,* and *observation.* You will find these skills invaluable as you cover meetings, speeches, and press conferences.

I often find myself peeling the telephone from my 14-year-old son's ear every evening. There are times I don't know he is on the phone because he is in the process of developing his listening skills. As he sits silently in his room with his textbook opened, the record player blasting and his siblings running in and out of his room, he is stoic, listening to the message coming in from the other end of the receiver. Occasionally, I might hear a chuckle, a "yeah," or a "right"—the only indication that he is involved in a conversation.

The point here is if you survived your preteen and teenage years at home, you've got some of the skills needed to cover a meeting or a speech.

For example, your parents go on and on about why you can't go to the movies next weekend. Your father says one thing about, "When I was your age . . ." and your mom adds, "I don't understand why . . ." and they both go on about, "If we've said it once, we've said it twice. . . ." But through all of the discussion, which could take several minutes, hours, or a couple of days, you get the key points in this conflict:

Who: You.

What: Can't go to the movies.

When: This weekend.

Where: At the mall.

Why: You brought home an F on an important test.

How: Only you can answer that, but your parents think it's because you spend too much time on the phone.

Welcome to listening and filtering.

Another important element in covering multi-source events is observation. During my professional career, I covered scores of meetings and speeches, and a handful of press conferences.

When then-presidential candidate George Bush spoke to a group of black GOP supporters at a Washington, D.C., hotel dinner, I noted what he wore, what was served, how long he spoke, how often the audience applauded or laughed.

During a speech in Cleveland by Massachusetts Gov. Michael Dukakis, Bush's challenger, I took note of how his travelling campaign workers placed themselves strategically throughout the audience, leading campaign chants: "Go, Mike," or "Duke, Duke, Duke" whenever the audience applauded.

I also remember how terrible Ronald Reagan looked in brown. The president, in Cleveland to speak at a fundraiser, was not so cleverly clad in a brown suit to show his support for the Cleveland Browns, the football team that was on a winning streak. Put it straight in my notes.

(continued)

TSITSI WAKHISI, UNIVERSITY OF MIAMI *(continued)*

At a speech in the Rose Garden at the White House, I wrote in my notebook that Jimmy Carter looked diminutive and pale. That description didn't appear in the story I filed (though I tried like heck to work it in). The experience taught me, however, that good observation and note taking do not oblige the good reporter to use everything in her [or his] copy. Carter already had been described millions of times as being short and pale looking, the latter especially so after he had been in office for a year. It wasn't unusual that he was short, therefore, that observation, though noted, had no place in my story about his speech to high school student leaders who were visiting Washington.

Back to you.

The basic information you need to know about covering meetings and speeches is explained quite well in this chapter. Every journalist, however, has a "like" and "dislike" list. Here's mine:

You called it the main idea in junior high, the theme in high school, and you're learning to call it the lead in your journalism classes. Learn how to find the central idea in a meeting or speech story, develop it, and support it.

Don't think that a story has to be reported in chronological order: First the mayor did this, and then he did that. You are not the organization's or the civic body's recording secretary. You will not be required to read the minutes at their next meeting. You will be required, however, to give your readers, viewers, or listeners an informative synopsis of what occurred.

Finally, be prepared. Do as much reporting as you can in advance of the meeting, speech, or press conference. Sources may be difficult to get for comment following a presentation, so call them a day before or the day of the event. Be as familiar as you can about the topic being discussed or debated.

However, there is the unexpected. You thought you were going to be covering a routine city council meeting, but all of a sudden, a council member accuses the mayor of pocketing city funds.

There you are, like Dorothy, no longer in Kansas but in Oz. Summon the lion's courage, and take plenty of notes.

Prof. Tsitsi Wakhisi (Garrison, 1990) is managing editor of the University of Miami News Service, a function of the graduate program of the School of Communication at the University of Miami. She spent 11 years as a reporter, editor, and editorial writer at the *Plain Dealer* in Cleveland, the *Miami Herald,* the *Detroit News, Kansas City Star,* and Richmond, Indiana *Palladium-Item.*

Conventions usually last only a few days. Usually there are one or two major scheduled events each day, but numerous smaller groups and events are scheduled around the most important events. As a journalist covering a convention, you must not let the significance bestowed on the event by the convention organizers determine whether it is the most newsworthy event of the day.

Seminars are usually shorter in duration and even more focused. Typically seminars run part of a day, a whole day, or even a few days. These events are held with focus on a narrow topic and usually draw experts who may create news by what they have to say.

Some seminar sessions feature just one major speaker. Others present panels of experts to discuss issues or subjects of interest to the group. There will be occasions when you must cover a convention or seminar featuring more than one speaker. This type of reporting assignment will require a special lead and organizational writing approach.

Paul Moses, reporter for *Newsday* on Long Island, illustrated how to focus on the comments of one key speaker at a convention with his story about the speech by a Catholic Church Cardinal to anti-abortion activists at their statewide convention in Manhattan. If you look closely at the story's structure, it is basically a speech story in a convention context. Moses used plenty of direct quotations from the Cardinal to support the generalizations made in the story. He described the audience size and reactions. He put the Cardinal's comments in a current events context by also telling readers about other archdiocese activities supported by the Cardinal. Although the Cardinal was the keynote speaker and main newsmaker, Moses summarized two other speakers' comments as he concluded his story in the final two paragraphs.

HOW PROFESSIONALS WRITE IT

Press Conference-Based Story

• • •

SOURCE: The *Miami Herald,* final ed., p. 12A
DATE: Friday, January 25, 1991
AUTHOR: Michael M. Phillips, States News Service
HEADLINE: Drug use among teens dropping sharply, report says; education campaign is working, U.S. health officials say

* * *

WASHINGTON—Cocaine, crack cocaine, marijuana and other illegal drug use among American high school seniors is dropping precipitously, according to a national survey released Thursday.

Federal health officials, who sponsored the study, say it is convincing evidence that drug education and enforcement have begun to turn back the onslaught of illicit drugs.

The survey showed 5.3 percent of the class of 1990 used cocaine at some time during the year prior to the poll, one fifth less than the 6.5 percent of the class of 1989.

The same trend held for crack. Annual crack use by seniors tumbled almost two-fifths, from 3.1 percent to 1.9 percent.

"This survey further substantiates that a significant attitudinal change has taken place in America, and we are beginning to loosen the grip that drug dealers and financiers have on our schools and our neighborhoods," said Secretary of Health and Human Services Louis Sullivan, who released the report at a Washington press conference.

For the first time in the 16 years the survey has been conducted, more than 50 percent of the students reported that they had never tried any illicit drug. And annual marijuana use fell from 29.6 percent to 27 percent of the class.

"Declines in this population now, today, promise still greater declines — in all types of drug use, in all age groups — for the future," said John P. Walters, acting director of the Office of National Drug Control Policy.

Former Florida Gov. Bob Martinez, President Bush's new choice to head the Office of National Drug Control Policy, attended the news conference but did not comment on the survey.

Health officials said the reductions are most notable among frequent drug users. Daily cocaine use, which peaked at 0.4 percent in 1985-86, dropped two-thirds from 0.3 percent in 1989 to 0.1 percent last year. Daily crack use fell by half, from 0.2 percent to 0.1 percent, and daily marijuana use fell by nearly one quarter, from 2.9 to 2.2 percent of the class.

Annual use of several drugs, including heroin and LSD, did not change significantly between the classes of 1989 and 1990, according to the survey.

Sullivan and other health officials warned that drug abuse — like cigarette and alcohol use — still constitutes a "major problem" in the United States. "We're not declaring victory," Sullivan said.

Reprinted with permission of States News Service.

• • •

Public Hearing Stories

SOURCE: *San Jose Mercury News,* morning final, p. 3B
DATE: Thursday, March 7, 1991
AUTHOR: Laura Kurtzman, staff writer
HEADLINE: Panel waits on 'McEnery Center' vote

* * *

Clearly uncomfortable at being confronted with such a hot issue, San Jose's historic landmarks commission on Wednesday voted not to vote on a proposal to rename the San Jose Convention Center after former Mayor Tom McEnery.

Instead, commissioners decided after four hours of contentious public hearing, they'll reconsider the center's name at their April 8 meeting so they will have time to study the issue.

A parade of speakers praised McEnery for his role in redeveloping the downtown.

"I say give him his roses while he's here," said Ron McPherson, who dismissed arguments that it was too early to honor McEnery for his accomplishments. "Let him smell those roses."

But others, including veterans and members of the city's Hispanic community, argued against naming the center after McEnery. In a long and passionate speech that evoked sparse but insistent applause, Mike Borquez, a member of the local chapter of the Veterans of Foreign Wars, urged the panel to adopt the name "San Jose Memorial Convention Center."

The plan to rename the $143 million San Carlos street facility was announced at a Feb. 6 news conference by a group of influential political backers who said the idea surfaced late last year as McEnery supporters were planning a going-away dinner for the former mayor, who held office for eight years.

The proposal was supported by Mayor Susan Hammer, but it drew fire a few weeks later from Councilwoman Blanca Alvarado, who said the landmarks commission, which considers name-change proposals and forwards recommendations to the council, didn't have enough guidelines.

Alvarado suggested that the city hold at least two meetings to help establish new criteria for naming parks or buildings in honor of people or groups. But her idea failed to win much support from her colleagues and she withdrew it at a Feb. 26 meeting.

• • •

Public Meeting-Based Stories

SOURCE: *Ocala Star-Banner*, final ed., pp. 1A, 6A
AUTHOR: Kelly Turner, staff writer
DATE: Friday, June 14, 1990
HEADLINE: Ocalans complain of crime; residents demand city council action

* * *

OCALA—If by some outside chance city council members never knew a drug and crime problem existed in west Ocala, they did after Tuesday's meeting.

More than 60 westside residents jammed into the council chambers, many of them lining the back and side walls, to tell the council they are fed up with current conditions and demand a change.

The results of the meeting, if any, won't be known for weeks. But the meeting did motivate the council to discuss tightening city ordinances to shut down businesses where drug dealers congregate. Council members also urged citizens to get more involved in reporting crimes.

The residents represented an interesting cross-section: older citizens, young children and middle-aged parents. The only group conspicuously missing was the teenagers, a generation some say is already lost to the nationwide drug problem.

At times, the meeting resembled a church revival, with many of the speeches punctuated by outbursts of "That's right!" and "Amen!"

Leading the group was Patrick Hadley, a westside resident who got the city's attention two weeks ago when he stood outside City Hall with signs saying he was concerned about the city's drug problem.

Hadley has even won praise from local leaders he hasn't even met. At an Economic Development Council luncheon last week, Phillip Van Hooser, of Van Hooser Associates, called him a "true leader" and said "he was willing to stand for something that so many other people haven't."

Local realtor Roy Abshier also commented on Hadley's efforts at the luncheon. "The entire community should be proud and join him," he said. "It signifies the community is tired and no longer accepts what is happening there. He's done a necessary job."

Hadley performed part of that necessary job Tuesday. After brief opening remarks, he turned the microphone over to the audience, who, during the 90-minute-plus discussion, related numerous tales of dodging bullets in their own homes, scattering drug dealers from their yards and being taunted by thugs.

Despite praise from some residents, the Ocala Police Department took its share of lumps during the discussion. One man complained that the police "always seem to arrive after the crime occurs," and another woman said when she calls to complain about disturbances in her neighborhood, she's always referred to someone else.

"It doesn't take a genius to figure out that when a semi pulls up on 17th Street then backs out on to the highway, that something is going on," said Brandon Cave.

Several residents also said the problem would never have gotten as bad as it is if it occurred on the east side of town.

"You all would call out the National Guard," said one man.

"Our hands are very, very tied sometimes," said Mayor Jack Clark in response to the accusations against the police. As mayor, Clark oversees the city police department.

He added that it's up to the residents to help, and he discouraged earlier threats from some about forming a vigilante group.

"I'd like to call Charlie Bronson and have him come in to clean up the place. But we can't do that and stay within the law," he said.

After the meeting, Police Chief Lee McGehee said he realized many of the complaints were born out of frustration.

"They're frustrated and we are too," he said. "A police officer is the most visible person to take frustrations out on. But were doing 110 percent of what we can do."

McGehee also said there are currently "long-term, intensive investigations" going on in the west side that will hopefully penetrate the upper levels of the drug trade in Ocala. He said the results of those investigations won't be known for months.

Hadley concluded with a rousing speech that contained a thinly veiled ultimatum for the elected city leaders.

"I hope this dispels the myth that black people don't care," Hadley said. "That's the biggest lie ever told."

"All these people out here are voters," he added. "They're taxpayers. They're what this city's all about. Without these people, the city wouldn't function. And my message is this to our leaders: Get up off your butts. If we don't get up and do something, then God's going to raise up new leaders."

Council President Gerald Ergle praised Hadley's efforts: "Politicians, a lot of times, have to be kicked to do anything. I want you people to get together and keep kicking until something is done around your community and your part of town.

Reprinted with permission of the *Ocala Star-Banner*.

• • •

SOURCE: WPLG-TV, Channel 10, Miami
DATE: Monday, March 13, 1990
REPORTER: Michael Putney, political editor
TIME: 6 P.M. newscast

* * *

03/13/90 22:09 mpu 1:40 #11 + 1P-DAWK1
P-DAWKINSRACISM (9A)
TALENT = MPU
WRITER = MPU
BOX GRAPHIC =
(NATS/DAWKINS)
CG = FILE VIDEO/MIAMI

	COMMISSIONER DAWKINS MADE HIS REMARKS LAST THURSDAY AS THE COMMISSION WAS DISCUSSING NEW MEMBERS FOR THE BAYFRONT PARK MANAGEMENT TRUST.
(PRE-PRODUCTION)	COMM. DAWKINS: "HOLD IT. I MOVE THAT THIS BE DEFERRED. I NEED SOME MORE INFORMATION. I CAN'T UNDERSTAND WHY YOU WOULD PUT ARTHUR HILL, A BLACK, OFF AND YOU DON'T HAVE NO BLACKS ON THERE. . . ." VO
	THE EXECUTIVE DIRECTOR OF THE BAYFRONT PARK TRUST, IRA KATZ, EXPLAINED THAT NOMINEE MARIO WILLIAMS IS BLACK.

(PRE-PRODUCTION)

IRA KATZ: HE'S A BLACK ATTORNEY. HE'S ALSO ON THE HISPANIC HERITAGE BOARD, A NUMBER OF CIVIC BOARDS IN THE CITY." DAWKINS: "OH, HE'S A HISPANIC."

VO

THE DISCUSSION CONTINUED WHILE DAWKINS APPARENTLY STUDIED WILLIAMS' RESUME.

(PRE-PRODUCTION)

DAWKINS: "MR. MARIO A. E. WILLIAMS. BORN MAY 2, 1957, LIMON, COSTA RICA. SO HE'S A HISPANIC. HE'S NOT BLACK."

VO

IN FACT, WILLIAMS IS BLACK . . . AND HISPANIC . . . AND OFFENDED:

CG = MARIO WILLIAMS/
ADVISORY BOARD
NOMINEE

"He's trying to keep me off this trust because of my ethnic makeup. In my opinion that's bigotry."

VO CG = FILE VIDEO

DAWKINS REFUSED TO DISCUSS HIS REMARKS TODAY. . . . BUT COMMISSIONER J. L. PLUMMER SAYS HE DOESN'T THINK HIS COLLEAGUE MEANT TO OFFEND ANYONE.

CG = J. L. PLUMMER/
MIAMI COMMISSIONER
(SOUND AT 15:44/SOT: 11)

"I think my colleague was doing what he thought was necessary to get the representation he felt was necessary. But I have to tell you I don't think there are any hard feelings among anyone here."

VO

BUT THERE ARE HURT FEELINGS. ELOY VASQUEZ NOMINATED WILLIAMS TO THE BAYFRONT TRUST BOARD.

CG = ELOY VASQUEZ/
NOMINATED WILLIAMS
(SOUND AT 24:31/SOT: 09)

"You can be Black and be Hispanic . . . and be born in the Bahamas or in New York. To me, it doesn't make any difference."

(BUTT WILLIAMS SOUND BITE
AT 18/SOT: 09)

"I've been in the U.S. since age 10. I grew up here. And I've been through many situations just like the Afro-Americans."

(PUTNEY STANDUP)

AT A COMMISSION MEETING A YEAR AGO DAWKINS OBJECTED TO A WHITE MAN SPEAKING FOR THE N-DOUBLE A-C-P. NOW, HE'S OBJECTING TO A BLACK MAN SITTING ON A CITY BOARD. . . . BECAUSE HE'S HISPANIC AND WASN'T BORN IN THE U.S.A. IN MIAMI, MICHAEL PUTNEY, CHANNEL 10 EYEWITNESS NEWS. . . . ON THE NIGHTBEAT.

Reprinted with permission of WPLG-TV.

• • •

SOURCE: *Philadelphia Inquirer,* final ed., p. B5
DATE: Friday, October 20, 1989
AUTHOR: Idris M. Diaz, staff writer
HEADLINE: Resolution approved backing transit aid for elderly

* * *

With more than 100 senior citizens watching from the sidelines, City Council yesterday approved a hotly debated resolution that commits members to endorse funding for a peak-hour discount for elderly SEPTA riders.

The measure does not require Council to provide additional city funding for the subsidy. But it commits Council members to investigate all possible state, federal or other sources of assistance, including the city's treasury.

"What this resolution would do would be to set forth that it is the policy of this City Council that the half fare for senior citizens at peak hours should be maintained," said Councilman David Cohen, who sponsored the resolution.

The resolution, passed by a vote of 16–1, demonstrated the power of senior citizens, who traditionally have a high turnout at the polls on election day, to win support for their causes.

Last spring, Council by a vote of 13–4 cut funding for the subsidy, which allows senior citizens to ride at half fare on SEPTA buses, subways and trolleys during peak hours. Senior citizens ride free during off-peak hours under a state program funded by the lottery.

SEPTA officials have said that without additional funding, they would have to end the discount for peak hours sometime next month.

The cut in the subsidy, from $2.4 million to $500,000 in fiscal 1990, was part of a package that included cuts in funding for a variety of social programs including those for the homeless and the prevention of AIDS.

Council members approved those cuts in May. But yesterday, all but one voted to approve Cohen's resolution.

Only Republican Leader W. Thacher Longstreth stood firm against the resolution; he was resoundingly jeered by the audience.

Longstreth, 69, argued that Council approved cuts in certain programs last fiscal year in an effort to avoid large tax increases proposed by the Goode administration. Those cuts require sacrifices by everyone, he said.

"It would seem to me that we who are senior citizens have the same responsibility to share in the belt tightening," said Longstreth, who added that he did not oppose programs targeted at programs for low-income elderly people.

Cohen, who had vowed to organize hundreds of senior citizens to demonstrate in Council chambers until the resolution was passed, yesterday acknowledged that fear of alienating elderly voters may have helped win support for his measure.

"I'm not suggesting that it (politics) is not a factor on this or any other bill," he said. "I suspect that there isn't a single bill or resolution that comes before this council in which Council members are not fully aware of the fact that they run for public office every four years."

Cohen had planned to introduce his resolution at Council's regular session last week. He held it until yesterday at the suggestion of some members who expressed reservations about the resolution and wanted more time to study the issue.

The Goode administration has been working on a program to use the $500,000 that has been appropriated for fiscal 1990 for a peak-hour subsidy program for low-income senior citizens only. But Cohen, echoing the criticism of senior-citizen activists, called that proposal unworkable and unfair.

During debate in Council's caucus last week, many members argued strongly against the resolution. Among them was Councilman James J. Tayoun, who told Cohen, "I'm going to have to vote against it because it makes no sense."

Tayoun, who as chairman of Council's Transportation Committee will have to hold hearings on the issue, voted for the resolution yesterday. In an interview yesterday, Tayoun said he changed his mind after Cohen made some minor changes in the resolution's wording.

• • •

Convention-Based Stories

SOURCE: *Newsday,* city ed., p. 19
DATE: Sunday, April 28, 1991
AUTHOR: Paul Moses, staff writer
HEADLINE: O'Connor blames media on abortion

* * *

Opposition to abortion is now considered "virtually un-American" because of the way it is portrayed in the media, Cardinal John O'Connor said yesterday in a speech to a convention of anti-abortion activists.

"You are the counterculture," he told the group. He said that Americans are convinced, "in large measure by the media, that the American thing is freedom of choice."

O'Connor was the keynote speaker at an annual convention of the New York State Right to Life Committee, an activist group that is not connected to the Right to Life political party.

He told the audience that abortion opponents are often criticized and unfairly depicted as fanatics.

"Are only those who support the taking of human life Americans?" O'Connor said. "Do I give up my citizenship because I want to advance the cause of human life?"

Referring to criticism of professional football players who made an anti-abortion film, he said, "If those same New York Giants went on television and accepted high fees for advertising beer, no one would think anything of it."

But O'Connor said that despite "enormous sums of money made available" to abortion-rights forces, studies show the number of abortions in America dropping. "How many lives have you saved?" O'Connor asked conventioneers, who filled a ballroom in Manhattan's Hotel Roosevelt. "You don't begin to know. Only God knows."

The speech came at a time when the Catholic Archdiocese of New York is starting a new effort in its anti-abortion program. O'Connor said a new religious order, the Sisters of Life, is to begin June 1. About 12 nuns have joined the order, which will seek to further the church's position on abortion.

O'Connor said he also has initiated a National Federation for Life, an umbrella organization for more than 90 already existing anti-abortion groups.

Other speakers at the convention included Dr. Kathryn L. Moseley, a Michigan neonatologist who likened the anti-abortion movement to the civil rights movement. "Abortion is really another example of discrimination," Moseley said.

Herbert London, former Conservative Party candidate for governor, told the crowd that he is starting a new newspaper, the *New York Guardian*, to supply news about the anti-abortion movement.

• • •

III REPORTING REGULATION AND CONTROLS

10 | Law Affecting Reporting

A Colorado television news reporter who had previously won two Emmy awards for her journalistic abilities went into state court as a key source for a news story. She was accused, and later convicted, for staging illegal dog fights so she could have her photographers record video for a "sweeps week" series. The dog fights, supposedly staged at her encouragement by a dog breeder, are felonies in Colorado. The reporter for KCNC-TV in Denver was also charged with, but not convicted of, felony counts of perjury for allegedly lying to a grand jury, and for conspiracy to commit perjury. The four-part May 1990 series called "Blood Sport" was aired on the Denver NBC affiliate during the spring sweeps period when stations typically strengthen stories to increase audiences during the week-long period when audiences are scientifically measured to set advertising rates for the rest of the year. Prosecutors had argued during the trial that the reporter, who was forced to resign from her job after 7 years, was driven by ambition and believed she was above the law. Her attorneys said she had violated journalistic ethics, but had not violated the law (Anon., 1991, July 29; Anon., 1991, August 8).

A Miami television station and an investigative reporter were found not to have libeled a commercial air transport company in a series of news stories that stated the Miami-based cargo company was linked to a Central Intelligence Agency plan to trade guns for drugs. The stories broadcast by ABC affiliate WPLG-TV said the company worked with Colombian cocaine cartel bosses in a plan to ship weapons to the Contras in Nicaragua. The air transport company sued the station and the reporter for $150 million in damages plus compensatory damages, arguing that the stories

Cameras and other recording equipment are now permitted in courtrooms in most states to capture courtroom action such as this attorney's arguments. Recording equipment is not permitted in federal courts, however (photo by the *Miami Herald* staff).

were false, malicious, and defamatory, and it had lost millions in business as a result of the negative publicity. A jury, at the end of a 6-week trial, decided otherwise (Lester, 1991).

A television station and a reporter in Texas found a jury not to be so supportive. Dallas station WFAA-TV and a reporter were ordered in 1991 by a jury to pay a record $58 million in damages to a former prosecutor in compensation for defamation damages caused by a series of stories that accused him of accepting bribes in return for dismissing drunken driving cases. The stories led to a federal investigation and indictment for racketeering, but he was acquitted 2 years after the stories aired. The attorney said his career was ruined and he deserved the damages. This time, the jury agreed (Anon., 1991).

Each of these cases was appealed, but they illustrate the complicated legal world that influences how reporters can and cannot do their work. If reporters violate criminal laws, as the Colorado reporter was accused of doing, they face fines and possible prison sentences. If the reporters' work causes damages to the reputation of an individual or a group of individuals, then the reporters and their news organization may be held liable for those damages in court. At the very least, as in the case of the Miami television news investigative series, there are countless hours of time and thousands of dollars in legal fees that must be expended to defend against allegations. There is no doubt such actions have a "chilling" effect on the news media.

It is important for reporters to be familiar with criminal and civil laws as they affect reporting approaches and techniques. As a reporter, you need to be aware of the legal and ethical environment in which you and other reporters work. Here's why legal scholars T. Barton Carter, Marc A. Franklin, and Jay B. Wright (1991) deemed it relevant:

> Presumably, an intelligent professional in any aspect of communications should know enough about the law to make some on-the-spot judgments (sometimes under deadline pressure), should know enough to alert a superior when a potential legal problem is spotted, and should know—particularly after reaching management level—when to seek the advice of an attorney. (p. 1)

This chapter, along with the following one about news ethics, creates a final section of this book which focuses on reporting regulation and controls to provide you with a legal and ethical foundation for your reporting. This chapter provides an overview of the First Amendment, First Amendment legal issues, and restrictive problems facing reporters in the 1990s. This discussion examines the specific legal restrictions placed on reporting, including description of the major laws relating to the First Amendment, free press and fair trial conflicts, libel, privacy, copyright, reporter–source relationships, trespassing, gag orders, censorship, open records and meetings, surreptitious recordings, broadcast journalism, and the interrelated issues of reporter's privilege, shield laws, and confidentiality.

Laws affecting the conduct of print and broadcast reporters and the content of their news reports have evolved over the past 200-plus years of U.S. democracy. Some laws exist to protect national security; others have been created to preserve personal privacy, to protect copyright, and to prevent defamation through libel and slander.

These rules—society's own controls—of journalistic conduct exist at both the federal and state levels. At the federal level, for example, broadcasting is regulated and policies are set. At the state level, great variation exists from state to state on many media-related regulatory issues.

Ethics, the moral conduct and standards of individuals in a society or in a profession, advance media law a level further. And as members of an evolving profession, reporters are becoming more and more concerned about development of a body of ethical principles to guide their work. Ethical standards and issues are discussed in the next chapter.

THE FIRST AMENDMENT

The U.S. news media operate under the protection of the First Amendment to the Constitution. This part of the Bill of Rights states in no uncertain terms that the press shall be *free* (italics added): "*Congress shall make no law* respecting an establishment of religion, or prohibiting the free exercise thereof; or *abridging the freedom of speech, or of the press;* or the right of the people peaceably to assemble, and to petition the Government for a redress of grievances."

Yet, with these freedoms there are laws that temper freedom of the press in relation to other constitutional and social rights. U.S. press freedom is not absolute. Carter, Franklin, and Wright (1991) noted that

> the lack of broad consensus concerning the philosophical underpinnings of the majestic words of the First Amendment does not mean that the courts and legislatures of the United States are released from the obligation to obey the Amendment's dictates. To the contrary, our Nation's lawmaking bodies have clearly acknowledged that the Amendment represents a constitutional bar to government action in numerous situations. (p. 46)

Many journalists believe the First Amendment is being seriously challenged by the actions of public officials, the courts, and even some private citizens. There are constant battles in legislatures and in courts to temper the meaning of the amendment and the freedoms it provides for responsible journalism. Attempts to pass new laws restricting the press, court decisions in libel and privacy cases, and other legal activity place increasing pressure on the freedoms guaranteed by the First Amendment. Although the First Amendment is now over two centuries old, numerous individuals wish to reinterpret it, redefine its guarantees, and rewrite it, and some even have suggested that it be repealed.

Many First Amendment issues involve problems to be discussed in later sections of this chapter. The following sections are designed to provide an introduction.

FREE PRESS/FAIR TRIAL CONFLICT

There is a basic conflict in the Bill of Rights. On one hand, the First Amendment provides the right of the press to be free. On the other hand, the Sixth Amendment guarantees a citizen the right to a fair trial.

There are times in our modern society when these rights come in direct conflict with each other. Because of the sophisticated forms of mass communication of the 20th century, the assurances of a fair trial are not always as secure as they were 200 years ago when these rights were amended to the Constitution. Modern mass communication can publicize events prior to a trial to such an extent that it may be difficult, perhaps impossible, to provide a defendant with a fair trial.

Many persons, including the defense team, believed that William Kennedy Smith, a medical student accused of sexual assault in Palm Beach, Florida, at the estate of the Kennedy family but later acquitted, could not be able to get a fair trial in state court — perhaps nowhere in the nation — because of pretrial publicity about the case. The effort by a court to seat an impartial jury in such a case is difficult if not impossible. Many times, such advance news coverage of a case before it goes to court results in motions to change the venue of the trial, but even this expensive effort does not assure the defendant of a fair trial. Responsible reporting during the highly competitive hours and days following a major break, such as an unofficial accusation or a more formal arrest in a case, is difficult to achieve. The circuslike atmosphere created by media coverage in Palm Beach County immediately after the incident became public and after Smith was charged, created difficult circumstances for any pending judicial procedure.

Gag Orders

One alternative that courts have chosen in situations where media coverage of a trial or pretrial activities are believed to be out of control is a gag order. Rulings of the U.S. Supreme Court have curbed efforts to prevent publication of news about a trial. But there are still rulings by judges in some cases that prevent participants in a case from talking about it, or at least control how they talk about it. Typically, jurors are instructed not to discuss a case with anyone, especially reporters. Other court officials such as clerks and attorneys may be temporarily instructed not to talk to the news media during, but not after, a trial.

To be able to apply a gag order, a judge must be satisfied the situation meets all three parts of a U.S. Supreme Court test. The defendant's representative, who typically initiates the request although a judge can do so, must show how the news publicity can damage Sixth Amendment rights, that no alternative means are available for a fair trial, and that the order will protect the defendant's interests (*Nebraska Press Association v. Stuart,* 1976; Kirtley, 1986).

Gag orders, although rare, directly confront an individual's First Amendment rights and are often contested. Reporters and news organizations that believe such an order might be out of line should contest the decision in a higher court. The Reporters Committee on Freedom of the Press recommends obtaining a written copy of the order from the court clerk, finding out who is specifically gagged, and determining the reason for it. Then contact your editor or news director, obtain legal representation, and decide if you can, and should, appeal (Kirtley, 1986).

DEFAMATION: LIBEL AND SLANDER

Law of *libel,* or a *malicious defamation,* exists to protect individuals and institutions against published information that unjustly damages or injures their personal or institutional reputation. Media law scholar and University of Washington professor Don Pember (1990) said libel "is undoubtedly the most common legal problem faced by journalists. . . . The very nature of contemporary journalism creates a fertile soil for the growth of libel problems" (p. 101).

For beginning news reporters, the prospect of libel may be scary. You can spend a lot of time worrying about whether something you write will or will not be libelous. Libel generally involves a defamation based on reporting, but it can also be in a photo, a sign, or information graphic that damages a reputation. With deadline pressure and complex subjects, errors are more likely to occur. Yet, for the most part, much of what you write will not be libelous. But think about what you are reporting because if it can damage someone's reputation, then you must be sure it is safe to publish or broadcast. Your stories, photographs, cartoons and other graphics, and picture captions may be libelous if they bring a person or institution shame, hatred, disgrace, or ridicule, or generally cause public opinion to become negative toward the person or institution.

As the *Associated Press Stylebook and Libel Manual* (French & Goldstein, 1988) advises, most libel cases are caused by news stories that "allege crime, fraud, dishonesty, immoral or dishonorable conduct, or stories that defame the subject professionally, causing financial loss either personally or to a business" (p. 289).

Under libel law, a person filing suit for libel must prove *at a minimum* that the libelous statement was published, that it was about the person filing the suit, and that there was defamation, or harm, done to the person's reputation.

The Florida First Amendment Foundation and the Florida Press Association recently held a "mock libel trial" based on a fictitious story. This story, and errors made by the news reporter, point to how libel can occur. In this mock case, a federal court reporter learns that a solar energy company begun in the days of the energy crisis has filed under Chapter 11 of the bankruptcy laws. He checks other sources, such as clips, and finds out that the company once received a great deal of publicity for its successes. The reporter writes this lead for the story headlined "Once bright solar firm/turns out its lights": "A one-time high flyer in the solar heating industry has filed for bankruptcy amid complaints of shoddy construction and misrepresentation in dealings with franchise holders."

The lead may seem accurate, but it is not. In the mock trial, the company complained to the court that its reputation had been damaged. The problem arises from the reporter's lack of knowledge of bankruptcy laws. The company had not filed for bankruptcy, but instead requested the federal court to approve its reorganization plan under bankruptcy laws. The newspaper could be held responsible for damages for such an error (and the mock court ruled for the plaintiff in this case).

Whereas libel has become more difficult in recent years to prove, there are two important common law defenses in any libel case. First, and foremost, is *truth*. You must be prepared to show that the information you use is the truth. Truth, however, is rarely used as a defense. Establishing truth is very costly and often risky as a defense. Recent court decisions have placed falsity of information in an alleged libel as the plaintiff's, or the accusing party's, responsibility in the context of speech of public concern. From the point of view of the media libel defendant, it is no serious concern whether the defamatory news story is truthful. "What does matter," according to Arizona State University media law professor Kyu Ho Youm (1991), "is whether the plaintiff, both private and public figure, can prove 'with convincing clarity' that the story is false. Media attorney Robert Sack observed thus: 'In the light of the constitutional cases, truth may *not* be a defense—falsity may instead be a part of the plaintiff's case.' "

The second defense is *privilege*. Absolute privilege protects some people at all times—this includes public records and the official public pronouncements of certain public officials. *Qualified privilege*, characterized by some legal authorities as the media's "bread-and-butter" defense, applies to the news media. This means, as the Associated Press explains, "that it [qualified privilege] can be lost or diluted by how the journalist handles the material" (p. 289). Qualified privilege is more frequently used as a defense. The defendant will try to prove the news story is privileged under libel law.

Other defenses include a *statute of limitations* (in most states, a libel suit cannot be filed after 1 or 2 years), *fair comment* (criticism about public performances or works in the arts, for example), and *mitigation* (some states recognize the importance of immediate or timely retractions and/or corrections).

Fair comment and criticism still can be useful as a defense in that they have been considerably subsumed into the constitutional defense developed by the U.S. Supreme Court in *New York Times Co. v. Sullivan* in 1964. Defendants must prove their opinions were grounded in a truthful set of facts and directed at the public performance of those under public scrutiny.

In recent years, cases such as the 1986 U.S. Supreme Court case

---

KYU HO YOUM, ARIZONA STATE UNIVERSITY
EFFECTS OF THE ACTUAL MALICE RULE

Arizona State University media law scholar Kyu Ho Youm (1991) explained the effects of the actual malice rule in the famed U.S. Supreme Court case *New York Times Co. v. Sullivan* in 1964:

"*The New York Times* 'actual malice' rule brought on a revolution in the libel law, both federal and state, by explicitly recognizing the First Amendment restriction on the common law protection of reputational interests.

"So far as they are not proved to have published a defamatory statement with actual malice — with knowledge of its falsity or with reckless disregard of whether it was false or not — the media defendant is now immunized from liability for the statement concerning public officials or public figures. Of course, in the context of privileged criticism of government officials and others under the actual malice rule, qualified privilege is now accorded First Amendment status.

"When it comes to the impact of the *New York Times* rule upon the common law defense of fair comment and criticism, the actual malice rule is broader than the common law defense for libel actions involving public officials or public figures."

Philadelphia Newspapers v. Hepps or the celebrated 1984 New York federal district court case, *Sharon v. Time Inc.,* have turned the burden of the truth or falsity of an allegedly libelous passage to the accusing party — especially those involving public issues and the news media (Smith, 1989). Clearly, however, reporters are better protected if they can provide proof of truth whenever it is needed. Smith (1989) suggested that libel damages can be reduced "by proof of mitigating factors, such as a retraction" (p. 11).

Libel laws vary from state to state, so you must find an authoritative legal source for your state's libel laws and its court rulings. Various libel handbooks have been published to help journalists in this regard, and these are usually available from each state's bar, newspaper/press, magazine, and broadcast cable associations.

The landmark 1964 case argued before the U.S. Supreme Court, *New York Times Co. v. Sullivan,* limited the power of individual states to enforce libel laws. The case introduced the *actual malice rule* by which states could not award damages to public officials for libel statements about their official conduct unless the officials could demonstrate the news organization, as defendant, published the libel knowing it was false or, that the defendants did not care about, or recklessly disregarded, the truth. Since this case, definitions of public officials and public figures have been refined by later court decisions.

ACCESS AND TRESPASSING

Trespassing is defined in *Black's Law Dictionary* (Nolan & Nolan-Haley, 1990) as "an unlawful interference with one's person, property, or rights"

(p. 1502). Furthermore, *criminal trespassing* is defined by *Black's* as "entering or remaining upon or in any land, structure, vehicle, aircraft or watercraft by one who knows he is not authorized or privileged to do so" (p. 1503).

Reporters, like any other citizens, have access to most *public* places. But without expressed or implied permission, reporters and other citizens do not have access to *private* places. It is important to remember that reporters generally have no more right to access to a particular public place than any other citizens. Of course, it can be difficult to obtain permission to enter private property to gain access to a source. Sidewalks, streets, and parks are most often public property. But corporate office buildings, factories, and homes are likely not to be. There are situations where private property is accessible if it is used for public purposes. This includes private universities, parking lots, or shopping malls. An event occurring on private property that is not open to the public may not be open to reporters unless by invitation. Similarly, if the event is open to the public but held on private property, it should also be open to reporters (Kirtley, 1986).

Many sites are posted against trespassing. Signs indicate it. Other places may not be as clear, and if there is doubt, you should always ask. Otherwise, you may be at criminal risk. There are numerous situations in which access to a story setting or a source may be questionable. Access to the executive offices of a major corporation, for instance, may be off limits to the public, thus making a source more difficult or impossible to locate. And the location of a crime, for example, may often be private property.

An automobile at the center of a major news story is about to be towed away. Reporters and photographers present when this occurred were able to observe the event because it occurred on a public street and not on private property (photo by Al Diaz, *Miami Herald* staff).

But regardless of whether it is on private or public property, law enforcement agencies legally restrict access to crime scenes because they usually argue such news media access interferes with the crime investigation.

Trespassing is illegal at both state and federal levels. There are various forms of trespassing, but criminal and defiant trespass are two that most concern reporters. Defiant trespass is disregard for notices posted on the premises and other indications such as police lines or barricades. Without permission to enter private property, a person, including a reporter, may be arrested. Most trespass penalties are fines, but can include liability for any damages caused by the trespasser.

In a recent example, an Associated Press reporter covering the breaking story of the 1991 airplane crash death of U.S. Sen. John Heinz from Pennsylvania, was arrested and found guilty of defiant trespass while reporting on assignment. The reporter, AP's Pittsburgh bureau chief, went to the Heinz home in Fox Chapel on the day of the accident for reaction comments from family members. The crash had occurred near Philadelphia. She was fined $351 because she used a neighbor's side yard, with permission, to reach the front door of the Heinz home after barricades had been placed by police to block the front gate of the private driveway. No one answered the door, but she was issued a citation by a police officer (Anon., 1991, May 8).

Reporting about a civil disturbance on public streets does not present an access problem for reporters as long as police lines and other public safety barriers are respected (photo by Al Diaz, *Miami Herald* staff).

In another recent case, a WNBC-TV reporter was cited by police for disorderly conduct when he supposedly interfered with officers breaking up a dispute between supporters for a Persian Gulf welcome home celebration and antiwar demonstrators. The reporter said he and his camera crew had permission to be at that location, but police officers told the reporter and his crew to move during the altercation. The reporter and crew were trying to get tape of the scuffle, but officers covered the lens of the camera. The reporter said he would fight the ticket and the president of the New York Press Club called it another case of "media bashing" (Anon., 1991, June 11).

CENSORSHIP AND PRIOR RESTRAINT

Censorship involves a number of acts. It has received the most public attention when it has involved examination of literature or motion pictures or other forms of mass communication *in advance* of distribution *to remove unsuitable content*. Typically this is done by authorities to prevent what is thought to be abuse of public morals. Such actions, however, can also include the news media. Under certain forms of government in other parts of the world, censorship of news media is a daily activity. But in the United States, it is extraordinarily rare when it involves the commercial news media in a time of international peace.

Censorship is unfortunately much more common when student news media are involved. A different set of legal guidelines has evolved in U.S. Supreme Court cases over the years, which has led to censorship of school and college newspapers and broadcast stations from time to time by school administrators. Cases such as *Hazelwood School District v. Kuhlmeier* in 1988 show that the Supreme Court sees a difference in student and adult press rights. Few student news media censorship cases reach the higher courts, but the problem still occurs frequently. The Student Press Law Center recently estimated as many as 300 censorship cases a year (Gillmor, Barron, Simon, & Terry, 1990).

Censorship is also known as prior restraint. Prior restraint is defined by law scholar Don Pember (1990) as "prepublication censorship that forbids publication or broadcast of certain objectionable material, as opposed to punishment of a perpetrator after the material was published or broadcast" (p. 615).

Government attempts to censor the news media have been routinely struck down by the U.S. Supreme Court on constitutional grounds. In numerous modern Supreme Court cases, any prior restraint has been presumed to be unconstitutional by the court (Watkins, 1990). Yet there are still efforts to censor news from time to time. The Reporters Committee for Freedom of the Press (Anon., 1986) listed five categories of possible exceptions to the court ban on prior restraint:

1. *National security*. In the interest of protecting the security of the nation, some information cannot be published or broadcast. But the

government must demonstrate harm before a court will stop the publication or broadcast.

2. *Obscenity.* U.S. Supreme Court decisions have permitted government bodies to regulate sale and distribution of material considered to be obscene.

3. *Commercial speech.* Advertising is not completely a First Amendment issue. Government restriction must be based on serving the public interest.

4. *Corporate information.* This information is covered by the First Amendment, although some corporations may try to prevent publication or broadcast of news about their activities.

5. *Government regulation.* At times, there is effort to stop broadcast or publication on the grounds that the news organization or its product does not qualify under government regulation. A recent example included an effort to stop a newsletter because it contained financial advice. The government said the publication had to be registered as a financial advisor through the Securities and Exchange Commission, but the Supreme Court ruled such publications exempt.

Efforts to censor or restrain publication in advance must be taken seriously. Although not common, they do occur. Reporters and news executives must seek legal counsel to determine whether the order to stop can be contested.

PRIVACY LAW

Privacy is generally a 20th-century legal doctrine. As more citizens become concerned about protection of their privacy in the modern, mass media-oriented United States, court rulings have led to a body of privacy law that news reporters cannot ignore.

Privacy law primarily focuses on *invasion of privacy*. The concept of invading privacy, according to Don Pember (1990), includes numerous activities such as wiretapping, illegal surveillance, misuse of retail credit agency information, use of two-way mirrors in stores, and collection of information by organizations such as research institutions, banks, and government agencies. The news media are often accused of invading personal privacy of individuals — from entertainers to politicians to rank-and-file employees in the factory down the street. The developing right to privacy does place some limitations on gathering news, although legal experts such as Pember feel these legal handicaps are minor at best.

Tort scholar William Prosser (1960) proposed that invasion of privacy involves four distinct legal wrongs:

1. Appropriation of an individual's name or likeness for commercial purposes, such as endorsements, without permission.
2. Intrusion into an individual's solitude and private life.

3. Publication of private information about a person, such as gossip, the content of private conversations, details of private tragedies, or medical conditions.

4. Publication of false information about a person, or placing a person in a false light.

Consent is the all-purpose defense in situations involving privacy. Whenever there is doubt, you should seek written consent from the person involved. But there are time limits to consent agreements in some states. After all, newsworthiness is the best defense for privacy actions involving news media because courts often interpret news liberally.

Many persons feel the news media oversteps the boundaries of propriety at times, thus the privacy issue is significant. Privacy rights require greater sensitivity on the part of reporters and they demand that you be better informed about the rights of individuals you seek to write about and photograph for your stories.

COPYRIGHT LAW AND PLAGIARISM

The 1976 federal copyright law protects property that is not always *material*—that means property such as creative works. This means you, as a reporter, cannot use someone else's copyrighted material without the author's or copyright holder's permission. This includes original reporting and other literary works, graphics, music or other sound, photographs, dramatic works, motion pictures, and other similar works (Pember, 1990). "Copyright is an area of the law that deals with intangible property—property that a person cannot touch or hold or lock away for safekeeping," wrote law scholar Don Pember (1990, p. 431). Permission may be granted on written request, but it may require payment of a fee, or specific credit, or both.

Just as copyright law specifies what can be copyrighted, it also outlines what cannot be protected. This includes trivial material in the public domain, as well as ideas. Events cannot be copyrighted, but your creative expression, or news story, about the events can be (Pember, 1990). Copyrights last for the life of the author plus 50 years.

Fair use is a doctrine that is part of the copyright law. This permits small amounts of copying in situations that enhance public knowledge—such as news reporting or teaching. It is often left to judges to decide what constitutes fair use, even though the law outlines four factors:

1. The purpose and character of the use, including whether such use is of a commercial nature or is for nonprofit educational purposes.

2. The nature of the copyrighted work.

3. The amount and substantiality of the portion used in relation to the copyrighted work as a whole.

4. The effect of the use on the potential market for or value of the copyrighted work (Pember, 1990, pp. 443–44).

Another related legal concern, probably of more interest to beginning news reporters, is *plagiarism*. Plagiarism, as you have probably been taught since elementary school, is an act of using ideas and words of others without credit, thus giving the impression that those ideas and words are your own.

Like schools, many news organizations have strong policies prohibiting plagiarism. It is an offense that will damage a news organization's credibility and may lead to an employee's dismissal. It is taken very seriously in the news media. A *Washington Post* reporter and bureau chief left her job after she was found to have used portions of a *Miami Herald* article without attribution or credit (Anon., 1991, July 13). In Fort Worth, Texas, the *Star-Telegram* said it fired a columnist for "substantial duplication" of a *Washington Post* article, although she said the dismissal was in retaliation for a column she wrote containing criticism of her former newspaper for publishing the name of a rape victim (Anon., 1991, July 30).

The best way to avoid plagiarism is to make certain credit is given whenever material from others is taken for your own reporting. In news stories, this can be done with attribution in the text. On television, this is often done with a credit on the screen that identifies the source of the tape, sound, or words.

REPORTER'S PRIVILEGE, SHIELD LAWS, CONFIDENTIALITY

There are occasions when news reporters enter into a very sensitive relationship with a source of information for a story. Guarding the identities of sources is essential to the work of reporters, especially those journalists involved in special investigations. To protect themselves or family members, news sources often reveal information in confidence. In return for the information for the story, the reporter agrees not to identify the source to the public or other interested individuals.

Journalists "claimed, and continue to claim, that the privilege is needed to ensure the flow of vital information to the public. Refusal to recognize the privilege would result in a 'chill' on the newsgathering process," argued legal scholars Donald Gillmor, Jerome Barron, Todd Simon, and Herbert Terry (1990, p. 347).

Other professionals, such as attorneys, physicians, and accountants, are given privilege or limited privilege in relationships with clients in some courts.

However, on some stories, when a reporter is ahead of the government in investigating a case, for instance, the reporter may be required by the government, through a judge, to identify the source. Just as doctors are protected in their confidential relations with patients and priests are protected in their confessional relations with parishioners, reporters have sought similar protection by arguing it is sometimes necessary to properly do the job of a reporter. If reporters refuse to divulge the source, they may be found in contempt of court and fined or imprisoned.

To that end, some states, but not all, have enacted various forms of "shield" laws, which offer limited privilege to refuse to identify sources in court testimony. At present, more than half the states have some type of shield law, but variation of the protection is so great that you should check the situation in your own state. Some states have no shield law, some have highly qualified shield laws, whereas others have strong protections for reporters. The Reporters Committee for Freedom of the Press (Kirtley, 1986) warned:

> Some shield laws protect reporters from forced disclosure of their confidential news sources, but do not protect unpublished material. Other laws protect reporters differently according to the type of legal proceeding involved and/or the role of the journalist in the proceeding. . . . Reporters should become familiar with the scope of their state's privilege to withhold confidential sources and information, as recognized by a shield law or in case law. (pp. 31–32)

A *Washington Post* reporter, in a 1991 case, was threatened with jail in the District of Columbia because she refused to disclose a source. A mistrial order by the judge caused by other circumstances eliminated the concern over her contempt of court at least until the case would be retried. Reporter Linda C. Wheeler wrote about a failed police undercover drug operation after the drug raid had occurred. She was held in contempt of court for refusing to testify about the identity of the individual who gave her a copy of a police handbook that outlined drug raid procedures. The District of

---

KYU HO YOUM, ARIZONA STATE UNIVERSITY
REPORTER LIABILITY FOR "BURNING" SOURCES

When a reporter voluntarily reveals the name of an anonymous source, what happens? "Burning" a confidential source may mean legal problems for reporters.

Kyu Ho Youm (1991), a media law scholar at Arizona State University, cautioned beginning reporters about their responsibilities:

"The U.S. Supreme Court ruled in 1991 that the First Amendment does not protect the news media from being sued for breaking their confidentiality agreements with their sources. Under the common law theory known as *promissory estoppel theory,* a promise, as distinguished from a contract, is legally enforced if breaking the promise creates an 'injustice.'

"The Court reasoned that 'generally applicable laws do not offend the First Amendment simply because their enforcement against the press has incidental effects on its ability to gather and report the news,' according to *Cohen v. Cowles Media Co.,* 1991."

Columbia does not have a shield law, but the Superior Court judge said he felt reporters should have a qualified right (Asseo, 1991; Rowley, 1991).

In California, the judge controlling the well-publicized Rodney King videotaped police-beating case fined a *Los Angeles Times* reporter $1,500 a day for refusing to reveal the identity of a source who provided the reporter with a copy of a 314-page report detailing a police internal affairs investigation into the King arrest incident. The judge later delayed additional fines after the first day. The newspaper defended the reporter, saying the reporter was protected by California's shield law. The judge believed the law did not apply because the reporter witnessed a crime while the reporter's source violated a court order prohibiting public disclosure of the report (Crane, 1991).

There is no federal shield law despite efforts by some news media organizations to enact one.

OPEN RECORDS, OPEN MEETINGS LAWS

From state to state, and on the federal level, there is a body of statutes that exists to set rules for access to public records and public meetings. These laws do not exist specifically for reporters; in fact, any citizen can take advantage of state laws to inspect public documents and to attend formal discussion by public officials.

Always remember that news writers and reporters have no more legal access to information contained in records and at meetings than anyone else. It seems, though, that news people use these laws to find information more than most citizens. Journalists most often seek information as the eyes and ears of the public.

As the states and the federal government have passed or amended these "government in the sunshine" laws over the past two decades, more specific guidelines have evolved. These include inclusion and exclusion of records and meetings, precise definitions of records and governing bodies, advance notice terms, and even penalties for those who violate these laws.

If you are ever denied access to records or to a meeting that the law says you can see or attend, you have a right to protest — usually to the local office of the state attorney general.

Clearly, some meetings and some records are not open to public review under these laws. These include matters of national security, public employee personnel records, health records, income tax records, and so on. It is really up to you to know the current federal law and the specific guidelines of your state. Copies of these laws can be obtained from the local office of the state attorney general, the state bar association, or a local press or broadcasters' association.

COMMENTARY AND CRITICISM

A libelous passage can be damaging to an individual. But it does not have to be contained in straight news reporting. It can appear in any type of news

Records and documents, such as traffic citations and arrest records issued by police, are open for public inspection under sunshine or open records laws in most states (photo by Al Diaz, *Miami Herald* staff).

reporting. In fact, in personal opinion pieces such as columns and reviews the potential for libel can be a particular concern.

If you write opinion—editorials, columns, or reviews and criticism—you have been given the right to comment on the news of your town by the editor or news director of your news organization. It is a significant role in the community that must be kept in perspective at all times. It is a form of public trust not unlike that of the city hall or statehouse reporters who cover—and often judge—government for the public.

It is also important to remember that broadcasting is considered by the courts to be the same as publication because there is likely to be a permanent record of the defamation. In fact, some persons have begun to use the term "defamacast" to refer to broadcast defamation. Television, *primarily* a visual medium, suggests libel problems rather than slander. So, slander is not the broadcast version of libel. Slander is generally a small-group, nonpermanent defamation. Another important consideration is the legal limitations of criticism under the First Amendment and various state constitutions. How far can an opinion writer go in expressing opinion before it is unacceptable?

In terms of law, an opinion writer must be concerned with libel because of the potential for defamation of character of a subject such as an artist, politician, or community leader. And because libel law varies from state to state, the limits of criticism will also vary according to each state's libel law. What a columnist or critic says might not be considered damaging by a jury in a major city as easily as it would be in a small town in the more conservative regions of the country.

Opinion writers are permitted to express their opinions, even defamatory, on topics that are interesting to the public. This is a conditional privilege of *fair comment,* a defense that has existed since the beginning of this century. Pember (1990) explained, "Opinion statements, supported by facts, about matters of public concern, are protected by this privilege" (p. 174). He added, "The fair comment defense only works when the opinion statements focus upon something of legitimate public interest" (p. 183).

Although the U.S. Supreme Court rejected a separate recognition of opinion as a privileged expression in 1990, it is still possible that state courts can retain the position that opinions are not, and cannot be, a ground for defamatory liability, pointed out Arizona State University's Youm (1991). This means there is no court action, depending on the state courts, that can be taken, he noted. "Given the burden of proof on the part of the defendant, the common law 'fair comment' defense is not so protective as the privilege of 'opinions' recognized by state courts," Youm explained.

Mass media law professors Harold Nelson, Dwight Teeter, and Don Le Duc (1989) stated that common law and state statutes extend to

> even scathing criticism of the public work of persons and institutions who offer their work for public judgment: public officials and figures; those whose performance affects public taste in such realms as music, art, literature, theater, and sports; and institutions whose activities affect the public interest such as hospitals, schools, processors of food, public utilities, drug manufacturers. Under fair comment legal immunity against a defamation action is given for the honest expression of opinion on public persons and/or matters of public concern. (p. 226)

Pember (1990) said the fair comment defense against libel in a review must be based on three factors:

1. The comment must focus on a subject of public interest.
2. It should reflect on the public activity, not the private life, of the artist.
3. The comment should have a factual basis.

Still, Pember cautioned, the difference between fact and opinion is not that clear. The courts, he said, still wrestle with the distinction. This makes life difficult for aggressive opinion writers; the best advice is to back up what you say in the public interest with evidence, and you should be concerned with context of the statement and the words themselves. This way, Pember explained, the public has the ability to develop its own opinion about the subject or the subject's work itself.

SURREPTITIOUS RECORDINGS

When using a tape recorder during an interview or conversation, should you tell your source that it has been turned on?

In most U.S. states, it is legal to record a conversation without informing the other party that the recording is being made. It is also legal in those states for a source to record an interview that you conduct without telling you. Thus, surreptitious recording can be a two-way street.

States where surreptitious recording is not permitted, or is restricted, include California, Florida, Illinois, Maryland, Massachusetts, Montana, New Hampshire, Oregon, Pennsylvania, and Washington (Middleton & Chamberlin, 1991).

Reporters find taping to be a very important tool in their work. But even when the action is legal, it becomes an ethical matter. Some editors and producers feel it is unethical to do so without informing the other person, yet the practice seems widespread in U.S. journalism. Virginia attorney and Old Dominion University journalism professor Frederick Talbott (1986) acknowledged that taping is often vital to the reporting process and taping without telling is necessary:

> The belief that reporters should always announce their intention to tape before taping—a belief reinforced in many newsrooms—is ridiculous. Reporters cover a world of fleeting events, a world of varied and sometimes extreme human behavior. How any newsroom managers can foresee *all* possible newsgathering circumstances and needs is beyond me and, I believe, beyond them. (p. 43)

Talbott recommended these steps be taken when recording:

1. Tape often. Get sources used to it.
2. If surreptitious taping is outlawed in your state, get the agreement to record on tape.
3. Know the law in your state or any state where you work on a story. Also find out if tapes recorded in a state that allows surreptitious taping can be used in a story published in a state where such taping is prohibited.

BROADCAST REGULATION

Broadcast regulation, like broadcasting itself, is a relative newcomer. Most U.S. broadcast regulation stems from the federal Radio Act of 1927. The

Federal Communications Act of 1934 expanded the Radio Act by including telephone and telegraph. Although it has been changed many times since its approval by Congress, the act is the basic body of regulation for radio and television. One group that the 1934 act created was the Federal Communications Commission (FCC). This five-person group, appointed by the president, sets broadcasting policy.

In an era of deregulation that began in the Reagan administration, the FCC has recently attempted to remove some of the rules affecting radio and television broadcasting. The leading example, perhaps, is elimination in 1987 of the "fairness doctrine." The fairness doctrine was, for a long time, controversial because of its apparent conflict with the First Amendment rights to free speech (Pember, 1990). The doctrine said broadcasters must devote reasonable amounts of time to discussion of public issues and that this discussion must be fair.

Even with these changes, however, the public is not satisfied: Some people argue for greater control of broadcast content and others argue for no control at all. But there are physical limitations to the public-owned airwaves—there is a finite number of stations in a given area—and regulation continues to exist to give some order to broadcasting in this part of the world.

Unlike in the print media, licenses are required to operate a broadcast facility. The limit of these licenses reflects the limited "air space" for broadcasting. To obtain, and then to retain, a license—which is renewed on the basis of performance—license holders must prove they will serve public need and public good. The individuals who can *best* serve the public are supposedly given licenses by the FCC. Radio licenses expire after 7 years and television licenses must be renewed each 5 years.

Regulation of program content is a major concern among broadcasters. However, it rarely is a concern of news departments. It can cause problems on occasion if content is not monitored. Many content guidelines center on indecent or obscene material and political material—particularly during a campaign period.

There is literally no *broadcasting* involved in cable television, so federal regulations are virtually nonexistent. The federal Cable Communications Policy Act of 1984 sets explicit rules for cable that delineate the jurisdictional division between the FCC and state and local authorities. Most cable regulation is by the franchise grantor; thus, it is highly localized. There is no limit to the number of channels for cable television as there is in broadcast television. Content is not regulated and is free to vary as well. Only local community standards dictate, or control, the availability and content of programming on cable television. These guidelines are often written into franchise agreements between communities and cable television companies. As the law is evolving quickly for cable programming, satellite transmission of information is also guided by a developing body of national and international regulation.

11 | News Reporting Ethics

Although it usually is only a professional issue, the ethical behavior of journalists came back into the national spotlight recently when William Kennedy Smith was arrested – he was later found not guilty – on a charge of sexual assault at his family's estate in Palm Beach, Florida. The name of Patricia Joyce Bowman, the woman involved in the alleged sexual assault – Florida's term for rape – was published in several newspapers and aired on a television network shortly after the alleged incident occurred.

Most news organizations chose not to publish or broadcast the woman's name even though it may have been legal to do so. However, to do so in Florida violated a rarely enforced and virtually unknown law preventing news media in the state from doing so. But in the nation's collective mind, the issue became important because many Americans felt news organizations were going too far, violating a time-honored national tradition of not identifying sex crime victims, but also simply destroying the woman's privacy.

In cases such as the William Kennedy Smith arrest, and in thousands of others at the local level, are questions about *how* journalists should do their jobs. What is the proper way to cover a sexual assault charge, even one involving a prominent family member in a city of extraordinarily wealthy individuals? There are ethical and legal questions that will be debated for years involving reporting about the William Kennedy Smith case.

Beyond the law is the level of performance standards for journalists called ethics. A principle of human conduct is an ethic. Some journalists consider the law to be the limit of their ethical judgments: If it is legal, then

A death that occurs at a public location is a very stressful situation for family members such as this woman who has just arrived at a murder scene. It is also a difficult time for journalists who need information about the victim and the incident and often have to interview grieving relatives and friends (photo by Battle Vaughn, *Miami Herald* staff).

it is acceptable to do it. Yet there are others who set performance standards in news writing, reporting, and editing that go well beyond the law. These journalists are ethicists.

Ethics is the study of human behavior involving standards of conduct and moral judgment or philosophy. There are many times each day when journalists are faced with decisions between right and wrong, not legal or illegal, conduct—at home, at play, and at work. Journalism ethics involves the continuing series of decisions that relate to your writing, reporting, editing, and production of your news work. The level of ethical performance of your journalistic duties should be important to you as an individual. It is also important to your employer and the public your news organization serves.

Ethics advance media law a level further. And as members of an evolving profession, journalists are becoming more and more concerned about development of a body of ethical principles to guide their work. This chapter examines reporting performance in the arena of professional ethics in terms of newsroom ethical standards expressed in codes. This chapter also discusses how journalists build public trust in their work through credibility and believability. Ethical issues to be discussed include fairness and objectivity, privacy, conflicts of interest, acceptance of gifts from sources, and problems peculiar to broadcast journalists.

THINKING ABOUT JOURNALISM ETHICS

There is a changing industry attitude toward ethics in journalism. Journalists have, for many decades, viewed ethics in a negative, or "red light" context. Ethics has been viewed as a system of rules used to restrict what journalists do in reporting about their communities. A new journalism ethic may be evolving to replace the "red light" approach. Poynter Institute for Media Studies Dean of Faculty Roy Peter Clark calls this new philosophy a "green light" ethic. It is based on what University of Alabama journalism professor Jay Black and Brigham Young University journalism professor Ralph Barney (1991) described as "ethically defensive insights, systematic decisionmaking processes, and positive moral philosophy. The end result may be a new journalism ethic . . . based in part on courage, ingenuity, democratic duty, compromise, pluralism, openness, independence, and mission" (p. 1). Black and Barney further explained:

> Rather than acting like fingerwagging scolds with pursed lips constantly chiding, "No, no, no!" whenever they encounter a journalist about to exercise news judgment, ethicists and media critics—and journalists—are encouraged to look at the decisionmaking process as a more positive enterprise based on a moral obligation to positively contribute to an informed populace. (p. 1)

You will find that the degree of virtuous conduct you display in your work will be noticed by your employer and your audience. Your ability to

ETHICS READING LIST

There are numerous excellent books and periodicals devoted to the subject of journalism ethics. The following books and periodicals will give you insightful discussions of the issues and examples of cases. If you have a serious interest in the subject, you might consider reading one or more of these:

BOOKS

Christians, C. G., Rotzoll, K. B., & Fackler, M. (1991). *Media ethics: Cases & moral reasoning.* (3rd ed.). New York: Longman.

Day, L. A. (1991). *Ethics in media communications: Cases and controversies.* Belmont, CA: Wadsworth.

Elliott, D. (ed.). (1986). *Responsible journalism.* Beverly Hills, CA: Sage Publications.

Fink, C. C. (1988). *Media ethics.* New York: McGraw-Hill.

Goodwin, H. E. (1987). *Groping for ethics in journalism.* (2nd ed.). Ames: Iowa State University Press.

Hulteng, J. L. (1985). *The messenger's motives: Ethical problems of the news media.* (2nd ed.). Englewood Cliffs, NJ: Prentice-Hall.

Kaidman, S. & Beauchamp, T. L. (1987). *The virtuous journalist.* New York: Oxford University Press.

Lambeth, E. B. (1986). *Committed journalism: An ethic for the profession.* New York: Hastings House.

Merrill, J. C. (1989). *The dialectic in journalism: Toward a responsible use of press freedom.* Baton Rouge: Louisiana State University Press.

Meyer, P. (1987). *Ethical journalism: A guide for students, practitioners and consumers.* New York: Longman.

Patterson, P., & Wilkins, L. (1991). *Media ethics: Issues and cases.* Dubuque, IA: W. C. Brown.

Rivers, W. L., & Mathews, C. (1988). *Ethics for the media.* Englewood Cliffs, NJ: Prentice-Hall.

PERIODICALS

FineLine: The Newsletter on Journalism Ethics, monthly, published by Billy Goat Strut Publishing, Inc., Louisville, KY.

Journal of Mass Media Ethics, quarterly, published by Lawrence Erlbaum Associates, Hillsdale, NJ.

Media Ethics Update, two times a year, published by Emerson College, Boston.

distinguish between right and wrong in a journalistic context will, in part, be affected by many different influences in your life.

Your professional values may be affected by your education. You may take an ethics course in either the philosophy or communication programs at your school. This course will help you to understand the most important values held by journalists in their proper conduct on the job.

Your family, your religion, and other major influences in your life have helped set your personal system of values that determine how you will react in certain routine situations. For instance, would you drive through a red light late at night if no other traffic was present? Some people would not, stating absolutely that laws should not be broken. Others would do so, arguing that no harm is done by this act.

Personal and professional standards change. In the professional world in the 1970s and 1980s, journalists closely examined their performance and gradually began to redefine how they should do their jobs. What was considered proper behavior several generations ago is unlikely to be acceptable in the 1990s. However, the debate over professional right and wrong continues as journalism's ethics are fine-tuned.

MAJOR ISSUES

There has been a strong growth in interest in journalistic ethics by professionals and by the public and the scope and depth of issues has also grown. Most journalists still do not make ethical decisions after extended thought simply because they do not have the chance. "The rush of events forces us to make ethical decisions by reflex more than by reflection, like drivers wheeling around potholes, mindful that a blowout sends them into a courtroom at one ditch and into public scorn at the other," wrote ethics scholars Clifford G. Christians, Kim B. Rotzoll, and Mark Fackler (1991, p. xiv).

There has been much interest in ethics at all levels in the past few years. In particular, the public seems to be more interested in the ethics of politicians and public officials, of businessmen and women, and of journalists. Widely publicized recent cases involving the behavior of elected and appointed public officials, and new guidelines for ethics in business, as well as those in journalism are the reason (Galvan, 1989).

Much of the professional discussion of ethics issues in journalism occurs at professional organization meetings. Typically, a panel of experts is assembled to discuss the current issues and problems facing the news media. Discussions often cover a wide range of subjects and situations, but rarely look beyond the practical side. In the past decade, several key journalism ethics issues affecting reporters have surfaced without resolution.

One of those recurring issues is the role of the journalist. The question of competing responsibilities is one that has led to many spirited debates among journalists. *Newsweek* columnist Meg Greenfield (1990) indicated that it is an odd and contradictory position, one that surfaced again during reporting of the Persian Gulf War in 1990 and 1991.

It sometimes seems to me that in these foreign crises we [journalists] are complaining either that (1) the government is calling us disloyal or (2) it wants our loyalty as advocates of what is it doing, which, by the nature of our jobs, we cannot give. In other words: please don't call us disloyal and please don't expect loyalty to inform what we write, say or do on the job. (p. 76)

What Greenfield said is not limited to just wartime international situations. The same "us versus them" attitude exists at city hall, in the home team locker room, and in the corporate board room down the street. When do reporters stop being journalists and begin being citizens, team fans, and customers? Perhaps there is room for both. Perhaps not. "The problem is that we are rightly obliged not to let those sentiments [about the subject] keep us from asking the lousy questions, from being a pain in the neck to governments that are trying (it is their nature and often their short-term interest) to orchestrate reality and fiddle with the truth," Greenfield said (p. 76). Greenfield also advised:

Some questions don't have good answers. American journalists who fashion themselves blank slates get written on by some pretty unsavory characters, that is, used. You have to call on some judgment and knowledge and instinct that can only be a product of where you come from and who you are. You don't have to renounce your citizenship at the door. You just have to be willing to risk some disfavor and misunderstanding if that is the price of covering the subject fairly (p. 76).

Whereas the public seems to be more aware of ethics and the professional behavior of journalists, there is effort to make more journalists aware of ethical standards. This awareness effort is occurring in journalism and mass communication education at the college and university level, as well as through professional seminars and in-house programs sponsored by news organizations. Professional organizations provide the material for discussion, but individual news organizations must provide reporters and other staff members with the guidelines for their work. Increasing awareness also comes through these written guidelines and in-house discussion sessions about them (Seals, 1990). Even less structured and often casual college media news staffs can produce codes or ethics policies and discuss them.

Other important issues debated in the 1990s include fairness in reporting. At one point not too many years ago, most journalists discussed *objectivity*. But it became apparent that objectivity is not really an attainable goal of news reporting. What most journalists were really describing was a desire to be *fair* in reporting by presenting all sides to controversies.

Truth is another issue that has arisen from cases in which reporters have made errors in not reporting truthful information. Although reporters may feel information is accurate, they not always challenge its truthfulness.

Privacy of individuals is not only a legal matter, but also an increasingly hot ethical matter. The issue became one of the most talked about in 1991 when the William Kennedy Smith case evolved over a period of several months. But it also involves other matters such as identification of AIDS victims and use of computer databases to search for information about private citizens as well as celebrities and public officials.

In *graphics* and *photography,* ethical issues surround developing technology that permits photographers, graphic artists, and picture editors to change reality. With digital images available in many newsrooms, the potential to change images tempts journalists daily. For graphics reporters, it becomes significant: Do you eliminate an undesired background item? Should you change the color of the carpet or the sky? Do you move people closer together? How much change is acceptable or is any change improper? These are some of the unresolved issues involved in this form of reporting.

A phenomenon known as "advertorials" is becoming more popular in the broadcast and print media. Whereas some seem less troublesome than others and not everyone agrees on what they are, some news organizations are presenting advertising copy—in full page ads, in special sections, or in special broadcast programs—as if the information were news. Advertorials, also known as "infomercials," have caused the line between news and advertising to become more difficult to find. *Philadelphia Inquirer* reporter Doreen Carvajal (1991) wrote that "given economic pressures, television, magazines and newspapers have been casting for new forms of revenue and in that struggle, ethical standards have become elastic" (p. 1).

Dave Gianelli, assistant managing editor of the *Phoenix Gazette* (1990) urged, "Given that the use of advertorials is increasing, and given that the question of whether these sections undermine public newspapers is unanswered, it's time we began examining the issues in a systematic way" (p. 24). The problem is also becoming serious for television news departments. Advertorials are troublesome when it becomes difficult for audiences to determine when a program that appears to be in a news documentary format on a given subject turns out to be a 30-minute or 1-hour program devoted to the virtues of an exercise machine, health food, a real estate sales philosophy, or some other product or service.

Discussion and eventual resolution of these and other ethical issues help build positive relations with the public. These efforts contribute to *trust* and *credibility* in news reporting. Without them, or if they gradually erode, audiences seek other sources for information that can be more reliable and credible.

Whatever the ethics problem might be, and whatever the cause of the issue, enforcement of ethics standards has been a long-term problem that shows no signs of immediate solution. There are few codes of ethics that even address enforcement mechanisms or penalties for clear violations. Some news companies have employee policies about ethics code violations, but there is no universal process such as those known to the medical or legal professions.

An incident that occurred at the *Washington Post* in 1981 is a benchmark in modern journalism ethics. That spring, the *Post* returned a Pulitzer Prize won by a reporter on its staff for feature writing. Why? The reporter, Janet Cooke, had written about a child drug addict who did not exist. The child was, the reporter eventually admitted, a composite of young persons she had met while researching her story. Journalism professors Jay Black and Ralph Barney (1991) recently looked at the progress made in developing journalism ethics since the Cooke episode and concluded:

> The challenges and opportunities have never been as closely aligned as they are today, a decade after Janet Cooke reminded the world that journalism has an ethic worthy of intellectual pursuit. Janet Cooke has made a major contribution to the field of journalism ethics, if only to sharpen the debate and focus attention on journalism's positive moral duties. The debate has become intellectually richer, and journalism cannot help but be the better for it. (p. 7)

CODES OF ETHICS AND NEWSROOM POLICIES

Journalists have tried to assemble evolving professional values into meaningful ethics statements. These statements, most often called *codes of ethics,* serve as behavior models for journalists. Major journalism associations have created codes, and some individual newspapers, magazines, radio stations, and television stations have created their own and placed them in employee handbooks.

Standards of acceptable professional behavior change over time. This is certainly true of law, medicine, business, and politics in addition to professional journalism. Some newspapers such as the *Milwaukee Journal* have even regularly published their codes of ethics in the newspaper for concerned readers to see and understand.

Mostly, however, these codes are distributed to members of professional societies and associations for occasional reference. Unlike medical and legal codes that have enforcement strength through license revocation procedures, no such penalties exist in journalism. The most severe penalties at present are loss of employment if journalists commit a serious violation of their employer's code or policy involving company ethics.

Regardless, the professional codes serve as models or ideals of professional conduct in the news media. Two codes of ethics are presented in the appendices. Appendix D, the Code of Ethics of the Society of Professional Journalists, is one of the most widely publicized codes representing the sentiments of an organization of journalists from both print and broadcast news media. Appendix E, the code of the Radio-Television News Directors Association, demonstrates the concerns of broadcast news managers.

Journalistic ethics, as Penn State University journalism professor Eugene Goodwin (1987) noted, are often studied in a situational context. This means rather than looking at the big picture through general philosophies or perspectives, most study and discussion of news media ethics focus on individual situations. Roy Peter Clark, dean of faculty at the Poynter Institute in St. Petersburg, Florida, created a practical model for ethical thinking, depicted in Fig. 11.1. The model is effective in situational ethics

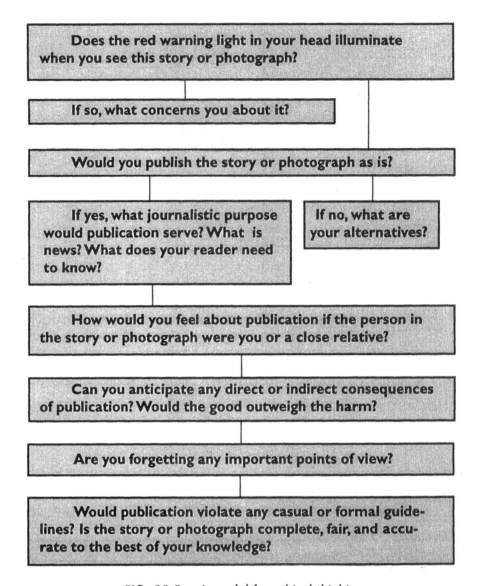

FIG. 11.1. A model for ethical thinking.

analysis. When facing an ethical dilemma, this model provides a track for thought and decision making.

ETHICS AND TRUST: CREDIBILITY

One of the most important characteristics of the news media's relationship with their audiences is trust. And to gain the public's trust, the news media must be credible and believable. These are two difficult-to-achieve and even more difficult-to-maintain goals. Numerous public opinion polls during the 1980s indicated eroding public faith in the news media. The public believes there is more bias and unfairness, more improper content, and more sensationalism in the news media, the polls tell journalists. The growing dislike for the news media has been called the "credibility gap" (Fink, 1988).

To be credible, a characteristic all media news organizations seek but some fail to attain, means the public feels it can put faith and confidence in the work that is done. In a news context, the public will be confident in your reporting and presentation of the facts over time if you are credible. Believability reflects the ability of your work to be accepted as the *truth*. It means that not only does an audience turn to a news organization for routine news, but it will rely on that organization for information in an emergency or potentially dangerous situation.

University of Georgia journalism professor Conrad C. Fink (1988) described the media credibility problem:

> Any discussion of media ethics today must acknowledge that many journalists are deeply concerned that the media have not used their power entirely wisely or professionally and that the transgressions by individual journalists are many and serious. Media ethics must be discussed also within the context of increasingly negative perceptions of newspapers and television held by readers and viewers. Inside the media and out, there is fundamental reassessment underway of the journalist's basic mission, the techniques of reporting and writing, and the morality of the manner in which they are employed. (p. 14)

For journalists, no characteristic of their work is more important. Journalists whose work is, over the long run, lacking in high ethical standards will lose credibility, believability, and ultimately the trust of their audiences. News organizations, which continue to convey a sense of arrogance, aloofness, insensitivity, and bias are asking for trouble with their audiences. Figure 11.2 displays the most common components of media credibility suggested by Chung (1991).

There are early signs of improvement in the 1990s. Coverage of the Persian Gulf War was one of the biggest tests of news media professional

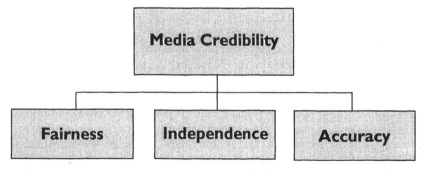

FIG. 11.2 Components of media credibility (from Chung, 1991).

performance in many years. The public was not only reading and watching in very large numbers, but also paying attention to how the work of journalists was done, especially those working for the U.S. television networks in Saudi Arabia, Iraq, Kuwait, and Washington. That, too, became news at times during the war. Robin Hughes, former editor of the journalism ethics newsletter, *FineLine,* wrote a postwar media ethics analysis. In it, Hughes (1991) argued that there are indications of increasing sensitivity to the people involved in the war, especially the families of the men and women who died in combat. Although news organizations sought the local "home front" angle on the war by reporting about soldiers from the home region, they also faced tough decisions about how to cover the effects of casualties of the war. Hughes (1991) wrote:

> On any given day, in any given TV newsroom, news directors and reporters will jump at the chance to beat their competition on a story. War—and especially death—can change that.
> Television stations across the country . . . jumped into pools for coverage of funerals of those killed in the Gulf war and for contacting and interviewing families of victims. In some cities, pool arrangements extended to POWs and MIAs. (p. 3)

Hughes said similar sensitive approaches to reporting about the war were seen in newspapers also. Efforts such as this will eventually make a difference. But it takes more than a war to effect long-term change in public perception about performance. The "credibility gap" is one of the highest prices all journalists pay for the unethical performances of just a few.

SOCIAL RESPONSIBILITY OF JOURNALISTS

Codes of ethics exist to help journalists to think about their behavior, said Casey Bukro (1989), an environmental reporter for the *Chicago Tribune* and one of the authors of the Society of Professional Journalists' widely distributed code of ethics. As a set of guidelines and not an explicit "yes or no" check list, codes address responsible conduct of journalists, Bukro argued. "The code of ethics is what it was intended to be: Guidelines and a statement of principles to usher us in the direction of responsible journalism, accuracy, objectivity and fair play," he wrote (p. 22).

Social responsibility, in the code of the Society of Professional Journalists, is at the top of the list. In the preamble and first section of the code, journalists are told their primary responsibility is to serve the truth and the public's right to know about events in the public interest.

Responsibility cannot be delegated. Louisiana State University professor Louis A. Day (1991) argued, "As moral agents we are all accountable for our actions and should not blame others for our ethical lapses" (p. 8). Social responsibility developed as an alternative to libertarianism, which endorses freedom without enforced responsibility. Advocates of the social responsibility approach to journalism also feel strongly about freedom, but argue that responsibility is essential especially for performance by institutions such as newspapers, magazines, or radio or television stations (Day, 1991). As a socially responsible press, journalists place high value on such concepts as duty, accountability, obligation, truth and accuracy, objectivity and fairness, professionalism, balance, and credibility (Black & Barney, 1991; Day, 1991).

Simply put, morality is conformity to a set of rules of proper conduct. Many social critics have bemoaned the decline in morality in the United States. Similarly, many observers of U.S. journalism feel there has been a serious disruption in morality in the news media. Whether or not you believe this is true, there is concern about morality in the media. Public awareness of the values represented in the news media as well as the values used in reporting news have been under fire for a decade or more. In the past 10 years, numerous incidents of improper conduct have perhaps created a greater concern for what is right and wrong.

ETHICS AND PRIVACY

One of the best known recent cases involving privacy was the national news media coverage of the Gary Hart–Donna Rice story. The *Miami Herald,* led

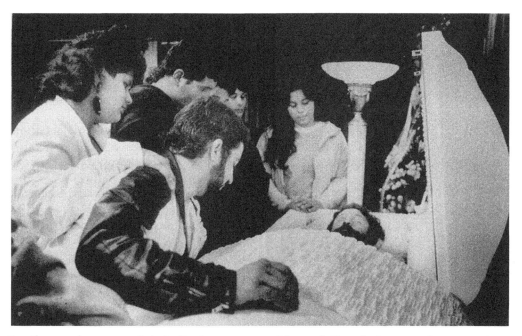

Family members spend their final moments with a relative during a wake at a private funeral home. Without permission from the family, the photographer and reporter at the event may be invading the family's privacy. But with permission, the photographer and reporter can record a poignant moment (photo by the *Miami Herald* staff).

by political editor Tom Fiedler and investigative reporter Jim McGee, discovered Hart's involvement with Donna Rice, creating a sensation during the 1987 campaign for the Democratic party's presidential nomination. Hart abandoned his campaign after his integrity was questioned — a married man apparently involved with a single woman. A number of individuals felt this was an invasion of Hart's privacy, not to mention Rice's, and the story should not have been reported. Others believed the story was a major news development because Hart's behavior had been questioned, he had invited reporters to watch him, and he was caught. The story gave significant insight into the character of a U.S. senator seeking the presidency.

Even while you follow the legal guidelines about privacy in your state, you may encounter decisions involving privacy that create ethical dilemmas while remaining within the law. Most codes of ethics advise responsibility and fairness in dealing with matters of an individual's privacy. For instance, the Society of Professional Journalists' code in Appendix D advises, "Journalists at all times will show respect for the dignity, privacy, rights, and well-being of people encountered in the course of gathering and presenting the news." It adds, specifically, "The news media must guard against invading a person's right to privacy." Similarly, the Radio-Television News Directors Association advises members in its code in Appendix E to "respect the dignity, privacy and well-being of people with whom they deal."

Ethical issues involving privacy can surround use of photographs or private communication such as memos or letters. They can also involve reporting about the private lives of public persons such as public officials, athletes, and entertainers. Privacy ethics can entail issues such as AIDS patient identification, the sexual orientation of an individual, the identity and the problems of troubled juveniles, the behavior of family members of widely known individuals, the victims of sex and/or violent crimes, and suicides (Goodwin, 1987).

Issues involving reporting techniques that invade privacy are important, remarked Penn State University journalism professor Eugene Goodwin (1987). During tragedies, for example, how far should you go to get a story? During emotional moments, do you shoot tape? Try to interview a grieving family member? Many times, these perhaps necessary acts are viewed by the public as insensitive. Journalists must think about the value of the information weighed against the intrusion, no matter how "legal" it might be.

Questions about how far stories should go to impose on privacy are often debated without resolution, even when publication of the information and techniques of getting the story are within the law.

FAIRNESS, OBJECTIVITY, AND ACCURACY

As professional journalism standards go, fairness and objectivity are highly valued. Fairness involves reporting that is just. Objectivity is perhaps more complex. One particular definition says it is "the journalistic decision-making process that encourages, if not demands, detachment from evidence, sources, subjects, and audiences" (Black & Barney, 1991, pp. 3–4).

In recent years, journalists have begun to talk more about fairness and less about objectivity in their news writing and reporting. This is probably because just about everyone involved, from writers to audiences, realize a reporter cannot be completely objective about a subject when reporting about it. Thus, the focus is properly placed on *fairness*. Fairness, as a concept, is more appropriate because objectivity had often been rigidly interpreted as reporting without explanation (Goodwin, 1987).

Fairness naturally evolved from the inadequacies of the concept of objectivity. Fairness in news writing and reporting entails a quality of justness, evenness, civility, and of "by-the-rules" journalism. It is news writing and reporting without bias, imbalance of perspective, deception, or prejudice. And because the values of journalism—codes of ethics, for example—advise journalists to represent all sides in controversies, to present all relevant points of view, and to be complete, it is more realistic to discuss writing and reporting in terms of fairness.

Along with this, Goodwin said, comes accuracy in writing and reporting. Accuracy is an unspoken given in the business. Accuracy is the most basic characteristic of the work journalists must do. Inaccurate or untruthful reporting undermines credibility and public trust. It is logical, then, that you consider accuracy and fairness at the same time. After all, would it be fair to report inaccurate information? Untruthful information? Of course not.

It is not, for instance, against the law to alter direct quotations for any of a number of reasons, such as cleaning up grammar. But is this accurate reporting? Is it unethical behavior? Some journalists routinely alter quotations to make what was said more readable. Others feel it is dishonest and unethical.

Most codes of professional journalism ethics address accuracy, truthfulness, objectivity, and fairness. Review the codes in the appendices, for example, for the particular sentiments of the profession's leaders on these issues.

ETHICS AND CONFLICT OF INTEREST

Conflict is disagreement, opposition, and incompatibility. And there are times when reporters find themselves in positions of possible conflict of their interests as journalists and as individuals. Conflicts of interest can be opportunities for journalists to take advantage of a situation for professional or personal gain. These situations will ultimately compromise their professional position with their audiences.

For instance, reporters who are members of special interest groups should not write stories about those groups. To illustrate, it would be wrong for a reporter who is an active member of the National Wildlife Federation to write about environmental issues involving that organization.

As with other ethical issues, conflict of interest concerns are traced to the importance of public trust in the news media. How can you trust and believe the news stories you are reading or hearing about the National Wildlife Federation if the reporter is a member? The reporter's point of view may be perceived as biased toward that organization, even if it is not.

Reporters covering politics should not serve in appointed or elected political positions, although they may have the opportunity to do so. Some news organizations even extend this rule to immediate family members. The usual way to avoid these situations is to change beats or regular assignments in the newsroom. There is no reason a reporter cannot continue to work in the community as a journalist, but the news work that individual does should not conflict with personal activities.

Conflict of interest policies include political involvement, outside jobs, memberships in some social organizations, business interests, and even personal romantic relationships with sources. When in doubt, check with a supervisor. Remember, your own interests are not all that are at stake. Your news organization's credibility may be at risk also.

DECEPTION AND IMPERSONATION

Deception and impersonation are ethical concerns arising out of the desire for truthful conduct by journalists. In simple moral terms, a reporter using deception or impersonation cannot be completely truthful. Therein lies the ethical problem.

There are numerous cases of participatory reporting discussed elsewhere in this book as well as hundreds of other examples in the literature of ethics and reporting. Often the question arises whether one particular form of participatory reporting, undercover reporting, is allowable because reporters do not readily identify themselves as journalists seeking information for a story. Some critics feel it is dishonest and categorically oppose its use.

Another form of participatory reporting that raises serious ethical debate is impersonation or misrepresentation. There are times when a reporter may feel compelled to impersonate or misrepresent to obtain information for a story. Usually this is done when the story itself is of high public value and the information is very valuable for a story and cannot be obtained by other more conventional means of reporting.

Deception and misrepresentation in reporting can take many forms. It could mean calling a hospital emergency room and identifying yourself as a physician or a relative of a victim to get information needed for a story about an accident. It could mean visiting a local restaurant without identifying yourself with the intention to write a review. It could mean teaching as a qualified substitute teacher in the public school system to get a true picture of what is happening at a troubled school. It can mean owning and operating a bar to learn about suspected corruption in local government, as the *Chicago Sun-Times* once did. Decisions to use deception and misrepresentation are not made in a vacuum. These are difficult choices often made under the pressure of deadline or pressure to produce a significant news story. The choice is not easy. Day (1991) offered one useful way of deliberating the matter:

> One question that often arises is whether journalists stand apart from the general population in ethical situations like the use of deception. If we assume that reporters act on behalf of the public, the answer must be no. Only if the average citizen, faithful to the ethical norms of society, would be willing to use deception to get a story could a journalist justify doing likewise. And regardless of what justifications are used for occasional deceptions, the line should always be drawn at violations of law, because illegal conduct by reporters undermines the respect for law. (pp. 76–77)

Dartmouth College Ethics Institute Director Deni Elliott (1991) pointed out that most reporters must walk a fine line between charming a story from a source and alienating them by being open about your purposes for talking to them. "Reporters don't want to tip their hands, but sources feel burned if they don't know from the start what the reporters have in mind. What do reporters owe their sources? In this case, other professions can't provide much guidance. Reporters *don't* owe sources the kinds of things that doctors owe patients or lawyers owe clients" (p. 2). Elliott advised, "Good reporters treat their sources with respect" (p. 3). "And people don't like to be fooled. They especially don't like it when reporters pretend to admire them while preparing to nail them to the wall. They don't like it when the context of quotes changes between interview and publication." Sources who have experienced such reporters are cautious in subsequent interviews or refuse to talk at all, Elliott observed. "A story that is won through seduction is sorcery, not sourcing. No professionals (except magicians) can last long if trickery becomes known as the usual method of operation" (p. 3).

SENSATIONALISM IN REPORTING

One of the contributing causes of the "credibility gap," discussed earlier in this chapter, has been sensationalism. The idea of news that is exciting or startling is not new. Publishers such as William Randolph Hearst and Joseph Pulitzer made their newspaper fortunes in the late 19th century with content that was nothing less than sensational.

Most professional conduct policies and codes of the 1990s state that sensational journalism should be avoided. For example, the Radio-Television News Directors Association code of broadcast news ethics in Appendix E states in specific terms that RTNDA members "will evaluate information solely on its merits as news, rejecting sensationalism or misleading emphasis in any form." The Society of Professional Journalists' code in Appendix D advises against pandering "to morbid curiosity about details of vice and crime."

Although most journalists agree sensationalism is not appropriate, the problem is defining what constitutes sensational journalism. Is a television "sweeps week" series on revealing summer bathing suits sensational? Is a radio station's use of a tape of an emotional plea for help just before a murder occurs on a 911 recording sensational? Is a newspaper's graphic details of the arrest of a television and film star who was accused of masturbation in a theater sensational? Is use of offensive language in a news story sensational? Is use of home videotape of violent acts such as a shooting, rape, or beating sensational? These situations are often overwhelming to ponder and often impossible to reconcile.

Visual images are often the most significant cause of sensationalism criticism in the news media. This is especially true of video. With the proliferation of home videotape cameras, more and more such video is available to the news media. The case of the police beating of Rodney King in Los Angeles is but one example, but the shock of the event itself overwhelmed any arguments about potential sensational intent when it was broadcast by networks and local affiliates countless times. A 1987 suicide with a gun by a Pennsylvania state official at a public press conference was another situation where decisions had to be made about the appropriateness of televising and publishing images of such a violent public act.

Usually sensationalism charges arise from less unusual news events. Often these charges arise from use of nudity, sexuality, and sexual behavior, atypical human relationships, and from strong language or certain forms of violence. One thing is clear: It is beyond the limits of today's ethics in the news media to determine what is and is not sensational. Day (1991) explained:

> On the one hand, a system of ethics based on moral prudishness would lead to such austere media content that it would probably be rejected by a majority of the audience. On the other hand, absolute freedom leads to moral chaos and destruction of cultural continuity. Practically speaking, neither extreme is workable. Thus, in a diverse society the strategy should be to reach some middle ground, an accommodation between the excesses of moral prudishness and moral chaos. (p. 237)

SOURCES AND FREEBIES

Years ago, journalists readily accepted gifts, often called *freebies,* from sources because journalists were poorly paid and most journalists considered the gifts as part of the benefits of the job. This type of thinking today may have a big price — your job. Acceptance of gifts of value because of your job can damage credibility, so most news organizations categorically refuse such offers. Freebies are troublesome because of the real influence-buying, or the appearance of influence-buying, that comes with the gifts.

DAVID B. OFFER, THE *NEWPORT DAILY NEWS*
THE REALITIES OF ETHICS AND THE LAW

Perhaps the most difficult thing for journalism students to understand about legal and ethical problems is that they are real and they don't just affect experienced reporters or editors or major newspapers and television networks. The problems you read about in textbooks happen daily in small cities throughout the nation.

Let me provide a few examples:

In La Crosse, WI, a city of 50,000 on the Mississippi River, a reporter walked across the street from the newspaper to the courthouse to cover jury selection in the trial of a local lawyer accused of defrauding clients. Everything should have been routine. The reporter had covered hundreds of cases in that courthouse with no problems. But that morning, the judge decided not to allow reporters to be present as prospective jurors were questioned. The reporter understood state laws regarding open courts, and the newspaper had a plan for what to do if anyone ever tried to close a courtroom. The reporter asked the judge to delay the case while the sought legal advice and he asked to place a preprinted statement about open courts on the official record. The judge refused both requests and began to question and select jurors behind closed doors.

The reporter notified his editor, who called a lawyer. The editor and the paper's attorney went immediately to the courtroom seeking to make a legal argument. The judge wouldn't let them in. Jury selection was completed in secret. The paper appealed to the Wisconsin appeals court and then to the state supreme court, where it won a unanimous decision requiring that in the future, jury selection be open to the press and public. The most important thing to understand about this case is that it was not very special. It was La Crosse, WI, not New York City. It was a routine part of newsgathering. The law is not just something for the books.

Another case in La Crosse illustrates the value of open records laws. A reporter attending a local school board meeting heard board members casually mention a concern about school bus safety. Not wishing to tip the competition—he said nothing. The next morning, he went to the school administration office and asked to see the files on bus inspections and all correspondence and reports about bus problems.

A secretary provided them, and the reporter started to make notes from material indicating that school officials were justifiably concerned about lax safety standards for the busses. Then the school superintendent emerged from an office, saw what the reporter was doing, and snatched the material away from him.

The reporter returned to the paper and told his editor, who called the superintendent to argue that the records should have been available under state law. Laws differ from state to state, but most states guarantee access to most court and governmental records and meetings, with exceptions for personnel matters. The school superintendent refused to release the documents. The newspaper sued and obtained a court order allowing the reporter

(continued)

DAVID B. OFFER, THE *NEWPORT DAILY NEWS* (continued)

to see and copy all the bus safety files. The result was a series of stories that were very important to the community. It wasn't Watergate or organized crime. But it was journalism at its best in real life.

Another basic area of the law that can affect every reporter is libel. No reporter sets out to libel anyone, but even the newest journalist can cover news that offers opportunities for libel. The best prevention is accuracy. Such simple things as taking careful notes may save reporters embarrassment and their newspaper thousands of dollars.

It is libelous, of course, to say that an innocent person is a criminal. So reporters covering courts must be very certain when they identify anyone. Names are often similar. That's why most news articles identify people by name, age, and address. There may be more than one John Smith, but there probably are not too many who are 19 years old and who live at 3456 Main St. That's why you often see police items reporting that "John W. Smith, 19, of 3456 Main St., was charged today with. . . ." Complete identification is safe and accurate.

In Wisconsin, a usually careful reporter incorrectly copied from a police log and found himself in a potentially libelous situation by naming a police officer as the person arrested and the suspect as the arresting officer. Fortunately, an apology and a correction settled the case—there was no libel suit—but it could have been a major problem.

Young reporters sometimes err by thinking that things are obvious, by making assumptions. For example, they assume that police records are properly spelled. Experienced reporters know that police officers are often poor spellers, and they check and double check. John Smith could be Jon Smith, John Smithe, or even Joan Smith. Even if it sounds silly, it is good practice to ask persons how to spell their names. When that is impossible, careful reporters check in phone books, city directories, or with other sources.

In addition to be alert to legal issues, reporters and editors at every level are deeply concerned with the ethics of journalism. In Newport, Rhode Island, a reporter had to consider proper journalistic standards in deciding how—or whether—to approach the widow of a man who had been shot to death by a police officer. The newspaper wanted to know something about the man, who attacked the police officer with a machete. But would a call be improperly intrusive? What about the widow's need for privacy in her grief? After discussion, the reporter called the woman, who said she was willing to talk and invited the reporter to her home.

In newsrooms throughout the country, reporters and editors have had to decide what to do when local servicepeople were killed in Lebanon, when local students died in auto accidents, when worldwide events meant local tragedy. Journalists, who agonize about making these calls, almost always find families are pleased to talk about their loved ones.

Ethics is a constantly changing way of evaluating what we do and how we act. For many years it was considered acceptable for journalists to accept gifts—free trips, liquor, expensive dinners—from news sources or people

(continued)

DAVID B. OFFER, THE *NEWPORT DAILY NEWS (continued)*

about whom they wrote stories. That attitude changed when younger reporters insisted that taking these "freebies" compromised their independence.

In 1976, the Society of Professional Journalists adopted a code of ethics prohibiting journalists from accepting favors, gifts, travel, or special privileges. Still, people keep offering them. Most honorable journalists and their employers turn them down. In Newport, the staff decided to save all the freebies that arrived in the newsroom and to donate them to charity. They regularly pass on T-shirts, hats, books, food samples, and other items. At many newspapers, senior editors meet with reporters, copy editors, and photographers to discuss ethical questions. In Newport, we gathered at deadline to decide whether to print the name of a woman who accused three college students of rape. The case was dismissed after a grand jury decided the woman had been a willing participant. The *Daily News* has a policy against publishing the names of victims of sex crimes, but after the case was dismissed, should this woman's name be published? The question was hotly debated before the editor decided that her name would not be printed. This kind of debate is far more normal in newsrooms than most people would believe.

Good reporting — accurate fact gathering and careful writing — and a concern for what is honorable will prevent most problems and result in good stories that best serve your readers (Garrison, 1990).

David B. Offer is editor of The *Newport Daily News* in Rhode Island. Offer was one of the authors of the code of ethics of the Society of Professional Journalists.

Sources usually send gifts to journalists as a manner of thanks for positive coverage (thus, reinforcement for the next story, too) or to register positive impressions for a story in progress. And, like other unethical situations described in earlier sections, acceptance of free gifts may damage the credibility of the journalists and their news organization. Readers and viewers simply cannot trust reporters to be straight with the facts if they are aware that the reporter just got a free meal for the positive restaurant review or a trip to the Caribbean for a glowing destination feature in the travel section. In this case, the appearance of influence is as damaging as the actual influence in terms of public perception. There are no freebies worth that price.

Because his newspaper does not want its credibility damaged by the taint of accepting free food or services, *New York Times* food critic Brian Miller spent $80,000 on restaurant meals and related expenses in 1987. That computes to about $219 a day (Modzelewski, 1988). Although Miller's expenses are rather extreme, this illustrates that news organizations are willingly paying for what used to be provided free by restaurants, theaters, politicians, sports teams, or record companies.

Who should pay for the entertainment you report about or review? The lunch meeting you scheduled with a source? Should you pay for free transportation offered by a source? Tickets? Records? Books? Food? Journalists who pay their own way—that is, their companies pay—are obligated to no one except their public.

Most news organizations require their reporters to reject freebies unless the free ticket or item is used by a legitimate reporter in the completion of an assignment. When the story is completed, if the item can be returned or donated, it is not kept by the reporter. Items such as books and records are usually donated to local charities when received from a source.

Why are freebies a concern? Usually there are expectations associated with free tickets, records, food, subscriptions, travel, and books. The expectations can range from simple recognition in print or on the air—news "publicity" for no or little cost with the added bonus of news legitimacy— to positive news coverage.

There has been a change regarding such expectations from sources in recent years. However, ethical standards have tightened, forcing this change. Sources now expect less but often offer less, too.

ETHICAL CONCERNS IN ELECTRONIC JOURNALISM

Whereas newspapers and magazines have much in common with radio and television in terms of ethics, there are some ethical issues that deeply concern electronic journalists. Research shows 4 in 10 radio and television stations have a code of ethics for reporters and producers, describing standards for performance (Wulfemeyer, 1990). These situations reflect specific broadcast situations of many of the issues discussed in previous sections of this chapter.

San Diego State University professor K. Tim Wulfemeyer (1990) ana-lyzed the ethical perspectives of radio and television news directors on ethics in their newsrooms. He found concern for ethical matters, but found some guidelines were "more likely to be followed than others" (p. 991). He found the most agreement in areas of fairness, balance, and accuracy in reporting, but less consensus in conflict of interest, privacy, and misrepresentation areas.

Wulfemeyer found news story production areas to reveal problems in the minds of news directors. Some of the production findings included dis-agreement on these items:

- 51% would "clean up" profane language used by sources
- 43% would correct factual errors made by sources
- 38% said there was too much sensationalism in radio and television news
- 35% said there was too much "fluff" on the air

In terms of reporting techniques used by broadcast journalists, the study also determined news directors believed:

- going undercover is not acceptable (84%)
- paying sources for information is not acceptable (88%)
- going live without any real reason is acceptable (31%)
- naming "daredevils" is not acceptable (34%)
- violating traffic laws is acceptable (24%)
- victims should be helped if possible is acceptable (59%)
- hidden camera and microphones is not acceptable (40%)
- ambush or surprise interviews is not acceptable (47%)

PROFESSIONALISM AS A GOAL

There is considerable ongoing industry discussion about whether journalism should strive to become a profession. Traditional professions such as law and medicine have standards that most U.S. journalists would not accept. Some individuals have argued it may not even be desirable to strive for professional status. A group of *Washington Post* reporters and editors, for example, failed in a suit against management to argue they were *not* professionals. These persons did not want to be called professionals because it meant the company could pay them less because overtime pay was not given to professionals (Black & Barney, 1991).

Although many people will argue that professionalism is a positive goal, the greatest barrier to journalism becoming a profession is licensing. And it may be insurmountable. Few journalists would ever permit licensing to occur because they view it as a direct conflict with the freedom of the press assured in the First Amendment. And any licensing agency would likely be a governmental body, so a conflict of interest would exist.

Yet there is no doubt in the past several decades that journalism has moved toward professionalism. Education, activities of industry organizations, and standards of conduct, for example, each an important characteristic of the professions, have improved dramatically.

Regardless of whether professionalism is ever achieved as a goal, it is important to consider the words of University of Missouri journalism professor Edmund Lambeth (1986):

> Reporters and editors, for their collective part, could do worse than heed the call of [Edmund] Burke and [Yale law professor Alexander] Bickel, which is the call of the classical liberal tradition placed in the modern context. It is for a journalism of commitment and humane truth telling. It is for a journalism watchful of its own ways but also alert to report injustice. It is for a journalism that respects its own independence, as well as that of others. It takes seriously its stewardship of free expression, and searches for better ways to report, and, therefore, help build the very community which can assure its own survival in a free society. (p. 179)

Court rules do not permit reporters to talk to jurors during a trial. But after jurors are dismissed by a judge, it is no longer illegal or unethical to request an interview with a juror (photo by the *Miami Herald* staff).

IV | APPENDICES

Appendix A: Confidential Sources and Anonymity

THE ORANGE COUNTY REGISTER
SANTA ANA, CALIFORNIA
SEPTEMBER 27, 1988

MEMORANDUM
To: News Division Associates
From: Chris Anderson
Subject: *USE OF CONFIDENTIAL AND ANONYMOUS SOURCES*

I want to remind you all of our policy and practices regarding confidential and anonymous sources.

In a nutshell, we want to avoid the use of anonymity in our news pages to the greatest extent possible. We also want to avoid making promises of confidentiality to sources when it is not in the best interest of the *Orange County Register* and its readers. Further, we make a distinction between anonymous sources and confidential sources.

Credibility is a newspaper's most important asset, and it is held tenuously.

Information attributed to real people is more credible because the reader is not required to accept its existence on faith.

Every inclusion of information attributed to anonymous sources erodes the overall credibility of the newspaper because some readers will refuse to believe it.

In addition, every inclusion of anonymous information tells news sources that we will accept anonymous information and makes on-the-record newsgathering more difficult.

Every decision on whether to include anonymous information in the newspaper must weigh the loss in credibility versus the value of the information to those readers who will accept it.

Here are our guidelines on anonymous sources in locally written articles:

—We won't use anonymous sources to express negative opinions or make negative charges about an individual or organization.

—We will use anonymous sources only when we are convinced that the facts they are providing us are of overwhelming news value and cannot be obtained in any other way from any other sources.

—To the fullest extent possible, we must explain why the source is anonymous. We also must identify to the fullest extent possible the nature of the source, including qualifications and biases which can aid the reader in determining the validity of the information.

—We will use anonymous sources only when approved by an editor at the level of assistant managing editor or higher.

Granting confidentiality is another matter—one we take very seriously. We distinguish anonymous sources from confidential sources. An anonymous source is one whose name we have agreed to leave out of an article, but who may later need to be identified. That need may come from legal action for example. A confidential source is one whose identity will not be revealed.

Therefore, we must be extremely careful about granting confidentiality. This promise is made not on behalf of a reporter or editor, but on behalf of the newspaper.

Generally, it is better to grant a source anonymity rather than confidentiality. If the source is not concerned about the possibility of legal action, he or she should not be troubled by this.

If it becomes necessary to discuss the issue of anonymity or confidentiality, make clear the distinction. Don't make vague promises. In the case of anonymity, use the following specific language: "I may use this information in my story but I won't reveal your name as the source, except to an editor or as required by law."

Approval of the editor or managing editor is required before granting confidentiality.

Because of the seriousness of this promise, we will grant confidentiality in the rarest of cases. And, equally important, we will publish information from confidential sources only in the rarest of cases.

This memorandum cannot possibly detail every instance in which we will be faced with the issue of granting anonymity or confidentiality. We will continue to use professional judgment, again with the guideline that we act in the best interests of the *Orange County Register* and its readers.

Reprinted with permission of the *Orange County Register*.

Appendix B:
Public Information Policy

University of Miami, Coral Gables, Florida

PURPOSE: To clarify the University's position regarding the release of information concerning the institution to the media and general public.

POLICY: The University recognizes that each employee has freedom of speech, however, the President is the official spokesperson for the University on matters of policy and official action. In most cases, this authority is delegated to the Director of Media Relations. It is the duty of the Director to release all information pertaining to controversies and emergencies, as well as to routine events to which the press has a reasonable claim, as quickly and fairly as possible.

It is the responsibility of the University Relations Office to compile, coordinate, and disseminate information to the media and to see that all media get the facts as quickly as possible. Deliberations of administrators, faculty and student boards, committees or councils must be distributed through the University Relations Office to ensure accuracy, prevent duplication of effort and avoid confusion.

It is the responsibility of all administrators to keep the University Relations Office fully informed about such matters in their areas of responsibility. The Medical Relations Director will then decide, in consultation with the persons involved, what information is to be released to the press and in what manner. The University Relations Office will assist individuals or groups on campus in the preparation of news material for the public.

There is no intent to censor or to prevent freedom of expression on the part of any individual connected with the University when the person speaks or writes as an individual. Unless given authority to do so, an employee is advised not to speak to the media concerning University affairs.

An employee should be careful to state when remarks are made as an individual and not as an official spokesperson of the University.

313

PROCEDURE: When the need arises to deal with the news media, University employees must realize that attempts to suppress bad news often lead to rumors far worse than the actual facts. By taking the initiative in releasing "bad news" to the media, the University Relations Office seeks to report the situations' positive points in a fair and balanced manner. A policy of candor enhances the University's credibility with both the press and the public.

The following are guidelines for University employees responding to press queries:

1. Ask the reporter's name and the publication/media outlet for which they are working. If you feel the request for information is reasonable, give the reporter your full cooperation, making every effort to be accurate, factual, and fair.

2. Normally, you would be asked to comment only on matters within your area of expertise. If asked questions which do not fall within the area you are comfortable commenting on, do not hesitate to tell the reporter so. Refer the reporter to the University Relations Office if the reporter's questions can best be answered by other persons within the University.

3. Some reporters may ask you to comment on a controversial issue, with the assurance that your name will not be used. Such reporting should be discouraged.

4. When your comments are personal opinion, make it clear to the reporter that you are speaking for yourself, and are not representing the University or your colleagues.

5. Do not assume that the reporter will check the story with you before it is used, as deadlines often make such double checking impossible. If technical or scientific data are involved, you might suggest that the reporter check back with you to ensure the accuracy of the story.

6. Broadcast stories can cover only the barest essentials of a story. If you are being interviewed by the broadcast media, make every effort to be succinct, avoiding detailed technical explanations and superfluous details whenever possible.

7. Most reporters dislike "off-the-record" information, as they may receive the same information later from another source. If, however, you feel it is essential to make "off-the-record" remarks, indicate clearly when you are speaking "off-the-record." Don't say belatedly, "The material I have just given you is off-the record."

8. After answering a press query, please inform the University Relations Office of the call and your response.

9. Queries should be directed to the Director of Media Relations when (a) the University Relations Office has already been provided information on the subject, (b) the query deals with an area where responsibility lies with or is shared with another department, and/or (c) the query deals with a matter of University-wide concern or policy.

Reprinted with permission of the Office of Public Affairs, University of Miami.

Appendix C:
A Writer's Bookshelf From
the *Orlando Sentinel*

No book will make you an accomplished writer, but each of the books on this list offers practical advice on starting, organizing, describing, explaining and stopping. They provide a beginning for reporters who want to improve their writing and for editors who want to help.

Seven of the titles likely to be used most widely are available for checkout in the *Sentinel* library. The seven are marked with a bullet (•). Three copies of each are stocked, and bureau reporters may call reference librarian Jill Sinser . . . for courier delivery. Some copies also are on order for permanent use in bureaus.

The books deal primarily with style and storytelling rather than with grammar and usage. Any one of them will prompt you to rethink your assumptions and encourage you to try new approaches. All of them, in different ways, explore the critical relationship between reporting and writing.

GUIDES

• Blundell, William E. *The Art and Craft of Feature Writing*. New York: Plume, 1988.

An almost scientific handbook that emphasizes the importance of analyzing your information continually as you report and planning your story before you write. A winner of the American Society of Newspaper Editors' Distinguished Writing Award, Blundell has been writing coach at the *Wall Street Journal* and has taught these techniques in the *Journal's* feature writing seminars. Don't be misled by the title: Blundell's process is as applicable to the news-side weekender as it is to the magazine profile.

• Cappon, Rene. *The Word: An Associated Press Guide to Good News Writing*. New York: Associated Press, 1982.

A collection of tips especially useful for the journalist who is just starting to concentrate on writing improvement. Brief (140 pages) and clearly subdivided, *The Word* offers cautions about avoiding common pitfalls in news writing and introductory lessons on tone, description and human interest. Cappon is former managing editor of the AP.

Franklin, Jon. *Writing for Story: Craft Secrets of Nonfiction.* New York: Atheneum, 1986.

A discussion, for the advanced writer, on how the traditions of short fiction can be applied to journalism. Franklin teaches that complication and resolution are at the heart of the successful feature story. To the extent that these elements are developed skillfully, he contends, reading a factual article becomes as satisfying as reading good literature. Franklin is the winner of two Pulitzer Prizes.

Graves, Robert, and Alan Hodge. *The Reader Over Your Shoulder: A Handbook for Writers of English Prose.* St. Paul: Vintage Books, 1979.

A cranky, eccentric collection of writing "principles," as the British co-authors call them. *The Reader Over Your Shoulder* is valuable for its guidelines on clarity ("No unintentional contrast between two ideas should be allowed to suggest itself") and grace ("Alliteration should be sparingly used").

• Murray, Donald M. *Write to Learn* (2nd ed.). New York: Holt, Rinehart and Winston, 1987.

An exploration of five steps essential to good writing: collect, focus, order, draft and clarify, a process Murray regards as circular. Although his approach is structured, it's not stuffy. Murray, a writing coach and a Pulitzer Prize winner, helps writers find their own answers to a question that all too frequently isn't asked: What's this story about? (Also see *Read to Write,* below).

• Murray, Donald M. *Writing for Your Readers: Notes on the Writer's Craft from The Boston Globe.* Chester, Conn.: Globe Pequot, 1983.

A compendium drawn from Murray's experience as writing coach of the *Globe.* Particularly strong are the chapters on developing ideas and writing leads. The latter includes a handy checklist of questions the writer can ask in deciding how to begin a story.

Scanlan, Christopher (ed.). *How I Wrote the Story* (2nd ed.). Providence, R.I.: Providence Journal Co., 1986.

Stories from the *Providence Journal-Bulletin,* one of the newspapers that began the "writing movement" about a decade ago. Each is followed by the writer's account of the reporting and writing process, and introductory chapters by *Journal-Bulletin* staffers focus on the theory and practice of writing improvement, including consultative editing. *How I Wrote the Story* provides unusual from-the-trenches testimony about how better writing can change a newspaper and the lives of those who work for it.

• Strunk, William Jr., and E. B. White. *The Elements of Style* (3rd ed.). New York: MacMillan, 1979.

Perhaps the best-loved single volume on writing to be found in American newsrooms. "Strunk and White," as this little book is often called, attempts to coach the writer with a handful of enduring tenets, and it succeeds as no other book has.

• Zinsser, William K. *On Writing Well: An Informal Guide to Writing Nonfiction* (3rd ed., rev.). New York: Harper & Row, 1985.

Wisdom, as opposed to instruction, from a writer, editor and teacher. Zinsser follows one of his most important preachings and keeps his book simple. In a conversational style that draws on his own experiences, he offers not a manual but a sensible framework for thinking about writing and evaluating it. Any journalist would be better for having read it.

ANTHOLOGIES

• Clark, Roy Peter, and Don Fry (eds.). *Best Newspaper Writing*. St. Petersburg: Poynter Institute for Media Studies, annually since 1979.

News and feature stories and columns that have won the American Society of Newspaper Editors' Distinguished Writing Awards, plus discussion questions and interviews with the authors about their thinking and technique. Volumes since 1986 are still in print, and the *Sentinel* library will carry 1987, '88 and '89.

Murray, Donald M. *Read to Write: A Writing Process Reader*. New York: Holt, Rinehart & Winston, 1986.

A companion to *Write to Learn* (see above). Murray presents several dozen pieces by authors ranging from George Orwell to Lewis Thomas, grouping them according to his steps in the writing process (collect, focus, order, draft and clarify). In each piece, Murray's notes illuminate and question the author's technique.

Sloan, Wm. David, Valerie McCrary and Johanna Cleary (eds.). *The Best of Pulitzer Prize News Writing*. Columbus, Ohio: Publishing Horizons, 1986.

More than 70 examples of superior writing selected from 2,000 Pulitzer-winning pieces, with brief introductory comments.

Wills, Kendall J. (ed.). *The Pulitzer Prizes*. New York: Simon and Schuster, annually since 1987.

A yearly collection of the pieces that win journalism's highest honor.

Reprinted with permission of the *Orlando Sentinel*.

Appendix D:
Code of Ethics of the Society of Professional Journalists

(Adopted by the 1987 national convention, Chicago)

The Society of Professional Journalists believes the duty of journalists is to serve the truth.

We believe the agencies of mass communication are carriers of public discussion and information, acting on their Constitutional mandate and freedom to learn and report the facts.

We believe in public enlightenment as the forerunner of justice, and in our Constitutional role to seek the truth as part of public's right to know the truth.

We believe those responsibilities carry obligations that require journalists to perform with intelligence, objectivity, accuracy, and fairness.

To these ends, we declare acceptance of the standards of practice here set forth:

• RESPONSIBILITY: The public's right to know of events of public importance and interest is the overriding mission of the mass media. The purpose of distributing news and enlightened opinion is to serve the general welfare. Journalists who use their professional status as representatives of the public for selfish or other unworthy motives violate a high trust.

• FREEDOM OF THE PRESS: Freedom of the press is to be guarded as an inalienable right of people in a free society. It carries with it the freedom and the responsibility to discuss, question, and challenge actions and utterances of our government and our public and private institutions. Journalists uphold the right to speak unpopular opinions and the privilege to agree with the majority.

• ETHICS: Journalists must be free of obligation to any interest other than the public's right to know the truth.

1. Gifts, favors, free travel, special treatment or privileges can compromise the integrity of journalists and their employers. Nothing of value should be accepted.

2. Secondary employment, political involvement, holding public office, and service in community organizations should be avoided if it compromises the integrity of journalists and their employers. Journalists and their employers should conduct their personal lives in a manner which protects them from conflict of interest, real or apparent. Their responsibilities to the public are paramount. That is the nature of their profession.

3. So-called news communications from private sources should not be published or broadcast without substantiation of their claims to news value.

4. Journalists will seek news that serves the public interest, despite the obstacles. They will make constant efforts to assure that the public's business is conducted in public inspection.

5. Journalists acknowledge the newsman's ethic of protecting confidential sources of information.

6. Plagiarism is dishonest and unacceptable.

• ACCURACY AND OBJECTIVITY: Good faith with the public is the foundation of all worthy journalism.

1. Truth is our ultimate goal.

2. Objectivity in reporting the news is another goal, which serves as the mark of an experienced professional. It is a standard of performance toward which we strive. We honor those who achieve it.

3. There is no excuse for inaccuracies or lack of thoroughness.

4. Newspaper headlines should be fully warranted by the contents of the articles they accompany. Photographs and telecasts should give an accurate picture of an event and not highlight a minor incident out of context.

5. Sound practice makes clear distinction between news reports and expressions of opinion. News reports should be free of opinion or bias and represent all sides of an issue.

6. Partisanship in editorial comment which knowingly departs from the truth violates the spirit of American journalism.

7. Journalists recognize their responsibility for offering informed analysis, comment, and editorial opinion on public events and issues. They accept the obligation to present such material by individuals whose competence, experience, and judgment quality them for it.

8. Special articles or presentations devoted to advocacy or the writer's own conclusions and interpretations should be labeled as such.

• FAIR PLAY: Journalists at all times will show respect for the dignity, privacy, rights, and well-being of people encountered in the course of gathering and presenting the news.

1. The news media should not communicate unofficial charges affecting reputation or moral character without giving the accused a chance to reply.

2. The news media must guard against invading a person's right to privacy.

3. The media should not pander to morbid curiosity about details of vice and crime.

4. It is the duty of news media to make prompt and complete correction of their errors.

5. Journalists should be accountable to the public for their reports and the public should be encouraged to voice its grievances against the media. Open dialogue with our readers, viewers, and listeners should be fostered.

Reprinted with the permission of the Society of Professional Journalists.

Appendix E:
Code of Broadcast News
Ethics of the Radio-Television
News Directors Association

The responsibility of radio and television journalists is to gather and report information of importance and interest to the public accurately, honestly and impartially.

The members of the Radio-Television News Directors Association accept these standards and will:

1. Strive to present the source or nature of broadcast news material in a way that is balanced, accurate and fair.

A. They will evaluate information solely on its merits as news, rejecting sensationalism or misleading emphasis in any form.

B. They will guard against using audio or video material in a way that deceives the audience.

C. They will not mislead the public by presenting as spontaneous news any material which is staged or rehearsed.

D. They will identify people by race, creed, nationality, or prior status only when it is relevant.

E. They will clearly label opinion and commentary.

F. They will promptly acknowledge and correct errors.

2. Strive to conduct themselves in a manner that protects them from conflicts of interest, real or perceived. They will decline gifts or favors which would influence or appear to influence their judgments.

3. Respect the dignity, privacy and well-being of people with whom they deal.

4. Recognize the need to protect confidential sources. They will promise confidentiality only with the intention of keeping that promise.

5. Respect everyone's right to a fair trial.

6. Broadcast the private transmissions of other broadcasters only with permission.

7. Actively encourage observance of this Code by all journalists, whether members of the Radio-Television News Directors Association or not.

Reprinted with permission of the Radio-Television News
Directors Association.

References

BOOKS

Balinksy, B., & Burger, R. (1959). *The executive interview: A bridge to people.* New York: Harper & Row.

Biagi, S. (1986). *Interviews that work: A practical guide for journalists.* Belmont, CA: Wadsworth.

Bittner, J. R. (1989). *Mass communication: An introduction* (5th ed.). Englewood Cliffs, NJ: Prentice-Hall.

Bleyer, W. G. (1913). *Newspaper writing and editing.* Boston: Houghton Mifflin.

Bogart, L. (1989). *Press and public* (2nd ed.). Hillsdale, NJ: Lawrence Erlbaum Associates.

Bush, C. R. (1929). *Newspaper reporting of public affairs.* New York: D. Appleton.

Cannon, L. (1977). *Reporting: An inside view.* Sacramento, CA: California Journal Press.

Cappon, R. J. (1982). *The word: An Associated Press guide to good writing.* New York: Associated Press.

Carter, J. M. (1986). Magazines: The new "hot" medium. In *Magazine publishing career directory 1986.* New York: Career Publishing.

Carter, T. B., Franklin, M. A., & Wright, J. B. (1991). *The First Amendment and the Fourth Estate: The law of mass communication* (5th ed.). Westbury, NY: Foundation Press.

Chancellor, J., & Mears, W. R. (1983). *The news business.* New York: New American Library.

Charnley, M. (1975). *Reporting,* Chicago: Holt, Rinehart & Winston.

Christians, C. G., Rotzoll, K. B., & Fackler, M. (1991). *Media ethics: Cases & moral reasoning* (3rd ed.). New York: Longman.

Day, L. A. (1991). *Ethics in mass communications: Cases and controversies.* Belmont, CA: Wadsworth.

Day, R. (1989). *Grand inquisitor.* London: Pan Books.

Dizard, Jr., W. P. (1985). *The coming information age: An overview of technology, economics, and politics* (2nd ed.). New York: Longman.

Donaldson, S. (1987). *Hold on, Mr. President!* New York: Ballantine Books.

Downs, C. W., Smeyak, G. P., & Martin, E. (1980). *Professional interviewing.* New York: Harper & Row.

Fedler, F. (1989). *Media hoaxes.* Ames: Iowa State University Press.

Fink, C. C. (1988). *Media ethics: In the newsroom and beyond.* New York: McGraw-Hill.

Finn, S. (1991). *Broadcast writing as a liberal art.* Englewood Cliffs, NJ: Prentice-Hall.

French, C. W., & Goldstein, N. (Eds.). (1988). *Associated Press stylebook and libel manual.* New York: Associated Press.

Gans, H. (1979). *Deciding what's news.* New York: Pantheon.

Garrison, B. (1989). *Professional feature writing.* Hillsdale, NJ: Lawrence Erlbaum Associates.

Garrison, B. (1990). *Professional news writing.* Hillsdale, NJ: Lawrence Erlbaum Associates.

Garrison, B. (1991). Entertainment and recreation. In R. J. Griffin, D. H. Molen, C. Schoenfelder, J. F. Scotton, D. Cassady, B. Garrison, T. Hueterman, F. McVay, R. Meier, & K. Rystrom (Eds.), *Interpreting public issues* (pp. 154–179). Ames: Iowa State University Press.

Giles, R. H. (1988). *Newsroom management: A guide to theory and practice.* Detroit: Media Management Books.

Gillmor, D. M., Barron, J. A., Simon, T. F., & Terry, H. A. (1990). *Mass communication law: Cases and comment* (5th ed.). St. Paul, MN: West.

Goedkoop, R. J. (1988). *Inside local television news.* Salem, WI: Sheffield.

Goodwin, H. E. (1987). *Groping for ethics in journalism* (2nd ed.). Ames: Iowa State University Press.

Jacobs, J. (1990). *Changing channels: Issues and realities in television news.* Mountain View, CA: Mayfield.

Johnson, O. (Ed.). (1991). *The 1991 information please almanac* (44th ed.). Boston: Houghton Mifflin.

Jones, C. (1983). *How to speak TV: A self-defense manual when you're the news.* Marathon, FL: Video Consultants.

Keir, G., McCombs, M., & Shaw, D. L. (1991). *Advanced reporting: Beyond news events.* Prospect Heights, IL: Waveland Press.

Killenberg, G., & Anderson, R. (1989). *Before the story: Interviewing and communication skills for journalists.* New York: St. Martin's Press.

Kirtley, J. E. (Ed.). (1986). *The First Amendment handbook.* Washington, DC: Reporters Committee for Freedom of the Press.

Kresch, S. (1986). The changing face of the industry. In *Magazine publishing career directory 1986* (p. 14). New York: Career Publishing.

Kubis, P., & Howland, R. (1985). *The complete guide to writing fiction, nonfiction, and publishing.* Reston, VA: Reston.

Lambeth, E. B. (1986). *Committed journalism: An ethic for the profession.* Bloomington, IN: Indiana University Press.

Lavine, J. M., & Wackman, D. B. (1988). *Managing media organizations: Effective leadership of the media.* White Plains, NY: Longman.

Marcus, N. (1986). *Broadcast and cable management.* Englewood Cliffs, NJ: Prentice-Hall.

Metzler, K. (1989). *Creative interviewing* (2nd ed.). Englewood Cliffs, NJ: Prentice-Hall.

Middleton, K. R., & Chamberlin, B. F. (1991). *The law of public communication* (2nd ed.). New York: Longman.

Mooney, S. E., & Trivedi, H. S. (1983). *Guidelines for newspaper libraries.* Reston, VA: American Newspaper Publishers Association.

Nelson, H. L., Teeter, D. L., & Le Duc, D. (1989). *Law of mass communications: Freedom and control of print and broadcast media* (6th ed.). Westbury, NY: Foundation Press.

Nolan, J. R., & Nolan-Haley, J. M. (1990). *Black's law dictionary* (6th ed.). St. Paul, MN: West.

Papper, R. A. (1987). *Broadcast news writing stylebook.* Columbus, OH: Publishing Horizons.

Pember, D. (1990). *Mass media law* (5th ed.). Dubuque, IA: Wm. C. Brown.

Peterson, T., Jensen, J. W., & Rivers, W. (1965). *The mass media and modern society.* New York: Holt, Rinehart & Winston.

Rivers, W. L. (1975). *Finding facts: Interviewing, observing, using reference sources.* Englewood Cliffs, NJ: Prentice-Hall.

Rivers, W. L., & Work, A. R. (1986). *Free-lancer and staff writer: Newspaper features and magazine articles.* Belmont, CA: Wadsworth.

Sherwood, H. (1972). *The journalistic interview* (rev. ed.). New York: Harper & Row.

Shook, F. (1989). *Television field production and reporting.* New York: Longman.

Sigal, L. (1973). *Reporters and officials: The organization and politics of newsmaking.* Lexington, MA: D. C. Heath.

Sohn, A., Ogan, C., & Polich, J. (1986). *Newspaper leadership.* Englewood Cliffs, NJ: Prentice-Hall.

Stewart, C. J., & Cash, W. B. (1985). *Interviewing: Principles and practices* (4th ed.). Dubuque, IA: Wm. C. Brown.

Stein, M. L. (1974). *Shaping the news.* New York: Pocket Books.

Stone, V. A. (1989a). *Careers in radio and television news* (6th ed.). Washington, DC: Radio-Television News Directors Association.

Turkel, S. (1974). *Working.* New York: Avon Books.

United Press International Broadcast Services. (1979). *United Press International broadcast stylebook.* New York: Author.

Watkins, J. J. (1990). *The mass media and the law.* Englewood Cliffs, NJ: Prentice-Hall.

Weaver, D. H., & Wilhoit, G. C. (1986). *The American journalist: A portrait of U.S. news people and their work.* Bloomington, IN: Indiana University Press.

Yoakam, R. D., & Cremer, C. F. (1989). *ENG: Television news and the new technology* (2nd ed.). New York: Random House.

PERIODICALS

Anderson, N. C. (1990). Personalizing 'products' is essential. *presstime, 12*(1), 30.

Anderson, N. C. (1991). What exactly are they doing at the *Orange County Register? ASNE Bulletin, 731,* 13–14.

Anon. (1990, October). *Cable television developments.* National Cable Television Association, Washington, DC.

Anon. (1991, January 9). *Hoaxster hoodwinks media on $35 million Lotto jackpot.* Associated Press national wire, n.p.

Anon. (1991, April 19). *Libel award.* Associated Press national wire, 9:38 P.M., n.p.

Anon. (1991, April 24). *Palm Beach woman in rape scandal angrily ends TV interview.* United Press International northeast regional wire, 9:08 A.M., n.p.

Anon. (1991, May 8). *Reporter guilty of trespassing at Heinz home.* United Press International northeast region wire, 9:44 A.M., n.p.

Anon. (1991, June 11). *WNBC-TV reporter ticketed at welcome parade.* United Press International northeast region wire, 10:30 A.M., n.p.

Anon. (1991, July 13). The *Herald* gets *Post* apology: Reporter's story omitted credit. *Miami Herald,* p. 8A.

Anon. (1991, July 29). *Pit-bull reporter wouldn't take 'no' for an answer.* United Press International national wire, 4:32 P.M., n.p.

Anon. (1991, July 30). *Columnist fired.* Associated Press national wire, 8:36 A.M., n.p.

Anon. (1991, August 8). *Reporter convicted in pit bull trial.* United Press International, 12:01 A.M., n.p.

Anon. (1992, March 23). Summary of broadcasting & cable. *Broadcasting, 122*(13), 84.

Asseo, L. (1991, April 22). *Post reporter–source.* Associated Press national wire, 12:30 P.M., n.p.

Aumente, J. (1989, April). Bauds, bytes and Brokaw: New PCs revolutionize the newsroom. *Washington Journalism Review, 11*(3), 39–42.

Bales, M. (1990). Missiles in tourist central. *The Quill, 78*(6), 14–19.

Blankenhorn, D. (1991). Stations weigh benefits of online services. *Electronic Media, 10*(9), 18.

Briskin, J. (1979). Research is a snap. *Writer's Digest, 59*(2), 26–28.

Buchanan, E. (1988, March 27). Retarded man's suicide baffles cops. *The Miami Herald,* p. 1B.

Bukro, C. (1989, October). The code is intended to make us think professionally. *Solutions today for ethics problems tomorrow.* Society of Professional Journalists Ethics Committee special report, p. 22.

Burke, R. L. (1990). Newspaper efforts have momentum going. *presstime, 12*(1), 22.

Camper, J. (1990, April 15). Loyola struggling to handle new racial tensions. *Chicago Tribune,* Sect. 2, p. 2.

Carvajal, D. (1991). Is it news, ad, or infomercial? *FineLine* [sic], *3*(4), 1, 8.

Casey, T. (1989). Computer-generated news opens catch viewers' attention. *RTNDA Communicator, 43*(10), 12–13.

Chichioco, T. (1989). Computer-assisted reporting: Newspapers are beginning to use it to their advantage. *Editor & Publisher, 123*(35), 20PC–21PC.

Christian, S. E. (1990). A shot across the masthead, *ASNE Bulletin, 725,* 38–39.

Coffey, R. (1987, July 14). Full disclosure? It's a yawn. *Miami Herald,* final ed., p. 15A.

Courson, P. (1989). Cellular telephones for radio electronic news gathering. *RTNDA Communicator, 43*(3), 15–17.

Craft, S. (1990). Covering the census and using federal statistics. *IRE Journal, 13*(4), 13–16.

Crane, A. (1991, May 31). *Judge delays further fines against reporter.* United Press International national wire, 5:28 P.M., n.p.

Criner, K. (1990). Storm clouds. *presstime, 12*(1), 28.

Crouse, C. (1991). Reporting for radio. *RTNDA Communicator, 45*(3), 26.

Davis, L. J. (1991, July 14). What's wrong with banks? Bankers. *Miami Herald,* pp. 1C, 6C.

Dean, C. (1986, September 29). Computer use for news raises legal questions. *New York Times,* p. A12.

Dennis, E. E. (1990). A prescription for economic health. *presstime, 12*(1), 20.

Donnelly, J., & Coto, J. C. (1991, April 17). NBC fuels media debate in Kennedy case. *Miami Herald,* pp. 1A, 13A.

Donovan, S., & Schalit, N. (1989). Death of the morgue: A user-friendly institution yields to a profit center. *Washington Journalism Review, 11*(6), 36–38.

Dufresne, M. (1991, May/June). To sting or not to sting? *Columbia Journalism Review, 30*(1), 49–51.

Elliott, D. (1991, July/August). Thou shalt not trick thy source: Many a slip twixt the promise and the page. *FineLine, 3*(7), 2–3.

Fletcher, C., & Ziomek, J. (1986, December). How to catch a star. *The Quill, 74*(11), 32–36.

Galvan, M. (1989, October). For journalists, inescapable impact of ethics. *Solutions today for ethics problems tomorrow.* Society of Professional Journalists Ethics Committee special report, p. 2.

Genovese, M. (1987). "Desktop publishing" spurs weeklies. *presstime, 9*(1), 18–20.

Gersh, D., & Case, T. (1991). 75th annual Pulitzer Prize winners. *Editor & Publisher, 124*(15), 7–9, 32–35, 44.

Gianelli, D. (1990, October). Newspapers grapple with "advertorial" issue. *Newspaper ethics.* Associated Press Managing Editors Ethics Committee report, Dallas.

Greenfield, M. (1990). Whose side are we on? *Newsweek, 116*(10), 76.

Hancock, D. (1991, April 17). Social service agency chief takes paid leave. *Miami Herald,* p. 1A.

Hansen, K. A., Ward, J., & McLeod, D. M. (1987). Role of the newspaper library in the production of news. *Journalism Quarterly, 64*(4), 714–720.

Hoge, J. (1978, February). The Mirage: A report on the 'fix' in Chicago. *Chicago Sun-Times* reprint of series.

Hughes, R. (1991). A kinder, gentler news media? Post-war coverage shows sensitivity to families. *FineLine, 3*(4), 3.

Isaacs, N. E. (1988). Only editors should decide whether to grant anonymity. *presstime, 10*(9), 12–13.

Jacobson, T. L., & Ullman, J. (1989). Commercial databases and reporting: Opinions of newspaper journalists and librarians. *Newspaper Research Journal, 10*(2), 15–25.

James, S. (1991, May 1). Talk of *The Times. Times News.* (newsletter of the *St. Petersburg Times* news department) *98,* 1–2.

Jennings, M. (1989). PCs help reporters track good stories through mazes of bureaucratic statistics. *ASNE Bulletin, 716,* 13–17.

Katz, J. (1990). Memo to local news directors: Re: improving the product. *Columbia Journalism Review, 28*(7), 40–44.

Kelly, T. (1987). Good grief! Even well-known journalists can relate a story of when their judgment failed them—and a lifelong lesson was learned. *presstime, 9*(11), 20–22.

Leslie, J. (1986). Tough calls: The pros and cons of cleaning up quotes. *Washington Journalism Review, 8*(4), 44–46.

Lester, W. (1991, July 30). *Southern Air-libel.* Associated Press national wire, 4:02 P.M., n.p.

Leusner, J., & Quinn, C. (1990, March 18–21). Missiles in Boomtown. *Orlando Sentinel,* special report reprint, pp. 2–10.

Leusner, J. (1985). "Give me your tag number and I'll tell you your life story," *Sentinel Communication Quarterly (Orlando Sentinel), 3*(3), 14.

Loudis, S. (1991, May 4). Living on streets a "terrible feeling." *Miami Herald,* p. 8E.

Maguire, W. T. (1990). Law and regulations. *presstime, 12*(1), 35.

Martin, P. (1986). Overview: Computers and newspapers in the mid-80s. *Editor & Publisher, 119*(5), 1C, 24C.

McManus, K. (1990). The, uh, quotation quandry. *Columbia Journalism Review, 28*(7), 54–56.

Meeks, B. (1991). New databases get behind the scenes. *Link-Up, 8*(2), 9, 12.

Miller, G. (n.d.). Reader is victim when source isn't named, *The Bay View* (newsletter of the *Miami Herald* news department), reprint, n.p.

Miller, T. (1988a). The data-base revolution. *Columbia Journalism Review,* *27*(3), 35–38.

Miller, T. (1988b). Data bases: Finding your world in the electronic newspaper. *Editor & Publisher, 121*(37), 34–35, 38, 40–44.

Modzelewski, J. (1988, January 13). The $80,000 expense accounts. *Miami News,* p. 1A.

Murphy, R. P. (1989, February 20). Celebs a sellout for magazines. *Miami Herald,* final ed., p. 1C.

Murrie, M. (1990). Computer cub reporter: Newsroom computers, on-line databases are where newspapers are scooping TV. *Television Broadcast, 13*(9), 28.

Murrie, M. (1988). Electronic databases in the newsroom. *Link-Up, 7*(2), 27.

Murrie, M. (1987). Information at your fingertips. *RTNDA Communicator, 41*(9), 36–40.

Naylor, R. (1991, April 29). *Credit reports.* The Associated Press A wire, 3:56 P.M., no story number available.

Nelson, S. (1990). The best in journalism: The winners of the 1989 SDX Awards tell how they did it. *The Quill, 78*(5), 19–20.

Ojala, M. (1991). Online broadcast news: From television screen to computer screen. *Database, 14*(2), 33–40.

Oppel, R. (1989). Here are eight basic tips on the basics of managing any beat. *ASNE Bulletin, 710,* 12–13.

Paul, N. (1991b). For the record: Information on individuals. *Database, 14*(2), 15–23.

Paul, N. (1991d). Hook up with a librarian. *IRE Journal, 14*(1), 3.

Paul, N. (1990). The killer left a paper trail. *IRE Journal, 13*(1), 11.

Paulson, B. (1991). A model for improving station-wide operations productivity: The computer-based newsroom. *RTNDA Communicator, 45*(3), 16–17.

Pearson, S., & Cohen, L. (1990). Contest winners: City pays off brutality suits, lets police off. *IRE Journal, 13*(3), 11.

Prosser, W. L. (1960). Privacy. *California Law Review, 48,* 383–423.

Rambo, C. D. (1987). Database searches. *presstime, 9*(3), 10–12.

Ramos, R. (1988, July 15). Chief Dickson expected to resign. *Miami Herald,* pp. 1A, 4A.

Rinehart, W. D. (1990). Laser disks and HDTV. *presstime, 12*(1), 26.

Rodman, J. (1991). Challenges facing radio news managers: Learning from our mistakes. *RTNDA Communicator, 45*(4), 28–29.

Rose, B. (1991, April 15). On writing. *The Bay View* (newsletter of the *Miami Herald* news department), *15*(91), 5.

Rowley, J. (1991, May 20). *Reporter–source.* Associated Press national wire, 5:00 P.M., n.p.

Rykken, R. (1989, August). Weeklies become a sought-after catch. *presstime, 11*(8), 20–27.

Samuelson, R. J. (1990). Let's blame the media. *Newsweek, 116*(20), 80.

Schmerler, D. (1989). Electronic paint systems tell the story pictorially. *RTNDA Communicator, 43*(10), 10–11.

Sommers, L. (1991). Confidential sources: Protection and prevention. *Editor & Publisher, 124*(11), 32.

Spikol, A. (1987). Non fiction: Before the interview. *Writer's Digest, 67*(9), 8–10.

Stephens, M., & Frankel, E. (1983). The counterpunch interview. *Columbia Journalism Review, 21*(6), 38–39.

Stone, V. (1989b). Upgrading tops developments in radio news. *RTNDA Communicator, 43*(3), 9–11.

Stone, V. (1991). Staff gains offset cutbacks. *RTNDA Communicator, 45*(3), 24–25.

Stumpf, M., & Jessell, H. A. (1991). What cable could be in 2000: 500 channels. *Broadcasting, 120*(13), 27–28.

Swanston, W. J. (1990). Changing times. *presstime, 12*(1), 32.

Talbott, F. (1986). Taping on the sly: Nasty business — or sound journalistic technique? *The Quill, 74*(6), 43–48.

Terrell, P. (1990). Full name, age, and address — or not? *presstime, 12*(12), 30–33.

Wagar, K. (1991). A lesson on property taxes. *IRE Journal,* 4–5.

Wall, C. (1991). Some 115 newspapers are on-line. *presstime, 13*(4), 46.

Ward, J., & Hansen, K. A. (1990). Newspapers and electronic libraries. *Editor & Publisher, 123*(44), 34–36.

Ward, J., Hansen, K. A., & McLeod, D. M. (1988a). Effects of the electronic library on news reporting protocols. *Journalism Quarterly, 65*(4), 845–852.

Ward, J., Hansen, K. A., & McLeod, D. M. (1988b). The news library's contribution to newsmaking. *Special Libraries, 79*(2), 143–147.

Webb, C. (1989). Government databases. *presstime, 11*(4), 18–20.

Weinberg, S. (1991b). Don't believe everything you hear: Investigative reporting is alive, well and ready to grow stronger. *ASNE Bulletin, 731,* 20–21.

Weitzel, P. (1991a). Hello sucker. *The Bay View* (newsletter of the *Miami Herald* news department), *14*(91), 5.

Weitzel, P. (1991b). On reporting — The JESCA memos and more. *The Bay View* (newsletter of the *Miami Herald* news department), *16*(91), 1.

Wulfemeyer, K. T. (1990). Defining ethics in electronic journalism: Perceptions of news directors. *Journalism Quarterly, 67*(4), 984–991.

OTHER SOURCES

Ambrose, J. (1991, May 16). Personal communication with author.

Anderson, C. (1988, September 27). Use of confidential and anonymous sources. Unpublished memorandum, Santa Ana, CA.

Anderson, B. (1991, April 29). Personal communication with author.

Anon. (1986). *Freedom of the press*. Washington, DC: Reporter's Committee on Freedom of the Press.

Anon. (1990, July 15). *The American media: Who reads, who watches, who listens, who cares*. Washington, DC: Times Mirror Center for the People & the Press.

Anon. (1991, April). *Facts about newspapers '91. Reston, VA: American Newspaper Publishers Association.*

Anon. (1991, April 28). *Fake crash report scrambles news reporters*. United Press International southwest regional wire, 2 P.M., n.p.

Bartimus, T. (1990). How I write. *Literacy, nut graphs, copy editing, the writing process, kickers*. Writing & Editing Committee Report. Associated Press Managing editors, national convention, Dallas, p. 10.

Bergen, L. (1990, August). *Characteristics of newspaper journalists' best work*. Paper presented to the Association for Education in Journalism and Mass Communication, Minneapolis.

Black, J., & Barney, R. (1991, March). *Journalism ethics since Janet Cooke*. Paper presented to the Association for Education in Journalism and Mass Communication Southeast Colloquium, Orlando, FL.

Calkins, M. (1990, May 15). Personal communication with author.

Chung, W. W. (1991, August). *Lay theories of media credibility*. Paper presented to the Theory and Methodology Division of the Association for Education in Journalism and Mass Communication, annual convention, Boston.

Conway, M. (1990, May 1). Personal communication with author.

Crockett, K. (1991, June 22). Personal communication with author.

Dotson, B. (1988, November 18). Professional development seminar at the national convention of the Society of Professional Journalists, Cincinnati, OH.

Freedberg, S. (1991, June 23). Reporting tips seminar at journalism workshop, School of Communication, University of Miami.

Godsey, W. (1980, summer). *If you are asked to leave a meeting*. Newsroom memorandum, WTMJ-TV, Milwaukee.

Green, D. (1991, April 22). Personal communication with author.

Horvath-Neimeyer, P. S., & Kent, K. (1990, August). *Stereotypes and news-gathering: Biases that guide reporters' information searches*. Paper presented to the Association for Education in Journalism and Mass Communication, Minneapolis.

Kellogg, J. (1990). Developing stories stand alone with help from nut grafs. *Literacy, Nut Graphs, Copy Editing, the Writing Process, Kickers*. Writing & Editing Committee Report. Associated Press Managing editors, national convention, Dallas, p. 8.

Kelly, T. (1989, March 6). Personal communication with author.

Kelly, T. (1991, April 18). Personal communication with author.

Kleinman, J. L. (1988, fall). *Miami Herald* Neighbors transportation beat book, unpublished library files.

Kramer, J. (1988, August). *Star Tribune* guidelines on anonymous sources and confidentiality. Unpublished memorandum, Minneapolis.

L'Amie, R. C. (1991, August). *The computerization of television news-rooms: A case study*. Paper presented to Radio-TV Journalism Division of the Association for Education in Journalism and Mass Communication, annual convention, Boston.

Leusner, J. (1991a, April 24). Personal communication with author.

Leusner, J. (1991b, May 10). Personal communication with author.

Markowitz, A. (1991, June 22). Personal communication with author.

Paul, N. (1991a, April 18). Personal communication with author.

Paul, N. (1991c, February 19). Researching the war. Unpublished manuscript, the *Miami Herald* library, pp. 1–3.

Potter, M. (1990, November 26). Personal communication with author.

Prince, A. (1991, June 11). Personal communication with author.

Rendfeld, R. (1991, June 21). Personal communication with author.

Soley, L. C. (1990, August 9–12). *The news shapers*. Unpublished paper presented to the Association for Education in Journalism and Mass Communication, Minneapolis.

Smith, E. B. (1989). *Libel law in journalism skills tests*. Paper presented at the Southeast Colloquium on Law, Association for Education in Journalism and Mass Communication, University of North Carolina, Chapel Hill, NC.

Splichal, S. (1991, March). *Florida newspapers and access to computerized government information: A study of how they are dealing with the new technology*. Paper presented to the Association for Education in Journalism and Mass Communication 1991 Southeast Colloquium, Orlando, FL.

Wadlington, D. (1991, April 19). Personal communication with author.

Walewski, S. (1991, April 4). Personal communication with author.

Wolfe, D. P. (1989a, August). *Newspaper use of computer databases and guidelines for access; A case study:* The St. Petersburg Times. Unpublished master's thesis, University of South Florida, Tampa.

Wolfe, D. P. (1989b, October). *Gatekeeping: New power for news librarians in the 1990s*. Paper based on speech given to the Florida News Librarians' Association.

Youm, K. H. (1991, August 27). Personal communication with author.

Index

For Product Safety Concerns and Information please contact our EU
representative GPSR@taylorandfrancis.com Taylor & Francis Verlag GmbH,
Kaufingerstraße 24, 80331 München, Germany

Printed and bound by CPI Group (UK) Ltd, Croydon, CR0 4YY
08/05/2025
01864500-0003